# On Freedom

## ALSO BY TIMOTHY SNYDER

*Nationalism, Marxism, and Modern Central Europe:*
*A Biography of Kazimierz Kelles-Krauz, 1872–1905*

*The Wall Around the West: State Borders and Immigration Controls*
*in North America and Europe* (ed. with Peter Andreas)

*The Reconstruction of Nations:*
*Poland, Ukraine, Lithuania, Belarus, 1569–1999*

*Sketches from a Secret War:*
*A Polish Artist's Mission to Liberate Soviet Ukraine*

*The Red Prince: The Secret Lives of a Habsburg Archduke*

*Thinking the Twentieth Century* (with Tony Judt)

*Bloodlands: Europe Between Hitler and Stalin*

*Stalin and Europe: Imitation and Domination, 1928–1953*
(ed. with Ray Brandon)

*Ukrainian History, Russian Policy, and European Futures*
(in Ukrainian and Russian)

*The Politics of Life and Death* (in Czech)

*Lessons on History and from History* (in Polish)

*The Balkans as Europe, 1821–1914* (ed. with Katherine Younger)

*Volhynia 1943* (in Polish)

*In Defense of Freedom* (in Portuguese)

*And We Dream as Electric Sheep: Humanity, Digitality, Sexuality*
(in German)

*Black Earth: The Holocaust as History and Warning*

*On Tyranny: Twenty Lessons from the Twentieth Century*

*The Road to Unfreedom: Russia, Europe, America*

*Our Malady: Lessons in Liberty from a Hospital Diary*

# On Freedom

## Timothy Snyder

CROWN
NEW YORK

Published in the United States by Crown, an imprint of the Crown Publishing Group, a division of Penguin Random House LLC, New York.
crownpublishing.com

CROWN and the Crown colophon are registered trademarks of Penguin Random House LLC.

Grateful acknowledgment is made to Random House, an imprint and division of Penguin Random House LLC and Curtis Brown Ltd. for permission to reprint an excerpt from "The Shield of Achilles" from *Collected Poems* by W. H. Auden, edited by Edward Mendelson, copyright © 1952 by W. H. Auden and copyright renewed 1980 by The Estate of W. H. Auden. Reprinted by permission of Random House, an imprint and division of Penguin Random House LLC and Curtis Brown Ltd.

Library of Congress Cataloging-in-Publication Data
Names: Snyder, Timothy, author.
Title: On freedom / Timothy Snyder.
Description: First edition. | New York : Crown, [2024] | Includes index.
Identifiers: LCCN 2023058629 (print) | LCCN 2023058630 (ebook) |
    ISBN 9780593728727 (hardcover ; acid-free paper) |
    ISBN 9780593728741 (paperback ; acid-free paper) |
    ISBN 9780593799048 (international edition) | ISBN 9780593728734 (ebook)
Subjects: LCSH: Liberty. | Democracy—United States. | Political culture—United States.
Classification: LCC JC585 .S556 2024  (print) | LCC JC585  (ebook) |
    DDC 323.440973—dc23/eng/20240529
LC record available at https://lccn.loc.gov/2023058629
LC ebook record available at https://lccn.loc.gov/2023058630

Hardcover ISBN 978-0-593-72872-7
International edition ISBN 978-0-593-79904-8
Ebook ISBN 978-0-593-72873-4

Printed in the United States of America on acid-free paper

Editor: Amanda Cook
Editorial assistant: Katie Berry
Production editor: Joyce Wong
Production manager: Heather Williamson
Managing editors: Chris Tanigawa and Liza Stepanovich
Copy editor: Janet Biehl
Proofreader: Janet Renard
Indexer: Jay Kreider
Publicist: Dyana Messina

9 8 7 6 5 4 3 2 1

First Edition

Jacket design by Chris Brand
Book design by Aubrey Khan

*For those who wish to be free*

# Contents

# Preface

"What do you think?" asked Mariia, smiling, in her bright dress, as I ducked under the doorframe of her orderly little hut and stepped back into the sunshine and rubble. "Everything as it should be?" It was. Her rugs and blankets, laid out in nice rectilinear patterns, recalled Ukrainian futurist art. The cords leading to her generator were tidily arranged, and water bottles were near at hand. A thick book lay open on her bed.

Outside her metal domicile, a temporary dwelling provided by an international organization, woolen sweaters were drying on a line. A pretty wooden drawer, lined in felt, rested on a bench, like an open Pandora's box. When I complimented her on it, Mariia offered the drawer to me as a gift. It was a lonely relic of her house, just in front of us, a ruin after bombs and shells. She looked up nervously at a passing plane. "Everything happened," she sighed, "and none of it was necessary."

Like every house in the village, Mariia's was destroyed during the Russian invasion of Ukraine. Posad Pokrovs'ke, in the far south of the country, was at the edge of the Russian advance. It rests among fields of sunflowers in this fertile region. The Ukrainian army pushed the Russians out of artillery range in late 2022, making it safe to return, or to visit, as I am doing now, in September 2023.

Taking a seat on the bench and listening to Mariia, I think about freedom. The village, one would say, has been liberated. Are its people free?

To be sure, something terrible has been removed from Mariia's life: the daily threat of violent death, an occupation by torturers and murderers. But is that, even that, liberation?

Mariia is eighty-five years old and living alone. Now that she has her neat little residence, she is certainly freer than when she was homeless. That is because family and volunteers came to help. And because a government has acted, one to which she feels connected by her vote. Mariia does not complain of her own fate. She cries when she speaks of the difficult challenges faced by her president.

The Ukrainian word *de-occupation,* which she and I are using in conversation, is more precise than the conventional *liberation*. It invites us to consider what, beyond the removal of oppression, we might need for liberty. It takes work, after all, to get one older woman into a position where she can greet guests and perform the normal interactions of a dignified person. I have trouble imagining Mariia being truly free without a proper house with a chair and without a clear path to the road for her walker.

Freedom is not just an absence of evil but a presence of good.


SOUTHERN UKRAINE IS STEPPE; northern Ukraine is forest. Visiting a de-occupied town in the north of the country, I had similar thoughts about freedom. Having dropped off my children at friendly schools in New Haven, Connecticut, I made the journey to an abandoned school building in Yahidne, which Russian occupiers had transformed into a small concentration camp. For most of the time that the village was occupied, the Russians had packed 350 civilians, its entire population, into the school basement, an area of less than two hundred square meters. Seventy of the villagers were children, the youngest an infant.

Yahidne was de-occupied in April 2022, and I visited that September. On the ground floor, Russian soldiers had destroyed the furniture. On the walls, they left behind dehumanizing graffiti about Ukrainians. There was no electricity. By the light of my phone, I made my way down to the cellar, and examined the children's drawings on its walls. I could read what they had written ("No to war"); my children later helped me identify the characters (such as an Impostor from the game *Among Us*).

By a doorframe were two lists, written in chalk, of the names of the perished: on one side, those executed by the Russians (of whom, best as I could tell, there were seventeen); on the other, those who died from exhaustion or illness (of whom, best as I could tell, there were ten).

By the time I arrived in Yahidne, the survivors were no longer in the cellar. Were they free?

A *liberation* suggests a woe that has dissipated. But the adults need support, the children a new school. It is so very important that the town is no longer occupied. But it would be wrong to end the story of Yahidne when the survivors emerged from underground, just as it would be wrong to end the story of Posad Pokrovs'ke when the bombing stopped.

The gentleman entrusted with the key to the Yahidne school asked for help to build a playground. It might seem like a strange desire, amid a war of destruction. Russians kill children with missiles, and kidnap them for assimilation. But the absence of these crimes is not enough; de-occupation is not enough. Children need places to play, run, and swim, to practice being themselves. A child cannot create a park or a swimming pool. The joy of youth is to discover such things in the world. It takes collective work to build structures of freedom, for the young as for the old.

I CAME TO UKRAINE during the war while writing this book about freedom. Here its subject is palpable, all around. A month after

Russia invaded Ukraine, I spoke with some Ukrainian lawmakers: "We chose freedom when we did not run." "We are fighting for freedom." "Freedom itself is the choice."

It was not just the politicians. Talking in wartime Ukraine to soldiers, to widows and farmers, to activists and journalists, I heard the word *freedom* over and over. It was interesting how they used it. With much of their country under genocidal occupation, Ukrainians would seem to have good reason to speak of freedom as a liberation *from*, as an absence of evil. No one did.

When asked what they meant by *freedom*, not a single person with whom I spoke specified freedom from the Russians. One Ukrainian told me, "When we say *freedom*, we do not mean 'freedom from something.'" Another defined victory as being "for something, not against something." The occupiers had gotten in the way of a sense that the world was opening up, that the next generation would have a better life, that decisions made now would matter in years to come.

It was essential to remove repression, to gain what philosophers call "negative freedom." But de-occupation, the removal of harm, was just a necessary condition for freedom, not the thing itself. A soldier in a rehabilitation center told me that freedom was about everyone having a chance to fulfill their own purposes after the war. A veteran awaiting a prosthesis said that freedom would be a smile on his son's face. A young soldier on leave said that freedom was about the children he would like to have. Their commander in his hidden staff room, Valeriy Zaluzhnyi, told me that freedom meant a normal life with prospects.

Freedom was a future when some things were the same and others were better. It was life expanding and growing.


IN THIS BOOK, I aim to define *freedom*. The task begins with rescuing the word from overuse and abuse. I worry that, in my own country, the United States, we speak of freedom without considering what it is. Americans often have in mind the absence of something: occupation, oppression, or even government. An individual is free, we think, when the government is out of the way. Negative freedom is our common sense.

To be sure, it is tempting to think of liberty as us against the world, which the notion of negative freedom allows us to do. If the barriers are the only problem, then all must be right with us. That makes us feel good. We think that we would be free if not for a world outside that does us wrong. But is the removal of something in the world really enough to liberate us? Is it not as important, perhaps even more important, to add things?

If we want to be free, we will have to affirm, not just deny. Sometimes we will have to destroy, but more often we will need to create. Most often we will need to adapt both the world and ourselves, on the basis of what we know and value. We need structures, just the right ones, moral as well as political. Virtue is an inseparable part of freedom.

"Stone Walls do not a Prison make / Nor Iron bars a Cage"—said the poet. Sometimes they do, and sometimes they don't. Oppression is not just obstruction but the human intention behind it. In Ukraine's Donetsk, an abandoned factory became an art lab; under Russian occupation, the same building became a torture facility. A school basement, as in Yahidne, can be a concentration camp.

Early Nazi concentration camps, for that matter, were in bars, hotels, and castles. The first permanent one, Dachau, was in an abandoned factory. Auschwitz had been a Polish military base meant to defend people from a German attack. Kozelsk, a Soviet POW camp where Polish officers were held before their execution, had been a monastery—the one where Fyodor Dostoevsky, in *The Brothers Karamazov,* set the dialogue with the famous question: If God is dead, is everything permitted?

No larger force makes us free, nor does the absence of such a larger force. Nature gives us a chance to be free, nothing less, nothing more.

We are told that we are "born free": untrue. We are born squalling, attached to an umbilical cord, covered in a woman's blood. Whether we *become* free depends upon the actions of others, upon the structures that enable those actions, upon the values that enliven those structures—and only then upon a flicker of spontaneity and the courage of our own choices.

The structures that hinder or enable are physical and moral. It matters how we speak and think about freedom. Liberty begins with de-occupying our minds from the wrong ideas. And there *are* right and wrong ideas. In a world of relativism and cowardice, freedom is the absolute among absolutes, the value of values. This is not because freedom is the one good thing to which all others must bow. It is because freedom is the condition in which all the good things can flow within us and among us.

Nor is it because freedom is a vacuum left by a dead God or an empty world. Freedom is not an absence but a presence, a life in which we choose multiple commitments and realize combinations of them in the world. Virtues are real, as real as the starry heavens; when we are free, we learn them, exhibit them, bring them to life. Over time, our choices among virtues define us as people of will and individuality.

WHEN WE ASSUME that freedom is negative, the absence of this or that, we presume that removing a barrier is all that we have to do to be free. To this way of thinking, freedom is the default condition of the universe, brought to us by some larger force when we clear the way. This is naïve.

Americans are told that we were given freedom by our Founding Fathers, our national character, or our capitalist economy. None of this is true. Freedom cannot be given. It is not an inheritance. We call America a "free country," but no country is free. Noting a difference between the rhetoric of the oppressors and the oppressed, the dissident Eritrean poet Y. F. Mebrahtu reports that "*they* talk about the country, *we* talk about the people." Only people can be free. If we believe something else makes us free, we never learn what we must do. The moment you believe that freedom is given, it is gone.

We Americans tend to think that freedom is a matter of things being cleared away, and that capitalism does that work for us. It is a trap to believe in this or any other external source of freedom. If we associate freedom with outside forces, and someone tells us that the outside world delivers a threat, we sacrifice liberty for safety. This makes sense to us, because in our hearts we were already unfree. We believe that we can trade freedom for security. This is a fatal mistake.

Freedom and security work together. The preamble of the Constitution instructs that "the blessings of liberty" are to be pursued alongside "the general welfare" and "the common defense." We must have liberty *and* safety. For people to be free, they must feel secure, especially as children. They must have a chance to know one another and the world. Then, as they become free people, they decide what risks to take, and for what reasons.

When Russia invaded Ukraine, President Volodymyr Zelens'kyi did not tell his people that they needed to trade liberty for safety. He told them that he was staying in the country. After my visit to Yahidne, I spoke to him in his office in Kyiv, behind the sandbags. He called deoccupation a chance to restore both security and freedom. He said that the "deprivation of freedom was insecurity," and that "insecurity was the deprivation of freedom."

FREEDOM IS ABOUT knowing what we value and bringing it to life. So it depends on what we can do—and that, in turn, depends on others, people we know and people we don't.

As I write this preface on a westbound night train from Kyiv, I know how long I have before I reach the Polish border. I have a bit of security in that knowledge, and a bit of freedom to work—thanks to the labor of other people. Someone else laid the rail lines and repairs them when they are shelled, someone else built the carriages and looks after them, someone else is driving the train. When the Ukrainian army de-occupies cities, it raises the flag and shares the photos. But Ukrainians tend to regard cities as liberated when rail service has been restored.

Russian propagandists claim that there is no right and no good, and so everything is permitted. The consequences of that view are all around me in de-occupied Ukraine, in the death pits I saw at Bucha, in ruined settlements such as Posad Pokrovs'ke, in concentration camps such as Yahidne. Russian soldiers in Ukraine speak of cities they destroy as "liberated." And indeed: all barriers, from their perspective, have been removed. They can bulldoze the rubble and the corpses, as in Mariupol, build something else, sell it. In that negative sense of *free,* they are free to murder and steal.

The wheels and tracks beneath me are not making me free, but they are carrying me forward, creating conditions for my freedom that I could not create myself. I would be a less free person right now were there no train, or had Russia destroyed the Kyiv rail station. People in Ukraine were not freer when Russia destroyed public utilities and public schools.

We enable freedom not by rejecting government, but by affirming freedom as the guide to good government. Reasoning forward from the right definition of freedom, I believe, will get us to the right sort of government. And so this book begins with an introduction about freedom, and ends with a conclusion about government. The five chapters in between show the way from philosophy to policy.

HOW DOES FREEDOM figure in our lives? The connections between freedom as a principle and freedom as a practice are the *five forms of freedom.*

The forms create a world where people act on the basis of values. They are not rules or orders. They are the logical, moral, and political links between common action and the formation of free individuals. The forms resolve two apparent conundrums: a free person is an individual, but no one becomes an individual alone; freedom is felt in one lifetime, but it must be the work of generations.

The five forms are: *sovereignty,* or the learned capacity to make choices; *unpredictability,* the power to adapt physical regularities to personal purposes; *mobility,* the capacity to move through space and time following values; *factuality,* the grip on the world that allows us to change it; and *solidarity,* the recognition that freedom is for everyone.

The labor of freedom begins after the labor of a mother. A baby has the potential to evaluate the world and change it, and it develops the requisite capabilities with the support of and in the company of others. This is *sovereignty.*

Coming of age, a young human being learns to see the world as it is and to imagine how it might be. A sovereign person mixes chosen virtues with the world outside to make something new. Thus *unpredictability* is the second form of freedom.

Our bodies need places to go. We cannot as young people create for ourselves the conditions that will allow us to be sovereign and unpredictable. But once those conditions have been created, we rebel against the very institutions that made them possible and go our own way. And this *mobility,* the third form of freedom, is to be encouraged.

We are free to do only the things we know how to do, and free to go only to places where we can go. What we don't know can hurt us, and what we do know empowers us. Freedom's fourth form is *factuality.*

No individual achieves freedom alone. Practically and ethically, freedom for you means freedom for me. This recognition is *solidarity,* the final form of freedom.

The solution to the problem of freedom is not, as some on the Right think, to mock or abandon government. The solution is also not, as some on the Left think, to ignore or cast away the rhetoric of freedom.

Freedom justifies government. The forms of freedom show us how.

THIS BOOK FOLLOWS the logic of an argument and the logic of a life. The first three forms of freedom pertain to different phases of life: sovereignty to childhood; unpredictability to youth; mobility to young adulthood. Factuality and solidarity are the mature forms of freedom, enabling the others. Each form has a chapter.

In the introduction, I draw on my own life, beginning with the first time I remember thinking about freedom: during the summer of 1976, the American bicentennial year. I will try to show, on the basis of five decades of my own mistakes, how some misunderstandings of freedom arose, and how they might be corrected. The conclusion describes a good government, one that we might create together. There I imagine an America that has reached the year 2076, its tercentennial, as a land of the free.

The chapters are divided into vignettes. Some of them include memories that sprang to mind as I was trying to address a philosophical issue. The flashes of recollection enable some reflection. They allow me to apply a humble version of the Socratic method to my earlier self: questioning the sense of words and the habits of life, to awaken what is, in some sense, already known. The point is to elicit truths about this country and about freedom that were not evident to me in the moment—and that would not be evident to me now had I not passed through those earlier experiences.

This is a philosophical method (I hope) fitting for a historian, which is what I am. I rely on historical examples and know more about the past of some regions than others. This is a book about the United States, but I draw comparisons with western Europe, eastern Europe, the Soviet Union, and Nazi Germany.

I am in discussion here with philosophers ancient, modern, and contemporary. Sometimes I leave the references implicit; those who care will catch them. I do cite explicitly five thinkers: Frantz Fanon, Václav Havel, Leszek Kołakowski, Edith Stein, and Simone Weil. These figures are not American and are not well known in the United States; with minor exceptions, they neither resided in the country nor wrote about it. A prodding from another tradition (or a term from another language) can shake us free of misapprehensions. I adapt from each thinker a concept that advances the argument; I do not claim that they agree with one another (or with me) on every issue.

This book is conservative, in that it draws from tradition; but radical, in that it proposes something new. It is philosophy, but it cleaves to experience. A few phrases in this book are text messages that I wrote to myself in intermittent moments of consciousness in a hospital bed, during an illness that nearly took my life. Arguments were conceived while teaching a class inside an American maximum security prison. I wrote much of what follows during three journeys to wartime Ukraine.

The fundamental questions were posed by readers. My books *Bloodlands* and *Black Earth,* studies of mass killing, led to public discussions that moved me toward the ethical subject of this book. If I can describe the worst, can I not also prescribe the best? After I published the political pamphlet *On Tyranny* and a contemporary history called *The Road to Unfreedom*, I was asked what a better America would look like. This is my answer.

Defining freedom is a different sort of ambition from defending it. I interrogate my former self; I interrogate others; and others interrogate me. The method is part of the answer: there may be truth about freedom, but we will not get to it in isolation or by deduction. Freedom is positive; getting words around it, like living it, is an act of creation.

This book is meant to exemplify the virtues it commends. It is, I hope, reasonable, but also unpredictable. It is intended to be sober, but also experimental. It celebrates not who we are, but the freedom that could be ours.

The sun rises outside my window. The border approaches. I begin my reflection on a summer day.

T.S.
Kyiv-Dorohusk train
Wagon 10, Compartment 9
6:10 a.m., September 10, 2023

# Introduction

## Freedom

### JUBILEE

It is summer 1976, a sunny afternoon on an Ohio farm. Wisps of cloud flit across the sky; gravel presses underfoot. A boy of six, going on seven, stands in line next to a farmhouse to ring a bell: the me that I once was, full of futures.

A gravel lane winds upward from the country road. It bends as the hill crests, between a maple tree that extends across the first few rows of a cornfield and an old sycamore that shades the farmhouse. On the maple hangs a swing, slowly oscillating now from my leap to earth. Past the house, the lane continues to two round corncribs and an old wooden barn, then fades into a path sloping downward to a pond. On both sides of the lane are fields of fossils and arrowheads, as I think of them, covered now in rising stalks of corn.

I am on the farm with my mother's family, to celebrate summer birthdays and commemorate two hundred years of American independence. Each cousin, in line from the oldest to the youngest, is taking a turn at the bell. Its distinctive double ring resounds through my childhood: a nice high peal, followed by an awkward lower one, as the bell's clapper meets the lip an unintended second time. The bell has a flaw.

My turn comes. The bell weighs as much as I do, but it is well mounted, and I know how to move it. Hands clenched around the rope, eyes closed, I lean back to make a lever of my body. Gravity does my work. The bell rings out, unmistakable and imperfect. I open my eyes, still leaning back, and see only blue. I am thinking about freedom.

After every kid has rung the bell, we all tumble through a white-washed screened-in porch, where a mastodon tusk hangs on the far wall. I pause there for a moment to find my sneakers, then tread into the kitchen, the last to join a circle formed for silent grace. I catch a glimpse of the basket of outgoing mail, mounted on the wall behind me. The Liberty Bell stamps cite the biblical injunction inscribed on the bell itself: in a jubilee year, "Proclaim liberty throughout all the land."

The Liberty Bell is cracked. The fissure was right there on the stamp. The bell in question was forged in 1752 for the Pennsylvania Statehouse in Philadelphia for a different jubilee, the half-century of the colony's Charter of Privileges. The flaw we see now appeared when it was rung on George Washington's birthday in 1846.

The next words of that biblical verse suggest a way to interpret the crack: "ye shall return every man unto his possession, and ye shall return every man unto his family" (Leviticus 25:10). In the nineteenth century, abolitionists read those words as a call to end American slavery. They took the bell at the Philadelphia statehouse as their symbol and gave it the name we know today. Later the Liberty Bell was used by the woman suffrage movement.

In 1976 the stamp codified a patriotic legend: that a Liberty Bell was rung as the Declaration of Independence was declaimed in Philadelphia in July 1776. Neither was the bell rung then, nor did it bear that name. The Liberty Bell was named in reference to those who gained no liberty. It was used to claim a better future, not to commemorate an ideal past.

The bicentennial was a tricky idea for a child. It called me to a world where freedom had been achieved two centuries before because something, a British Empire, had been removed. We, the Americans, were then supposed to be liberated eternally. As a bicentennial symbol, the Liberty Bell was stripped of its reference to women and Black people, suggesting a perfect achievement of freedom long ago complete.

It might at first seem logical that freedom is an absence and seem fair that the government should leave each of us equally alone. This intuition draws its plausibility from a history of exploitation. Traditionally, some people have regarded themselves as free because they exploit the labor of slaves and women. Those who believe themselves free because they dominate others define freedom negatively, as the absence of government, because only a government could emancipate the slaves or enfranchise the women. The conflation of a Liberty Bell with the American Revolution dodges the issue of what freedom is, and for whom that bell tolls.

As a boy of six going on seven, I had heard the phrase *underground railroad* and had wondered what it would be like to hide in the farmhouse cellar. But it would not have occurred to me to ask whether American independence meant freedom for everyone. Black kids my age would not have needed to ask, since the answer was out there, in life itself.

## FLIGHTS

The bell rings. Time for freedom. Time for dinner. Since my birthday is closest, I jump to the head of the line. The buffet starts by the door that leads from the porch, then follows the counter around the perimeter of the kitchen: sweetcorn (still boiling in the pot) first, then meat and vegetables and mashed potatoes, then casseroles and bread, and desserts and coffee. For those who want it, there is a watermelon on the porch, to be sliced later and eaten outside.

One table is set in the kitchen, others are spread through the ground floor, some under portraits of ancestors. Amid the portraits is a framed deed to the property and a certificate from the state of Ohio confirming a century of continuous ownership. My mother's family lived here through the War of 1812, the Civil War, the First World War, and the Great Depression. My mother was born here in the middle of the Second World War. My father was born on the other side of the county, in another farmhouse.

My mother gave birth to me in a hospital named after an Ohio inventor, in the midst of the Vietnam War, a few weeks after the moon landing of 1969. The Wright Brothers' projects for heavier-than-air flight had been realized a few miles north, in their Dayton bicycle shop.

Dayton was a great American center of innovation and industry. It was the site of the first commercial cargo flight and the first helicopter flight. It became a rail hub in 1900, with dozens of stops at its Union Station each day. Charles Kettering, the hospital's namesake, invented the electric starter for the automobile. He started work at National Cash Register (today NCR), founded DELCO (Dayton Engineering Laboratories Company), and headed research at General Motors.

Along with Wright-Patterson Air Force Base, these three companies were the major local employers in the 1970s, when I was a boy in southwest Ohio. Workers were unionized. The farmers called National Cash Register "the Cash" and Wright-Patterson Air Force Base "the Field" (while the city kids said "NCR" and "Wright-Pat").

Neil Armstrong, the first man to walk on the moon, was from Wapakoneta, Ohio, north of Dayton. As kids we visited his museum there and met him in person. My maternal grandmother had a signed photograph of the astronaut. Her younger brother was a pilot and engineer who worked on the space shuttle; the launch of the *Columbia* was the ecstatic moment in my childhood. I watched it on television and then went outside to look up at the sky. Heavier-than-air flight in 1903, a moon landing in 1969, a space shuttle in 1981: this trajectory promised a future of adventurous mobility.

My parents grew up on farms in Clinton County, Ohio, before making the leap to Ohio State University. I spent a good deal of my childhood on those farms. During the summer, my paternal grandfather put me and my brothers to work and took us to the county fair. He kept his old baseball bats and gloves by the porch door, as though a game might break out at any moment. I brought my own glove and found ways to practice baseball in the barnyard. The Cincinnati Reds might be playing on television inside while I was playing an imaginary game outside. My paternal grandmother taught me not to cook the sweetcorn too long, shared her historical novels, and was thoughtfully critical about how one spoke. She had taught my father in a one-room schoolhouse.

On the other side of the county, in my maternal grandparents' house, the one with the bell, I liked to take refuge upstairs. Amid my maternal grandmother's fossil collections, I immersed myself in her books about the past, the present, and alternative futures: paleontology, zoology, *A Wrinkle in Time*.

On New Year's Day 1982, that attic was cold and drafty as I read about the imposition of martial law in communist Poland. In the newspapers, Americans worried about instability and nuclear war, but I had the sense of something lively and interesting. In the photographs in magazines, the gray of armored personnel carriers and dirty snow contrasted with the bit of red ink for the banners of the suppressed labor union, Solidarity.

## HOLOCAUSTS

In my childhood, the Soviet Union always seemed close, a few minutes' flight by intercontinental ballistic missile. *Reader's Digest* featured articles on Soviet and American nuclear arsenals. The obsession with the superpowers' destructive capacity was a way to ignore the people who suffered directly in the Cold War, such as the Latin Americans we kept invading and the east Europeans the Soviets kept invading.

In the 1980s, as social mobility in the United States slowed, talk of nuclear confrontation grew. In 1984 I answered the phone—a landline, of course—and took a survey. The pollster asked me two questions: "Is it safe to work in convenience stores?" and "Are you afraid of nuclear war?" I found nothing strange about that.

American nuclear missiles were called "Minutemen," after the militias of the Revolutionary War. In the 1970s and 1980s, the vision of a nuclear exchange between the United States and the Soviet Union was an element of everyday life. Behind our house (to the west) a meadow stretched all the way to railroad tracks a quarter-mile away, where freight trains passed at sunset when I was a small child. A stream ran through the meadow, watering a little copse where we tried to fish. To the south of our house, across the road, a cornfield rolled uphill to a seminary. A siren atop its bell tower practiced tornado warnings, but the local kids associated it with air raids. Looking up from the creek ("crick") where we were trying to catch crayfish ("craw-dads") in Styrofoam cups, we thought of mushroom clouds and knew that it was midday.

It was a shock when my maternal grandmother, Lucile, told me that danger doesn't come from afar. For the fortieth anniversary of D-Day in 1984, a teacher sent me to interview her about the Second World War. Sitting across from me at the kitchen table, Lucile suggested that researching relatives was not the way to understand the war. Herself a teacher, she had taken my school assignment as an opportunity to make sure I learned. She always laughed and offered gumdrops; at fourteen, I scarcely knew what she looked like with a serious expression. That day I found out. Her eyes were wide open, and her cheek muscles taut, as she remonstrated with me about where my thoughts should be. If I was to write about the war, I should remember "all those Jewish people." She sighed and then smiled again.

The Holocaust of the Jews had happened not so very long before. I had read Anne Frank's diary, found by chance on a school bookshelf in fifth grade. Yet at the time when I interviewed my grandmother, the mass murder of the Jews was a smaller part of the memory of the war than it later became. The word *Holocaust* in this sense came into broad American use after a 1978 television series, but in the 1980s the term was still ambiguous. *The Day After,* a 1983 made-for-television movie about nuclear holocaust, was watched by one hundred million Americans. One December afternoon in 1985, sitting on an orange couch in the local public library, I listened to some older kids expound upon their plan for nuclear war: get a six-pack, drive to Wright-Pat, and die in the flash rather than from the radiation.

Perhaps that hypothetical nuclear holocaust drew attention away from what the Jewish Holocaust might have taught us. A possible catastrophe involving long-range missiles overshadowed the recent demonstration of how easily a partially democratic system like ours could collapse, how quickly big lies could create restive alternative realities, and how callously humans could kill one another. During the Cold War, American and Soviet propaganda relentlessly associated the other side with the Nazis; the decades of mutual accusation perhaps hardened everyone to the actual risk, which was that fascism might arise at home.

I did have the idea, as a teenager, that fear was making the country less free. When I went to college in 1987, I planned to become a nuclear arms negotiator. Though there was nothing ignoble in this career aim, I was turning away from American reality. I was ignoring the sources of fear that were right in front of me.

## BELLS

In the late 1980s, as a college student, I was fascinated by people who had found a politics beyond fear: the east European dissidents. Andrei Sakharov, one of the founders of the Soviet nuclear program, was urging Westerners to think less about nuclear intimidation and more about human dignity. I remember raising my eyes from his text and looking up at the sky as the point came home. We should remove the causes of fear if we can; we should also take responsibility for our fears. Freedom cannot be just an absence; it must arise from us and grow into the world.

In the autumn of 1989, during my junior year in college, my planned career in nuclear disarmament was taken away from me. Communism in eastern Europe came to an end, and arms control negotiations with the USSR proceeded quickly to treaties. It was thrilling to read the dispatches of American reporters from eastern Europe. Thanks to a student job at the Center for Foreign Policy Development at Brown University, I met some of the dissidents as they came to power.

I was responsible for the Czechoslovak foreign minister Jiří Dienstbier during some meetings in Washington, failed to get him to any of them on time. He paid no attention to the schedule and kept pausing to have a smoke. We made the vice president and the secretary of state wait. My idea of freedom at that point was all about efficiency, and I was a little flummoxed that his was so different.

I had written a senior essay on nuclear arms control as a sophomore; as a junior, I focused more on economics, starting projects that would become senior theses on Soviet defense reform and Soviet monopoly. In November 1990, the autumn of my senior year, I was invited to Moscow to present some of my work. It was my first transatlantic flight, following the trajectory of all those imagined missiles. As the aircraft descended, I looked down at a patchwork of collective farms.

This was deep into Soviet leader Mikhail Gorbachev's period of reform, I was feckless and twenty-one, and I treated the Soviet capital as a place to explore. I dropped the heavily fobbed room key at the reception desk of the Hotel Akademicheskaia and took the fast escalators down to the deep metro platforms that were meant to double as bomb shelters, memorizing station names and asking strangers for help. The hurried glances of fellow passengers, the empty shelves in the stores, the unkempt farmsteads: these impressions confirmed what I had written in my paper, which was that this country would not go on for long.

People did give me directions, which was good; the city was large, the days were cold and short, and the buildings seemed to repeat from district to district. A Russian scholar at the conference kindly took me in, and his two children, about my age, gave me better tours of Moscow. When I spoke tactlessly about the coming collapse of the USSR, their faces showed a simple sadness. They did not doubt it, if the young American scholar said so. But the post-Soviet Russia that they imagined was an empire with a tsar. In the apartment, they showed me treasured relics of the Russian Empire, of a pre-Soviet past.

It was snowing the day the three of us visited the Kremlin. The flakes melted on a bell of improbable size: the "Tsar Bell." It was about as large as the family's apartment and weighed about two hundred tons. Meant to glorify an absolute ruler, the ferrous enormity rested on the ground and did nothing. The songless object got me thinking about the disproportions in the Soviet economy that I was meant to address at the conference in Moscow.

## EQUILIBRIUM

In the language of physics, a bell that hangs on a post on a farm is in equilibrium: the force of gravity pulling it down is matched by the force of the ground pushing back on the structure. Getting a bell in the air so that it can be rung requires some careful work. Not every equilibrium is the same. The Tsar Bell is in an equilibrium in which it cannot be rung.

Economists also speak of equilibria. They like situations when things seem to be in balance, as the result of an aggregate of human actions that can be characterized as a larger, impersonal force. For example: supply, the amount of stuff, is supposed to balance demand, how much people want that stuff. An equilibrium is like a happy ending: everything turns out right. We don't have to think about people as individuals with purposes: markets do the thinking for us. We do not have to ask how people come into the world, why they want what they want, or what it means to be free.

In autumn 1990, when I traveled to the Soviet Union, I was working on projects in economics, but that semester I was also taking graduate classes in history and had applied for a fellowship to continue those studies in a doctoral program. I liked history's inexhaustibility—a surprise awaited in each new book, behind each half-understood event, within each new language. The past is full of wild possibilities that were actually realized, such as the Bolshevik Revolution, or the American one. The east European revolutions of 1989, unpredictable as they had been, made me wonder whether other surprises might be coming.

In Moscow in November 1990, history gave me a common language with Soviet scholars. We talked about the Russian economy in the late imperial years, before the revolution, and about the crash industrialization of the 1930s. I could agree with Soviet participants that the problem of transforming their planned economy into something else was not foreseen in textbook economics.

In the cold and drafty conference room, my mind wandering, I doodled little bells in the margins of my notes. In the Russian Empire, in 1591 and 1771, bells had been sentenced to Siberian exile, on the theory that they precipitated public gatherings. In 1510, after Moscow conquered the town of Pskov, the new rulers did away with the bell used to call public meetings.

I drew some manacles around the bells. In the Soviet Union, as I knew from my own research on Soviet monopoly, Pskov was where they made all the handcuffs. (In 2014 troops from Pskov invaded Ukraine; in 2022 they murdered civilians at Bucha.) The rest of the Soviet economy was similarly centralized: critical products were made in a few sites or even in a single factory. Natural gas and oil were also extracted and distributed in a very centralized way.

As an initial condition for a market economy, I was trying to say, monopoly was unpromising. Capitalism's radical critics (Vladimir Lenin) and radical supporters (Friedrich Hayek) agreed that monopoly meant oppression. Markets are supposed to enable competition, spread information, and separate economics from politics. But what would happen when giant Soviet enterprises came into private hands?

Monopolists would seek to prevent competition, own media, and corner political power. Once the Soviet Union began to come apart (I was arguing), its industrial concentration would accelerate the process of disintegration, because locals who seized control of valuable assets would seek to protect their new holdings by trying to control new states.

So any shift to capitalism in the Soviet Union had to be understood as part of a longer political history, not as a clearing of the slate that would generate perfect markets. From the starting point of the Soviet reality around me in November 1990, laissez-faire was not going to lead to the right result. Oligarchy, rule by the very wealthy, is also an equilibrium. A heavy bell can just stay on the ground.

I don't think I managed to get much of this across in Moscow: the huge meeting room turned all utterances into echoes; men in scarves shivered during the presentations; the secondhand cigarette smoke was uncannily warmer than the air.

No one was thinking much then about the non-Russian nations. Americans said "Russia" for the USSR and "Russians" for Soviet citizens. I was little better, though I knew the geography from studying military sites and big factories. Half of the population of the Soviet Union was not Russian, and a quarter of the territory was in the non-Russian republics. The Russian republic itself was described as a federation because of its tremendous variety: it contained, for example, the Tatars, one of the largest Soviet nationalities. Ukraine was, after Russia, the second-largest in population. In Moscow, American conference participants saw the opera *Mazepa,* about the Ukrainian hetman and his break with Tsar Peter; during the intermission, the economists in the group asked the Russia hands whether Ukraine was a separate country. Not really, was the consensus.

Jet-lagged and reading at night for a college seminar on Marxism, I thought in Moscow about the uncanny similarity between the prophets of communism and the prophets of capitalism. Capitalists *knew* that communist societies would automatically right themselves once private property was restored, just as Marxists had once *known* that capitalist societies would automatically right themselves once private property was abolished. I felt the draw of the first view: Would it not be nice to simply start again, free of the past? But the appeal was just too similar to the confidence of Marx and Engels, or for that matter that of Lenin and Trotsky when the Soviet experiment began.

I worked as a student at the Center for Foreign Policy Development between spring 1989 and spring 1991, in Washington at *Foreign Policy* magazine in summer 1990, and in Washington again at the Institute for International Economics in the summer and autumn of 1991. I had a sense of the elite consensus between the end of communism in eastern Europe in late 1989 and the disintegration of the Soviet Union in late 1991. Very few of the wise heads expected either. The George H. W. Bush administration supported Gorbachev to the very last moment. U.S. policy was to hold the Soviet Union together. President Bush went to Kyiv on August 1, 1991, but only to urge Ukrainians not to declare independence.

On August 18, 1991, I went to bed early in my Georgetown sublet. I had worked all day on Russian economics and German language, then made a meal for some friends to celebrate my twenty-second birthday. A Russian friend awakened me with a telephone call: "Massive revolution!" He meant the coup attempt against Gorbachev that would be the beginning of the end of the USSR. Ukrainian communists declared the independence of their republic on August 24. A month later, I finished my study of Soviet monopoly and departed for graduate study in history at Oxford. The formal dissolution of the USSR in December found me in Czechoslovakia. Right after New Year's, I took the night train from Prague to Warsaw. When I presented a paper on Soviet monopoly in Vienna in April 1992, the economists from what had been the USSR now represented newly independent states.

As the Soviet Union came to an end, American anxiety yielded to an odd euphoria. Americans hadn't expected revolution and disintegration. And yet many were now speaking with confidence about what must follow: a durable capitalist equilibrium would bring with it democracy and freedom. In fairness, the better economists were concerned about structures. But negative freedom set the tone: once the barriers of Soviet central planning and state ownership were cleared away, only good things could follow. This odd confidence about the future was one reason I decided to study the past.

## EXCEPTIONALISM

The Cold War had been a moral challenge for the United States. Anti-communism led to the denunciatory excesses of McCarthyism. It also became a justification for supporting right-wing dictators, invading Caribbean and Latin American countries, and overthrowing democratically elected rulers.

I was brought up in this knowledge. My parents had been serving in the Peace Corps in the Dominican Republic when the United States intervened in 1965. They were then transferred to El Salvador. A Salvadoran girl spent six months at our home when I was small, taking care of my brothers and me. My mother kept visiting Latin America throughout my childhood, and she taught Latin American studies at a local university.

The Soviet challenge had also pushed America toward some strengths. It led to the moon shot of 1969 and to important technological spin-offs. It encouraged Americans to engage with European and Russian culture, and it brought government investment to universities, including in languages and the humanities. American universities taught classes on Russia and the Soviet Union (though rarely on eastern Europe and almost never on Ukraine). Avant-garde American art, music, and literature were propagated abroad, to show that democracy could be hip and vibrant. Soviet reminders of American inequality bolstered the American welfare state and helped the civil rights movement. So long as Marxism was a present alternative, Americans tried to justify their own system with ideas and safeguard it with structures.

The disintegration of the USSR in 1991 was like a judo move, turning the United States against itself. Arguments gave way to verities: capitalism would replace communism and bring democracy to the world. As negative freedom became common sense in the United States, one determinism replaced another. If the absence of private property had not brought freedom, then the presence of private property surely would. Since the iron laws of history would liberate everyone, there was no need to know the past—even the details of communism and fascism, the two great political alternatives of the twentieth century, could be forgotten. At the moment I chose history, it was deemed irrelevant. And yet freedom must be about possible futures, and any possible future exists on a line from an actual past. How were we to draw those lines without history?

## OLIGARCHY

Unexpected events did take place in the early 1990s: racial violence in Los Angeles, which I read about in Polish newspapers as I was learning the language on the Baltic coast; the billionaire Ross Perot's first campaign for president, which became real for me on a BBC electoral map in an Oxford common room; the Yugoslav wars, which drove refugees to Vienna, where I befriended a few of them. Yet in this mood, each crisis seemed exceptional, and each challenge seemed technical. History was not to be learned but blamed—ethnic cleansing in the Balkans was supposedly a result of "ancient hatreds." America was to be the timeless measure of freedom.

If freedom is negative, then politics becomes the practical work of clearing away the junk of the past: in the jargon of the 1980s and 1990s: *deregulation, privatization, welfare reform.* Economics or nature is expected to do the rest. The conception of freedom as negative led Americans to give bad advice to east Europeans: privatize as quickly as possible; portray the welfare state as a communist deformation; ignore culture. It also led the United States to some dreadful domestic policies in the 1990s, such as the prison industrial complex and wealth hoarding.

Negative freedom also hovered over errors of the 2000s. After spending a few more years in eastern Europe, I moved in September 2001 to

New Haven, Connecticut, for my first real job, at Yale University. I was in New York in the early morning hours of September 11 (to watch the Yankees lose to the Orioles in a long, ugly game delayed by rain). When I learned in New Haven what had happened, I tried to return to New York, but the trains had stopped running.

The attacks of 9/11 were presented as something unprecedented, the dawn of a new world in which freedom must be sacrificed for safety. At my very first class at Yale, I talked about the destruction of the Twin Towers in the light of what I understood from east European episodes of terror and counterterror. A provocation works when a less powerful entity turns a more powerful actor against itself. The attack of 9/11 was one of the most successful provocations of all time.

After 9/11, Americans were told that the attackers "hate freedom," but our response suggested that we misunderstood it. The ostensible exchange of freedom for security meant less of each. Surveillance became normal. The 2003 invasion of Iraq killed hundreds of thousands of Iraqis and left the United States poorer, less secure, and less trusted. That war was an adventure in negative freedom, waged to create an absence. Destroying the Iraqi state and dissolving the ruling party and army, it was assumed, would automatically bring capitalism and democracy. It did not. The war strengthened Iran and created a series of security problems that extended deep into the new century.

Our misunderstanding of Russia in the 1990s and 2000s also had to do with negative freedom. In 1993 the Russian president, Boris Yeltsin, had dissolved the Russian parliament by force. This was understood in the United States as necessary for economic reform. In fact, Soviet industrial concentration was becoming capitalist monopoly. A few people were taking control of the profitable enterprises. After 1999, Yeltsin's handpicked successor, Vladimir Putin, became the boss of bosses, consolidating power through terror and wars.

Seen through the lens of negative freedom, Putin seemed like a technocrat interested in money. The assumption was that wealth would bring rationality, and rationality would bring democracy. During my first spring at Yale, I was invited to a meeting where a major international hydrocarbon firm was being advised about Russia. A colleague with experience at high levels of government said that U.S. policy was grounded in the assumption that capitalism would bring democracy to both Russia and China. I said that this was absurd. I was not invited to such meetings for a while.

Russian oligarchy instead brought a new politics, an alternative during an epoch when there were supposed to be no alternatives. In 2004, Putin's Russia attempted to rig the vote in Ukraine. Ten years later, it invaded southern and eastern Ukraine. Before and during the invasion, Moscow's propaganda slandered Ukraine and Ukrainians. The basis of the attack was not evidence or even ideology, but rather estimations of what would arouse negative emotions in consumers of social media. Knowing something about what people believed about the world, Russia could target specific vulnerabilities. Considered in their totality, Russia's claims about Ukraine were contradictory: there was no Ukrainian language, but the Ukrainian state was making everyone speak it; the Ukrainian state did not exist but was repressive; Ukrainians were all Nazis, but they were also gays and Jews. I was living in Vienna at the time and was in contact with Ukrainian friends and colleagues. The simple fact that Russia had invaded a neighboring country got lost in social media. Americans and others wasted outrage on phantoms even as a real war of aggression began.

In Russia, we see the transition from the definition of freedom as the lack of barriers to a politics of fascism in which there are no barriers to the Leader's whims. Yet Moscow's own propaganda position—that nothing is true and nothing is good—was not perceived as a danger. The invasion of Ukraine demonstrated the fallacy of economic determinism: oligarchic Russia was an aggressive empire, not an emerging democracy. For people who believed that freedom was negative, Russian nihilism did not seem hazardous. It was, of course. Any vacuum of facts and values will be filled with spectacle and war. The fascist nature of the Russian regime ought to have been clear well before Russia's full-scale invasion of Ukraine in 2022.

The Russian case might serve as a warning. In the twenty-first century, American capitalism has also been driven toward monopoly, wealth concentration, and decadence. When we think that we are exceptional in our devotion to freedom, our overconfidence makes us vulnerable to the propaganda of tyrants pitched at what we want to hear. If we believe that freedom is negative, the problem is only a barrier outside, and never our own lack of judgment. When I returned to the United States in 2014 after a year away, I was struck (as were my Ukrainian and Russian friends) by how well Russian social media functioned in American politics. That Americans had been fooled by Russia about Ukraine was bad enough. But in 2015 and 2016 Americans were fooled by Russians about other Americans. In 2016 the oligarchical American presidential candidate won, with Russian assistance.

Donald Trump, Putin's submissive client, is a hero of negative freedom, wealthy through undertaxed inheritance and comfortable denying everything. In 2018 he traveled to Helsinki and told the world that he trusted a Russian dictator more than his American advisers. In 2019 he tried to bully an elected Ukrainian president to get dirt on his rival in the coming presidential election. When Trump lost the election of 2020, he lied about the outcome and tried to stage a coup d'état to stay in power. Despite a constitutional ban on insurrectionists holding office, he purports to be running for president in 2024, keeping alive Putin's hopes that he can win his war in Ukraine.

Deep into a century that was the stuff of dreams in the 1970s, and the subject of confident predictions in the 1990s, we find ourselves at a turning point. Whether we will be free will depend on us—not just on what we do, but on why we do it: our ideals.

## STAYING

Without ideals, it is impossible to be a realist. If you forget about freedom, you misunderstand the world and change it for the worse. The initial American reaction to Russia's full-scale invasion of Ukraine in February 2022 clarifies the point.

As Russia massed its troops on the Ukrainian border, I was in New

Haven, where I had been teaching for two decades. On the Monday before Russia's full-scale invasion, I took part in a remote meeting, a doctoral dissertation defense in Ukraine. Illia Chedoluma was defending a history thesis about a Ukrainian literary critic of Jewish origin who translated *Hamlet* while hiding from the Nazis. Illia passed his exam, then enlisted in the Ukrainian territorial defense.

On the Tuesday before Russia invaded, I was invited to join a class at Yale's School of Management. The colleague leading the class had seen me on television the prior Sunday and knew that I held an unusual opinion about Ukraine's president, Volodymyr Zelens'kyi: that if Russia invaded, he would stay, and that Ukraine would fight. My colleague had invited security advisers to former presidents Barack Obama and Donald Trump to participate remotely in the class, and he asked them to comment on my prediction. Talking down from the big screens, they all disagreed with me. For them, it was self-evident that Zelens'kyi would flee. Like the people inside the Kremlin, the people inside the Beltway believed that Ukraine would fall in three days. The Russian and American conventional wisdom was identical.

On the Thursday, Russia invaded, and my student reported to his unit. Zelens'kyi stayed in Kyiv, and Ukrainians fought. The American experts had excluded freedom as a factor in the world, so their prediction was incorrect. They had patiently explained that Zelens'kyi would leave the country; American intelligence officers advised him to do so. All were representing an American consensus. Americans had told themselves for decades that freedom was negative, that it represented a clearing-away of barriers by larger forces. If you believe in the primacy of the larger forces, then you have no choice when they seem to turn against you: you run. And you cannot imagine that others would behave any differently.

On the Friday, Zelens'kyi posted a video of himself and other high government officials in Kyiv: "The president is here." This was a transformative example of the freedom of speech. Like freedom in general, freedom of speech is not negative but positive, not about the barriers but the person, not about an absence but a presence. We protect free speakers because truth threatens the power of tyrants. Zelens'kyi was speaking truth amid the lies of Russian propagandists who claimed that he had abandoned the city. He was speaking his truth to power, because Russia was invading with terrifying force. Zelens'kyi was putting his body at risk for what he knew to be true. Indeed, it was what he was doing with his body—staying—that *was* the truth.

His refusal to leave gives a hint of what positive freedom—true freedom—might be. Barriers to freedom were no doubt present, in a most radical form. Even as Zelens'kyi spoke, Russian assassins were tracking him. The Russian army was at the gates of Kyiv, Russian bombs and missiles were falling, and virtually everyone outside Ukraine expected Russia to win the war within hours or days. And yet for Ukrainians, it was not so much the objects that were the issue— the bullets and the explosives—but the intention behind them, the elimination of a society. Russian weapons had to be met with Ukrainian weapons, but they also had to be met with commitment. The Ukrainians defeated the Russians at Kyiv and then at Kharkiv. Bucha would be de-occupied, Yahidne and Posad Pokrovs'ke as well, within a year after Russia's full-scale invasion. Ukrainians would regain more than half of the land Russia took in February 2022. But only because people decided to stay.

When I asked Zelens'kyi why he had remained in Kyiv, he said that he "could not have done otherwise." Explaining his choice, he began not from the specific predicament, dramatic though it was, and not even from himself. He spoke of his love for his parents, and what he had learned from them. He had not chosen them, and yet in his love for them he was free. He compared that love to the decision to remain in the capital as the war began: something self-evident. Staying was not something he did alone: he was in the company of those who had taught him when he was younger and those who had elected him. He was in the company of others who were also taking risks. He understood the situation, he said, because of what it meant to represent others. A president, he said, was only the first grain of sand in a turning hourglass.

We talked about how, over time, beginning in youth, an accumulation of decisions makes us who we are. Then a moment comes when we do what we must because of what we have chosen to become. An unfree person can always try to run. But sometimes a free person has to stay. Free will is character.

# Sovereignty

The German philosopher Edith Stein put her own body forward during the First World War. A graduate student, she took leave to volunteer as a nurse. When she returned to her dissertation, her time with the wounded guided her argument about empathy. "Do we not," she asked, "need the mediation of the body to assure ourselves of the existence of another person?"

The word she used for "body" was *Leib*.

The first form of freedom, as I hope to show, is sovereignty. A sovereign person knows themselves and the world sufficiently to make judgments about values and to realize those judgments.

For Stein, we gain knowledge of ourselves when we acknowledge others. Only when we recognize that other people are in the same predicament as we are, live as bodies as we do, can we take seriously how they see us. When we identify with them as they regard us, we understand ourselves as we otherwise might not. Our own objectivity, in other words, depends on the subjectivity of others.

This is not how we are accustomed to seeing things. We imagine that we can just take in information ourselves, as isolated individuals.

We believe that when we are alone, we are free. This mistake ensures that we are not.

The word *Leib* gets us to a new standpoint. The German language has two terms for "body," *Körper* and *Leib*. The word *Körper* can denote a person's body but also a "foreign body" (*Fremdkörper*), a "heavenly body" (*Himmelskörper*), the "racial body" (*Volkskörper*), and other objects thought to be subject to physical laws. A *Körper* might be alive, but it need not be (compare *corpse*). Stein says, "There can be a *Körper* without me, but no *Leib* without me."

The word *Leib* designates a living human body, or an animal body, or the body of an imaginary creature in a story. A *Leib* is a *Körper*, subject to physical laws, but that is not all it is. It has its own rules and so its own opportunities. A *Leib* can move, a *Leib* can feel, and a *Leib* has its own center, impossible to graph precisely in space, which Stein calls a "zero point." We can always see some of our *Leib*, but we can never see all of it.

Our liveliness is shared. When we understand another person as *Leib* rather than *Körper*, we see the whole world differently. The other person has a zero point, just as we do; those zero points make connections, creating a new web of understanding. It is thanks to the *Leib* of another that we are liberated from thinking of ourselves as outside the world, or against the world. A little leap of empathy is at the beginning of the knowledge we need for freedom.

If it is just me against the world, then all my grumpy late-night pronouncements are justified and true and deserving of attention. But let us imagine that my daughter (also) gets cranky when she is tired and says entirely unreasonable things. Seeing her, seeing that, I recognize a phenomenon in the world, and suddenly know more about myself. That example I owe to questioning my son about the argument of this book. Knowing me and knowing his sister, he immediately knew what I meant, and then he could also see that this is objective knowledge, of the kind we cannot get alone.

Thanks to the *Leib*, phenomena come into view, those that are essential for life and for freedom: birth, sleep, waking, health, breathing, eating, drinking, sheltering, lovemaking, illness, aging, death. None of us remembers being born, but all of us were born. None of us will remember dying, but we remember others dying. Empathy is not just some vague urging to be kind. Empathy is a precondition for certain knowledge of the world. The isolated individual, trying to contemplate the world alone, has no chance at understanding it.

Because the *Leib* is at the source of knowledge, it is also at the source of a politics of freedom. When we see other people as subjects like ourselves, we begin to gain objective knowledge about the world. If we see others as objects, we will lack essential knowledge not only about them but also about the world and about ourselves. This makes us vulnerable to those who would abuse us and rule us. We will see ourselves as objects, and we will be manipulated by others who treat us as such.

In this light, negative freedom is the self-deception of people who do not really wish to be free. Those who present freedom as negative ignore what we are, ignore the *Leib*. If we are just *Körper,* physical bodies, then the idea of negative freedom would make a kind of sense. Objects can be restrained by other objects. Freedom could just be freedom *from,* without aspirations or individuality, without any sense of what life is or should be. But when we correctly apprehend ourselves as a body in a human sense, as a *Leib,* we understand that freedom must suit that special state. It must be positive, not negative. Barriers are bad not because they block us as objects, but because they hinder us from understanding one another and becoming subjects.

Negative freedom is not a misunderstanding but a repressive idea. It is itself a barrier, a barrier of an intellectual and moral kind. It blocks us from seeing what we would need to be free. Those who want us unfree create barriers between us, or dissuade us from building the structures that would allow understanding. When we see ourselves as *Leib,* and understand the world, we see what we would have to build together in order to become free.

## LIFE

Edith Stein only ever held one university job, for a single academic year. She lost it when Adolf Hitler came to power. In April 1933 she wrote a letter to the pope, in which she tried to explain, in language he would understand, the position of Germany's Jews: "We have seen deeds perpetrated in Germany which mock any sense of justice and humanity, not to mention love of neighbor." She called the Church's silence about Jewish oppression a "black mark" on its history.

Hitler took a view of the human body utterly opposed to Stein's. In *Mein Kampf,* he wrote of *Fremdkörper,* "foreign bodies," infesting the *Volkskörper,* the German racial organism. Rather than seeing each person in Germany as a distinct human body, Nazis portrayed the German race as a single organism and the Jews as the foreign objects, bacteria or parasites.

When my children were smaller, we lived in Vienna. When my daughter was in first grade and my son in third, we commuted to school on scooters across the Heldenplatz, where a huge crowd had welcomed Hitler just before Germany annexed Austria. That year I took my son to soccer practice in a stadium twice a week. One day, the coaches passed out violet jerseys, *Leibchen,* a word that sounds like "little body." The boys threw off what they were wearing, pushed their arms and heads into their new shirts, and suddenly looked like a team.

Five years before that, when we waited for the bus for kindergarten, my then-three-year-old son was fascinated by the machines used to dig into the sidewalk and to spread tar on the exposed areas. The workers were preparing to lay *Stolpersteine,* "stumbling stones," palpable memorials to murdered Jews. These inscribed metal plates, embedded in the pavement, remind us of where Jews once lived. The information they carry—names, addresses, sites of death—give us a chance to rehumanize, to restore, at least in imagination, what they lost. Before the Jews were killed, they were stripped of everything: first their property, then their clothes. Like the million or so other Jews murdered at Auschwitz, Edith Stein had to disrobe. This was theft, of course, but mainly humiliation, treating a *Leib* as a *Körper*, preparing everyone for murder.

Before my son's birth in Vienna, German was for me a language of death: of Hitler's speech at the Heldenplatz, of the sign over the gates of Auschwitz, of all the thousands of sources I had read in order to write about the Holocaust and other atrocities. *Körper* in all its forms was familiar, *Leib* less so. With my son, German became a language of life. I heard the word *Leib* in a Vienna maternity ward, from a nurse trying to teach breastfeeding.

Mothers remain in Austrian hospitals for ninety-six hours after giving birth, to learn to wash and feed the baby. In that space with those bodies for four days, I learned things I would not otherwise have known. The predicament of nurse, mother, and infant was different from mine, but I could understand something about it, then about myself and the world. I am freer as a father for having been there.

Your *Leib* pushes back into the world, changing it. It translates physics into pain and pleasure, chemistry into desire and disappointment, biology into poetry and prose. It is the permeable membrane between necessity and freedom. It is a *Leib* that is capable of the kind of concentration that marks a free and sovereign person. *Körper* we concentrate in a camp.

## NEIGHBOR

Stein was unable, as a woman in interwar Germany, to earn the credential and keep the job that would have suited her. After publishing her dissertation on empathy, she turned her energy to publishing the work of a friend and teacher who had been killed in battle, and then to editing that of Edmund Husserl, their supervisor. Husserl wrote letters of recommendation to the effect that she ought to be a professor of philosophy were it an appropriate role for women.

Jewish by upbringing, Stein had converted to Catholicism. After Hitler came to power and she lost her academic job, she took orders as a nun. Recasting her philosophy in biblical terms can help us see what is special about our bodies. Unlike contemporary German, Martin Luther's first German translation of the Bible always uses *Leib* for the human body. As a *Leib*, we are neither gods nor objects, but nor are we just a dilution, something in between. The universe neither gives nor denies us freedom. It sets before us restraints that we can know, and it offers us the possibility of adding something new.

Because we are imperfect, we see the universe in ways appropriate to the limits of the human body. This is positional knowledge that God cannot have. Unlike God, we can choose to see ourselves and the world through others of our own kind. A familiar biblical verse makes Stein's point about knowledge through the *Leib* of another: "For now we see through a glass, darkly; but then face to face: now I know in part; but then shall I know even as also I am known" (1 Corinthians 13:12).

God has no *Leib* and is aware of the attendant limitations: "My spirit shall not always strive with man, for that he also is flesh" (Genesis 6:3). Stein put it this way: "We have to admit that if God rejoiced over the repentance of a sinner, he would experience no pounding of the heart."

Our hearts do pound from excitement or exertion. Unlike God, we can be free, in the precise sense of turning the restraints of our universe into opportunities. God knows no adversity, and adversity has uses. Facing a law of necessity He does not face, we expand a law of freedom He does not know. And so:

The limits of an object are its limits.

The capabilities of God are His capabilities.

The limits of a *Leib* are its capabilities.

Jesus of Nazareth certainly had a *Leib*. He forgave the sins of a weeping woman who "began to wash his feet with her tears, and did wipe them with the hairs of her head" (Luke 7:38). When Jesus says that "the spirit indeed is willing, but the flesh is weak" (Matthew 26:41), we can relate. He suffered physical pain and knew that he would die. Unlike God the Father, Jesus is neither litigious nor vengeful, emphasizing instead the simple laws of loving God and loving one's neighbor.

Whereas God quickly lost patience with his creations, exposing their imperfection by killing them, Jesus spoke patiently in riddles and allegories, forcing his listeners to think again. When asked whom we should regard as our neighbor, he told a story about a suffering *Leib*.

In the parable of the Good Samaritan, a Jew who has been "stripped of his raiment" is lying "wounded" beside the road. Other Jews walk by and do not help him. A non-Jew, a Samaritan, recognized the injured Jew as a fellow person, "had compassion on him" (Luke 10:30–33), tended his wounds, and found him shelter. Who is thy neighbor? He that showed mercy. Go and do likewise.

In the story, it is the Samaritan who is free. He is sovereign, in that he is acting according to his own values and is able to realize them in the world. The road that he walked was material, but not only. We are in nature but not entirely of it. Our bodies are subject to inertia, but we can choose to stop by the side of the road. Our bodies are pulled down by gravity, but we can raise someone else up from the ditch.

## MYSTERY

For the French philosopher Simone Weil, acknowledging the existence of another was an act of love. For her, loving one's neighbor as oneself meant reading "the same combination of nature and the supernatural" in another person's body that we experience ourselves.

The Bible also asks us to love "the stranger that dwelleth among you" as we love ourselves (Leviticus 19:34). "To love a stranger as oneself implies," says Weil, "that we love ourselves as strangers." Like many of her formulations, this one is a challenge. It is not just that we do right when we love a stranger. It is that we see ourselves as a stranger might see us, see what is strange in us, which is what we need to see. When we see ourselves as others see us, we know ourselves better. This is liberating. We experience the restraints of the external world and push against them, in the company of others who are doing the same. We are free when we know in which direction we wish to push and how we can do so.

Weil felt the restraints acutely. She suffered from migraines and physical awkwardness. That one academic year when Stein was able to teach, 1932–33, Weil spent in Germany. In 1934–35 Weil worked as a machinist and a packer in factories in France, to understand workers; the labor exhausted her. She volunteered to fight in the Spanish Civil War in 1936 but injured herself immediately. During the Second World War, working in London for the French Resistance, she asked to be sent to occupied Europe with a group of nurses. Her supreme commander, Charles de Gaulle, thought she was crazy. Weil had trouble eating and died of illness during the war.

Weil called our bodies "a source of mystery that we cannot eliminate." We are here as our bodies or not at all; we are free as our bodies or not at all. In notebooks that she kept during the war, Weil wrote of gravity and grace. We are a special sort of creature, subject to the laws of physics but able to understand them—and to bend them to purposes that are not reducible to them. The body wends its way between the world of things *as they are* and the world of things *as they might be*. Weil's "mystery" was the presence of the body in both realms, the *is* and the *ought*. To be sovereign means to have a sense of what ought to be and how to get there.


## STADIUM

Simone Weil liked sports. She thought that physical coordination enables "thought to enter into direct contact with things." Practice creates, she thought, "a second nature, better than the first." Like Weil, I was a poor athlete by nature, so I had to practice. I can swim thanks to a local swim club and instructors and a patient mother reading novels poolside. I could never do all the things in gym class that other kids found easy, so I trained myself. My mother recalls my jumping rope in the garage by myself for hours each day. I excelled at baseball because it was a sport I could practice alone or with my father.

As a kid, I loved to watch baseball live. It was a special treat to be in the stadium, my body with other bodies. I played the game and so could identify with the players. I idolized the Cincinnati Reds, the Big Red Machine of the 1970s. I played make-believe games of baseball with a friend, batting as all the Reds players, imitating their stances.

The 1975 World Series between the Reds and the Boston Red Sox is the first I remember. In game one, the winning pitcher for the Red Sox was the ageless Afro-Cuban Luis Tiant. During the game, which I watched on television, one of the commentators mentioned that Tiant had worried about raising his son in the United States. I was barely six and not sure what the word *prejudice* meant.

A stadium is a site of education. The word comes from Greek and has to do with a fixed measurement. A stadium is an objectively defined site where intensely subjective things happen. In a group bigger than we can count, we learn things that we later find difficult to question. At Riverfront Stadium in Cincinnati, I learned the national anthem, "The Star-Spangled Banner." I can't remember not knowing the lyrics.

Awed by British cannons during the War of 1812, Francis Scott Key asked:

> O say does that star-spangled banner yet wave
> O'er the land of the free and the home of the brave?

The Reds brought together talented white, Black, and Latin American players. I don't think I ever asked myself what it might mean for African American players to stand for a song about liberty that was written when their ancestors were enslaved. I do remember wondering what it meant for the players who were not American to stand for the anthem of another country.

Considering the *Leib* of others (as Stein put it), or seeing the strangers among us (as Weil said), we attune ourselves differently.

Thinking about that physical act of standing at attention from other perspectives, we hear the anthem's lyrics differently. The questions it poses become less rhetorical: Does the American flag wave today? Most assuredly it does. This is the easy part. But does it fly over "the land of the free"?

It is easy to imagine that freedom will be brought to us by a song, by jets over a stadium, by the land, by the ancestors, by the Founders, by capitalism. But is the notion that we are granted freedom right for a "home of the brave"? Is it not more courageous to ask what Americans have done, could have done, should do?

We say that a symbol *stands for* something, but all too often a symbol merely *stands in for* something. The American flag is supposed to *stand for* freedom, but it can very easily *stand in for* freedom. In singing the anthem, we treat its values as permanent, or as if they were enacted by song. But praise is not practice.

By no meaningful index are Americans today among the freest peoples of the world. An American organization, Freedom House, measures freedom by the criteria Americans prefer: civil and political liberties. Year after year about fifty countries do better than us on these measures.

Our northern neighbor Canada stands far above us. In a recent ranking, the United States shared a place with South Korea (a country Americans fought for), Romania (a post-communist country that few Americans would see as a peer), and Panama (a country that the United States called into existence in order to get a canal built).

The truth about the "land of the free" is more sobering still. Most of the countries with higher rankings than ours in civil and political liberties would surpass us by still greater margins in the measures that their citizens would consider elements of freedom, such as access to health care. If such measures were included, we would fall even further down on the scale.

The countries where people tend to think of freedom as *freedom to* are doing better *by our own measures,* which tend to focus on *freedom from.* That should give pause for thought. Political systems that are oriented toward *freedom to* are doing better than we are on *freedom from*. This suggests that there is no contradiction between the two. Indeed, it suggests that *freedom to* comes first. That is not what we are used to thinking or want to think. It helps to look at others if we want to understand ourselves.

We tend to think of freedom just as *freedom from,* as negative. But conceiving of freedom as an escape or an evasion does not tell us what freedom is nor how it would be brought into the world. *Freedom to,* positive freedom, involves thinking about who we want to become. What do we value? How do we realize our values in the world? If we don't think of freedom as positive, we won't even get freedom in the negative sense, since we will be unable to tell what is in fact a barrier, how barriers can be taken in hand and become tools, and how tools extend our freedom.

*Freedom from* is a conceptual trap. It is also a political trap, in that it involves self-deception, contains no program for its own realization, and offers opportunities to tyrants. Both a philosophy and a politics of freedom have to begin with *freedom to*.

Freedom is positive. It is about holding virtues in mind and having some power to realize them. Insofar as such a thing can be measured, Americans could be doing better. As I write, in self-reported well-being, Americans are fifteenth in the world. In about fifty countries, people live longer lives.

## DEATH

Not long after I reached the age of fifty years, it seemed that I would die. When I was close to death, I thought about baseball.

One of my clearest memories from childhood is the first home run I hit, at the age of thirteen, in May 1983. The team uniforms were baby blue and navy, the white lettering advertising a local orthodontist. The team was stacked with talent at almost every position. That day we were playing on one of the few local fields that had a fence. The pitch to me was a fastball down and on the inside half of the plate, but too close to the middle. I stepped, turned on the ball just right, and hit it. The left fielder turned, took a step, and watched it clear the fence. The ball bounced on the asphalt of the parking lot and disappeared into the woods. My teammates whooped.

What I remember is the way the bat felt in my hands when I struck the ball. I knew that I had hit it just right. I had that feeling of rightness on my palms, in my wrists, up my arms, and into my thin chest. I was an alienated teenager who could program a computer; earlier that year, in school, I had created a game called "Lifegame" and was excited and then a little disturbed by how it could take over players' attention. I had been obsessed since early childhood with the possibility that everything could be a simulation and that therefore I was not really alive.

But when the bat hit the ball, I knew that I was.

In moments of distress, my body calls for that memory, as it did during a serious illness in late 2019. That December an infection of my appendix spread to my liver and then to my blood, bringing about the often-lethal condition known as sepsis. As my body's immune system tried to resist, it attacked my own nerves. My hands felt hot and tingled intensely, as though I were wearing mittens of heated steel wool.

At year's end, in an emergency room in New Haven, I could feel my body floating between *Leib* and *Körper*. When I closed my eyes, I saw things that weren't there. The burning that I felt had no connection to the world outside. I was exhausted and breathing hard, but not because of any effort I had made.

Some of the fault was mine. I had been raised to think of the body as just one more external constraint, to be resisted. Pain was to be ignored. If I injured myself during a game, I was never to touch where it hurt. And so when my appendix burst on December 3 during a visit to Germany, my first impulse had been to pay no attention. I was in the German welfare state to attend a board meeting and discuss a hospital, but somehow none of that seemed directly relevant to me.

I was also to give a lecture in Munich that evening on the question "Can the United States Become a Free Country?" I did it, covering my discomfort by telling jokes, and the pain seemed to release me from inhibitions. After the lecture, I found I was not very hungry and left dinner early for the hotel. I went to bed, but then the thought of my distant family induced me to call a cab and go to a hospital. I was proud of myself for doing that. Once there, though, I did not complain enough. The doctors released me with the wrong diagnosis and without prescribing antibiotics. I went to my board meeting.

If freedom is just negative, an absence of barriers, then the body comes into the story negatively, as just one more restraint. My own unfortunate attitude toward my body was consistent with a broader American mistake.

From regarding the body as an object, it is a short step to regarding it as a commodity. It seems normal in the United States to see the body as a source of profit. And that was my next problem.

I flew home from Germany with a burst appendix and peritonitis, then managed (at my wife's urgings) to go to the doctor a second time. After being seen on December 15, I was referred to a New Haven hospital. This time the burst appendix was diagnosed, as was a lesion on my liver. But in their haste to get me out the door after the appendectomy, the doctors forgot about the liver. I left with an insufficient prescription for antibiotics and no referral for the liver abscess, about which I knew nothing at the time. (I learned about the detection of the liver growth long after the fact, reading my own medical records.) The infection then spilled into my blood.

## RACE

One problem was me; another was commercial medicine; a third was race. In the emergency room in New Haven on December 29, I needed a Good Samaritan, I needed someone to recognize me through my body, and I had such a person. Her presence, sad to say, might have made things worse.

The physician friend who met me at the emergency room had no trouble seeing my *Leib*. We had run a race together in a thunderstorm.

My convulsive trembling and high fever meant something to her. She understood that it was hard for me to communicate pain. She was not sure what was wrong, but she knew that my body needed more attention than it was getting. She spent the night in a chair beside me.

When my friend spoke up for me, though, she was deflected. Her colleagues saw the color of her skin rather than hearing her words. It was a cold December night, and she was wearing a purple fleece zipped up to her neck. I kept thinking that if only she would pull her hospital badge from behind that fleece, her colleagues might see her as a doctor rather than as a Black person. The nurse, the resident, and the attending physician set themselves up in opposition to my friend. If my friend said I was very ill, they were predisposed to think the contrary. They took my body less seriously than they should have. I almost lost my life—or, as people say in German, my *Leib und Leben*.

After more errors, I was eventually diagnosed with sepsis and treated for it; after a few more weeks and much more bungling, the liver infection subsided as well. Once I could walk around, I did. As in most American hospitals, there was nowhere really to go. So I walked up and down the corridor: one lap at first, eventually ten laps, twenty.

I needed to move. One day a nurse touched my arm as I was making my rounds and whispered to me that I was doing the right thing, as though the pursuit of happiness were a secret we shared.

## HAPPINESS

Having nearly died in that American hospital, I gave some thought, pacing its corridors, to the "right to life." In the Declaration of Independence, Thomas Jefferson's right to life is followed by a right to liberty and a right to pursue happiness. Liberty is in the middle.

Life comes first, which makes sense. We can only be free as a *Leib*. No *Leib,* no freedom. There can be a *Körper* without me, but no *Leib* without me, as Stein said. Negative freedom makes a *Körper* of us, one object of many, supposedly free when other objects are not in the way. That will not do. Whatever our freedom is, it must begin from what kinds of creatures we are, involve how we differ from the world beyond, and suggest how we make contact with that world and change it.

Liberty and life are connected, if perhaps not in the way that we are usually told. It is not that we have to trade the one for the other, freedom for safety. Had I been freer when I was sick, I would also have been more secure. The absence of freedom threatens life, just as threats to life undermine freedom.

In Jefferson's list, the pursuit of happiness comes third. Contemplating happiness teaches us important things. It is different for each of us. This can be irritating. But the implacable diversity of ideas of the good demonstrates the possibility of freedom.

Jefferson thought that happiness required virtue. His contemporary the Marquis de Sade made an unforgettable case for vice—which Jefferson's happy life was not without.

Schopenhauer says that happiness is given, Balzac that it is made.

Bentham says that happiness can be legislated, Dostoevsky that laws displace the thing itself.

Lafargue says that idleness brings happiness, Fourier proposes labor.

Burke says that beauty promises happiness, Kawabata and Murakami (like Ovid) that it brings woe.

Leopold Staff says that we are happy when we give the most, Irène Némirovsky when we give the least.

Lammenais says that we are happy when we expect much, Goethe when we expect little.

Epictetus says that happiness returns from whence we direct our love, the Buddha teaches us to expect no such reward.

Mickiewicz says that happiness is impossible amid suffering, Tertullian that this is our chance.

Żeromski says the young are happy, Cicero the old. (According to polling data, both are right, and it is the middle decades that are the unhappiest.)

Jean-Paul Sartre defines hell as other people, his contemporary Simone Weil as loneliness.

This irresolvable disagreement about how to pursue happiness affirms a right to liberty. Happiness has to do with what we value. The things we hold dear are real, but none of us values the same things in the same way as anyone else, nor is there a single correct way to order all the virtues. There is no one good thing of which all the others are just parts or examples. If there were such a singular good, our universe would be different, and freedom would be impossible. Were humans to agree on the sources of happiness, we would be far simpler creatures, subject to programming, incapable of freedom.

On only one point do we find agreement about happiness among thinkers at all times in all cultures: health favors it. When we are well, each of us wants different things. When we are sick, we all want to get well. The *Leib* comes first; only with the *Leib* healthy can we move on to other desires and claims and values. Illness not only hinders our pursuit of happiness, it jeopardizes our lives and constrains our liberty.

## HEALTH

Freedom is about the body. The Founders knew this, but they knew little *about* the human organism. John Locke, an English philosopher important to American constitutional thought, treated health as an element of good government. Thomas Jefferson thought that after ethics, health was the most important thing in life. The Founders bemoaned the epidemics that plagued their young republic, but they had no remedies. We do. George Washington inoculated his troops the best way he knew how. We know better. He died after being bled by his doctors. We wouldn't do such a thing.

The Founders held a variety of views about slavery, but even some of those who opposed its spread (such as Jefferson) owned slaves themselves. As a general matter, we can say that early American elites often did not see the body of an African as a *Leib*. They generally believed that people from Africa were not fully human, that their bodies were different from their own. This belief remains with us, and it makes it harder for us all to be healthy.

The racism was clear to me in the emergency room because I was dying. White people in the United States know about race, but they suppress that knowledge in an everyday covenant of ostensible ignorance. I did not learn about racism from the incident in the hospital; when I was at death's door, *what I already knew* surged forward to clarify the situation, because it was relevant to my own survival. Only at the extreme did I need ordinary knowledge. Black Americans cannot deny what they know, because they need it to get through the day. When white people deny what we know, we turn situations where we might all do better into situations where we all do worse. While the doctors ignored my friend, I was dying a truth I hadn't lived.

Slavery was conceived of as negative freedom: a right of the slaveowner to own property, with which the government was not to interfere. It is this tradition that leads some of us to think that government action must work against non-Black people if it is working for Black people. Negative freedom invites white people to think of themselves as self-sufficient, like plantation owners, with no need for government assistance. Then many white people (and other non-Black people) reject a right to health care since it means sharing it with Black people. This failure to recognize the *Leib* of the other leads to self-deception and unfreedom. In the end, one's own *Leib* is also ignored and abused, or even killed. We die sooner when we live a lie.

I had three problems when I was very sick: my own attitude toward my body; the commercialization of medical care; and racism. These really amount to one problem. If we do not recognize the general predicament of illness and death, if we do not recognize all bodies, then we do not recognize our own predicament when we are sick and what it means for freedom. If we conceive of liberty only as freedom *from,* we don't think expansively enough; we think only of ourselves, or about ourselves against the world. When we don't see the bodies of others, we don't really understand our own, and we end up giving away our own freedom and our own lives.

With respect to health, the idea of negative freedom is a dangerous relic of the past, of a time when the most that could be hoped for was property, slaves, and women to surround an ill man. We can do so much now, and for everyone. A revolution in medicine and hygiene began after the Civil War. Physicians—and following them, governments around the world—implemented policies of hygiene, vaccination, and preventive care. These programs created not only the reality but the expectation of a much longer life.

Advances in medicine made possible a profound gain of freedom. People who are more confident about health will have greater ambitions for life. People who expect to live short lives are more likely to risk them in violence that, in turn, shortens the lives of others.

We can bring Jefferson's thought to its logical conclusion and unite his three basic rights in a fourth: the right to health care. But we will only achieve that if we manage something that the Founders did not: recognizing other bodies as equally human.

## CATCHING

Thanks to illness and inactivity, in 2020 I was clumsy. My limbs followed my directives imprecisely, and I sensed objects that were not actually there. Home from the hospital that spring, I looked for simple jobs that I could do with my body. While sweeping out the garage floor with my right arm, a catheter for antibiotics in my left, I happened across a Wiffle ball and a red plastic bat. My daughter grabbed the bat, and I put down the broom and tossed her the ball with my good hand. She hit it on the first try.

My daughter was about to turn eight. She did not even know which sport had been invoked. Teaching her to play catch as I convalesced, I had an odd feeling. Because my body had unlearned much of what it once knew, I was uncannily aware of all the motions I made to throw and receive the ball. I was more conscious of space and time, or rather of how, in its humble neuromuscular self-regulation, my body had at one time mastered them. As I got well, I slowly returned to a state that I had achieved long before by practice. I was free in that I no longer had to think about what I was doing. Simone Weil called this *habitude*.

Practice does not make perfect. Nothing makes us perfect, fortunately. But practice does lead us to *habitude* and to grace, a quality otherwise absent from the universe. By June 2020, four months after I left the hospital, two months after the tube came out of my arm, my daughter could play catch, and so could I. The half-perceived arc of her throws sublimated into my half-aware certainty of when and where the ball would cross the plane of my body, and into the half-conscious movement that brought it unerringly into my glove. In my lack of awareness of what I was doing, I was free.

## PITCHING

When I played baseball in the early 1980s, I was a pitcher. Pitching is a bit like declaring freedom. You are alone, elevated on a mound, in your little chalk circle of honor, labor, and despair. The game turns on what you do next.

On the pitcher's mound, as I came to a set before my windup, I visualized what would happen next. I imagined the pitch I was about to make—let's say a fastball up over the inside corner—and I saw, in my mind's eye, the batter hesitate and lose time judging whether it was a ball or a strike, swing late and too quickly, and miss. I even saw his grimace. In a visualization of this sort, which Stein called "an intention permeating the whole," another world appears, a beat ahead of this one. Not always, but often, I could bring the two worlds together, pitch as I wanted to, and cause the reaction I expected. In a phrase of Roger Angell's that I treasured as a kid, the baseball was my "little lump of physics."

We are neither gods nor objects. We are humans who can become sovereign. Freedom is neither the lack nor the acceptance of constraints, but rather the use of them. The mound is sixty feet and six inches from home plate, and it is elevated ten inches above the ground; that both restrains and enables a pitch. We are free to do only the things we can do, which are usually things that others taught us to do and that we practice. What a pitcher does on the mound is a result not only of choices appropriate to a game situation, but of all the repetition that came before.

The same holds for any choice we make. Just thinking about the virtues is not enough; as Aristotle said, we have to practice them by working them into the world. "Nature resists," says Simone Weil, "but it does not defend itself." You feel that resistance when you pick up a baseball or touch the strings of a guitar. The guitar strings resist the pick but yield the chord. The baseball resists as you lift it but yields as you place a middle finger on a stitch, a forefinger against the middle finger, snap your wrist, and throw a curveball. Nature gives way in beauty. When we know how to play, and that we want to play, the resistance and the yielding are the same thing.

Pitches follow rules that we did not make, and arcs that we do make. I know my throw by how my daughter receives it, and I adjust; that is knowledge I cannot attain by myself. The ball leaves my hand with my purposes attached. They are not in the first four dimensions of space and time but in a fifth, in what Edith Stein called "the world of values." Behind all my throws to my daughter are also my thoughts about how she might grow up, and in each of my throws is every throw from my own father. I do not make the world of values or the world of things, but I do sometimes make small passages between them. In this humble way, I am sovereign.

Stein wrote that the person belongs to both worlds, subject both to the "law of necessity" and to the "law of freedom." I belong to two realms, and I can stand with one foot in each. I can bring the ball through from necessity to freedom. It is still *my* lump of physics. My daughter is a pitcher now, too, in softball, so the lump of physics is also *hers*. She has chosen how to perform a task that is both very much like and very different from pitching a baseball. That decision is hers, and yet it has something to do with what she saw in me.

When we play catch, the targets are not all in the physical world. The hand that throws and the hand that catches is *Leib*. My daughter holds up her glove, and I can put the ball in its web, from a shorter distance or a longer one. I hold up my glove just before her throw reaches me, directed not only by her strength but also by her purpose. A little arc of aspiration trails behind the arc of a ball, like the tail of a comet.

In describing how physics treats us, Simone Weil spoke of "a double law, an evident indifference and a mysterious complicity." The universe is unaware of us, yet it sometimes plays along. The example of the thrown ball is hers.

## BREATHING

One day the next summer, of 2021, my daughter and I were playing catch on a running track at the edge of an old shtetl, now a Polish town near the Lithuanian border. Then we went to the main street to get ice cream. While standing in line at the soft-serve kiosk, we saw some saxophonists taking a break in front of the (former) synagogue, the White Synagogue of Sejny.

I know, and my daughter knows, that the town's Jews were murdered after the Germans expelled them at the beginning of the Second World War. After the war, in communist Poland, the synagogue was used as a warehouse. In 1989, as communism came to an end, the building was taken over by a small troupe of actors, artists, and musicians who called themselves Borderlanders. They had a peculiar idea: that people would be freer if they could use art to see themselves, others, and the past.

The Borderlanders then began to teach local children, Poles and Lithuanians, how to play klezmer, the Jewish popular music that was widespread in Poland before the war. Day after day, year after year, local boys and girls accepted the gift of music, practicing and changing instruments. Every year new kids, as young as five or six, joined the older ones. I have been listening to the orchestra play in that synagogue for longer than my daughter has been alive. I have seen the young kids become teenagers, and the teenagers become young women and men.

Each new capacity contributes to our sovereignty and so belongs to freedom. Because they can play instruments, the musicians express themselves as they would not otherwise have been able to. The music they play is Jewish, and they practice in what was once a largely Jewish town, and they perform in what was once a Jewish temple. Their breath connects them to a world of values that one day will come to them. When the moment arrives to ask what it means to have a synagogue without Jews, those Jews are not entirely absent. They are, in some way, present in the music, and the music is present in the kids—present in their bodies, in their muscles as well as in their minds.

People cry in the White Synagogue in Sejny, listening to the music. I am brought to tears when young people in the audience have the courage to dance. Much of this music was meant to be joyful, after all. Some of it is wedding music. Some of it, come to think of it, was played at my wedding.

My daughter's relatives, three or four generations earlier, were murdered in the nearest big city. The Jews of Białystok, her mother's father's people, were shot and gassed to death by the tens of thousands, having been rounded up in the local stadium. As I write this vignette, my daughter is there, in Białystok, attending the university graduation ceremony of a Polish babysitter who has become a friend.

My daughter exists only because her ancestors on her mother's father's side left Białystok, and those on her mother's mother's side left Ukraine. The first graduation ceremony she attended was in Białystok, the first wedding in Ukraine. She was a flower girl.

Sovereignty has to do with the body, with what we learn to do. It also has to do with the past, with the world we inherit. "The past and the future," says Weil, "are man's only treasures."

## RECOGNIZING

When Russia invaded Ukraine in February 2022, my daughter donated all her money to Ukrainians. During the first few weeks after Russia's full-scale invasion of Ukraine, I kept getting phone calls from American Jews, people whose ancestors had fled Ukraine, asking how they could help. They were able to recognize the injustice.

Ukraine, today the site of Putin's war of destruction and extermination, has long been an object of empires. For Stalin, it was a "fortress" of resources that were to be extracted for "internal colonization." Hitler wanted Ukraine as *Lebensraum*, living space. In these colonial fantasies, Ukrainians were not seen at all, or were seen as subhuman.

*Leib* first reverts to *Körper* in the mind. In Nazi propaganda, east Europeans were subhuman beasts. On Soviet posters, rich peasants were pigs. Russian television today takes this notion to a postmodern extreme: Ukrainians are to be exterminated because they are Nazis, Jews, gays, Satanists, ghouls, zombies, vermin. The next step is violence, the opposite of recognition of the *Leib*. When we torture or humiliate a body, we further objectify it. After the body has been degraded and the person humiliated, the killer finds the work easier to bear. Some enjoy it.

In dehumanizing others, we make ourselves unfree. If we see others only as *Körper,* we cannot see ourselves as *Leib*; we lose the promise of our own freedom. So we can only get to freedom with the help of those we might otherwise demean, mistreat, or ignore. At a rehabilitation facility in Kyiv, I watched a soldier with two prosthetic legs work out on a treadmill while practicing boxing. Another young man, who had left a safe job in another European capital, lost his left arm and leg. He worked his right arm with a forty-kilo barbell. Talking to these men, I see myself in a different way, recognize a bit better how I reside in my body.

My own arguments about freedom would be impossible without the physical presence of others. I am writing by myself, but I am not really alone. Zelens'kyi told me that "we never really speak, others speak through us," and with these words he was making some of Edith Stein's points. We learn from people with whom we spend time, whom we respect—a word that, in its origins, means "look back, look attentively." We understand their thoughts in a different way when we have acknowledged them as people. We are more aware of our own thought processes when we think together with others. Even the books that stay with us are often given to us by people we know.

Some of the thoughts at the origins of this book arose in conversation with an admired historian friend who suffered from the neuro-degenerative disorder known as Lou Gehrig's disease or ALS. By late 2008, my friend was no longer able to write in the typical sense, since he could no longer raise his hands.

I wanted him to work, so I proposed that we compose a book together on the basis of recorded conversations. I took for granted that we would have to be in the same room. Only with him could I acknowledge and challenge him. Only in the presence of the disease could we work around it. My friend felt the same way: when I called him to propose the idea, he just said, "Come over."

We worked together during the two years before his death.

My presence did work on my friend, whose name was Tony Judt, as a provocation, in a positive sense. He needed answers that were better than my questions. He wanted to remember everything that he had ever read, and he just about could. Talking to Tony, I concentrated, tapping capacities that otherwise would have lain dormant. With our phones put away, with cases of books around us, with Tony's eyes on me, I recalled citations and passages with him. Together we achieved something that would have been beyond either of us as individuals: the book that Tony titled *Thinking the Twentieth Century*.

## ACKNOWLEDGING

One of the thinkers Tony and I found ourselves discussing was Edith Stein. She could not have written her dissertation on empathy and knowledge without the wounded soldiers. She started from the assumption, basic in philosophy since Immanuel Kant, that others were her equals, that the German men she treated were her fellow human beings.

Equal dignity is easy to grant in theory. But how do we recognize others in practice? Tending the wrecked bodies of men wounded at the front, Stein found that we acknowledge others through the *Leib*.

In the spring semester of 2022, ten years after Tony's and my book was published, I assigned Stein's dissertation to incarcerated students. We would read it together for the seminar in the philosophy of freedom I taught in a maximum-security prison. Though in a different way, this encounter with Stein was also inflected by illness: a pandemic. The course was supposed to have begun several weeks before it did, but prisoners and guards were sick in large numbers. I had to wait for the prison's Covid protocol to change before I could get inside. In January and February 2022, the students had their course packets and were doing the reading and did not want to wait.

I knew that I had to be in their space, at least in some limited way. That was, after all, Stein's point. Twenty years of classroom teaching had taught me the same. The students appreciated the contact, when it came, when I could enter the prison and join them in the classroom. They were quite ceremonious about the seminar; part of the ritual was that skin touched skin. Coming from different cellblocks, called over the loudspeaker by their numbers, they were happy to be bodies in the same space. Each arriving student gave the others hugs. Each one of them wanted to touch me when the class began and ended: I got white-guy handshakes.

We used the word *Leib* a lot. One of my incarcerated students, Dwayne, seemed captivated by Stein and summarized her arguments beautifully. You "have to see the body of others to see your own body," and so objectivity "is not being yourself without distractions, it is recognizing the other body as being like your body, and then seeing the world." "When I am imprisoned in my own self," wrote Stein, "I can never get beyond the world as it appears to me." But "thanks to empathy I get repeated appearances of that same world that are independent of my perception." It is empathy that allows us to know that the external world is real.

Empathy, in other words, is not a condescending concession of a rational person to the emotions of others, but the only way to become a reasonable person. To acknowledge the corporeality of others is not a gift to them but a step toward our own reason. "The constitution of the foreign individual," wrote Stein in her dissertation, "was a condition for the full constitution of our own individuality." The bodies of others allow us to see them as subjects, as in the same predicament as we are. Empowered then by empathy, we can see ourselves as others see us. That helps us both to know ourselves and to know the world. That knowledge, in turn, makes us better subjects, more sovereign.

We have to see the bodies of others as subjects, because otherwise we cannot see *ourselves* as subjects. And if we fail to do that, we cannot be free.

## SEEING

In Ukraine, meanwhile, other bodies I knew, friends or colleagues or students, were in trenches or bomb shelters or in flight from the Russian invasion. At the time of that first class in prison, March 2022, Ukrainian friends with families were trying to find a way to flee Kyiv.

My incarcerated students wanted to hear about the war. I was not supposed to turn my back on them, but I did so the first day to draw battle maps on the whiteboard.

We imagined a disaster thousands of miles away, in a country that none of my students had visited, and that to them at first was all but unknown. The application of what we were discussing, though, was clear enough. If Russian invaders believed that Ukrainians were less than human, then raping women and executing men was no crime: Ukrainian bodies were objects to begin with. In acting this way, of course, the Russians opened the logical possibility that they, too, were simply objects: to be sent somewhere to die pointlessly on the basis of lies. If we do not recognize one another through the *Leib*, we not only cause suffering to others but bring unfreedom to ourselves.

What if I think that my body is something more than a *Körper*, but no one else agrees? Then (my students pointed out) others can attach and detach meanings to me as they will, and my own values will never make their way out into the world. I can be enslaved, tortured, segregated. If I do not exist as a *Leib* because the existence of my group is denied, I can be subjected to genocide.

The students appreciated Stein's contention about the *Leib* but wondered how far she would have taken it. After all, the soldiers she treated in the First World War were her fellow Germans—or fellow white people, as my students saw it. Most of my students were Black, and all of them expressed this suspicion.

Meeting during the first four months after Russia's full-scale invasion of Ukraine, my students came to see that Europeans can colonize other Europeans—that is, that white people can colonize other white people. Their realization calls into question the universality of the American notion of "white people"—or, when construed positively, provides an example of empathy.

The students extended their literary and philosophical references to Ukraine and applied their personal experiences to those of Ukrainians. My student Alpha expressed solidarity in the highest degree when he said, "The suffering of Ukrainians affects me as a Black man." By the end of the class, Alpha said that he admired Ukraine's president Volodymyr Zelens'kyi as an anti-colonialist.

In their querying of Stein, the students were onto something, though I resisted them at the time. Stein was certainly a German nationalist when she wrote about empathy in 1917. She considered it "out of the question that we will now be defeated." She was probably not thinking critically then about the German war aim of conquering Ukraine and treating it as a breadbasket. In her field hospital, though, she was treating soldiers of the multinational Habsburg army as well as German soldiers. Ukraine did not exist at the time, and its lands were divided between Russia and the Habsburg monarchy. So young Ukrainian men were fighting on both sides. Confronted with their wounded bodies, Stein empathized with their predicament.

Would she have empathized with Black men? That's where the students had their doubts. For their part, though, they were able to imagine her position and to empathize both with her and with Ukrainians past and present. One student, Michael, was aware of another moment when Ukraine was treated colonially: the political famine in Soviet Ukraine. After the First World War, the Bolshevik Revolution, and a series of other wars, most of what is now Ukraine was incorporated by the Soviet Union. Joseph Stalin saw Ukraine as a territory to be tamed and exploited. As a result of the collectivization of agriculture, millions of Ukrainians were brought to the verge of starvation. Stalin then took a series of decisions in late 1932 that ensured that about four million people in Soviet Ukraine in fact died. Michael knew a poignant detail: that Ukrainians during Stalin's starvation campaign referred to Harriet Beecher Stowe's novel *Uncle Tom's Cabin*. Having once cried for the slaves in the book, Ukrainians now identified with them. In one of his papers, Michael mentioned his own aged mother, whose African American son was in prison and had been for thirty years. In early 2022, Michael told me, she watched the news about Ukraine and cried. She could see.

The world in which Russia invades and tortures and America impoverishes and humiliates is one world, and it can be understood, especially when people are physically present. My incarcerated students learned the names of Ukrainian writers. When I took this manuscript to Ukrainian colleagues in Ukraine, they learned the names of my incarcerated students. There was something pleasing about conservative Ukrainian humanists sitting around a table in Lviv discussing the views of Alpha, a radical young African American thousands of miles away. They could see him. Thanks to everyone who was discussing the book, whether they were in an American prison or in a Ukrainian city mourning its dead, I gained a broader view.

Russia has become a genocidal fascist empire for many reasons, but one of them is negative freedom. This concept made it hard to see that its oligarchy was the antithesis of freedom (rather than a side effect) or that Putin was a fascist (rather than just a technocrat seeking wealth). And America has become a flawed republic threatened by oligarchy and fascism for many reasons, but negative freedom is among them. It leads us to think that we have solved our problems when we have privatized them, when in fact all we have achieved is separating ourselves from one another.

## SWIMMING

My country is also my incarcerated students' country. They had done what they had done, and I have done what I have done, but there is a larger logic behind my being at Yale and their being in prison. The land that celebrated its bicentennial in 1976 was on the way to locking up more of its citizens than any other, as a matter of racial policy. That I was only about one-fifth as likely to go to prison as a Black person was due to no merit of my own.

One June day in 1976, a few weeks before I rang that bell, I was sitting in a yellow school bus, alone on a bench seat near the back. It was the last week of first grade, and I was looking at the elementary school yearbook.

It was a simple stapled affair, with a two-color cardboard cover, one glossy page for each class, black-and-white photographs in rows and columns, the teacher at the top left. In her picture, my teacher sported a tremendous Afro, thick round glasses, and a turtleneck sweater beneath a plaid overall dress of the sort she favored. A third-grader peering over my shoulder mocked me for the race of my teacher, calling out the standard term of abuse. It was the first time I had ever heard the word. I didn't know what it meant, but I had a notion, since I knew the kid and his attitudes.

The bus route took us past the local swim club. As a boy, I wondered why it was a "club." I took lessons and spent pleasant summer afternoons there with my brothers. Driving there in my father's tiny convertible, top down, was an unforgettable pleasure. When I got older, I found it annoying to carry the membership card, especially since I was always losing things. It seemed strange to me that kids would brag about the different kinds of privileges afforded by the different colors of their card. A bored teenager checked the laminated credentials at the entrance.

It was a nice place. Perhaps no one had any bad intentions. And yet the swim club reflected an unmistakable national reality. Our subdevelopment was built after Supreme Court rulings and the 1964 Civil Rights Act made it illegal for cities to exclude African Americans from public swimming pools. Around the country, municipalities then filled in their public pools with cement. Public goods like swimming pools passed to the private sector, where membership rules could informally enforce prejudice. This was a minor element of a larger political reaction to the Civil Rights Act.

When we choose not to recognize other bodies as human, we create specific social situations, which we then define as the state of nature. Having been excluded from swimming pools, Black kids were less likely to learn to swim than white kids. And so white kids were instructed that Black bodies were not buoyant. This was "common knowledge."

There were at most one or two Black kids at the pool that summer of 1976, maybe none. There were certainly no Black kids on the bus that day. A social arrangement, the creation of zoned suburban neighborhoods, was keeping certain bodies apart.

In a space without Black people, the point of yelling a racial slur was to create a group: everyone against the absent teacher and against anyone who defended the absent teacher. If we use language to treat others' bodies as objects of one color, we define ourselves as objects of another. We enter into a mindless physical collectivity, a racial mob. We sacrifice our own *Leib* to the cause of denying the *Leib* of another.

School might help, but we have to be taught to acknowledge the *Leib* of the other. I was lucky in that I was challenged at home and saw African Americans in settings chosen by my family. But I do not remember being challenged at school. What we learned about Jim Crow was that it had come to an end. We should have known that Jim Crow inspired German racial laws, which made Jews (such as Edith Stein) second-class citizens. Along with the laws came initiatives from below, such as banning Jews from swimming pools.

It might seem like a small thing, but no one ever taught me about the swimming pools.

## CONTRACT

Freedom begins with sovereignty, and sovereignty has to do with bodies. And so the philosophy of freedom begins with a baby's cry. Babies pull us to the philosophical issues that are so basic that they escape attention. I began to see the world differently when I cut my son's umbilical cord.

We are all born into a blurry storm of circumstance. This is an experience we all share, though none of us recalls it. We know about birth and can consider it only thanks to others. Recalling that we all begin with a shriek can deliver us from philosophical errors that stand behind American oppression.

In American culture, birth is surrounded by taboos. The silence around the most significant moment in life shields our prevailing notion of negative freedom from some basic critiques. Birth reveals its absurdity. A newborn is not going to become free thanks to the absence of something. You can summon others to a journey toward freedom with a beautiful declaration, but you cannot abandon a baby at the foot of a mountain with a benediction of liberty.

A negative idea of freedom seems plausible when we begin our thought process from an idealized image of adults and forget the bodily predicament that we all shared as newborns. If we begin from magical maturity, we can assume that freedom is only a matter of defending what we already have, of what already exists. Defining freedom only as something that can be lost, we never ask how it was gained, how people become sovereign in the first place.

*Sovereignty* usually means the sovereignty of the state, its capacity to dominate or at least to set the terms of life. But if we regard freedom positively, we can think of sovereignty differently, as being about the person rather than the state. We then take the first step toward a better justification for government.

How did we come to think of a government as sovereign? To imagine a situation in which citizens have some sort of standing or rights, we treat sovereignty as inhering in political institutions. The notion, in traditions such as ours, is that at some point there was a social contract, in which people—idealized adults, of course—met and agreed to form a government. The problem with this move is that such a thing never happened.

The American case comes about as close as can be: people met and agreed upon the Constitution. But the men who wrote that document can hardly be thought to be representative of everyone. Even had they been perfectly representative of the wealthy white landowner class, the exclusion of the non-landed, the African Americans, the women, and the Native Americans means that their covenant can hardly stand on its own in modern times. And why exactly should newborns be subject to an ancient order that they could not possibly have chosen? How is that freedom?

Fascists pointed out the problems with this tradition of sovereignty. The most intelligent of them, the legal theorist Carl Schmitt, argued that true sovereignty resided not in following the rules, as laid down by the contract, but in making an exception to them. Whoever could make the exception was the true sovereign. An Adolf Hitler taking advantage of a Reichstag Fire to declare a state of exception was thus an ideal sovereign.

Schmitt's view, though, was nothing more than cleverness. Rule breaking, though it appeals to the emotions, cannot be sovereignty. Negating an illusion does not generate substance. To say that he who makes an exception is sovereign is at most a statement of fact about power, leaving entirely open what sovereignty means or ought to mean. The fascist notion of sovereignty is puerile, a boyish joke. We need to begin not with overgrown boys but with actual children.

The fascist solution is incompatible with freedom, but the fascist critique of the social contract does reveal a problem. If we expect people to accept the institutions into which they were born, on the basis of an agreement that is largely (or totally) fictional, how can that be generative of freedom? A constitution must not only constitute but reconstitute, over and over again. This can be done.

The solution is to relocate the idea of sovereignty in the person. Freedom is the value of values, because it is the condition in which all other values may be exercised. A government is not legitimate just because it has power and uses the word *sovereign* to embellish decrepitude and deception. It is legitimate insofar as it enables freedom, enacting policies that allow young and coming generations to become sovereign.

A person has a beginning, and that is the opportunity. To enable freedom, a government must begin at that beginning, with birth and with youth. Practically, this is indispensable to freedom; ethically, it is indispensable to legitimacy, since freedom is the value of values.

Governments do not produce children, but a good government can make child-rearing more likely to ease the way to a life in freedom.

A government that does not claim to be sovereign, but that aims for the sovereignty of its children, legitimizes itself by its work for freedom. And it does so with respect not to a myth of the past or to people who are dead but with respect to each coming generation and to people who are coming to life.

## CONTACT

In thinking about freedom, we tend to leave out the time between birth and maturity, the formative period of life. The first form of freedom, sovereignty, is blocked out. We have no chance to consider what a baby's body is, what efforts and policies that *Leib* will need.

A baby will need nourishment, shelter, and warmth. A baby will need other people, an upbringing, an education. The Roman historian Livy defined freedom as "standing upright oneself without depending on another's will." At some point in the logic of life, this definition is true—but not while we are in the womb or at the nipple, unable physically to stand upright. When we are very young, we all need someone else's goodwill if we are to learn to stand at all. Because we live in time in a certain direction, we cannot make up later for what we were not given earlier.

We are born undeveloped compared to other mammals. Our large heads (for our large brains) require us to leave the womb early, before we are capable of much of anything. Yet with time and attention, especially in the first months and years, those large brains can become capable minds.

Humans evolved to be patient and evaluative, as hunters, gatherers, nomads, and farmers, and as parents, siblings, cousins, and grandparents of children who need years of attention. Patience and evaluation continue to serve us in our modern world. But such capacities arise only if young people make contact with people around them. The creation of individuality must be a social act.

Just bearing a child does not bring the knowledge that mothers (or parents or a family) need, nor the time needed to apply it. Babies are thrown into a world that, if governed by negative freedom, must be senseless and grotesque. They cannot be raised by the absence of barriers. They need things they cannot themselves know. No infant can liberate its parents, or give them time, or set policy. Freedom works as a larger cooperative project, over generations, or not at all.

Those who care about childhood should care about freedom, and those who care about freedom should care about children. This means caring about the society into which the next American baby will be born. Individual freedom is a social project and a generational one. For people to grow up in freedom, the right structures must *already* be in place when they are born.

And so not just the philosophy but the work of freedom begins with birth. We labor, though, under a tradition of philosophy that looks away from life's most fundamental moment. The existentialists and their teacher Martin Heidegger thought that our problem was that we ignore death. That conclusion, meant to be grim and bare and masculine, actually skirts the issue, as Edith Stein pointed out. The real problem is that we ignore life.

My wife, Marci Shore, who is writing a book about the larger tradition of which Heidegger and the existentialists were part (phenomenology), was deep into it during her pregnancy. When she was in labor, a nurse complimented her on her German. She answered, in German, gasping, "I am good on obstetrics and phenomenology." Heidegger has the idea of "being toward death." I (later) told Marci that she should write a pregnancy memoir called "being toward life."

"Beginning, before it becomes a historical event, is the supreme capacity of man," says Hannah Arendt. "Politically, it is identical with man's freedom." Sovereignty begins with birth and arises as a child is held, loved, reared, and educated. For the universe, a human birth is nothing special; for us humans, natality is the possibility of a life in freedom. We close that potential when we limit freedom to avoiding other objects, or begin our philosophy with death rather than life.

## LOAN

Edith Stein was the youngest of eleven children. Her father died when she was young. Four of her siblings died before she was born. Growing up in these conditions, she understood that the "creation of capabilities belongs to freedom."

Reading Stein in prison, my students seized on the point that children need to spend time with adults to become sovereign. As children, they themselves had wanted attention from adults that they could not get. The research is on their side: negative childhood experiences correlate strongly with adversity in later life.

Simone Weil wrote that "the one thing that man possesses that is essentially individual, that is absolutely his own, is his capacity to think." And yet in the million years our species has trod the earth, this "essentially individual" capacity has never been developed individually. Babies who are left alone learn nothing. This is, sadly, not just a hypothesis. Historians have all too much confirmatory evidence—from the Gulag, for example, or from the orphanages of communist Romania.

Our knowledge of early childhood development can enable sovereignty. We know that the *Leib* gains most of its capacities during the first five years of life, as the brain grows to nearly full size. And we know that the process is social. The brains of infants are primed for contact, but infants cannot make contact by themselves. Neural pathways emerge when babies are physically touched. Babies are good at recognizing faces when they are held so that they can see them. Their throats, tongues, and lips are capable of forming words, but do so only when they can imitate someone else's speech.

Putting alternatives in front of very young children is easy. Teaching them to evaluate and choose is harder. It takes caring people who have the time to care. Choice is a reality outside but also a capability inside. We need the ability to see alternatives as well as the external capacity to realize them. An American way to make people unfree is to wax on about choice but deny children the capacities they will need to make choices (or to realize that they have been denied them). The richer our capacities, the more alternatives we see, and the more choices we can make.

How many alternatives present themselves to us has to do with how we feel. Positive emotions broaden the range of choices we see and extend our experience of time. Negative emotions limit that range to immediate fight or flight. Fear is like that, limiting us to the binary. It turns our minds into circuits, our bodies into objects: *Leib* recedes into *Körper*.

With help, small children learn to name and regulate their emotions. Fear is sometimes appropriate, but knowing it and naming it are steps toward controlling it—and toward preventing others from manipulating it. Regulating emotions is a step toward the evaluation that enables freedom. If we are nothing more than our first reactions, we are prey to the people who arouse those reactions. Only individuals can resist pressure from others, yet it takes others to create such individuals. We can learn to govern ourselves only with the right kind of guidance, at the right stage of life.

Abundant research indicates what helps small children to gain these basic capacities: constant physical and vocal contact; trusting relationships; unstructured play; and choices about things and people. The attributes we need to be free individuals are available to us only through coordinated action. Babies can be raised and educated to become free, but babies cannot create for themselves the setting where this is possible. Since freedom requires capacities that we cannot develop by ourselves, we owe our freedom to others. Every free adult had manifold help as a child.

When we think of jobs that are associated with freedom, the first that comes to mind might be pilot or cowboy. Motherhood belongs to freedom. As the Ed and Patsy Bruce song reminds us, all those cowboys had mamas. The occupations that are most relevant to freedom are the caregivers: the elementary school teachers, the preschool teachers, the childcare workers. A society concerned with freedom would respect such people and pay them well.

Freedom requires capacity, capacity requires attention in child-hood, and attention requires time. It follows that parents' time, the mothers' above all, belongs to freedom. Adults lend to children a spe-cial kind of time, one that children cannot give adults, one that chil-dren cannot give children, one that adults cannot give adults.

Simone Weil said that everything precious in us comes from others, not as a gift but as "a loan that must be constantly renewed." Children borrow from adults a special kind of time. They can repay the loan only much later, when they are adults, by giving time to someone of the next generation. Government serves as a kind of guarantor of the loan, creating the conditions in which those who raise children can have time. A land of the free pays it back and pays it forward.

In leaving out birth from the account of freedom, we also make it impossible to accommodate the *Leib* of women. Because women can be impregnated by rapists, the orientation of their *Leib* has to be dif-ferent from that of men. In previous understandings of freedom, this issue did not arise, since it was assumed that women and slaves served the freedom of a powerful few.

Treating freedom solely as the absence of barriers gives us no instruction about rape. An idea of negative freedom as freedom from violence can seem to help here. It understates the stakes, though: it is not just that we have the right not to be raped, but that we should be able to live lives without the trauma or anticipation of rape. What people can become is limited by both the prospect and the memory of rape, and we can fully grasp this idea only when we take the bodies of others seriously.

Acknowledging the *Leib* of women also means understanding that they think about childbirth in a way that men generally do not. Women have to decide whether and when to have children, and they have to adjust other parts of their lives. Negative freedom leaves them to make those adjustments alone. If we make accommodations for childbirth, we remove a source of unfreedom for women and improve the chances that children can grow up free.

## OPENING

Death is simple and tempting. Fascism beguiles us with meaning drawn from the death of others and from our own. It is much easier to philosophize when we ignore what is most alive about us, when we fail to confront what Weil called the mystery of our bodies.

The death principle crept into philosophy early, in Plato's cave. Plato's conviction was that the things we experience in this world are not fully real but are rather imperfect copies of some ideal version of each thing. And so each bell, for example, is somehow just an emanation of a perfect bell that exists somewhere else, as is each tree or each bed in each maternity ward. We live under the illusion, Plato thought, that these things are fully real; it is the task of philosophy, he taught, to deliver us from this mistake. For this purpose, he provided (in his *Republic*) the memorable allegory of the cave.

Imagine that people are in chains, deep in a dark cavern, and can only look forward, at one cave wall. Behind them is a fire, and between them and the fire, people walk back and forth behind a wall, holding up a succession of "carved objects." All the enchained people can see are shadows cast on the wall before them. This, says Plato, is what our existence is like. We are shackled in a cave, gazing at a play of shadows, believing that we are in reality. We must think our way out, to a world where each thing exists in an ideal form.

This is a very evocative notion, and of course it cannot be proven false. Its plausibility, though, depends on ignoring basic experiences of life.

If you watch a childbirth, it is hard to think: *This is a shallow, partial replica of something else, only a reflection of some ideal birth taking place on an ideal plane.* When my wife experienced complications after the birth of our son, I did not think: *This blood is not actual blood and this red is not actual red but just a hint of what blood and red might be.* When the nurses left our newborn son with me while doctors sprinted from another wing of the hospital to operate on her, I did not think that the violet of his eyes was nothing more than an emanation of some ideal violet or eye, nor that the sound of the rushed footfalls in the hall was anything other than the only reality. And what is true of birth is true of the moment after birth and of all the moments thereafter. There is no cave, except the one we enter when we close our eyes to the world and our hearts to others.

There are indeed ideals, but they are not ideal bells or beds. They are virtues, notions of how the world might be different from and better than it is. As sovereign individuals, we learn to care about these ideals, and balance them, and bring them to life. We can also learn to create them. We don't borrow from an ideal world. We reach toward it and expand it.

If we think, though, that the world we experience is not the real world but is only a cave or (as people say now) a computer simulation, then we might conclude that such activity makes no sense. If we believe that life is elsewhere, then freedom is senseless, since we have no power to exist on that other plane, let alone to change it. Our only chance at freedom would seem to be to reach that elsewhere by shedding our imperfect bodies by dying (or as people imagine now, becoming one's own digital avatar).

This is the primal form of negative freedom: we can be free only by removing a barrier, and that barrier is our own bodies. We reject *Leib* and seek *Körper*. We embrace the death principle.

This conclusion haunts Plato's argument. In the *Republic,* Plato has Socrates, his teacher, describe the cave. Socrates is the archetype of the lonely philosopher, whose truths are beyond this world. After Socrates is sentenced to death, he calls the separation from his body a "release," a liberation. This cannot be right. Our body is not just one *Körper* among others, blocking some other life that is elsewhere and preventing us from reaching that higher state. Our *Leib* is special in that it touches both the realm of *what is* and the realm of *what should be.*

The allegory of the cave, properly understood, makes this case. As told by Plato, it wrongly conveys what people would experience. It makes no corporeal sense. Socrates says that "such captives," the people bound in the cave, "would consider the truth to be nothing but the shadows of the carved objects." No, they would not. Socrates ignores the bodies of the shackled people. If people were in fact shackled in a cave, their first reality would be their own bodily suffering, the iron on their flesh, not the shadows on a wall. When they noticed the shadows, the ones to which the shackled people would attend first would be their own. The shadows they would actually see on the wall, most consistently and most intelligibly, would be those of *their own bodies*.

The shackled people would have the truth of their own suffering. Within seconds, they would also apprehend the connection between certain shadows and their own bodies. Before long, they would also understand that they were not alone. They would see the shadows of other bodies and identify them as such. Even were they somehow chained so that they could not turn their heads to see the other people's bodies, they would quickly apprehend that the shadows on the wall that were similar to their own led back to other bodies, other people. They would understand that those others must be in a similar predicament, sharing a similar experience. And as they understood others, they would better understand themselves. This is what would actually happen in Plato's cave. The shadows of the "carved objects" would seem dubious and artificial, and rightly so.

So the cave allegory, if we do the optics correctly, leads to an entirely different conclusion from the one proposed by Plato and accepted by tradition. As a thought experiment, it actually shows that knowledge begins with the body, and that understanding begins from recognizing the presence of other bodies. The story of the cave, which is the story of Western philosophy, developed the way it did only because the body was written out of existence.

And so a correction must be made. Plato knew Socrates as a highly individuated adult, someone who was indifferent not only to prevailing opinions but to his own body and its pains and pleasures. No doubt Socrates was an admirably free person. He risked death for what he believed. But it is his capacity for freedom, rather than what he said about freedom, that interests us. Freedom is not about being right, which is elusive, but about trying to do right. How did Socrates come to be free? The answer cannot really begin from his thinking, right or wrong as it might have been. It has to begin with his life.

Socrates himself gives us a hint. Like all of us, Socrates had a mother. He spoke of her in one of his philosophical inquiries, comparing his own work as a philosopher to hers as a midwife. Toward the end of his life, Plato tells us, Socrates compared philosophy to childbirth, and thoughts to children.

His mother's name, Phaenarete, means "realizes virtue," a touching promise. We cannot realize virtue on our own, but we can learn to do so with the help of midwives and mothers and other people. Socrates, wrong as he was on other matters, rightly said that none of us is self-sufficient. Children need help from mothers, mothers need help from midwives, everyone at the beginning of life needs the help of others.

Natality, not fatality. Better a womb than a tomb. Thinking of Socrates's mother, we begin the philosophy of freedom not from an enclosing cave but from an opening world.

# Unpredictability

## IMPROBABLE STATES

My world opened up through reading, a capability I owed to others. People brought me to books, and books brought me to people. As I came of age, I was fascinated by the Czech dissident Václav Havel and his account of freedom, so different from the one I had imbibed in school or from movies. I was reading Havel in 1989 as communism came to an end in his native Czechoslovakia and throughout eastern Europe. The texts that captivated me arose when I was a child, in 1975 and 1978, around the time that I was ringing that bell and first thinking about freedom.

Havel started as a poet and ended as a president, with time as a playwright and a prisoner in between. Born in an interwar Czechoslovakia that was still democratic and independent, he was a small child when Nazi Germany dismembered his country in 1938, and a boy of twelve when communists took it over in 1948. Havel was fortunate in the care taken with his education, despite the circumstances. During the Prague Spring of 1968, a brief moment when Czechoslovak communists permitted freedom of assembly and of speech, Havel spoke up for multiparty elections.

After the Soviet Union (and its Warsaw Pact allies) invaded Czechoslovakia that August, Havel was blacklisted and could no longer legally publish his plays. He moved from Prague to the countryside and eventually took a job at a brewery. In 1975 he wrote a two-character play "about" the experience, to be performed among friends. *Audience* is set in a police state occupied by its superpower neighbor, both of which are ruled by communist parties notionally following Marxism. Yet the play has no ideology and no soldiers, and only a single policeman, who is present only in conversation.

The play is about what we do to each other within such structures. In *Audience,* a dissident employed by a brewery is summoned to meet the brewmaster. The brewmaster must, of course, inform on his politically suspect employee. From frothily roundabout conversations, it emerges that the brewmaster is friendly with the secret police officer to whom he submits the reports. The brewmaster wants to help his policeman friend, but he could use some assistance himself. He is not a good writer, and reasons that time could be saved all around if the dissident wrote the reports on himself, the brewmaster signed them, and the secret policeman filed them. The dissident eventually accedes to this.

In this brilliant bit of theater, Havel captured something of the Czechoslovakia of the 1970s. This was the period known as "normalization." No one believed in Marxism. Many Czechs and Slovaks did as late as 1968, during "the Prague Spring" that allowed free expression and promised reform. After Soviet tanks crushed the Prague Spring that August, the idea of socialism remained as excuse rather than as aspiration. The system was present everywhere not so much as ideology but as conformity; the temptation was simply to let it function. To be sure, it was easier when the dissident reported on himself. Yet doing so was to give up on dignity; as the dissident and the brewmaster agreed afterward, "Everything is shit." Cynicism about the system slips into nihilism that serves the system.

It might seem harmless to concede that there are no virtues, nothing to value in life. It might even seem to be consistent with freedom:

If nothing is true, then surely everything is permitted? On this basis, we would oppose barriers to our impulses—but we would lack an argument against the powerful whose impulse is to control us. If we accept that "everything is shit," if nothing is any better than anything else, we have no basis for sovereign choices, and gain no practice in the building of a self. We will mutter under our breath and accept our place in a system.

In 1975 Havel also wrote an open letter to Gustav Husák, the leader of the Czechoslovak communist party, about "the gradual erosion of all moral standards." Havel was a Bohemian in every sense; by "moral standards" he did not mean buttoned-up self-righteousness. He meant freedom, beginning with an affirmation of humanity. Only on that terrain do meaningful choices exist. Without a sense of *what should be,* we cannot be clear about how *what is* could ever change. In communist Poland, Adam Michnik, another dissident, read Havel's open letter and was impressed. A meeting was planned. It was delayed by Havel's arrest and imprisonment in 1977, but the next year it took place.

On a sunny day in August 1978, Havel eluded the secret police, made for the Czechoslovak-Polish border, and hiked to the top of a mountain. There he and other Czechoslovak dissidents met Michnik and other Polish ones. They built a fire, ate, and drank vodka. In the photographs, they look happy. Michnik asked Havel to write. Three months later, an underground courier delivered Havel's manuscript to Michnik in Warsaw. From a moment of contact at a border on a mountaintop arose Havel's essay "The Power of the Powerless," a profound meditation on freedom.

In the essay, Havel translated the experience of "normalized" Czechoslovakia into general political lessons. "Normalization" meant adaptation to the party line, even though no one believed it expressed anything beyond the convenience of the powerful. Normality in this sense of "normalization" has no substance, only form. It is the habit of saying (and then thinking) what seems necessary, while agreeing implicitly (and then explicitly) that nothing really matters. Life becomes an echo chamber of all the things we never dare to say.

The pretending was what Havel called "unfreedom," the concession of the authentic self. All the authorities needed was for people to react to stimuli: positively to consumer goods, negatively to the threat of prison. Modern tyranny, Havel concluded, required not devotion but predictability. Normalization forced life into "the most probable states."

## DECLARATIONS AND ACCOMMODATIONS

I loved this text in 1989, and still teach it decades later, because it helped me to see how "normal" could mean two different things. If what is normal is what everyone else does, then conformism can collapse to a single, meaningless, dark point. But if normal is what one should do, then an aperture opens instead, into a realm of dreams, aspirations, and judgments. If Havel is right, and unfreedom means predictability, then freedom must involve *unpredictability*. It is the second form of freedom, arising from sovereignty, or what Havel called "autonomy."

Sovereignty (or autonomy) takes work. Havel did not dwell on this, having been raised in a prosperous family and having had an excellent education. We need support to become autonomous people, sovereign individuals. Freedom requires a positive presence, not a malign neglect. Youth is a chance for freedom that must not be wasted. By the time brain functions are complete, at the age of about twenty, sovereign young people can show the world their unpredictability.

Havel was concerned with the power of the state to make us predictable. But what is such a state working against? How does our human unpredictability arise? The choices of each sovereign person will be in a unique combination, grounded in a unique set of commitments. But uniqueness at a given moment is only the beginning of unpredictability. No choice is ever final, not just because the world changes around us, but because different values will suggest themselves to us at different points.

A sovereign person, in making choices, is acting not only within the physical world, but in a realm of good and evil, right and wrong, virtue and vice. That zone, which Stein called "the world of values," is not an extension of the world of things. It is a kind of fifth dimension, with its own rules, and as such a reservoir of unpredictability for our own world of four dimensions, of space and time. The virtues do not interact with one another, or with objects, as objects do with other objects.

The fifth dimension, so to speak, has its own physics, its own geometry. When we make choices and affirm values, that different geometry of the fifth dimension seeps into our world, making us and it less predictable.

The values cannot be judged in the same terms as physical objects: we can say that a thing is bigger than another thing, but we cannot say that loyalty is bigger than honesty. Another difference: choosing between values is an act of affirmation, not of consumption. When we choose beauty, there is more beauty, not less. We leave behind the unchosen thing, whereas the unchosen value always awaits us. We might affirm it later, or even find some way to combine it with other values. As we move forward in time, we not only leave a trace of our choices behind us but also accumulate a new capacity for combining values within us.

Meanwhile, every sovereign person is doing the same thing. Everyone we encounter is facing an unceasing succession of choices in their own arrangements of unique circumstances, applying their own combinations of values. When people are sovereign together, they generate unpredictability. As they do so, they recognize this in one another, welcome it, and gain from it. When we apprehend others as *Leib*, we see them doing what we are doing, making choices in the zone between the world of things and the world of objects.

Working together, people bring human unpredictability into the world, and joyfully. This helps us to be free of all the people and forces who would rule us by predicting us or by making us more predictable.

Free people are predictable to themselves but unpredictable to authorities and machines. Unfree people are unpredictable to themselves and predictable to rulers.

Such unpredictability allows us to become our individual selves, together. The texture of the world of values enters our own world.

## ENTROPY AND GRAVITY

Havel strained toward that world of values, that fifth dimension, which he called "moral standards." Yet he also had in mind the physical world, the first four dimensions, the restraints we need for creativity.

Havel was preoccupied with the Second Law of Thermodynamics, according to which disorder, quantified by entropy, grows over time. "Moral standards" meant a limitation of chaos by ethics. "Just as the constant increase in entropy is the basic law of the universe," he wrote to Husák, "so it is the basic law of life to be ever more highly structured and to struggle against entropy." Normalization, by contrast, was a politics of entropy, a decomposition. Life was pre-death.

The freedom that Havel had in mind was a "life principle," resistance to a deadening politics of predictability. When we have access to ideas of the good, of virtue, we bring something fresh to the universe: "Life rebels against all uniformity and leveling; its aim is not sameness, but variety, the restlessness of transcendence, the adventure of novelty and rebellion against the status quo." A single improbable act "illuminates its surroundings" and makes possible other such acts.

Like Simone Weil, Havel was seeking a descriptive transcendence, a language that respected the truths of the physical world, including the truth that we can get beyond it. Whereas Weil had a brother, André, who was a renowned mathematician, Havel's brother, Ivan, was a noted cyberneticist. Where Weil wrote in the 1940s of a "law of freedom" and a "law of necessity," Havel wrote in the 1970s about "the law of life" and "the most probable states." Where she said "gravity," he preferred "entropy."

We cannot be neutral: we either deaden the world around us, or we make it more lively. Both Weil and Havel were convinced that we can be manipulated into making the physical world more predictable. Yet we can also make it less predictable, by finding passages to the improbable realm of "freedom" or "life." We learn about our *Körper* and the physical world to reach its edges, to better understand our own *Leib* and extend our chances. We need knowledge of both *what is* and *what should be* to experience that "restlessness of transcendence"—a phrase of Havel's that sounds very much like Weil.

## OUR MACHINES

Unlike Weil (1909–43), Havel (1936–2011) lived to see a world of screens. In the 1970s, the Czechoslovak communist party shifted to television as the primary means of political instruction. The aim was not to persuade people of the truth of Marxism but to induce them to see the present order as the only possible one. Communists on television dramas were portrayed not as engineers of a bright future but as regular guys doing their jobs, which just happened to be collectivizing agriculture or knocking down historic town squares. Violence hovered in the background of the entertainment, in the form of the recent Soviet invasion and in the certainty of prison for any overt resistance.

Communists had ruled by open violence: terror in the 1950s, invasion in the 1960s. As Weil wrote, and as Havel and other Czechoslovak dissidents said, violence against our bodies is meant to make the victim a predictable object—and it has a similar effect on the perpetrator. And yet, as the novelist Aldous Huxley prophesied, tyranny can be based less on "hitting" than on "sitting"—or really, on the alternation between them: lash, then leash. In the 1970s, the violence was never forgotten, but it was blurred by pleasure. Czechoslovak television could engineer a situation in which trams were empty because everyone was watching the same serial, in which conversations about plot displaced conversations about life. Those in power could use technology to make people more homogenous and less threatening to power.

Donna Haraway cautioned in 1985 that "our machines are disturbingly lively, and we ourselves are frighteningly inert." Like Havel, she was writing in the age of television, before the arrival of the internet. Social media today are far livelier than television. In our century, inertness is a feature, not a bug. Some people, of course, can nimbly exploit the internet to convey their personality and achieve their ends. The machine is built, though, to manufacture probability. Our screens seek our most probable states, refine them, and reinforce them. Algorithms herd us into categories defined by our least interesting features and distract us from the choices to be made in the physical and social world around us. Social media make us more predictable than we need to be and so easier to rule. Havel anticipated just such a digital future. He called computerized predictability an example of the "death principle."

Normalization in Czechoslovakia followed the end of faith in Marxism in 1968, the collapse of a certain view that technological change must bring human freedom. Like the Czechoslovak communists, the Silicon Valley libertarians first promised a brave new world, then told us that there were no alternatives, then invited us to live inside a screen. Like the communists, they passed from great certainty about utopia to total nihilism about everything, to a world in which "everything is shit."

And then they ask us if we are not, perhaps, living in a computer simulation ourselves—or, in an older language, inside Plato's cave. Unfortunately, wealthy and important people who speak of simulations are searching for an excuse to be irresponsible. If we decide that we are not real, that life is elsewhere, we can drop into a cave where morality has no sense and freedom is impossible.

## OUR COSMONAUTS

In 1976, America's bicentennial year, communist Czechoslovakia was at the height of official conformism and consumerism. The communists suppressed alternative culture, including rock and roll music, on the correct suspicion that it brought new values. The secret police had been surveilling rock musicians. That March, it arrested nineteen people from the underground scene, including members of a band called the Plastic People of the Universe as well as some other individual performers and members of other bands. This got Havel's attention. Blacklisted himself as an artist, he came to think that rock musicians embodied the "hidden life of society" that he had described the year before in his open letter to Husák.

When contemplating the art of youth, Havel made an unpredictable move. In 1977 the musicians were put on trial, first in Plzeň, then in Prague. He attended the second trial, in Prague, in which a member and the manager of the Plastics were accused of "disturbing the peace." Havel took the risk of publicly supporting their cause. Believing that they spoke a truth that was personally experienced and avouched, he signed a petition called Charter 77, linking the persecution of the musicians to the idea of human rights. "The freedom to play rock music," he wrote, "was understood as a human freedom and thus as essentially the same as the freedom to engage in philosophical and political reflection."

Havel became one of the spokespeople of the Charter 77 movement that emerged from the petition. Like his fellow spokesperson Jan Patočka, a noted philosopher, Havel wished to protect the self-education of young people. The musicians' ascent (in our terms) from sovereignty to unpredictability was the right kind of adulthood, precisely because it generated values that challenged older generations.

Patočka (1907–77) wished to protect the unpredictability of those much younger than himself. Taking the band name Plastic People of the Universe as an invitation to a philosophical riff, he called young musicians "our cosmonauts," generating values by remaining true to their young selves. In the essay, Patočka referred to two bands; the trial was directed at a more diffuse scene. The secret police interrogated Patočka for ten hours; he died shortly thereafter. Havel was sent to prison. It was after his involvement in protecting the musicians, and the corresponding term in prison, that Havel met Michnik in the mountains and wrote his anti-conformist essay.

Havel ended up writing about unpredictability thanks to his own unforeseen decision to risk his bodily freedom for the sake of others. "The Power of the Powerless" was a guide to the lure of unfreedom and a suggestion of how to become less probable. How did this text arise? Some people who were momentarily not in prison met on a mountaintop and talked. But what were the deeper sources of that encounter?

## HUMAN RIGHTS

Some causes lead us back to the Soviet Union, whose leader, ironically, wished to export predictability. As in its Czechoslovak satellite state, so in the USSR itself: after 1968, no one in power cared about Marxism. The dream of a communist future gave way to endorsement of the status quo, which Soviet leader Leonid Brezhnev called "really existing socialism."

Specifically, Brezhnev wanted acknowledgment of the Soviet empire gained by victory in the Second World War and consolidated by military actions in eastern Europe: antipartisan campaigns in Poland, the Baltic states, and Ukraine beginning in 1945, and invasions of East Germany in 1953, Hungary in 1956, Czechoslovakia in 1968. This he got. The Helsinki Final Act, signed in 1975, acknowledged the postwar territorial order and initiated new discussions on arms control. Soviet and east European communist rulers also signed on to a few paragraphs about human rights, which they considered meaningless.

The Helsinki Final Act affirmed the signatory states' commitment to earlier human rights treaties: the International Covenant on Civil and Political Rights and the International Covenant on Economic, Social, and Cultural Rights. These were ratified by the Soviet Union and its communist satellites in early 1976, technically becoming the law of the land. Communist regimes lacked the rule of law; their constitutions gave the communist party a leading role in society, which nullified the rest of the document. But communists liked to pretend to abide by the law, and this created a certain opening for Havel, Patočka, and others.

Human rights meant a universal recognition of equal human dignity. Once that idea was formally incorporated as law, it became an argument for the legal autonomy of a citizen of an actual communist state. Communist regimes treated law as subordinate to the party, as the written emanation of the power relations of a given moment. But law could also be understood differently, as an aperture to a world of values, in which *normal* meant "following moral standards" rather than "accepting normalization." Courageous people in the USSR and throughout eastern Europe decided, in this spirit, to take their regimes' new legal obligations seriously. They saw in human rights an opportunity to draw attention to the plight of their friends, whose imprisonments for speaking and writing could be chronicled as violations of human rights.

In Moscow, the editors of a samizdat publication called the *Chronicle of Current Events* had since 1968 been using a language of human rights to report on conditions in the Soviet concentration camp system (the Gulag) and in Soviet psychiatric prisons. After the Helsinki Final Act, new groups were formed in Soviet Ukraine and throughout the satellite states with the purpose of recording human rights violations. After the two Covenants had been published in the official law gazette, Czechoslovak citizens formulated the Charter 77 petition to document the regime's violations of human rights. The Czechoslovaks who signed Charter 77 were taking part in a larger movement. Brezhnev's desire that nothing change led to a change of concepts.

This is not just irony, or what Marxists called dialectics. It is a reminder that what might seem normal, predictable, and inevitable can be resisted, and that resistance begins with a definition of what might be. Sovereign people will see chances where others might not and will help to wrench the rest of us from our most probable states.

## PLASTIC PEOPLE

There would have been no trial, and no text, without the music. Another chain of causes that brought Czech musicians and thus Havel to that courtroom leads back to American history.

Rock and roll is part of the cultural aftermath of slavery, post–Civil War Reconstruction, and industrialization. It arose from the "race music," or rhythm and blues, of African Americans who moved to the industrializing North and met white audiences. Without that American encounter of the 1940s, rock and roll could not have been an important part of the alternative Czechoslovak culture of the 1970s.

A mediator between America and eastern Europe was a band called the Velvet Underground. Front man Lou Reed was a child of postwar American music—Little Richard, Ornette Coleman, Otis Redding, Al Green, Hank Williams, Elvis Presley. The Velvets were one of the most influential rock groups of all time—inspiring more bands than they sold records, as the saying went. One of these bands was the Plastic People of the Universe. The Plastics started covering the Velvets in 1968, the year Brezhnev ordered an invasion of Czechoslovakia, when violence begot "normalization." At that point, the Velvet Underground had released only two albums. For a couple of years, from 1970 to 1972, the lead singer of the Plastic People was the Canadian Paul Wilson, who could sing the English vocals of the Velvets.

The Velvet Underground was as New York as New York can be—but their trajectory owed something to eastern Europe. Reed was the grandchild of a Jewish family from the Russian Empire. The Velvet Underground was "managed" and their first album was "produced" by the pop artist Andy Warhol. The Velvets were the house band for Warhol's multimedia show *The Exploding Plastic Inevitable*. Warhol's parents spoke a Ruthenian (or Rusyn) dialect of Ukrainian. Like Havel's parents, they were born subjects of the old Habsburg monarchy, the central and east European empire that collapsed in 1918. Warhol's parents hailed from lands that became far eastern Czechoslovakia after 1918—and far western Soviet Ukraine in 1945. The recognition of the extended Soviet border was one of Brezhnev's goals at Helsinki.

The Plastic People of the Universe took their band's name from the song "Plastic People" written by Frank Zappa and performed by his band, the Mothers of Invention. ("I think that love will never be / a product of plasticity.") "Plastic People" was the first cut on the A side of the album *Absolute Freedom*.

The Mothers of Invention played "Plastic People" to the tune of "Louie Louie," a song made famous to the point of prom-night cliché by the Kingsmen (who were once investigated by the FBI on the suspicion that the song's incomprehensible lyrics might be obscene). As I did not know when dancing at my own prom, "Louie Louie" was written by Richard Berry, an African American born in Louisiana who made music in Los Angeles.

Berry penned the song on toilet paper in the bathroom of a club, having just heard "El Loco Cha Cha," by René Touzet. The unforgettable hook of "Louie Louie" is lifted directly from Touzet's composition. Touzet, for his part, was making a career in the United States after his club in Cuba was destroyed by a hurricane.

Without this improbable panoply, beginning with a hurricane (and therefore a butterfly?), there would have been no song titled "Plastic People," and no band called the Plastic People of the Universe. We can see all this as a causal chain that begins with African American and Cuban music and leads to Havel and his commitment to human rights and his defense of unpredictability. But some of the links in the chain, taken in hand, prove to be woven of the supple stuff of accident and choice.

Zappa's lyrics end with an admonition: "Go home, check yourself! You think we're singing about someone else?" It is us or no one. Freedom is not a drama we watch. It is a play that we write on a stage that we build for an audience of everyone. Responsibility, said Patočka, is something we always carry with us. Patočka did not choose the circumstances that led to communism or to rock and roll, but he chose the occasion of the Plastics' trial to write that "the only real help and care for others comes when I step forward and do what I have to do."

Necessity is the mother of invention; the better we understand necessity, the more inventive we are. As we choose over time, working from the law of necessity to the law of freedom, we invent ourselves.

As our choices mix with the universe, they render it more unpredictable, and us more responsible.

## NORMAL DISSIDENTS

Havel did not like the word *dissident* because it suggested a separate vocation. He thought the "dissidents" were just being themselves, living their truths, sovereign and unpredictable. Dissidence was just a matter of trying to live according to virtues rather than conforming.

The virtues themselves need not be exalted ones. Havel's two examples of dissidence in "The Power of the Powerless" were speaking up in your brewery about the quality of beer and taking down a propaganda sign from the window of your shop. Although Havel was a formidable dramatist writing in extreme conditions, the examples are human and accessible. The typical Americans of the 1980s knew nothing but bad beer. By the time I read the essay, I had worked cleanup on construction sites, in telemarketing, and in restaurants. The conformism of the workplace was easy to grasp.

*Normal* can mean what everyone does, as in *normalization*. But it can also mean what everyone *should* do. In his book on Poland's Solidarity movement, Timothy Garton Ash gives the word to a Polish peasant who says *normalnie!* in the sense of "great!" Mariia of Posad Pokrovs'ke, when she asked me how I liked her little hut, actually said *vse normalno?* ("everything normal?") in the sense of "as it should be." She meant by *normal* not the routine of rubble around us but the virtuous order that a home represents. Human rights restored to the word *normal* its ethical direction: what one *should* be doing. Although the punishment for trying to live normally in this sense could be drastic, the self-presentation was modest.

The appeal of human rights throughout the communist bloc was this everyday humanity, the banality of good. Myroslav Marynovych, a member of the Ukrainian Helsinki Group, noted a normal Ukrainian life, where *normal* meant pursuing the activities that seemed normal to him, such as speaking or singing in his own language. Writing to his mother and sister from the Gulag in 1984, he spoke of "an embargo on normal human aspirations." There is something fresh in the way that each of us combines values, and it was this freshness that was to be defended, not any sort of exalted abstraction.

Another human rights group, the Workers' Defense Committee, was established in Poland in 1976. Polish workers striking against rising prices had been humiliated and imprisoned by the communist regime. The Workers' Defense Committee found it abnormal that workers were beaten and fired by a regime that claimed to rule in their name, and normal that such workers would receive a legal defense and financial support. Human rights meant a handful of people trying to tell the truth about elemental matters, behave decently, and demonstrate solidarity. These realizations of human rights might seem prosaic: a defense of prisoners in Russia, of culture in Ukraine, of music in Czechoslovakia, of labor in Poland.

The everyday quality of human rights was the point. It was not one ideology against another. The dissidents made no grand claims and advanced no grand worldviews but rather tried to tell everyday truths, advance everyday causes, realize everyday virtues. Human rights did not mean the self-contradictory determinist "freedom" in the communist (or capitalist) sense: it was not what happened automatically when private property was taken away (or restored). The notion of human rights did not defer or delegate freedom. It opened up the space for the human exploration of virtues. It stood for *all* the values that actual individuals living in an actual historical moment might choose to hold and to try to realize. People earned respect, not for making an argument against communism in favor of some alternative, but for "living in truth" (Havel) or for living "as if they were free" (Michnik).

If the cause was so humble, why did people go to prison (Havel, Michnik) or the Gulag (Marynovych) or even die (Patočka) for it? From the outside, sovereignty and unpredictability can look strange; someone is standing up or standing out for reasons that are not immediately clear. From the inside, they can feel like a need to act consistently with value choices made over the course of a life. As in Havel's case, an unexpected decision that attracts public attention can be preceded by years when nothing striking takes place. This was the point Zelens'kyi was trying to make to me in September 2022, when we spoke about dissidence, resistance, and his choice to remain in Kyiv at the beginning of the war. You feel free when your prior choices make sense of a moment. Your actions are then predictable to you, though unpredictable to the world.

An action that seems odd or risky from an external perspective can seem normal and necessary to the person concerned. The Welsh theologian Rowan Williams contended that "spiritual maturity" means that "there isn't very much choice." For him, "that's not a diminution but an expansion of the personal because here is someone who by a long and hard route has become someone whose seeing and responding is instinctively truthful. You don't have to think about it." Writing in prison, Havel put it this way: "By the fact that today I vouch for what I did yesterday, that I vouch here for what I did elsewhere, I acquire not only my identity but through it I am also located in space and time; if on the contrary I lose my identity, space and time must perforce also collapse around me."

When members of the Workers' Defense Committee, or Charter 77, or the Ukrainian Helsinki Group, were sentenced to prison in the 1970s and 1980s, they tended to say that they were only doing what they felt they had to do.

## EMANCIPATION

The unrest in eastern Europe in 1968 was not limited to the Czechs and Slovaks of the Prague Spring. In Warsaw, Polish students took to the streets that March to defend freedom of speech. And, of course, 1968 was a time of youthful revolution not only in eastern Europe but around the world. Events in Paris, Berlin, and Berkeley were no doubt more important for the dominant understanding of freedom.

The American, German, or French claim for emancipation from prior sexual and gender norms seemed radical and was significant. It, too, was a more than plausible understanding of the message of, say, the Velvet Underground. Yet emancipation is a negative notion of freedom: it is always "emancipation from" something. It does not call into question the whole structure; it asks instead for inclusion within it. It need not mean freedom for all; it tends to mean, rather, joining a set of emancipated groups. In 1968 it often meant "emancipation from the older generation."

Contrary to appearances, this notion of liberation lets the old off the hook. Because sovereignty and unpredictability require work over generations, freedom for each coming one will always depend (in part) on the actions of older people. If the older generation is just a barrier to be set aside, what comes next? The young who grow old consider that they have done their work of freedom when they, in their turn, get out of the way.

Many people formed by 1968 easily moved, in the 1970s and 1980s, from the idea of emancipation from the elders to the notion of emancipation from the government. This is the dead end of negative freedom, the notion that we are free if the government is small and weak. It delegitimates the assistance to families that children will need to have a chance at sovereignty and unpredictability. This move by the generation of 1968 made it harder for their own children and grandchildren to grow up free.

To be sure, many east European rebels also liked the idea that freedom was sexual and that sex brought emancipation from the stuffy older people. In Warsaw, the students beaten by batons looked different from the policemen doing the beating. One of the striking features of the Prague Spring was the long hair and the short skirts. Beautiful youth irked Brezhnev, whose notion of communism was paternalistic and sexually repressive.

Young people in Prague got normalization, a consumerism without politics. This led some of them to creative thinking about freedom. In Warsaw, protesters were sent to prison, publicly shamed as Jews ("Zionists"), and told to leave the country. As in Czechoslovakia, the Polish communist authorities of the 1970s offered consumer goods in exchange for mindlessness. This led certain Poles, such as the dissident Adam Michnik, to argue that freedom resides in both rebellion and responsibility. That discussion about freedom crossed generations. Throughout eastern Europe, younger rebels looked for older mentors and found them.

## GLASS CANE

Individuality has to come from somewhere. The dissidents might have been sovereign and unpredictable, but they did not achieve this on their own. They were in milieus with recognized moral authorities, such as Jan Patočka for Havel or the philosopher Leszek Kołakowski for Michnik. Kołakowski was Poland's outstanding philosopher before being forced into exile after the events of 1968.

The "world of values," Kołakowski had written, is composed of "antagonistic elements which cannot all be recognized simultaneously, and each of which demands full recognition." Any single virtue has an absolute claim on us, but we can never realize it absolutely, not least because it clashes with other virtues. It is good to be consistent and good to be merciful, but nonsense to be consistently merciful, since to be merciful is to make an exception. It is good to be honest and good to be loyal, but over the course of a long friendship the statement "You're looking good" shifts from exemplifying the first virtue to exemplifying the second.

Totalitarianism offers an appealingly simple resolution: all the apparent diversity can be reduced to a single good. But this solution, said Kołakowski, is simply not true. The "world of values" is not a puzzle in which every piece has its proper place. There is no greater whole. Negative freedom also offers an easy dodge: once the barriers go down, all is permitted, and somehow all will be well. But this approach provides no definition of freedom and gives no sense of how a free person behaves. The story of freedom cannot be told without virtue, since freedom is the state in which we can affirm what we think is good and bring it into the world.

Aristotle was a value pluralist—like Kołakowski, he believed that there were many good things, not one or zero. When we are exercising judgment about which virtue applies in which situation, said Aristotle, we are doing right. This is true, but not quite all the truth. More than one virtue applies to almost any situation, so we have to choose. Since there are many good things, as Kołakowski argued, we must do some wrong even as we do right. The world of values is simply structured in this fashion. Since we are always deferring some virtue when we are affirming others, freedom assumes, in Kołakowski's words, "the reality of evil."

As we gather from his use of the word *evil,* Kołakowski's value pluralism means not relativism but a commitment to creative courage amid the clash of absolutes. We do right when we combine values and compromise with others, and when we accept that the concomitant evil leaves us responsible. As the philosopher Thomas Nagel concludes, "There can be good judgement without total justification." A graduate of my high school, Hannah Beachler, put it this way when she accepted an Oscar: "Do your best, and your best is good enough."

The possible combinations of virtues are infinite, and so our actions as free people are not predictable. Kołakowski also thought that we could invent new virtues, and that they were the most important ones. They emerge when we do things that no one has the right to expect of us. His value pluralism was an adventure directed toward the future. We believe in the possibility of new values because we believe that there is new good to be discovered in the world. This adds still another layer of unpredictability.

Leszek Kołakowski (1927–2009) was formed as a young man by the German occupation of Poland, and he married a Holocaust survivor. He met his future wife, Tamara, in 1948 when, as a student, she sought him out in a café in Warsaw to ask his advice about an exchange program.

Tamara was from Łódź, only about a hundred miles from Warsaw, but she had already journeyed thousands of miles before enrolling as a student. She was alive because her family had fled Łódź all the way to Uzbekistan. Before the Holocaust, Łódź had been one of the great Jewish cities of Europe, home to about as many Jews as Palestine. When she returned after the war, she found that "all of our Łódź family had perished. Three girls from my class at school survived." She married Leszek in 1949, left Poland with him in 1968, and remained with him to the end of his life. In her memoir, Tamara entitled the chapter in which she met her future husband "Accident," but it was accident followed by commitment.

Shakespeare has Hamlet say: "Where joy most revels, grief doth most lament / Grief joys, joy grieves, on slender accident." There is chance in the universe, and there are chances that we take. Kołakowski wrote, "My existence is realized only as permanent contact with the border of the unpredictable." When I knew him at Oxford and afterward, his rueful but mischievous smile reminded me that life can be full of rough chances, which we soften with humane choices.

Each of us enchants the world unpredictably or not at all. Kołakowski enchanted with a black hat, a glass cane, and a lopsided smile. He wrote me letters by hand, with a form of address that suggested interbellum collegiality. When we met, he would point the cane at my chest, smile, and call out "Snyder!" as if my existence made the world slightly richer, or at least slightly more comical. That made me smile, too.

No God, no person, no machine could have anticipated my teacher's marriage, his glass cane, or his lopsided smile, or what I do with his teaching: that, for example, I would go from writing about Marxism, one of Kołakowski's subjects, to writing about the Holocaust, a subject of his wife's memoir—or for that matter, that my own wife would write the book that Tamara would read to Leszek in his final days.

What I write is unpredictable, but it is not random. It rests in larger structures, physical and moral, even as it acts within them and alters them. It owes something to twentieth-century people whom I admired. It expresses values that I have learned from the past (when else?), which I am combining and applying in my own particular way. This chapter, about unpredictability in the twenty-first century, is what I must write.

## SERVANT

I read those nice letters from Leszek Kołakowski in a dodgy student hostel in Warsaw, with leaky pipes and frequent break-ins. As I carried out research for my dissertation in 1992 and 1993, I limited my possessions to what fit in a backpack, which I placed under my pillow at night to prevent theft. The most important thing I owned was the heavy gray Apple laptop I carried with me to the archives. My friend Andrzej Waśkiewicz, a Polish social thinker, would point to my computer and ask, "*Kto komu służy?*"

*Who is serving whom?* Is the human serving the machine, or is the machine serving the human? At that point, before wi-fi and smartphones, I could set the backpack in a corner of Andrzej's tiny apartment, one object among others, have a beer or three, play darts, and talk. During a brief visit to the United States in May 1993, my laptop was stolen, along with all the backup copies of my dissertation research. On my way to a New Haven crack house to try to get it back, Andrzej's question came to mind, an unbidden memory. Panting as I ran, I still had to laugh.

To be sure, machines can serve our purposes, enabling us to assert our own values. I did get the computer and the research back, and I did write my dissertation on it. Tony Judt and I communicated by email attachment as we edited our conversations into a book. My 2017 pamphlet *On Tyranny* began as a Facebook post. Right after the 2020 presidential election, when I told American CEOs to prepare for a coup attempt by Donald Trump, I was on Zoom. A class I taught at Yale on Ukraine in fall 2022 reached millions of people thanks to YouTube and Spotify and Apple podcasts.

I don't always succeed, but I try to keep in mind Andrzej's who/whom question. I try to see the computer in front of me as a tool to reach other people, and to motivate them to think or act differently. I know that readers of *On Tyranny* took action on the streets and in parliaments. On the basis of my notes, the CEOs quickly drafted a statement about respecting the outcome of the 2020 presidential election that became a model for others and that made it harder for Trump to stage his coup. That said, I would not have had to resort to the internet for these defensive maneuvers if Trump had not been elected, and had democracy around the world not crashed—developments enabled by social media.

I might be able to turn the machine to my purposes, and I know that others do. I fear, though, that overall the machine creates a special kind of entropy (Havel) or gravity (Weil). Because portable networked microprocessors—our ever-present phones, tablets, and laptops—can seem to do everything, they draw us into a messy mental world where we are not sure what we are doing. We leave behind the gifts of the *Leib* as we retreat toward the more predictable *Körper*. We lose our quiet, individual *why* amid the superabundance of *how*. And then the world shifts.

Who is serving whom? Or what? The purpose of most tools is self-evident. As Martin Burckhardt points out, the networked microprocessor has no clear purpose; it is less a tool for us than an invitation to us, or a seduction of us. It can be a pan-tool, capable of everything; but also an anti-tool, making its users less rather than more capable. If we do not thoughtfully engage the machines, we will find that they are disengaging us: from one another, from our values, even from our bodies.

## BIOGRAPHY

We have to be very mindful if we want to assert our purposes through social media. We have to manipulate software that is designed to manipulate us. If we are not careful, social media will turn our sovereign capacities to declare and accommodate against us, leaving us predictable and easy to rule. This is, sadly, not a hypothesis. Surveilled, harried, and nudged, I am undoubtedly less free than I was when I was sitting in Andrzej's apartment, backpack set aside, computer quiet in a corner. We are all less free.

In remembering that scene, I am freer than I would be had I forgotten it. Freedom involves possible futures, unpredictable to aspiring tyrants and uncaring machines. And any plausible future must be connected to a remembered or historical past. Knowledge of the past is therefore a reservoir of power and self-liberation. The future might flow down many channels, but its sources are in the past. Many things are possible, but not everything is possible. When we know nothing about the past, we think anything is possible but are quickly disillusioned. When we know something about the past, we know about some things that might be possible, and we have a chance at realizing them, a chance at freedom.

An element of ironic unpredictability in my own career is that unemployment enabled my historical work. I spent most of the first half of the 1990s in England, Poland, and France, writing a dissertation. After I finished my doctoral degree, I was unable to find a job as a professor for six years, so I spent much of the rest of the 1990s living in Warsaw, Prague, and Vienna, with journeys elsewhere in the region, including Belarus and Ukraine. I read books, learned languages, had some fellowships, translated for pay, and did other gig work. Living in Europe, I appreciated the access to public health systems. I suffered from disabling migraines and tended to break bones but did not have to worry about whether a doctor would see me.

As a result of some luck, I finally did get a job, at Yale. This had little to do with any merits of mine, or with any logic of hiring in American universities. It had been in New Haven that my laptop (with my dissertation research) had been stolen, and it was in New Haven that I was able to publish the next book, *The Reconstruction of Nations*, about Poland, Lithuania, Belarus, and Ukraine. Though it concerned the grand question of the origins of the modern nation, it was populated with unpredictable characters who saw the larger processes and worked with them. Like my later book *Bloodlands,* which was a history of Nazi and Soviet mass killing policies, it drew heavily from the time I had spent in the territories it described.

I was attracted to the unfashionable genre of biography, which captures some of the unpredictability that is essential to history—to what actually happened. Individuality tends to get washed out by retrospective accounts of what must have been according to the schemes we happen to believe right now. Writing about individuals restores some of the richness of the past and makes the present and future seem more open to choice. My dissertation had been a biography of a Polish Marxist exiled from his homeland by Russian imperial oppression. In New Haven, I wrote biographies of a Polish scenographer who plotted Ukrainian independence, and a Habsburg archduke, Wilhelm, who wished to become king of Ukraine.

## MAIDAN

Wilhelm von Habsburg's was an unpredictable sort of life; it ended in prison after interrogation by the Soviet secret state police. He signed his interrogation protocols with his chosen Ukrainian name, Vasyl Vyshyvanyi. His chosen nation, Ukraine, has taken on a significance that few had foreseen.

After the end of the USSR in 1991, most people continued to speak of Moscow and Russia, but in some respects Kyiv and Ukraine were more important. Historians appreciated that Ukraine kept its archives open; this seemingly small and everyday fact is at the root of much that we have learned about the Soviet Union. Protesting for freedom of speech and the counting of votes in the 2000s, Ukrainian citizens established a functioning democratic system. By the early twenty-first century, most Ukrainians were thinking of Europe as their political future. For Ukrainians growing up after the end of the Soviet Union, the European Union generally meant freedom, the possibility of a life with better prospects, less bounded by a Soviet past.

In November 2013, as Ukraine was about to enter into an agreement with the European Union, Putin managed, through bribery and blackmail, to dissuade the Ukrainian president from signing the relevant document. By then, all major Russian television stations issued coordinated propaganda. The message in late 2013 and early 2014 was that Ukraine did not really exist, and that Ukrainians and Russians were one people. I predicted on that basis that Russia would invade Ukraine, which it later did. I was apparently alone in doing so, at least in prominent forums. It was perhaps important that I was not on social media and was instead listening to people who were in Kyiv and attending closely to Russian propaganda. The same held later for my prediction in 2020 that Trump would try a coup, which he did. I just listened to what he said.

In Ukraine, the pro-European protests of 2013 were led at first by students and young people, those who had the most to lose if Europe was out of reach. After the students were beaten by riot police, the journalist Mustafa Nayyem summoned people to Kyiv's Independence Square, known as the Maidan. Nayyem closed his Facebook post with the words "Likes don't count"—only living bodies count, only the *Leib* counts. He was using the machine for an unintended purpose. The rule of law and human dignity would be protected, in the last instance, by the assembly of human bodies in a public place.

Isolation and algorithmic targeting summon the predictable *Körper*; people meeting one another rediscover the *Leib*. On the Maidan over the next few months, new and durable friendships were made. People founded civil society organizations that led to habits of cooperation and trust that would endure when Russia invaded Ukraine first in February 2014 and then in February 2022. In May 2014, along with friends and colleagues, I invited intellectuals, journalists, and policymakers from Europe and North America to Kyiv for a conference called Ukraine: Thinking Together. Its premise was that people who saw what was happening for themselves would understand better than people who stayed behind screens.

The idea for that conference began when friends in America called me in the middle of the night in London, and I realized, in the disinhibition of half-sleep, what had to be done. Colleagues and I organized the Kyiv gathering in a few turbulent and largely sleepless weeks, and my recollections are a little blurry. What everyone seems to remember is that I did some of the live interpretation and that I made the coffee. I don't remember deciding to do those things. I had waited tables before I had interpreted before. I was doing what I had chosen and what I could, which was what I had to do.

The circumstances that bring us together are unpredictable. And then in our encounter we bring unpredictability to one another. At the same time, in order to be together, we all need certain things: the time, the space, the language, the capabilities. It took work to get everyone together at that time and place. But I was animated by purposes that I understood and aided by institutions that others had made. I certainly felt free.

## CONFINEMENT

That conference in Kyiv was the first time my wife and I had both spent nights away from our children. My son had just turned four, and my daughter was not yet two. (And so there was a babysitter back in Vienna, of course. My wife had left the kids with me previously, which prompted this stunned reaction from a female east European colleague: "You left your children *with a man*?") Russia had invaded Ukraine, but the front was hundreds of miles away. We were in no danger in Kyiv in May 2014, but we were there to think about (and think with) people who had taken risks with their bodies. A poet and novelist I admired, Serhiy Zhadan, had refused to kneel before Russians in Kharkiv—and got his skull broken. His personal courage, as real as the batons, was part of what brought me to Kyiv. The young historian Bohdan Solchanyk was critical of my approach in *Bloodlands,* thinking that I had not gone local enough, had not accounted for specific motives of specific perpetrators. He had a point, though I never had a chance to talk to him about it. Bohdan was murdered by a sniper as Russia invaded Ukraine.

Another young Ukrainian historian later remarked that in *Blood-lands* I attended only to policies of mass killing, leaving incarceration in the background. This was true: I wanted my book on mass killing to have a clear focus and thought that the familiar notions of "Gulag" and "terror" overshadowed policies of political murder. When he made the point, Zhenya Monastyrs'kyi was speaking from experience. He had been taken prisoner during the first Russian invasion. The improvised jail in which he had been kept was part of a growing system of holding facilities, concentration camps, and torture chambers that Russia built (and builds) in the Ukrainian territories that it has seized since 2014.

Prison is a traditional place to contemplate freedom. Writings by prisoners help us to consider confinement not only as a set of barriers around the individual but as a specific condition of the human body. From the beginning, prisoners themselves have documented the vulnerability of the *Leib* to too little human contact—and to too much. In the first important book about Russian prison, the novel-as-memoir *Notes from a Dead House,* Fyodor Dostoevsky complained of "forced communal living," the unceasing presence of bodies not chosen for their company. James Davis III made the point that prison is an "unnatural space peopled by so many men, too many men." In the first important book about American prison, the memoir-as-novel *The Life and Adventures of a Haunted Convict,* Austin Reed complained of solitary confinement. The philosopher Lisa Guenther argued that our need for encounter makes forced solitude a specifically inhumane torture.

When kept in isolation, Zhenya recited poetry to keep his sanity. Solitary confinement is bad, but sharing a cell meant for one person is also bad. Those who oppress us either sever or overload the *Leib*'s connection to the world. As my students in the American prison explained to me, they do both, one after the other. There can be *too much* and there can be *too little,* with never a moment of *just right.* I hoped that our class provided such a moment.

## CELLY

Whereas in American English a *celly* is a cellmate in prison, outside the United States it can be slang for a cell phone. Watching people leave their cells and get cell phones can be disconcerting. A former prisoner released in the early 2020s asked a reasonable question about his new iPhone: "How do I get this thing away from my face?"

Another formerly incarcerated person I know, a man about my age, began his sentence in the twentieth century, well before smartphones were invented. When he was released after twenty-six years, he was troubled by the spectacle of people staring at the little screens. "I've seen more unfree people out here than I ever saw inside" was his comment. When I repeated it, that remark annoyed some of my incarcerated students: a touchscreen is no prison wall. But the perspective of the middle-aged man who had never encountered the portable internet is valuable: it provides a view of what has happened to us, from someone who was not eased gradually into our brave new world but encountered it all at once.

The algorithms of social media keep us online with a painfully elegant formula: *too much* contact with (apparent) others in the form of rapid affirmation, yet also *too little* contact with the actual *Leib* of actual humans. We feel as though we are recognizing and learning, but without the *Leib* we are disoriented, stressed, and prone to poor judgments about ourselves. We get used to all the dopamine hits, but they are delivered without any bodily sense. We get more psychological reinforcement from the device than we could possibly get in real life— and then get depressed because all the contact lacks tangibility. That experience of *too much* and *too little* leaves us trapped.

What might seem like a quaint human detail, that we spend ever more time looking at ever more seductive content, changed the world in the mid-2010s. The tipping of one convention into another, from looking at people to looking at screens, enabled a whole series of events that would otherwise have been impossible. In 2014, I realized that the actual stories of actual Ukrainians counted for little in the public conversation about the war, because mechanically amplified prejudices took up all the space. I started writing a book then, *The Road to Unfreedom,* about the hybrid tyranny that was emergent in Russia and its spread westward.

In 2016, exactly the same Russian institutions exploited exactly the same social media strategies to attack Hillary Clinton. Some Americans were told over social media that Clinton was a racist, others that she liked Black criminals. The contradiction did not matter, just as it had not mattered with respect to the 2014 Russian invasion of Ukraine, because the different messages were targeted at different people. An important Russian actor in the campaigns of 2014 and 2016 was Yevgeny Prigozhin, who ran Russia's Internet Research Agency. Prigozhin also directed a private military company called Wagner. (The name is the call sign of its founder, a Russian Nazi, who meant it as a reference to Hitler.) During the full-scale Russian invasion of Ukraine in 2022, Wagner recruited tens of thousands of incarcerated Russians to fight and die in Ukraine.

It is disturbing to think that our emotions, and even our actions, arise from the work of such people. But they do, and that makes us less free. Our emotions can be automated because our networked portable microprocessors ceaselessly communicate data about us. It is easy to calculate our vulnerabilities—to find our most probable states. When my Ukrainian student Zhenya was taken prisoner, he managed to erase his cell phone data while locked in the trunk of a car, so that he would not put his friends in danger. On a macro scale, though, we cannot easily protect others or ourselves. The agglomeration of data about our social media use makes us vulnerable, as groups, to targeted propaganda.

Data collection can become the structure of unfree politics. China has a smaller incarceration system (at least officially and proportionate to its population) than America or Russia; perhaps this is because the entire country is a kind of prison. Chinese authorities judge you quantitatively, with a numerical rating that determines which spaces your body can inhabit. Your body, rather than enabling unpredictable connections to others, becomes a part of a system of measurement. Your qualities are turned back into quantities and turned against your freedom. The physical world closes down around you. In a certain way, every citizen of China then becomes a celly.

## LOST TIME

"Do the time, don't let the time do you" is a phrase I learned in a prison, but it has a broader application. When we are not thoughtful about how we engage with social media, time is one of the first things we lose.

We give away the hours of the day. Our time without the machine is broken up by our time with it. Even if we are not using a phone or tablet, we forget what we are doing when we see one. If someone else glances at a device, we look at our own. We live as if in suspension, awaiting an interruption. In everyday life, our sense of time dissolves into a permanent rush. Even the precious moments just after wakefulness and just before sleep are sacrificed in the tiny glow. A *Leib* needs sleep in order to be sovereign and unpredictable; when we give sleep away to the screens, we are less ourselves and less free. Few things are more important than sleep to our maturation, happiness, and memory. Sleep has been the quiet casualty of our unfreedom.

For humans, time can resolve itself into subjective moments that we experience and then can remember. We lose time by not focusing, by not encoding moments from the flux. Simone Weil thought the "quantity of creative genius of an epoch" was measured by attention span. By her measure (and our own), we are becoming stupider. The twenty-first century is, let's face it, very dumb. Much is wrong with IQ tests, but the people who praise the digital world seem to approve of them. They like to speak of the Flynn Effect of increasing IQs. This is odd, since the internet age is in fact the time of the Reverse Flynn Effect, of decreasing IQs. We may have already dropped through the floor, too dumb to see how dumb we have become.

Time is also the time of life. Our sense of the continuity of our own biographies comes from our unpredictable capacity to go back and forth, to recall what was encoded, to link memory to experience. Some conjuncture in the present summons a rich memory of the past, perhaps of something we did not know we remembered—a taste of watermelon, a glimpse of sky, the sound of gravel under tires, the lyric of a song, the voice of a friend. The lines cast back are unpredictable, and yet very real, substantiating the present and thus the future. The solidity of those unexpected passages back ensures the navigability of our individual way forward. These involuntary memories are another form of time that the machine lacks and tends to deny us.

On social media, our attention is divided into fragments that are the right size for analysis *of* us but not *by* us. Our minds flutter hither and thither, landing nowhere. Attention is no longer about a special state of mind but about eyeballs on screens. Things *get* our attention, but we no longer *pay* attention. And then we do not remember. When memory fails, our future has no past, and we are not really present.


## REGAINED TIME

An involuntary memory can move us to see, think, write. Where did my bicentennial bell come from? As a three-dimensional object, it has its own trajectory in the fourth dimension of time: forged in Cincinnati; hung in a one-room schoolhouse at an intersection of country roads; one farm; another farm. It did stand next to the farmhouse in 1976, and I did grasp the pull and ring it. That happened. But how does my past reach me? How do I get back to a moment? How do we regain time? How does the bell mean something to me, stand for other things, appear in the fifth dimension? Unpredictably.

At around the time I rang that bell in Ohio, and the Plastic People of the Universe were arrested in Czechoslovakia, a teenager called Michael Stipe happened across a Velvet Underground album in the discount pile of a record store in southern Illinois. The band he started in 1980, R.E.M., was one of many with debts to the Velvet Underground. They covered four of the Velvets' songs, and Stipe would later cover a fifth.

My youngest brother discovered R.E.M. in 1984. We had a copy of their albums *Murmur* and *Reckoning* on cassette tape and excitedly bought *Fables of the Reconstruction* when it was released in 1985. I was fascinated by the cut "Driver 8," a song about trains, with the lyric "The children look up, all they hear is (sky blue) bells ring." Rightly or wrongly, I always heard "sky blue" not as the color of the bells, but as the color the children saw when they looked up. I was reminded of something: darkness, a loud peal, blue skies. I couldn't quite place it.

In September 1986, after R.E.M. released *Lifes Rich Pageant,* my father drove my two brothers and me to Cincinnati to see their concert at the Taft Theater. "Driver 8" was the fifth song R.E.M. played. "The children look up, all they hear is (sky blue) bells ring." Hearing those words with my brothers, I suddenly recalled being in line with them ten years before, leaning back, hearing the bell, and seeing the sky. What if we hadn't seen that show? What if Michael Stipe had never pulled the Velvet Underground album from the discount bin? What if my grandfather had never hung that bell? Where would this book be?

The unpredictability of biography flows into the unpredictability of history.

In September 1989, not long after a non-communist government formed in Poland, I listened to R.E.M. close a concert with a Velvet Underground cover. A week before the first big march in Prague, R.E.M. played "After Hours" again. The Czechoslovak protests that autumn were called the Velvet Revolution. They ended with Havel as president. Havel would never have reached the presidential palace without his decision to defend the Plastics, and the Plastics would never have been a band without the Velvets.

Nor would R.E.M. have existed without the Velvets, and so neither would I, at least not the I who listened to the music, remembered the bell, and wrote these lines.

As a graduate student in England, I had the CD of R.E.M.'s *Automatic for the People*. Once I was listening to it while I read a text Havel had written as president. The translator was Paul Wilson, once the Plastics lead singer. But who was translating whom, really? Havel would not have become the president writing that text without Wilson's Lou Reed imitation a quarter-century earlier.

In 2018 I was asked to write a new introduction to Paul Wilson's translation of "The Power of the Powerless," where I tried to formulate an argument about unpredictability. I met Paul in person in Prague in 2019; at a conference about Havel in Maine in 2022 I talked to him about music and chance. Right before that, I had been in Kyiv, asking Volodymyr Zelens'kyi how he defined freedom. And he said, "We all have our own values. Live in truth. Maybe you want to play the guitar. Learn to play the guitar. Start a band."

As the soft circles of memory open and close, we regain time. The chaos melds back together with choices, yielding a sovereign, unpredictable self. The machines corral us in harder pens: race, sex, income, residence. They define us by our most probable states, by what we do online or under surveillance, not by what we do on the mountaintops or under the water or when the music is loud or in our dreams. The algorithms get in among people and transform the energy of the *Leib* into enervation for the *Körper*. We don't encode what happens, or we don't recall what we encoded. The gossamer whirl of memory flattens on the screen.

## INHUMAN BARRIERS

When I saw R.E.M. perform in 1986, 1987, 1989, and 1995, I was in high school, college, and graduate school. No one expected much of me. Now I love live performance because someone else is occupying the stage. I empathize with artists acquitting themselves with their bodies of what they owe to their art, bringing what they have within to an audience awaiting without.

Teaching is performance, and it is work. The screens make my job harder. I have taught kids to read and to field ground balls. I have taught computer languages, Slavic languages, English as a foreign language. I have taught theater to kindergarteners and philosophy to prisoners. I earn my living as a history professor behind the lectern.

But where is that lectern today, in almost every American university classroom? As I travel around the United States for invited lectures, I notice the same shift everywhere. The lectern has been moved from center stage to extreme stage left, so that the human lecturer does not block the students' view of the huge, wall-sized screen where slides are to be projected. People pay me to speak, then bargain down the time of my lecture, then ask me for my slides (which I never have). The daring impulse of inviting a stranger to lecture gives way to increasing fear that something might actually be said.

We are being tamed by the machine, dulled to one another. The American university class is yielding to the screen, to the cave, to the death principle. Let us all pretend that something is happening while another hour passes, do that for four years, get the piece of paper, and move on to a world of further fakery. The university should enliven, and at its best it still does; certainly there is no substitute for it. But teaching is about the *Leib,* not the machine.

At the World Economic Forum in Davos, the pressure to have a visual presentation is intense. Flashy presentations are called "memorable," but no one actually remembers their content. I never use visuals, and people report that, to their own astonishment, they actually remember what I have said from year to year. I once had the rare pleasure, at Davos, of taking part in an event with two other historians, both of whom shared my attitude and refused to use slides and screens. The outcome was a rapt audience. In boardrooms as well as classrooms, elite and less so, machines stupefy. When the lights dim and the first slide goes up, we relax into zombified calm, knowing that nothing lively is expected of us.

In hospitals, patients are separated from nurses and doctors by giant computer caddies or handheld digital apparatuses. The screen has the power to separate people even when they are in the same place. The time we spend every day with screens teaches us to disregard our bodies, which is preparation for their disregard by others. We fail to notice when machines occupy space needed by our bodies, even when our lives depend on it.

## RATIONALIZING ZOMBIES

Our thinkers can help us resist predictability. Stein argued that bodily empathy leads us toward reasonability. Weil made the case that our corporeality allows us to ask the important questions. Kołakowski said that human existence is about pushing beyond the edge of a predictable world into one that is not. Havel warned that we can be tempted into thinking like machines, or even into thinking that we are machines. All of them insisted on the *why*, on the search for the "world of values."

As we engage with the digital world, we grow comfortable with the *how* questions, the inhuman ones, and we find awkward the *why* questions, the human ones involving judgments about good and evil. We phrase *how* questions in terms of "efficiency," "maximization," and "optimization." The idiom of productivity is senseless in itself; it can be meaningful only when we know what we value. No notion of means-ends rationality (if you value *a*, you should do *b*) coheres without a value judgment; no amount of *how* can get you to *why*.

The *how* questions generate quantitative propositions that computer programs can handle. As we translate the experience of life into machine language, we risk our minds becoming something like satellite servers to make things easier for the computers—which do not and cannot care. When we confuse the convenient with the significant, the death principle descends like a cold fog.

A major political challenge in this century is to get out from under the legacy of empire, a theme of the next chapter, on mobility.

And yet we seem to be building a new sort of empire instead. Frantz Fanon, the psychiatrist and anti-colonial thinker, observed that empire transforms humans from *why* creatures into *how* creatures. A colonizer portrays other colonizers as having agency, and colonized people as without agency, and therefore as instruments. As we lose our sense of *why,* we are being colonized by our machines—with the vertiginous twist that our mechanical colonizers have no agency. We are submitting to an entity that cannot even enjoy its domination.

Simone Weil predicted that "capitalism will be succeeded by oppression exercised in the name of function." In "surveillance capitalism," as Shoshana Zuboff rightly calls it, rationality means constant monitoring, so that an invisibly tiny group of people can profit. Their empire is not visible in territory like the empires of old, and they (usually) stash their wealth in tax shelters rather than flaunting it in marble palaces. The digital oligarchs themselves often have no idea what they are doing, aside from indulging in some vague competition with one another. They monopolize everyone's future and fill it with inbred silliness.

When we forget the *why* and have only the *how,* our imagination seeps into the gully of the status quo. We rationalize, using our residual intelligence to explain that the world cannot be otherwise than it is, and that we cannot do otherwise than we have done.

In so doing, we collaborate in our own unfreedom. Taking responsibility for past decisions is necessary for constructing future freedom; if we rationalize the past, we are trapped in a story, a narrative of what must be that others will use against us. Our digital nemesis (and its human acolytes) train us to be "rational," in just that sense of rationalization, of making excuses for the very process that is humiliating us. We are to accept the world as the elites and the machines have given it to us, and we are to praise our ascribed place. Such self-subjugation is a return to a feudal world, in which a divine order has been replaced by a digital one, one sort of priest by another. This is not enlightenment but darkness.

Weil warned that the *how* of life can crowd out the *why*, that "utility becomes something which the intelligence is no longer entitled to define or to judge, but only to serve." When humans call on other humans to turn their minds into rationalization circuits, the gist is that we should be functional, like machines. We should sacrifice the capacities that make us different from computers and instead become poor imitations of them. Rather than seeking freedom by thinking reasonably with facts and values, we fade into the status quo. We should not call into question the parameters of our existence but simply make the best of what we are given.

Freedom is positive; it needs the vivifying world of values. If we have no purpose, we serve someone else's, or we serve a purposeless machine. We have been assigned a senseless task: to adjust, to adapt, to normalize, to internalize the death principle before we die, to regard ourselves not as *Leib* but as *Körper,* to consider ourselves as nothing better than a computer simulation, to die without having lived, to self-zombify.

A human intelligence that asks *why* before it asks *how,* that is directed toward freedom rather than utility, is not rational so much as *reasonable*. It does not waste its energy rationalizing the existing state of affairs or its own weakness. It reasons instead, with the help of values and others, toward better futures. It operates in the borderland of unpredictability, considering values and facts. It seeks to understand the world as it is and to bend it toward the way it should be.

## BRAIN HACKS

It is hard to be free alone, sovereign alone, unpredictable alone. If I ever became reasonable, it was thanks to people around me, neighboring sources of human intelligence. When I was with my teacher Leszek Kołakowski, or even when I read his books today, I have a sense that I am in "contact with the border of the unpredictable." Free people who push up against that border are expanding the fifth dimension, the realm of virtues.

To throw our weight in that direction, to become free, we have to recognize the sources of predictability and our vulnerability to them.

When we understand the physical regularities outside ourselves, we can turn them to our own purposes. We cannot wish gravity out of existence or claim that it is just one opinion among others. If we exploit what we know about it, we can (to take a simple example) build counterweights and elevate. Elevators use gravity against itself, so to speak. Every step we take as we walk (or move in a wheelchair or on crutches) is a negotiation with gravity; we are free insofar as we move without thinking. The restraints of the universe are also opportunities in a broader sense: gravity, which seems to hold us down, is also the source of the energy and diversity that enables life and grace.

We must also understand the regularities of the built mental world around us, the network of microprocessors within which we spend so much of our lives. We can use that world in many ways, including some that allow us to realize our values. But there is, as yet, no equivalent in the digital world to walking, no form of engagement in which our knowledge of what we are doing fades into healthy habits. The rules of the digital world can be altered and must be.

Until then, social media's pulse of predictability will draw us in. The algorithms locate the parts of us that are most predictable, nourishing them until they suppress our character. They carry out what the mathematician Ada Lovelace (1815–52) long ago called a "calculus of the nervous system." Their dread superpower is to *predictify,* to dominate people by making them predictable as individuals and classifiable as groups. One mind at a time, this nemesis pushes the border of the unpredictable back, contracting the fifth dimension, making us unfree. When we see ourselves as *Körper,* we might not see the problem; when we see ourselves as *Leib,* we do.

We can use what we know about the mind to make ourselves sovereign and unpredictable. But we can also use such knowledge to find brain hacks that disable many human beings for the profit of the few. Social media draw from such knowledge. Facebook (and other social media) exploits brain hacks that arose decades ago in laboratories full of rats and pigeons.

## EXPERIMENTAL ISOLATION

In one set of experiments, a lone animal was placed before a lever, which might or might not (depending on the experiment) release a pellet of food. The purpose was to ascertain whether the animal was intelligent, in the sense of being able to understand the connection between pushing the lever and getting the food. Although it was not initially appreciated, the isolation of the animal was crucial to the results of the experiment. This experiment continues every time you place yourself in front of a display connected to a networked micro-processor. You, too, are being tested, on the basis of what was learned from the animals.

The first brain hack is *experimental isolation,* getting you alone, out of bodily contact with your fellow creatures. It generates an artificial loneliness that enables four more brain hacks, four more kinds of manipulation.

In the experiments, the isolated rat or pigeon works one end of the tool but does not see its other end, nor the actions and intentions of the experimenters. We similarly set our eyes on the display of a computer or a phone. We are ignorant of what lies on the other side: the tangle of algorithms, the vacuum of purpose. Fingertips on a keyboard, we fall into a trap. We speak of "my computer" or "my phone," but these objects are not ours, any more than the lab belongs to the rat—unless we figure out how they work on us.

Could animals tap a lever to get food? They could. In a variation of these experiments, pushing the lever might or might not yield a pellet of food. This led to a finding that has served advertising and oppression ever since.

Facing a device that sometimes but not always reacts to action by releasing a source of pleasure, the animal in the experiment will push the lever over and over, forgetting everything else. In this artificial situation, the external world has all the unpredictability, and the poor animal is suffering and predictable. *Intermittent reinforcement* is the second brain hack. It depends on experimental isolation—if the animal has company, the device is less beguiling.

We overestimate the difference between ourselves and other animals at our peril. Identifying with their predicaments can sometimes help us to understand our own. After all, the box into which we dropped rats or pigeons was the template for the computer programs that seem to dominate our lives. They are designed to isolate and then deliver intermittent reinforcement.

Though clearly disabling for the animals, intermittent reinforcement was lumped together with "rationality" as a normal way to treat people. It would be "rational" for people who control systems to intermittently reinforce others in this way, to get them to gamble at slot machines or to buy things. From gambling and advertising, isolation and intermittent reinforcement spread to social media, where the profit model is to keep you online to view advertisements. Social media dose you with what you like—and then, occasionally, with what you fear. The paradigm in which these experiments were developed, known as *behaviorism,* was indifferent to motives and purposes, let alone values and virtues. Those who exploit its findings tend to present *why* questions as signs of irrationality.

Some animals might be wiser than we are. When octopuses were subjected to behaviorist experiments, they reacted with less interest than did rats and pigeons. The octopuses seemed to understand that they were in a made environment and wished to pass judgment on their predicament. In one case, an octopus tried to break the machine, then raised itself out of the pool to squirt water at the experimenter. From this behavior, the human scientists concluded that octopuses were not rational—a conclusion that suggests their own mental limits. Such behaviors perhaps demonstrate that octopuses are reasonable, in the sense of judging an overall situation and reacting. We should be more like that.

Behaviorism can be applied to politics, as, for example, in the communist "normalization" that Havel described. Late communism was based on the assumption that people were beasts without values, easily manipulated to work for the few. Its logic was simple: give people what they want some of the time; throw in some fear; never ask what it all means, and make sure no one else does either. The totalitarian dream having proven empty, the single value of communism having been abandoned, communists shifted to zero values and intermittent reinforcement. Our silicon prophets have followed the same arc from hysteria to nihilism. There is no innovation in the ideas on offer, only familiar pyrite baubles rolled downhill into dreary disillusionment.

Havel saw in the normalized Czechoslovakia of the 1970s a "warning to the West, revealing to it its own latent tendencies." He thought that late communism presented the typical modern problem of "unfreedom" wherein we participate by reacting predictably to a pattern of stimuli. Experimental isolation and intermittent reinforcement bring us to our most probable states.

## ICY TUMULT

When we think with values, we are drawing from the past, but we are not stuck in it. We are considering the present, but we are not sanctifying it. We are oriented toward the future, and we are making it.

We like to think of ourselves as reasonable creatures, and sometimes we are. Our individual reasonability is unpredictable, because it arises in unique combinations of facts that we find salient and values that we affirm. Our collective unreasonability is predictable, because (unlike values and facts) impulses and lies can be mechanized. Our collective unreasonability has general patterns, which computers trace and amplify. It is not so much that they outthink us; they unthink us.

One form this unreasonability takes is *confirmation bias*. This means that we treat information as evidence when it seems to confirm what we already believe. In our better moments, we are aware of this tendency and try to correct for it: by creating political institutions that confront us with the opinions of others; by following social conventions that generate exchanges of views; by forcing ourselves to hear someone out; by having friends from different backgrounds; or by reading a surprising book.

Confirmation bias is an easy seam for a brain hack. The program simply follows where we click and nudges us along. It supplies more of the same, attaching a bit more emotional content. It keeps our eyes on the screen, while making us narrow-minded and sure of ourselves. Everything we feel turns out to be true and important. This gets worse as search engines merge with "AI" text-generators. "What we need is warm silence," wrote Simone Weil, "what we get is icy tumult." The cold stream of manipulation erodes us into caricatures of ourselves.

Confirmation bias, the third brain hack, works together with the fourth, *social conformity*. In real life, we tend to accept what people around us say; on the internet, the algorithms nestle us in an environment where we seem to be with like-minded people. Of course, some of the apparent people are bots, and others are pseudonymous fakes. (In the 2020 presidential election, the biggest Facebook group for American Christians was run by non-American non-Christians.) Even were there no non-people and no fake people, a silo is not a consensus—let alone the truth about the world. Our social media nemesis just groups clickers into conformist cocoons.

For us, the experience of having our brains hacked is emotional and political, even as our emotions hollow and our politics narrow. Our opinions, showered upon us, must be correct. Our feelings, repeatedly reinforced, become obsessive. We grow unshakably certain on matters about which we have zero knowledge. We come to believe that people who think differently are malicious. If we hear other people speak their minds, we are instantly suspicious. We are presented with images of the enemy on the internet, but rarely have contact with the bodies of other people in real life.

Our prejudices, confirmed when our social media nemesis doses us with fear, begin to harden. We control them until we feel attacked: social media regularly provide a splash of offense and violation, even when nothing has actually happened. We are sure that we are the victims: right now, in the future, in the past, always. My tribe never did anything wrong. *They* are the real racists. It was not my side that suppressed the vote. It must have been *the other side* that stole the election.

Our fears are cultivated to conform to what others in our categories fear. If you are a middle-aged white male and you fear exactly what other middle-aged white males fear, you have been had. When your fears are predictable, then so are you, which means that you (and your digital demographic) are ripe for manipulation. When you are predictable, you predictably bring your country down.

## LED LEADERLESS

Conforming, you are easily led. Having withdrawn from the rugged borderland of the unpredictable into the cozy cove of your digital demographic, you await orders, or nudges. You have exposed your buttons, and you wait for them to be stroked and pushed. Anyone (or anything) that caresses your naked anxieties will also be arousing those of the legion of cowards in which you have enlisted. The more people there are who fear the same things, the easier tyranny becomes. Unfreedom is efficient.

Our social media nemesis is thinking without being a thinker. It is conspiracy theorizing without there being a conspiracy theorist. To be sure, there is a human intelligence (at least so far) inventing the lies that the machine amplifies: Russians in St. Petersburg, for example, who claim that Hillary Clinton kidnaps children. But the amplification is digital.

As wealth is distributed ever more unevenly, the fantasies and whimsies of oligarchs get pride of place on our screens. Putin says Ukraine does not exist, and Elon Musk boosts the lie; hydrocarbon companies claim that global warming is not a problem, and Elon Musk boosts the lie; Trump says that he won the election of 2020, and Elon Musk boosts the lie. These lies then grow within us thanks to mental vulnerabilities that machines find and exploit.

When our brains are hacked, we can be led without a leader. As we expose our vulnerabilities, we become more vulnerable. As we come to feel more lonely and helpless, we are more likely to believe in ideologies that explain everything, conspiracy theories that make sense of the world, big lies that reassure us of our place in it.

The data about us, generated for advertisers, is sold to politicians or to oligarchs wishing to support them. Candidates can win elections by having superior knowledge of citizens' beliefs and fears, or by having others deploy the data for them. Politicians test phrases online before uttering them in real life. Talk radio hosts gain popularity by following what gets attention on social media during the day and then repeating it in the evening.

A politician who wins office with the help of algorithms is unlikely to lead us into a human future. Such a person is a character in a digital story, not its author, a mouthpiece of a politics of "us and them," contributing dwindling creativity to brain hacks. It is less shocking now than it was just a few years ago when a presidential candidate calls people "vermin," promises to imprison political opponents, plans to disassemble the government, and glorifies concentration camps. For the algorithms to get our attention, they need ever more drastic material.

Americans do disagree about many things, but why do so many of us seem ready for violence? Why did people storm the Capitol in January 2021 on the basis of falsehoods from screens? The lies invented by a few individuals were directed, by practiced algorithms, toward mass vulnerabilities. Why are we, so predictably, setting ourselves up for another scenario in which a presidential candidate loses the vote and then claims the office? We are being led leaderless into a calamity.

## SELF-BUILT CAGES

A sovereign person declares and accommodates. Values are declared and accommodated with one another. Others are recognized as they do the same thing. We become unpredictable—free—together.

Declaring and accommodating are the basic capacities of a sovereign person. Exercised alongside other sovereign people, declarations and accommodations generate an unforeseen realm, a land of the free. Coming to know other people, we know the world and ourselves better. Our values, our sense of what is right and what is wrong, are tested along with this everyday knowledge. This is what is best about us and what enables us to be free.

Our capacity for freedom, though, has a tragic flaw. Those capacities for declaration and accommodation, which are meant to greet and judge values and people, can also be drawn in another direction. Our nemesis captures these capacities and turns them against us, shifting us away from one another and toward our most probable states. Online, we declare ourselves, and social media extract data. We accommodate algorithms, and social media extract more. Our digital nemesis takes hold of our capacities, draws us into its fold, and beats us down for good and all. It acts, and we react, and we come to treat this as normal. It subdues our will without having a will of its own. We are predictified.

At first, the machine demobilizes. It takes up the time we need to attend to the bodies of others. It consumes energy and imagination. It tends to provide us with reasons not to act: not to exercise, not to make love, not to make friends, not to help our neighbor, not to vote, not to demonstrate. But at some point, when the algorithms locate our political fantasies, we find ourselves acting on the basis of unreality.

This fantasy, predictably, will have to do with a threat from others. A fearful world of "us and them" suppresses our capacities to see diversity and express empathy. Our fear is there to meet physical threats, planting us firmly (and predictably) in the first three dimensions. There is no time for evaluation, no fourth or fifth dimension. We feel that we must act immediately and that the choice is binary. Can we flee, or should we fight? We feel that we must act *right now*.

The fantasy arises from untruth. A lie belongs to someone else, and believing it puts you in someone else's thrall. You are predictable to the person who writes your lines. As the Indian novelist Arundhati Roy put it, the danger is not that the chatbots replace us but that we become the chatbots. The Russian thinker Mikhail Bakhtin said that "he who is deceived is turned into a thing." In the digital age, this can mean becoming objects that serve other objects. We cannot expect our nemesis, the pied piper of objects, to feel remorse about this.

Our nemesis moves us via fiction to do something in the real world, such as voting for a candidate who plays on our fears over Twitter, or invading the sanctuary of democracy for a big lie we read on Facebook. Then a line has been crossed. Having been recruited by algorithms for action in the real world, we rationalize, using our dwindling ingenuity to give our recruiter an alibi. Our minds become inferior search engines, set to find excuses for superior ones.

This is *cognitive dissonance,* the fifth and final brain hack, the machine's coup de grâce. We use what is left of our human reason to defend actions that were based on an alien one. We retreat from the borderland of the unpredictable and surrender the realm of freedom: not just for ourselves but for others who must endure our preprogrammed rants, senseless violence, and tiresome rationalizations.

The philosopher Lev Shestov wrote of "living automata, which some mysterious hand has wound up." Our nemesis winds us up, like toys. We are physically immobile while our emotions tense, then uncoil into action for reasons that are not our own. We become unfree in the simplest of matters, not doing what we would if we were thinking for ourselves.

Freedom needs human thinkers, sovereign and unpredictable. Unfreedom needs yielding and predictable creatures, quaking from fear in self-built cages, dreaming of enemies they never meet, and of friends and lovers they do not have.

When we see how the brain hacks work, we can escape predictification. That will involve changing the internet, but it will also require doing other things with our bodies than staring at screens. It is our move.

## RADICAL TRADITION

My friend Adam Michnik, the onetime Polish dissident, was a visitor at Yale in spring 2016. When I asked how he was doing, he responded that his fellowship at the law school was "almost as good as prison."

The joke had a point: it was the first time since his own release from prison that he had had the time to sit and read books. His best work had arisen during a long period of incarceration. Reflecting later on what he said, I realized that, in a much smaller way, I owed some concentration to prison as well.

In my prison class in 2022, the students did the assigned reading carefully, and I did the same. I was not allowed to have any electronics in the prison classroom, and of course neither were they. It was just us and the authors, without any distraction. When there was a break between the morning and the afternoon sessions, I would sit with this manuscript and edit it by hand.

By the standard of people on the outside, my students were quite radical. By the standards of what they would themselves have chosen to read, their syllabus was quite conservative. The point of teaching philosophy in prison is not that the thinkers are correct about every-thing, or that the students were always correct in their criticisms. Tra-ditions are an enriching restraint. In order to build on traditions, to correct them, we have to know them, and that takes time. Our current mood of discarding the past, usually on some self-righteous ground, has to do with our engineered inability to concentrate and tolerate. We are trained by our social media nemesis to join the herd and cull the herd. If we refuse to read, though, we are not trading the past for the future. Without the past, there can be no future. We are trading the past for quibbly static.

Past thinkers have warnings for us, including a warning precisely about that. We live amid devices that make us predictable, that predic-tify us. For thousands of years of literature, from ancient Greek poems through contemporary science fiction, writers have been concerned that we might create such machines. As this is now happening, we are forgetting the traditions meant to protect us.

George Orwell saw vocabulary as enabling what we are calling sovereignty and unpredictability. The plurality of virtues is real, but in his novel *1984,* people lack the words to name them. People are unfree not simply because their bodies are always observed but because their language is famished. In *1984,* the reduction of the number of English words is a cumbersome affair, drudge work carried out by people in offices. In our lives, social media reduce our vocabulary (and thus our references) at terrifying speed. Colonized on our couches, we accept a pidgin of English.

In Ray Bradbury's novel *Fahrenheit 451,* firefighters burn books while everyone is expected to spend leisure time in front of a screen. Its protagonist, a fireman, is able to gain distance from what he is doing as he reads books and regains words. The story closes with his escape to a wandering group of people who preserve literature by learning whole books by heart. The small band of people doing this are articulate, humble, and spontaneous. They have decided to stick together. This is how the greatest of books arose and endured.

One such was the *Iliad,* the story of a Greek attack on the city of Troy, preserved for hundreds of years by groups of poets and performers before it was set down in writing. For this chapter, a word I needed was *nemesis*: our own self-involved actions now create for us an enemy that can overcome us later, in a way that we darkly deserve, and that we can overcome only by knowing ourselves. That notion of nemesis comes (for me at least) from the *Iliad,* and from the Greek dramas set after the destruction of Troy. The long poem was codified in about 500 B.C. Its Greek manuscript was then preserved by hand copying for about two thousand years. A few copies reached Italy from Constantinople a few years before Byzantium fell in 1453. After the *Iliad* was finally published, heroes such as Achilles, Hector, and Odysseus populated tapestries, paintings, and poems.

In the *Odyssey,* a story that follows the *Iliad*, crafty Odysseus faces a series of trials as he seeks to return home after the victory at Troy.

One of these was the Island of Lotus Eaters, where endless pleasant stimulation extinguishes personality. Odysseus was held on another island by Calypso, who gave him everything except the freedom to go where he wished. The most apposite test was that of the sirens. Their song was irresistible because they adapted it to each listener—like the algorithms of today. Anyone who yielded to their summons would die, as the skeletons on the shore of their island attested. We are drawn by what seems to be about us, even to entities that we know we cannot trust.

Odysseus wanted to understand the sirens, but he also wanted to live and move on. He knew how vulnerable his body was, but also what it could do. He made a plan with his men. He had his sailors stop their ears with wax and tie his body to the mast. He heard the sirens, he felt his limits, he learned, and he persisted.

That is where we are. Like Odysseus and his ship, we have the technology we need to live and move. We have also created a digital siren song that will tell each of us what we want to hear, until we are no more, forgotten skeletons on a nameless shore. Together, though, we can understand our nemesis and ourselves, and move on.

It took him twenty years, the time we need to become sovereign and unpredictable. But Odysseus made it home.

# Mobility

## WOLF'S WORD

As a little kid, I was lucky to have a babysitter, Donna, who told me Greek myths as bedtime stories. Later I checked out books of mythology from the public library. I read Edith Hamilton's summaries under my desk in elementary school. The *Iliad* and the *Odyssey* followed, first in summaries or illustrated abridgments from the public library, then in full form. I read a few of the Greek dramas that began where the *Iliad* ended, such as *Iphigenia in Tauris* by Euripides. My father thought I should get out more.

And I was fortunate to grow up in a family that took me on journeys, whether I wanted to go or not. My parents knew Spanish and were comfortable in Latin America. As a fourteen-year-old on a trip to Costa Rica, I felt free, thanks to them. In the cloud forest of Monteverde, in May 1984, my brothers and I hiked every day, guided by a local kid, Ian. We walked or ran the paths from morning to evening, water and food and knives in backpacks, feeling self-sufficient and happy. We saw sloths and monkeys and the elusive quetzal.

One day Ian promised us something special, a mysterious quest. We walked on and on, but he remained taciturn. After three hours or so on a dirt road, we wandered through a maze of cloud forest paths, some visible, some of which seemed only to exist in Ian's imagination, some where I wished I had brought a machete. Then we heard the rush, everything opened up, and we saw the waterfall. It had a clear pool, both in front and behind, where there was a cave. We could swim into the cave and look out at the green world through tons of falling water.

That evening, too tired to speak myself, I sat at the edge of a conversation of older men. I heard a term that fascinated me after a day on the paths. The people my family knew in Monteverde were Quaker Cold War refugees who had managed to establish a dairy commune on a plateau. The English they spoke was right out of the Midwest, in some cases right out of my parents' home county in Ohio. The topic was the protection of habitat.

Two of the older gentlemen (Roy Joe and Wolf) got to talking about a path in the cloud forest, about whether it was available for public use. The term they used was *right of way*: Was this path a "right of way"? Did anyone have the right to use it? They pronounced the phrase like "right away," which only added to its appeal.

That's what I wanted, at fourteen. I wanted a right of way, right away. I wanted to know that there would be a path. As I didn't quite then understand, someone else would have blazed it. I took what I could get. A public high school was awaiting me in Ohio, with a few teachers who could deal with me, and a debate team with a patient coach. The country highways, empty at night, invited me to speedy calm, as they had my father. And when the time came, I claimed my right of way, my right to get away, my little American Dream.

I visited Costa Rica twice more, once in my early twenties and once in my late forties. During those later visits, I continued to appreciate the beauty and gave some thought to the politics. Here is a country that designates more than a quarter of its territory as park or refuge, that generates its electricity from renewable sources, that provides health care to its citizens. Costa Ricans live longer than Americans. Their political system scores much higher on freedom than the American one (on the American measures kept by the American organization Freedom House).

Costa Ricans do far better than Americans on all the happiness scales. And though it is impossible to quantify, people there do seem to feel more free.

## LIFE'S ARC

When I was hiking in Costa Rica as a kid, it was the paths through the cloud forests that liberated me. They existed, of course, only because of the work of other people, and they opened to me thanks to a guide and encouraging adults. If a trail is blazed, then someone else blazed it; if you blaze a trail, it's for someone else. It's still true that moving my body helps me to be free, to the point of enabling me to write. That I can do so, though, is the result of the labor of others.

We all need a right of way. Mobility is the third form of freedom: capable movement in space and time and among values, an arc of life whose trajectory we choose and alter as we go. For all of us, mobility means access to food, water, hygiene, health care, parks and paths, roads and railways, to help us make what we can of our bodies. Access includes safety: we are not free to go where it is not safe to go, especially when we are responsible for children.

For some of us, mobility means the time and encouragement to take care of our bodies. For others, it means more substantial support for our ability to move. None of us is capable of mobility without assistance. Those who require more assistance remind us of our general condition. We all need some help; beyond this general realization, it is all a matter of degree.

Although the individual *Leib* is mobile, mobility for all can be achieved only together. Mobility for individuals requires collective political attention to the logic of life: the risk of injury and illness, the progression from infancy to old age. Mobility is a form of freedom because we are free when we structure society with this in mind. It is not so much a final state as an accumulation of capacities and imaginings over the course of a life.

One of my relatives is blind and has limited movement. The better the technology around her, the better she can express herself. My friend stricken with ALS was more free, I like to think, when we were together doing something. Physical presence could generate a sense of spiritual freedom. But as I learned to operate his gear, another simple truth struck home: he was freer when he had a functional wheelchair (and would have been freer still had it been provided by American health care). Soldiers in Ukraine who have lost limbs to artillery are aided by prostheses and time and care. Rehabilitation belongs to freedom, and so does attention to aging. As the average population age, geroscience—preventive treatment of the afflictions associated with old age—becomes important to our liberty.

Care is important, as is the prior confidence that it will be there. We are more mobile when we can count on certain basic human requirements being met. If we knew that we had access to health care and a retirement pension, we would live more interesting lives. Lacking such confidence, we will be stuck where we are. Most Americans report receiving medical bills they cannot pay, which means being stuck in illness. For middle-class people, dependence on private health care makes it difficult to change jobs. This drastic restraint on mobility—and thus on freedom—is, sadly, taken for granted in the United States.

Poverty forces people into their most probable states. It impedes mobility. This is a point my students in prison made repeatedly. My student Marquis called poverty "the daily basis of unfreedom" and said that for many people he knows, freedom would begin with three meals a day and a decent school.

The first three forms of freedom—sovereignty, unpredictability, and mobility—should be present throughout our lives. There is nevertheless an order of development. In childhood, we attain sovereignty, with the help of others; in youth, we sustain unpredictability as we realize our own combinations of values. As we become adults, we need somewhere to go and the ability to get there.

Mobility is the challenge of maturity. To break free means to move in all five dimensions. It means having a waterfall to find or a mountain to climb, a day to do it, another to reflect on it. In the romantic imagery of freedom, we get to that idyll ourselves. In reality, all of us have help.

I love the places I am from, but I am glad that I could leave when I did. We all need mobility, but young adults need it in a special way. If everything goes as it should, they become sovereign and unpredictable, then break free of the structures (and the people) that allowed them to become so. But when those structures of mobility are not present, or when the structures are designed to immobilize and humiliate, rebellion takes on a different sense.

## CAN YOU IMAGINE?

Irene Morgan came of age in America during the Second World War. In 1944 she was a working mother. She commuted from Maryland to work for a defense contractor in Virginia that was building American bombers. In Maryland, she could sit where she liked on the bus, but in Virginia, she was required by law to move to the back. One day, particularly tired after a doctor's appointment, she was asked to yield her place in the back of the crowded bus to a white couple. She was then removed by force from the bus and beaten. But her case went all the way to the Supreme Court, and she won. In 1946 segregation in interstate travel became illegal, in theory. Nothing much changed in practice.

It was humiliating for African Americans to be segregated while traveling. Rather than simply moving from place to place, for purposes of their own, they were singled out. What should have been unreflective motion became a series of encounters (and the anxious anticipation thereof) that were meant to be reminders of inferiority.

Black people had to sit at the back of the bus or in a certain part of a certain wagon of a train. At each station, they had to use a different restroom and order food at a different counter.

Irene Morgan was helping to build airplanes. During the Second World War, a few African American men were trained to fly them. As one future pilot crossed the Mason-Dixon Line on his way to Alabama for training, he had to leave one train car and board another, just behind the locomotive. He and the other Black men on the train noticed that their places were then taken by German prisoners of war. The enemy was given more consideration than they. This sort of thing was recalled by a number of African American veterans.

Leon Bass, who volunteered to serve in the army, was humiliated as he trained for service on military bases in the South. He recalled a restaurant beyond the base where German prisoners could eat but he could not.

Bass fought on the western front of the European Theater, including in the Battle of the Bulge. He ended up in a group of American soldiers who reached the German concentration camp at Buchenwald. (As a nurse pointed out at the time, *liberation* was not the word for it, since former inmates kept dying and the survivors needed much more than the departure of their guards to be regarded as free.) Recalling Buchenwald, Bass said, "Racism is at the root of all of this. Under that umbrella comes bigotry and prejudice and discrimination. We haven't come to grips with that institution called racism. And we have to, because we see the ultimate of racism, which was what I saw at Buchenwald."

More than a million African Americans served in the segregated American armed forces during the Second World War. Black veterans returning home found an unchanged Jim Crow regime, regulating where their bodies could be. Leon Bass was refused service at a restaurant. "Can you imagine?" he said. "I put in three years of my life, put it on the line to make it possible for people like that young lady and that manager or whoever owned that store to function and enjoy the rights and privileges of Americans, and they were saying to me, just like the Nazis did, just like they told me down in the South, what they told my father, 'Leon, you're not good enough.' What a damnable kind of thing to say to somebody."

Some returning Black veterans challenged customary immobility. Wilson Hood sat where he liked on a bus from Atlanta to Washington, D.C., though on the way he was threatened with murder in Chapel Hill, North Carolina. As Isaac Woodard tried to return from a military base in Georgia to his home in North Carolina, he was severely beaten and permanently blinded. Both of his eyes were gouged out by a white man using a billy club.

## FREEDOM RIDES

In 1960 the Supreme Court ruled that racial segregation in bus terminals was unconstitutional. In May 1961 a group of "Freedom Riders" tested the new norm on the stops between Washington, D.C., and New Orleans. This first Freedom Ride was organized by the Congress of Racial Equality. One of its founders, Jim Peck, had watched the rise of Nazi Germany from Paris. Another Freedom Rider, John Lewis, wrote in his application to join the group of bringing "freedom to the Deep South." The Freedom Riders sat on buses and used facilities heedless of local custom and state law. In South Carolina, Lewis and two other Riders were attacked. In Alabama, one bus was bombed and set aflame, and the passengers were beaten when they escaped.

When the Freedom Riders reached Montgomery, Alabama, they took refuge in the First Baptist Church, where they were received by Martin Luther King, Jr. The church was besieged by a white mob, and the Riders were rescued only by federal marshals. When they reached Mississippi, many were arrested. John Lewis sat for thirty-seven days in a Mississippi prison.

Comparisons to Nazi Germany were made by all sides. After the siege of the First Baptist Church in Montgomery, Martin Luther King, Jr., said that "Alabama has sunk to a level of tragic barbarity comparable to the tragic days of Hitler's Germany." American Nazis responded to the Freedom Rides by riding in their own "hate bus." They proposed sending the Freedom Riders to "gas chambers."

From prison, the cause might have seemed lost. But some of the Freedom Riders pressed on to their destination and made it to New Orleans. Jim Peck, bruised and beaten, spoke at Xavier University with Charles Person. And other groups of Freedom Riders had already started their own journeys. More than four hundred people from both North and South took part in Freedom Rides in 1961, about 40 percent of them Black and about 60 percent of them white. That fall the federal government issued orders integrating bus stations.

## PUBLIC TRAUMA

Freedom means movement, and movement means encounter. But what does it mean to encounter one another?

To enter into a public conveyance and be judged by your appearance is a common experience. When I moved to Europe at the age of twenty-two, I learned how to blend in: get rid of the Cincinnati Reds baseball cap; wear leather shoes; sit and stand up straight; keep the hands out of the pockets; save the smiles for moments of significance. My father is always asked for directions, wherever he goes. In my twenties, I found that this was true of me as well: from Cornwall to Minsk, everyone seemed to think I knew the way.

But this amusing experience reflected a certain basic advantage. I had the color of my skin. I did not look anxious. Other travelers have a harder time.

I rode the bus in middle school with a Korean friend who lived a few blocks beyond the swim club. He never got to be himself. He was the Asian kid on the school bus, just as his two older brothers had been before him. They had worked out which remarks were to be ignored and which ones had to be resisted. If the school bully made fun of their eyes, fists flew. My friend later played linebacker and went to West Point.

The inability to move without being frozen in stereotype was theorized by Frantz Fanon. In the world Fanon describes, colonialists could move freely across great spaces, whereas people of color could be coerced and traumatized. He was concerned with the mental health of those seeking to pass unnoticed or just to be left alone.

Like Leon Bass, Fanon fought against the Germans in the Second World War. In 1943, as a teenager from the French colony of Martinique, he volunteered to join the ranks of the Free French. Like Simone Weil, he was thus part of the French Resistance. Fighting German racism on the battlefield, he found French racism among his comrades in arms. After he was wounded in action, his unit was purged of people, such as himself, who were not of European origin.

When the war was over, Fanon studied medicine in France. On public transport in French cities, Fanon could not escape the words that he heard to describe his skin. He could not help seeing himself as others saw him: he had the "sense of always looking at oneself through the eyes of others," as the American social scientist W. E. B. Du Bois put it. Fanon found that anyone, even a child, could trap his mind by attending to the exterior of his body. "I was coming into the world," Fanon wrote, "wanting to make sense of it, to be at its origin; and suddenly it was revealed that I was nothing more than an object among objects." His *Leib* became a *Körper*.

Past experience, Fanon's own or that of people seen as his group, made it impossible for him to be neutral in the present. He could not freely move from place to place; he was buffeted by the winds of the past. My incarcerated student David made a similar point about the future. In a paper for class, he argued that incessant external reminders of Blackness are a kind of threat. Because a young African American anticipates violence, every reaction to his skin suggests future pain. For David, "thinking without the threat of trauma" comes before freedom.

Mobility feels personal, but is political. A fourteen-year-old longing for a right of way may or may not get one, but the outcome is unlikely to result from his own personal efforts. My experience as a student in France was different from Fanon's. My experience of being a teenager in America was different from David's.

## THREE DIMENSIONS

For Fanon and Stein and Weil, a central enigma was Germany. Even for Havel and Kołakowski, who experienced the Nazi period as children, the human possibilities that fascism revealed could never be ignored.

One way to understand its special form of unfreedom is as immobilization and mobilization, rather than mobility. Within Germany after 1933, Nazis immobilized German Jews by making them second-class citizens, then setting other Germans against them. As the historian Peter Longerich has shown, to be a good German was to take advantage of the mobility Jews lost: a child's place in kindergarten, a parent's profession, a family's home. Such personal and familial gains made it easier to mobilize Germans as a *Volk,* a race.

Hitler identified Jews with the fourth and fifth dimensions. He portrayed political imagination as a Jewish rather than a human capacity. It was only Jewish concepts, he claimed, that drew Germans away from their racial destiny: the permanent mindless struggle for land and food. Jews were responsible for every structure that might initiate nonviolent human interactions that extend over time.

Hitler wanted Germans in the third dimension. No range of possible futures (no fourth dimension) awaited, and no society could be better than natural selection (no fifth dimension). Any virtue that enabled people to accommodate one another was Jewish, be it constitutionalism in a state, contractualism in a market, class consciousness under Marxism, or the mercy of Christian gospels. For Hitler, it all came down to Jews hindering Germans from seizing what they could as a race. Jews had to be removed from the planet so that nature could be redeemed. This was a hideous version of negative freedom: the freedom was conceived of as racial, and the barrier as the Jews.

The earth in *Mein Kampf* was populous and poor. Germans had to be mobilized to seize land before they were starved out by others. If most peoples were doomed anyway, went the logic, then it might as well be we who survive and prosper. Nature wanted humans to starve one another, and doing so was the only good. Technology offered no hope of escape. For Hitler, the notion that science could improve the condition of humanity was a "Jewish swindle." If there were no scientific solutions to human problems, all that remained was force. With time running out, Germans must compensate by seizing more land: *Lebensraum,* living space. This was a kind of imperial mobility: the world was covered by empire; Germans should impose their own.

Stripped of the fifth and the fourth, the first three dimensions are left barren and tragic. When Hitler spoke of "living space" for Germans, he meant killing space for others. As the strongest race, Germans should seize the rich soil of Ukraine, the most fertile in Europe. The idea was to dominate the western Soviet Union: "Our Mississippi must be the Volga River, and not the Niger River."

Hitler had in mind a frontier colony created by conquest, murder, and slavery. Germany did not aspire to retake its lost colonies in Africa, Hitler was saying, but to found an empire in Ukraine, one where Ukrainians would be treated as Africans and Natives had been in the United States.

## STALIN'S FUTURE

Mobility, as a form of freedom, has to do with values and time as well as with space. In dispelling the future and denouncing the virtues, Hitler created a politics in three dimensions, one of mobilization and demobilization. Killing the Jews and dominating eastern Europe became the only preoccupations. Mobility in only three dimensions means desperation and colonization.

In Stalinism, there was a future, a glimmer of the fourth dimension, but it was a single future, defined by the few. There was a hint of the fifth dimension, but it was the single value of communism, jealously crowding out all the others. The trouble began with Marxism.

Although Marx's analysis of capitalism was valuable, his proposed solution depended on the assumption that there was a single human nature to which we would return. In Marx's view of the world, private property was a singular evil, and its abolition would restore to each person that lost essence.

This is a negative form of freedom: remove a barrier; consider no ethics; plan no institutions; expect miracles. When Marxism led to liberating policies, as in the Vienna built by social democrats in the 1920s and 1930s, it was not as a program of total transformation but as a series of everyday ameliorations, directed toward freedom. Even today Vienna is often ranked as the best city in the world.

Marx argued that history was moving in the direction of a dictatorship of the proletariat, as capitalism had built the great factories that the workers would one day liberate. The Bolsheviks (unlike the Austro-Marxists in Vienna) took the view that history should be hurried along, and they made their revolution in the Russian Empire, a land of peasants and nomads. They thought that they were sparking a world revolution; when that proved not to be the case, they were left to build "socialism in one country." This was, again, not so much mobility as mobilization. Convinced that history could take only one course, they believed that they had to drive the USSR through an imitation of capitalism before they could create socialism.

Stalin had to plan an industrialization. His chosen measures, the crash industrialization of the Five-Year Plan of 1928–33, mobilized peasants to become workers, for about a generation. Millions of those peasants died of starvation or in the distant concentration camps of the Gulag, which was created at this same time. They suffered most in Soviet Ukraine, where about four million people were starved. Death had to have a meaning, and the available one was progress toward communism. Since there was only one future, and it was known to be good, then mass death along the way must have been necessary. At the 1934 congress of the Communist Party of the Soviet Union, that was exactly what Stalin's supporters said.

The certainty of a single future justified tyranny in principle, and it created a tyrant in practice. The classical form of tyranny was given the modern dress of scientific certainty. Until communism was reached, and all were liberated, people were just *Körper* to be manipulated. The consequences of this single future, which of course was never reached, swept through the twentieth century and into our own.

The Stalinist race against time provided the example for a Chinese revolution in 1949, which brought its own great famine in the 1950s and 1960s, killing at least forty million people. Without the certainty of a single future and the example of Stalinist mobilization, China's Great Leap Forward would not have taken place. Indeed, without the Stalinist singularity, China could never have taken the form that it takes today.

Along the way, the idea that economics had to yield a single communist future engaged with and encouraged the idea that economics had to yield a single capitalist future. The Soviet version of Marxism was a copy of capitalism; capitalists (as we shall see) later returned the favor.

## AMONG EMPIRES

Mobility is about the free movement of individuals toward their own individual futures; mobilization is about everyone catching up (Stalinism) or returning (Nazism) to how history or nature must be. Both Nazi Germany and the Soviet Union were ersatz empires, late attempts to exploit the European colonial experience of previous centuries. Hitler drew examples from the colonization of India and Africa; Stalin believed that the USSR should exploit its periphery as capitalist empires had exploited their maritime colonies. Imperialism, said Lenin, was the highest form of capitalism, and that was what had to be imitated. Both Hitler and Stalin drew inspiration from the imperial mobility they saw in the United States.

This view from the outside, partial and exaggerated though it might be, can help us to see ourselves. For about four hundred years, from the arrival of Columbus in the Americas in 1492 through the beginning of the First World War in 1914, European powers could expand thanks to their technological and immunological advantages. Twenty generations of Europeans had an unprecedented degree of imperial mobility (although, to be sure, much of the migration was flight from poverty or persecution or was a form of criminal punishment).

The United States emerged during the age of empires, which accustomed some Americans to an experience of mobility via dominance. The backdrop of American independence was the Seven Years' War, a global conflict between the British and French empires, of which the American Revolutionary War was an epilogue. The British won the Seven Years' War in 1763, extending their empire elsewhere, but also running up debts and accumulating arrogance.

The Declaration of Independence of 1776 was directed against a British Empire that was making financial and political claims on its American colonies. The rebellious colonists defeated the British in the Revolutionary War with the help of a French empire, which thereby gained a measure of revenge on Britain. Colonists loyal to the British Empire emigrated north to what became Canada. Americans established a republic in 1787. With the British and the French nicely out of the way, it was a republic marked for imperial expansion.

That same year, 1787, the United States organized the Northwest Territory, lands around the Great Lakes that France had just ceded to Britain in 1763. That is the Midwest of my youth. After American arms defeated Native peoples, a treaty at Greenville in 1795 opened Ohio to settlement. My maternal ancestors left North Carolina, where slavery was legal, to settle in Ohio. In 1803, the year Ohio was added as a state, Thomas Jefferson negotiated the Louisiana Purchase from a French empire. This opened settlement to the Mississippi River and a next wave of conquest and dispersion of Natives.

In the War of 1812, between the British Empire and the new United States, the British backed certain Native peoples, then withdrew. This separated Natives from their last European ally and generated justifications for revenge. American power spread westward, displacing

Native populations. In 1846 the United States declared war on Mexico, where Spanish imperial rule had ended less than thirty years earlier. American expansion to the southwest followed the victory of 1848.

It is typical for former colonies to display imperial features. The global norm was (and is) for new postcolonial regimes, even as their leaders spoke of liberation, to introduce scaled-down forms of exploitation. The American case was exceptional in that the former colonies had enormous potential for territorial expansion. For more than a century after 1776, Americans had tremendous technological and immunological advantages over Natives. In effect, the United States took the place of the European powers—the British, the French, the Spanish, the Russians.

An issue in American politics after 1848 was whether slavery should be allowed in states that were added to the Union. That question was settled by the northern victory in the Civil War in 1865 and the associated abolition of slavery. African Americans were allowed to join political life in the South, for just over a decade. In the Compromise of 1877, Union troops were withdrawn from the South, and racial authoritarian regimes were established (by the then all-powerful Democrats). The Union Army then returned to combat Native Americans in the West. As the West became a land of displacement, the South became a land of repression.

The late nineteenth century, then, set certain expectations for how mobility was achieved: by suppressing some, and by driving out others.

## CLOSED FRONTIER

The famous appeal "Go west, young man!" expressed an American spirit of imperial mobility. The vagueness of *west* and *frontier* suggested that there was always somewhere to go. A life can be shaped amid the certainty of superiority and the uncertainty of new terrains. The young man of European origin brought to the frontier his bravado and his hopes—and his bullets and his germs. (It was harder for African Americans to get land, even if they were not enslaved. African Americans did become cowboys, which was seasonal, transient work.)

The American frontier was vast but not unlimited. The U.S. border to the east and west was an ocean; to the north and south, it changed little after the middle of the nineteenth century. Spain ceded Puerto Rico, Guam, and the Philippines to the United States after its defeat in the war in 1898. The last great imperial drive was the "race for Africa" by European powers of the 1880s through 1914. In the First World War, some European empires (aided after 1917 by the Americans) defeated other European empires. This led to some reshuffling (Germany lost colonies in Africa and the Pacific, Ottoman land was placed under the care of France or Britain) but no change in the system.

The First World War brought about revolution in the Russian Empire, made by people convinced that imperialism was collapsing around the world. The Bolsheviks then updated empire, destroying young republics along the way and taking control of most of the territories of the former Russian Empire. Stalin then promoted "internal colonization," forced collectivization, and industrialization. Germany was ruled from 1933 by a Nazi Party bent on making a new empire in eastern Europe. The Nazis saw the Soviet Union (or its western part) as a future colony, intending to reverse Stalin's modernization and exploit Ukraine for food.

From 1941 to 1945, Nazi Germany and the Soviet Union fought a colonial war for Ukraine, which we remember as the Second World War. The fact that two European powers were contesting an east European borderland indicated that territory elsewhere was unavailable. Ukraine was now the focus of global colonialism.

Hitler treated the Soviet Union as a fragile state and Ukrainians as a people destined for domination, but that did not make it so. The differences in technology between Nazi Germany and the USSR were minimal. Germany had no immunological advantages; indeed, Germans were afraid of pathogens as they invaded. The Soviet Union was supported by American economic power, which made the difference.

Having defeated Nazi Germany, the Soviets regained control of Ukraine and restored empire. It lasted only forty-six years.

Around the world, the immunological and technological advantages ran out during the third quarter of the twentieth century. After 1959, when Alaska and Hawai'i became states, the United States would add no more territory. The United States often lost the actual wars that it fought in what came to be called the Third World. In this respect, it was typical. France could not return to its prior imperial holdings in Indochina: Laos became independent in 1949, as did Cambodia in 1953. Even funded by the United States, France had to concede northern Vietnam in 1954. The United States took over the war in Vietnam directly in 1965, killed about a million Vietnamese, then departed in defeat in 1973. After withdrawing from Vietnam, France fought a colonial war in Algeria until it was defeated in 1962.

British, Dutch, Spanish, and Portuguese empires left Asia and Africa in the third quarter of the twentieth century. The USSR was on a slightly different schedule. It expanded its own territory and added an external empire of east European replicate regimes in and after 1945. It was able to intervene militarily in Hungary and Czechoslovakia in 1956 and 1968. Yet when the Soviet Union invaded Afghanistan in 1979, it suffered defeats. Soviet leaders pushed Polish communists to suppress the Solidarity movement in 1981 on their own rather than ordering the Red Army to invade Poland. In 1989 the USSR was forced to retreat from Afghanistan; it lost its external empire in Poland and eastern Europe that same year.

If what Stalin and Hitler tried in the 1930s and 1940s was neocolonialism, then Putin's wars on Ukraine of 2014 and 2022 were neo-neocolonialism. Russia's leaders applied every argument from the history of imperialism, including Nazi and Soviet neocolonialism, to Ukraine and Ukrainians. The state did not exist; the nation did not exist; international law did not apply; borders were not real; Ukrainians were colonial people yearning for domination whose alien elites were to be destroyed and whose food and other resources were to be plundered. The scale of Russian atrocities after 2022 was comparable to that of the worst colonial wars of the past.

As a military struggle, however, the Russo-Ukrainian war followed the usual pattern. Without major technological and immunological advantages, even countries that regard themselves as superpowers will have difficulty seizing and holding much territory. In our historical moment, the larger country (the empire) tends to lose wars. Imperial mobility is no longer viable.

## SOCIAL MOBILITY

A free person ranges through the borderland of the unpredictable. But how to do so in our crowded century?

Imperial mobility brought to bear some powerful weapons of predictability: superior arms and infectious diseases. Both immunity and technology spread, eventually aiding the victims of colonization.

Anti-colonialists, generally victorious against overseas metropoles from the late 1940s, fastened on national sovereignty as the response to empire. National self-determination became the global norm, codified by the new United Nations.

The language of national self-determination was borrowed from liberal ideas of individual freedom; the notion of sovereign states, nevertheless, left open the question of how individuals become sovereign. Nationalism was effective as resistance, defining freedom collectively and negatively as the removal of imperial rule. But it provided no formula for the freedom of the individual.

The anti-colonial struggle *in* Europe, against the Nazi empire in 1939–45, took a different form than the anti-colonial struggle beyond Europe against European rule. Aiming to restore rather than create states, west Europeans could think about how not to repeat the mistakes of the 1930s. Those who resisted German occupation were almost never fighting just for the removal of the Germans, and certainly not for a return to the prewar status quo. The freedom that they had in mind was usually positive, about a future with a broader sense of possibility.

Americans helped Europeans adjust to a postwar era, which was really a postimperial era, by encouraging European economic cooperation. They indirectly subsidized the health care systems, social services, redistribution, and state investment of the European welfare states. That created an idea of mobility that did not depend on imperial expansion. The new *social mobility* improved on imperial mobility, while reducing the exploitation of some people by others.

The one form of mobility bled into the other. Germany, having lost its imperial war in 1945, was suddenly home to more than ten million refugees, most of them driven from Poland and Czechoslovakia. But they did not find a land of stasis. Expelled Germans who arrived in a democratic West Germany found themselves in the midst of a new project of social mobility. The same could be said of the French who arrived later from Southeast Asia and North Africa, the Dutch who arrived from Indonesia, the Belgians from the Congo, and the Spanish and Portuguese from Africa. Europeans who left former colonies in the 1950s, 1960s, and 1970s found new possibilities for movement in Europe itself.

The European (and Canadian) welfare states created after 1945 built infrastructure and public transport, trained workers, and spared citizens anxiety about the difficult passages of life. Public education, health care, and pensions also allowed Europeans (and Canadians) to choose more freely throughout their lives. Such policies helped to generate the first three forms of freedom: sovereignty, unpredictability, mobility.

Beginning in 1957, European states joined in a project of economic and political cooperation that in 1992 was named the European Union. The EU permitted not only free trade but also freedom of movement. It subsidized roads and agriculture and financed student exchanges. Imperial mobility was forgotten as social mobility became the rule.

The process was far from innocent. Europeans suppressed (and forgot) their own colonial pasts, which was frustrating to others. That

lack of historical self-reflection made it harder for Europeans to recognize Russia's colonial wars of 2008 (Georgia), 2014 (Ukraine), 2015
(Syria), and 2022 (Ukraine) as such. Wealthy Europeans found ways to
extract their cash from their former colonial homes and stash it out
of sight of European tax authorities. This made economic development in postcolonial states more difficult, and it created a culture of
tax avoidance that spread globally. It now threatens freedom in the
United States.

## MIDDLE CLASS

For about four decades in the twentieth century, the American trajectory resembled the European: imperial mobility gave way to social
mobility.

Beginning in the 1930s, an incipient American welfare state took
shape. Franklin D. Roosevelt's "New Deal," John F. Kennedy's "New
Frontier," and Lyndon B. Johnson's "Great Society" described the
shift from imperial expansion to social mobility. For many Americans,
these were the decades of the American Dream. Through the 1970s,
the gap between the richest and the rest was closing, enabling ever
more Americans to join a broad middle class.

The American Dream meant social mobility. Rather than promising more land forever, it offered a sense of unpredictable but possible
social advancement on the present territory of the United States.
Mobility was no longer about families settling down on land but
about new generations creating new kinds of lives. In this conception,
the permeable borders were those of social classes.

In the American Dream, society was fluid, subject to achievement
by individuals over the course of a single life. Unlike historical
estates, such as the peasantry or the nobility, the middle class was
defined not by ancestry or vocation but by life. Entering the middle
class was not only about individual Americans achieving a certain
level of prosperity but about the general possibility that everyone
could live unpredictably and end up somewhere new. Children would

not be stuck in the estate or profession of their elders, as in previous centuries, nor caught in a race or class mobilization, as in the Nazi or Soviet regimes.

Although sometimes presented as the natural result of capitalism, the American Dream depended on social policies developed after the capitalist collapse of the Great Depression. It lasted until its origins were forgotten and capitalism itself was enthroned as the lone source of freedom. That happened in the 1980s.

During that decade, the west European and American responses to the postimperial age diverged (though Britain was more like the United States, and Canada was more like western Europe). Beginning in 1981, under the presidential administration of Ronald Reagan, American policies of social mobility were reversed. Union busting weakened workers' ability to bargain. The neglect of antitrust law suppressed small business. A relaxation of taxes on the rich placed burdens on everyone else. The explicit rationale was negative freedom: President Ronald Reagan maintained that government can never help, only hurt.

The end of communism in eastern Europe in 1989 was taken as confirmation of this American version of negative freedom. Interestingly, in America's northern neighbor, there was no such turn. In Canada, no ideological case was made against the welfare state. In 1981 Canadians on average lived 1.5 years longer than Americans. The difference has increased to 5 years. If we multiply that out over the population, the price that living Americans will pay is about 1.5 billion years of being unnecessarily dead. And that's not the price of freedom, as some like to think. Pointless dying is unfreedom.

Social mobility into the middle class was a matter of positive freedom, a mixture of values and institutions, the notion that each life might have a unique trajectory thanks to enabling structures. In the United States, the elevation of negative freedom in the 1980s set a political tone that lasted deep into the twenty-first century: the purpose of government was not to create the conditions of freedom for all but to remove barriers in order to help the wealthy consolidate their gains. Wealth was allowed to flee the country, to the postcolonial tax havens.

The oligarchical turn made mobility very difficult and warped the conversation about freedom. The more concentrated the wealth became, the more constrained was the discussion—until, in effect, the word *freedom* in American English came to mean little more than the privilege of a few wealthy Americans not to pay taxes, the power of a few oligarchs to shape the discourse, and the unequal application of criminal law.

## MASS INCARCERATION

Prison halts movement in space and takes away time. In the late twentieth and early twenty-first centuries, prison deprived millions of Americans of the years when they might have been educated, found a job, or had children. It also stripped many of them of the vote, their voice in the political future.

Denying the franchise to felons is morally hazardous. It incentivizes aspiring tyrants to define felonies in a way that suits their own political aspirations—in short, to lock up people who might vote against them. More fundamentally, it is inconsistent with any program of freedom to create urban zones of hopelessness as a matter of policy. Those Americans who were incarcerated from the 1970s through the 2010s were disproportionately Black. A Black man was about five times more likely to be imprisoned than a white man.

A second moral hazard is the American procedure known as prison gerrymandering. Incarcerated people are counted as residents for the purposes of deciding how many elected representatives a given district will have. When prisons are built and filled, the bodies of prisoners increase the electoral power of the nonincarcerated people around them. Urban Americans are extracted from cities where they would have voted and placed in the exurbs or countryside where their bodies magnify the voting power of others—very often others who vote for politicians who run on the platform of building prisons.

The Connecticut prison where I taught was beyond the electoral districts of the cities from which my students came. In my home state of Ohio, people are moved from counties with big cities to rural counties. In this way, not only are the incarcerated denied a voice, but their voice is taken by others—and precisely by those who have an incentive to see prisons as a source of jobs and of political power.

*Leib* becomes *Körper* here in an especially sinister way: what people might want counts for nothing, while the physical existence and location of their bodies count in someone else's quest for power.

The historical precedent of counting bodies against people does not go unnoticed by imprisoned Black people. By the terms of the Constitution, slaves could not vote, but their bodies were reckoned (as 60 percent of a body each) in the calculations of how many representatives the slave states could elect. Representation in Congress was therefore structured directly by slavery to the benefit of the slaveholders and to the detriment of those enslaved. The more slaves lived in a state, the more people could be elected to preserve and expand slavery.

When state political authorities plan to build a prison, they are also planning to remove democratic representation from one area and supply it to another. What does it mean to vote for such candidates? Or to vote in a district where your voice counts more than others' because a prison is nearby? For people purporting to live in a democracy, it is a failure to "live in truth"—as Evan, one of my incarcerated students, pointed out after reading Havel's "The Power of the Powerless."

Prison gerrymandering is a phenomenon that Black and Latino people know and white people do not, or at least convince themselves that they do not. But for Black people and for Latinos, who tend to live in cities and who together comprise the majority of the imprisoned, the logic of the situation is clear. Their imprisoned bodies are converted into someone else's right to elect people who build more prisons.

It is true that individuals commit crimes, and that they should be held responsible. It is also true that others can create larger injustices around those individuals that make crime more likely and its punishment more political. Both of these things can be true at once. The truth we have to live in is not a single, comfortable one.

## BIG ZONE

In the class on freedom I taught in prison, we read works by dissidents under communism. Soviet political prisoners spoke of the "little zone," their concentration camp, and the "big zone," the USSR itself. American incarcerated students, once they heard this formulation, picked it up and applied it to the United States. They were not doing this to provoke me, though I did find it startling. It just fit an experience.

The extreme immobility of prison (little zone) seemed to them to be the focal point of the immobilization they had experienced their whole lives (big zone). These incarcerated students were not cynical: they had competed to be admitted to the university program, they wanted to earn a degree, and they were working at a high level. It was rather that they had begun their lives in an America where social policies to aid mobility had largely collapsed, in a way especially unfavorable to them. The idea that Black people were proto-criminals worked against the welfare state, even as white politicians defined policies of social mobility as a benefit for Black people.

In fact, white politicians had designed the welfare state to create a *white* middle class. Black people were often excluded. The National Housing Act (1934) created the Federal Housing Administration, which guaranteed mortgages, making it easier for Americans to purchase a house. But it only did so for white people in white neighborhoods. If a Black family could afford to move into a white neighborhood without federal assistance, the Federal Housing Administration would no longer guarantee the mortgages of white families in that neighborhood.

The result was the segregation of neighborhoods known as redlining, which mutated into new forms after housing discrimination as such was later banned.

The Wagner Act (1935) created the legal basis for private sector unionization, but it also allowed unions to exclude Black workers. Like the Social Security Act of the same year, the Wagner Act excluded agricultural and domestic workers, who were disproportionately Black. Unions did become one of America's important multiracial institutions by the 1970s—which was one of the reasons they were attacked in the 1980s.

In his "I Have a Dream" speech of 1963, Martin Luther King, Jr., meant the American Dream as a dream for everyone. An American Dream for everyone would have to involve a reconception of freedom as positive. Without an understanding of the past (which takes a sense of sovereignty), some of us will (if we are predictable) seek forms of mobility that are no longer available. In a sad symphony of misunderstanding and vice, we can reproduce the mental habits of empire, this time with no material benefit to the exploiters. Those who seek to immobilize others end up immobilizing themselves.

In positive freedom, we recognize that there are many good things, and we try to bring them together. Social justice and entrepreneurship were brought together as the American Dream. Under a regime of negative freedom, we imagine a tragic choice, whereby we must sacrifice everything else for a small, dysfunctional government. Racism stops us from being pluralists and so prevents us from being free.

## RACIAL UNFREEDOM

The American idea that we must choose between entrepreneurship and social justice is racist. It works in politics insofar as white (and other non-Black) people think of themselves as entrepreneurs, and of Black people (or immigrants, or other groups) as slackers.

The image of work-shy or inherently criminal Blacks dates back to the period before the Civil War, when enslaved people of African origin were performing the hard labor, and their main "crime" was their attempt to escape. This lingering racist specter displaces the reality that the welfare state served the American Dream. Seduced by a sense of ethnic honor, whites (and other non-Blacks) looked away as the world's largest prison system grew up around them, replacing a welfare state that, in many cases, had helped them or their families.

Socrates thought that disabling others prevents us from enabling ourselves. As Toni Morrison has argued, punishing a minority educates a majority. My lifetime has been the mass incarceration period of U.S. history, and this half century has left a mark on the minds of Americans. The imprisonment of Blacks communicated that being white was superior and safer. White Americans have accordingly grown up with a racialized notion of freedom as negative: as not going to prison. That absence of oppression, though a poor sort of privilege, is nonetheless awkward to acknowledge. And so the very subject of law and order immediately triggers angry emotion. It becomes hard to talk about freedom at all.

Was I freer as a teenager because the police did not arrest me in circumstances where someone else, someone Black, would likely have been detained? Certainly, I was better off than a Black peer who entered the criminal justice system. But if such an experience taught me to define freedom as just the absence of state power, I was enticed into making a huge mistake. The notion that what was good about the state was that it arrested other people was a trap laid for white Americans, a preparation for social stasis and anger.

Tyrannies make anxiety seem normal. They attach a threat to a group (in this case Blacks) whom the authorities don't really fear, then boast to their supporters of having protected them from that threat. They substitute relief from fear for freedom and teach citizens to confuse the two. The cycle of anxiety and release is not liberation, of course, but manipulation.

It is not immobilizing the way that prison is. It is nevertheless a policy of immobility that extends from the Black bodies on the inside to other American minds on the outside.

## IMMOBILIZATION POLITICS

In the final quarter of the twentieth century, rhetoric about Black criminality and laziness convinced some American whites that they were too good for social policies that had enabled *their own* social mobility for two generations. Wrongly convinced that economic justice was for other people, they settled for the self-deception that independent spirits such as themselves needed no help from the government. This was certainly a very strong sentiment in my high school in the 1980s.

In 1968 Richard Nixon, then a presidential candidate, brought together the concepts of crime and race. Ronald Reagan then linked welfare and race (which, thanks to Nixon, was already associated with crime). Reagan publicized the idea of the "welfare queen" during his failed 1976 presidential campaign and then again in his successful 1980 one; it was a stereotype that white kids growing up in the 1970s and 1980s were bound to hear. I can't remember not knowing what it designated: a stereotype of Black women claiming the tax dollars of hardworking white people to raise delinquent broods. In accepting this logic, and in voting against the welfare state, white Americans brought anxiety into their own lives—thereby making themselves and their children more vulnerable to future racist tactics.

A white person growing up in the late twentieth or early twenty-first century was taught to associate welfare with something that Black people exploited; yet very likely, it had earlier allowed his parents or grandparents to join the middle class. American kids now lost the American Dream, in large part thanks to their parents' and grandparents' votes. As the philosopher Richard Rorty mused, "It is as if, sometime around 1980, the children of the people who made it through the Great Depression and into the suburbs had decided to pull up the drawbridge behind them."

Many Americans of European origin were accustomed to mobility. They were, generally speaking, used to the system working for them.

Told that the system was working for other people, they voted against it—and thus against the social mobility of their children and grand-children. In the 1980s, Americans blocked themselves from complet-ing the transition from imperial to social mobility, then looked around for people to blame. Resentment arising from bad policy became a political resource for the very politicians who had designed that pol-icy. Immobility created an opening for politicians who claimed that one race was innocent and another was guilty, and that the only prob-lem in America was the presence of those others.

Since the late twentieth century, the ghostly prestige of empire has gotten in the way of lively freedom. The prestige of a past of imperial expansion, a time when we were "great," is attractive because of its mixture of affirmation and rejection. It promises people that they are part of a winning group by reference to a triumphant past, then makes them losers in their own unconsidered futures. This addictive mix, *postimperial immobility*, leads to stagnation and isolation. In the United States of the early twenty-first century, it brought suicide and addiction.

Postimperial immobility summoned a tragic echo of the age of imperial mobility. Where once prison inmates were forced to work, now they are forced to do nothing. Where once disease was a tool of empire, now drugs have become a means of self-oppression. Where once guns allowed men to tame a frontier, now they are instruments of self-annihilation. Postimperial immobility is not simply personal tragedy but the birth of tyranny.

## RUSSIAN GUEST

We don't live in truth as often as we might. White Americans know more about race than they admit they do, but the knowledge tends to emerge only when they are talking about white suffering that is Black-adjacent, as in my hospital story. Still, it is helpful to be "shaken," as the Czech philosopher Jan Patočka put it. The moments when we do live in truth, when we do glimpse the predicament of the other, can stay with us. My stories come from a certain position, the recognition of which enables a general point to be made.

In October 1990, as a junior in college, I was helping to run a conference of Soviet and American officials and security specialists in Washington, D.C. At the end of its first day, a friend and I were sent to fetch an important guest for an evening reception: Giorgy Arbatov, a prominent Soviet specialist on the United States and an adviser to Soviet leader Mikhail Gorbachev. As we entered the hotel where he was staying, we passed a sign in the lobby welcoming the Philadelphia Eagles, the professional football team, in town to play the Washington Redskins. My friend and I were in high spirits. Arbatov had graciously agreed to be interviewed for the *Brown Foreign Affairs Journal,* which we edited. We had an interesting conversation in his room. Afterward, the three of us were in a cordial mood as we took the elevator down.

It stopped after a couple of floors, the opening doors revealing two large men wearing green hoodies, obviously Eagles players. Even without the clues of the sign and the jerseys, I think I would have guessed. I had gone to a high school where football was king. Eight of its graduates have played in the NFL. I remember from the weight room the feats of a couple of other guys, two years older than me, who went on to play football for Ohio State and UCLA. The kid who sat next to me in driver's ed in high school was, in that fall of 1990, maybe third on the depth chart at quarterback at Ohio State, where he would start his senior year. After that he would become ESPN's best commentator on college football. The kid who sat next to me in Physics 1 in high school was, that fall, playing linebacker at Kent State; he would play pro football with the Eagles, and become an all-pro linebacker.

Arbatov did not have this background. And while his English was excellent, he had no way of knowing certain American usages around race. The two men entering the elevator were Black. Arbatov, who was about five feet tall in his shoes, looked up at them and offered a surprising overture: "My, you are certainly very big boys!"

One football player turned to the other: "Did you hear that?" His teammate had indeed heard the words but had registered something else, maybe the accent. "Let it go, man," he said quickly and almost inaudibly; the words were little more than a quick breath. Then he looked at the wall, as though nothing had happened. But the first man then turned to me, still angry: "Did you hear what he just said?" I had. A little nod, meant to suggest that I was listening and not confronting but that maybe there was more to be said. One kind of America, confident late–Cold War America, confronted another America, perplexed and injured racial America. Our job of getting the scholar to the banquet had become complicated.

The elevator bell dinged as we passed each floor; it seemed to take forever to reach the lobby. When we did, the angry football player got out, turned toward us, crossed his arms, and blocked the way. He wanted an explanation. His teammate put a hand on his shoulder, in a gesture that could have been support or restraint and was probably both. I took a little step forward, looked up to make eye contact, and said quietly, "He's Russian, man. He didn't know."

The body in front of me relaxed. Arms uncrossed. The second football player stepped away, threw his shoulders back, and fell into an everyday saunter through the lobby and toward the exit.

Arbatov didn't grasp what was happening but knew he had given offense. He came out of the elevator with outstretched arms. This time the first football player greeted him with a huge smile, put an arm around the academician's shoulders, and started making small talk about D.C. nightlife. Suddenly they were guys going out on the town.

Now I had a new worry: Arbatov was following the athlete's stream of schmooze into the wrong car. "You like cigars? Have one of mine. These are excellent, man." The word *excellent* was extended, like the arm. Arbatov gave him a beautiful smile back, eyes alive behind the thick plastic glasses, and took what was offered. My friend and I had to disentangle the two men to get the Soviet scholar to his conference.

When the football player got angry at Arbatov, he was reacting not only, I take it, to Arbatov's words. He was presumably experiencing one in a lifelong series of reactions to his body. No matter what he wore or how he comported himself, he was a Black man in America and would be treated as such. In this sense he was unfree, immobile, the way Fanon described. In a world in which there had been slavery and we all knew that there had been slavery, the word *boy* could not be neutral: he had to react or not react, and either would have risks and costs. He could not just move along.

As a twenty-one-year-old American from the (let's call it lower) Midwest, I knew that Arbatov would be seen as white and that a white person can't say "boy" to a Black man, and I knew more or less why. In a flash, I knew what I needed to know about race, though most of the time I didn't think about it at all or suppressed what I knew. Right then, I grasped that disassociating Arbatov from American ways of seeing and speaking was the only exit from the situation. My part was easy. The heroes of the story are the football player who dropped his guard when he realized his mistake and the bespectacled, diminutive foreigner who hung in there and kept smiling.

As the elevator descended the last few floors, I had been silently rehearsing what I would say: *Russian, Russian, Russian.* I told the football player that Arbatov was Russian because I knew that would be understood. *Soviet* might have been more accurate. Back in the Soviet Union, Arbatov was seen as Jewish, a characterization he could not escape and never did.

Arbatov's father, Arkady, was from a poor Jewish family in what is now the Dnipro region of Ukraine, then in the Russian Empire. As a boy, Arkady Arbatov migrated to Odesa, where he worked as a laborer. In 1918, Arkady joined the Bolsheviks and fought on their side in the Russian Civil War, which brought most of what is now Ukraine into the Soviet Union.

Giorgy Arbatov was born in 1923 in Kherson, Soviet Ukraine, six months after the founding of the Soviet Union. Germany invaded the Soviet Union in 1941; Arbatov came of age just in time to be drafted into the Red Army and sent to the front. Romanian occupiers and local Soviet collaborators murdered the Jews of Odesa. German occupiers and Soviet local collaborators murdered the Jews of Kherson and Dnipro. Arbatov never knew anything about the Jewish side of his family; by the time he asked, they were all dead.

In late 1941, Arkady Arbatov was sent to a Soviet labor camp. The year 1942 was hard for Giorgy Arbatov's mother: her son at the front, her husband in the Gulag. In his memoir, which he was writing at the time of our interview, Arbatov wrote about his father's grotesque predicament: a Jewish communist imprisoned in a Soviet camp, even as invading Nazis claimed to be liberating locals from a Jewish regime. Arbatov referred to George Orwell's *1984*—adding only that Orwell did not go far enough in his description of totalitarian perversity.

After the war, Stalin began a purge directed at Jews. Propaganda presented Jewish bodies as different, as cowardly. It became "common knowledge" that Jews had not gone to the front. Arbatov's Jewish background did not help him in his postwar career in the Soviet Union. But he remained, by the standards of the Cold War, an optimist about politics: learning English, trying to point the USSR away from confrontation, always ready to give the conversation another try.

## CONVERGENT STAGNATION

When my friend and I spoke to Arbatov in that hotel room in 1990, he said, "I do not rule out convergence." He had in mind a positive scenario, that the United States and the Soviet Union might meet somewhere around social democracy: unhindered elections, markets, the welfare state. This optimism was one reason the three of us were in a good mood when we entered the elevator.

As the years and decades pass, I keep his words in mind in a broader sense. In the moments when Russia and America seem very different, they might have hidden similarities. One of these is the collapse of social mobility, first in the USSR, then in the United States.

Soviet crash industrialization created mobility from the peasantry into the working class. Peasants who were not starved to death during collectivization or worked to death in the Gulag became workers. The Great Terror of 1937–38 killed much of the communist elite and much of the secret police command, allowing younger people—such as future Soviet leaders Nikita Khrushchev and Leonid Brezhnev—to quickly advance. It also allowed Soviet citizens to denounce their neighbors, move into their apartments, and take their possessions.

Stalin's alliance with Hitler in 1939 allowed Soviet citizens to make careers in territories annexed from Poland, Lithuania, Latvia, and Estonia. After 1941, the Germans (with local Soviet collaborators) murdered Soviet Jews (such as Arbatov's father's family) in cities, opening apartments for non-Jewish Soviet citizens from the suburbs and the countryside. Victory in the German-Soviet war of 1941–45 brought the opportunity to rebuild the western Soviet Union, to annex (again) the Baltic states and eastern Poland, and to plunder the east and central European territories occupied by the Red Army after its victory. And so for a time there was postwar mobility in the USSR.

Stalin's successor Khrushchev and Khrushchev's successor Brezhnev agreed on one thing: there would be no more murderous terror against communist party cadres. The bloody mobility that had enabled their own careers ceased. The Stalinist economic transformation was complete by Brezhnev's time. Peasants could become workers once; this mobility could not be repeated for a second generation. Brezhnev reoriented the Soviet economy toward the export of natural gas and oil, a policy shift that could not be imagined as heralding some kind of positive social transformation. There would be no territorial expansion and so no more plunder and seizure of empty residences.

By the 1970s, the Soviet Union was in the grip of postimperial immobility. Even the vision of a different future was gone. No one believed in a promise of future communism, least of all Brezhnev. He wanted to sustain the Soviet state by consumerism, while making it plain that no alternative was possible. He offered Soviet citizens a mythical past: nostalgia for the victory of communism over fascism in the Second World War. But as communism lost its meaning in the

USSR, so did fascism. It designated Moscow's chosen enemy, losing all connection to a specific political regime or ideology. The reference to the victory of 1945 enabled a simple politics of "us and them."

Insofar as Brezhnev's rule involved class war, it was one of the old against the young. Brezhnev's generation then, much like Putin's now, blocked younger generations from attaining power. In the 1980s, President Reagan, no young man himself, complained that Soviet leaders kept dying on him. Brezhnev died in November 1982, his successors Yuri Andropov and Konstantin Chernenko quickly following suit. Mikhail Gorbachev was borne to power in 1985 on this progression of wakes.

After four years of Gorbachev, Soviet collapse began in the outer empire, in the satellite states of eastern Europe. Poland was in a deep crisis generated by the lack of social mobility. The consumerism of the 1970s reached its limits, in part because Poles were comparing themselves to west Europeans in prosperous welfare states, in part because of the inherent flaws of central planning. The strikes of 1976 resulted in the Workers' Defense Committee; those of August 1980 brought the labor union Solidarity.

Gorbachev believed that the east European states would remain acceptably communist even without the threat or use of Soviet force. The Polish communist party took this as an invitation to legalize Solidarity and negotiate with its members. After roundtable talks, Solidarity won partially free elections in June 1989 and formed a non-communist government that September. Other east European communist regimes then also held elections. The new governments that emerged opposed the presence of the Red Army and preferred a "return to Europe." In 1990 the Baltic states of Lithuania, Latvia, and Estonia, annexed by the USSR in 1945, declared their independence.

Within the Soviet Union itself, vested interests in the communist party blocked Gorbachev's attempts to reform the economy. He wanted to put the state above the party and govern as president rather than general secretary, but that meant defining the state. The USSR was nominally a federation of national republics, and the leaders of the non-Russian ones now demanded recognition. The non-Russian nationalities believed that they had been exploited by the center; predictably, Russians believed that *they* had been ill used by the periphery. Communists in Russia itself, led by Boris Yeltsin, spoke out for a greater role for the USSR's largest republic.

In summer 1991, as Gorbachev prepared a new union treaty among the Soviet republics, reactionaries tried to remove him from power. Their coup attempt that August brought about the very outcome they had feared: the disintegration of the Soviet Union into its constituent republics. While the coup plotters held Gorbachev in his dacha, Yeltsin led the resistance to the coup, which led to an assertion of Russian power within the USSR. With the cooperation of Ukraine and Belarus, two other founding republics of the USSR, Yeltsin extracted Russia from the Soviet Union that December. The Soviet Union was no more.

The deep source of Soviet collapse was the end of mobility. Prewar Stalinist mobilization had never given way to anything like the postwar social mobility on display in western Europe. Brezhnev was right that the system would be hard to reform. Gorbachev was right that nostalgia could not go on forever. The West might have taken the collapse of communism as a warning. Instead, in a convergence of the worst sort, Americans chose to repeat the basic failure of the Soviet Union.

President Ronald Reagan was right about the ethical emptiness of Soviet rule. His description of the USSR as an "evil empire" was apt. But he and his successors brought stagnation to the United States. The worst possible analysis prevailed: the collapse of the USSR was somehow the fault of the welfare state. Having won the Cold War with social mobility, Americans cast it away. They brought the emptiness of failed empire home.

Since the decade of Reagan, Americans have been drowning in the syrup of a postimperial immobility: sweet references to a time when Americans could move forward and upward, the 1940s through the 1970s, to distract from the crystallization of an oligarchical social order. The political trick was to swap real social mobility for just the intimation of imperial mobility, which was no longer possible. Reagan's cowboy hat and boots brought an image of conquest but no frontier to conquer.

## ROADS AND TRACKS

At an elemental level, mobility involves building roads and keeping them up, a project the United States neglected in my lifetime. When I visited Poland for the first time in January 1992, a few weeks after the dissolution of the Soviet Union, Polish roads were horrible. As a young historian, I knew that this had been true for a millennium—and it remained the case for another decade. As the twenty-first century began, a journey eastward from Warsaw, on the terrains of the old Russian Empire, was still bumpy misery. After Poland joined the European Union in 2004, its roads were finally built. It was entering a Europe of social mobility, and its people benefited tremendously. I have visited the country every year of the twenty-first century and so have experienced the change firsthand.

In 2022 and 2023, when I needed to get to wartime Ukraine, it was impossible to fly over its territory. So I would get myself to Warsaw, then drive east to the border to catch a Ukrainian train to Kyiv. Polish roads, even in this easterly direction, are now impeccable. The contrast with the drive from New Haven to New York is discomfiting. So, for that matter, is the fact that Poles now live longer than Americans. My Polish friends would have found this unthinkable when I met them in the early 1990s. Now they take it for granted.

For thirty years, I have been riding the trains of post-communist Europe, which even in the rougher years of the early 1990s afforded an easy mobility I never knew in the United States. The railway also opens our eyes to society: As the Ukrainian poet Serhiy Zhadan asks, "What don't you see in a train station?" It has been impressive, if also unsettling, to benefit from the superior performance of the Ukraine railways during the Russo-Ukrainian war. Despite regular bombing and missile attacks, Ukrainian trains are incomparably more functional than American ones. While disposing of much greater wealth than Poland and Ukraine, the United States has found ways to have worse infrastructure.

## SADOPOPULISM

How did Americans come to think of immobility as normal? Postimperial immobility involves a sleight of hand, a trick that might be called *sadopopulism*. In the twenty-first century, politicians who claim to oppose "the system" are often called "populists." That is not always accurate. Some of them are rather sadopopulists.

Populism offers some redistribution, something to the people from the state; sadopopulism offers only the spectacle of others being still more deprived. Sadopopulism salves the pain of immobility by directing attention to others who suffer more. One group is reassured that, thanks to its resilience, it will do less poorly than another from government paralysis. Sadopopulism bargains, in other words, not by granting resources but by offering relative degrees of pain and permission to enjoy the suffering of others.

Donald Trump proved to be a compelling sadopopulist, teaching his supporters contempt for others during his campaigns, then declining to build infrastructure as president—precisely because it would have helped people. When sadopopulism works, the majority is satisfied with what is, never asking for sensible things like roads or railroads. My roads are bad, but yours are worse. I am trapped in my social class, but you are trapped in a ghetto.

Sadopopulism replaces the American Dream with that American nightmare. It directs the attention of a fragile middle class toward those who are doing still worse, rather than toward those who collect the wealth and decline to be taxed on it. It activates racism as the substitute for a better future. It creates barriers that block the many, then defines freedom as their absence for the few. Putting Black people in prison offers no social mobility (except to newly employed guards), but it might leave white people feeling less stuck than others.

Sadopopulism normalizes oligarchy. If I am comfortable with stagnation because others are drowning, my attitude to the highfliers will be one of supplication.

## TIME WARPS

Social mobility has three meanings. Politically, it is the alternative to postimperial immobility and its sadopopulism. Historically, it was the twentieth-century alternative to mobilization and imperial mobility that allowed European societies to flourish. Philosophically, it is an example of the third form of freedom.

Though every person's path is different, everyone's mobility depends on a sense that the future is open. Since the 1980s, American politics has succumbed to three time warps that deny us any such confidence: (1) a *politics of inevitability* after the end of communism; (2) a *politics of eternity* in the early twenty-first century; and (3) a *politics of catastrophe* emerging now.

After the revolutions of 1989 in eastern Europe, Americans took up the *politics of inevitability*. Capitalism was expected to fill the world with democracy. The market shifted from being a source of alternatives in life to a jealous behemoth that permitted no rivals. Americans traded a future full of possibility for a false sense of certainty. Negative freedom was enough: lift the barriers, and all would fall into place. History was over, only one future was possible. The politics of inevitability sucks the life from values as well as facts, then presses the dry shells together. It abolishes the difference between *what is* and *what should be*: the world as it is supposedly brings the world as it should be.

Facts about the present, for example, about inequality, were finessed into a narrative of progress. The propaganda of the politics of inevitability was "rationality" in the sense of "be rational": accept that things are good even if they don't seem so; everything is objectively good even if you experience it subjectively as bad; dismiss your values and personality and do what I say. Such "rationality" was contrary to the facts and obviously self-contradictory. Freedom cannot be inevitable, because in a world governed by inevitability, there can be no freedom. The politics of inevitability generates passivity, dampening the fighting spirit of individuals. Free people resist impersonal forces or turn them to their own purposes; they do not kneel before abstractions.

The politics of inevitability created the conditions for its own collapse. The American prison population more than doubled in the 1980s, and nearly doubled again in the 1990s. Whatever this was, it was certainly not the inevitable rise of freedom; nor was it democracy, since it involved mass disenfranchisement. Twenty-first-century wars were justified by the false premise that destroying bad states would generate the conditions for good ones. The disastrous invasion of Iraq in 2003 and the twenty-year defeat in Afghanistan proved that liberation was not a result of inevitable laws that come into operation when something is destroyed. Some Americans were shocked by a financial crisis in 2008, others by an election in 2016, or a pandemic in 2020, or an attempted coup in 2021.

Purporting to guarantee mobility, the politics of inevitability closed it down. Family by family, personal experience undid the story of inevitable progress. Faith in negative freedom brings staggering inequality, which freezes social mobility. The politics of inevitability, though it promised a better future for everyone, delivered imperial immobility, which is to say nothing or less than nothing for almost everybody. The claim that everything is getting better for everyone justified policies that left most people worse off than they had been before.

## 1 PERCENT OF 1 PERCENT

Freedom is positive, not negative. It is a presence, not an absence. The American Dream does not come true on its own. Older people have to enable younger people to be free. Young people do not choose the conjuncture in which they come of age. If they are sovereign and unpredictable, they will have the capacity to make choices. But they will be frustrated when mobility has been halted and few options are available.

Born in 1969, I had the sense, as the twentieth century gave way to the twenty-first, that I'd had an easier time than my brothers, born in 1970 and 1973. When I began teaching university students in 2001, at the age of thirty-two, I was dealing with undergraduates who were not so much younger than my youngest brother, and graduate students who were the same age as he. Since then I have had a steady view of the experiences of people ever younger than me, as the age gap between me and my undergraduates has widened from one decade to three. The unmistakable trend, even before Covid, was increasing anxiety and accordingly greater reluctance to learn things that might complicate a planned life path.

As the corner was turning on wages, the welfare state was disassembled, and labor unions were besieged. The American Dream had been a combination of earnings and institutions, and both were in decline. The statistics bear this out. Children born in America at the end of the Second World War were almost certain to earn more money than their parents. An American born in the 1980s had only about a fifty-fifty chance. Since then, inequality has only gotten worse.

I graduated from high school in 1987. Since the 1980s, new wealth generated by the U.S. economy has remained in the hands of an almost invisibly minuscule fraction of the population. The number of the oligarchs is numerically insignificant. The people in question are not really the 1 percent made notorious by the Occupy Wall Street movement, but the 1 percent *of the* 1 percent. Not 1 percent, but *0.01 percent*. Not 1 of 100, nor even 1 of 1,000, but 1 of 10,000.

Essentially all new wealth generated by the American economy since 1980 is in the hands of that tiny percentage of the population. The group of Americans who control as much wealth as half of the population is even smaller: as numerous as my high school class. And those few hundred oligarchs are paying less tax now than the actual members of my high school class—which is to say they have a lower effective tax rate than working-class and middle-class Americans.

Mobility depends on distribution. If I own everything and put a fence around it, you will not be very mobile. If I own a huge company that can prevent competition, you are unlikely to have an exciting first job. If a few pals and I can control a market with our monopoly power, we can keep prices up, making it very hard for people to break free into a new social class. In monopoly conditions, earnings will come from stocks rather than from wages, keeping the wealthy up and the rest down.

The politics of inevitability normalized this situation. Since capitalism was identified with freedom, any suffering was interpreted as necessary. Since freedom was negative, there was supposedly nothing government could do. In any event, there were, we were told, no alternatives. Politicians of inevitability presented growing inequality as a side effect of progress rather than its contradiction. The future was supposedly known and certain and good; once this premise was accepted, it seemed logical that pain in the present must be a meaningful step along the way.

## UNSPEAKABLE WEALTH

The truth was simpler. Inequality meant immobility. And immobility meant unfreedom.

Politicians of inevitability and their acolytes like to talk about averages, but they are worse than meaningless. If Jeff Bezos is in a room with a hundred impoverished working mothers, their average wealth is north of $1 billion, but that means nothing to the women. If you have $12 million, and each of your ten friends has $100,000 in college debt, you and friends are, on average, $1 million in the black. But your friends can't pay off their debts with that average.

It only seems that the typical American has some money because the wealth of a few hundred families—again, a group the size of my high school class—gets into the mix and spoils the math. Since half the national wealth is owned by an irrelevantly small group of people, the country is only half as wealthy as the numbers present it to be. If we remove oligarchs from the sample, it becomes brutally clear that the national wealth is spread thin. Typical Americans live from paycheck to paycheck, which is a polite way of saying that they are poor. A typical American cannot come up with $1,000 in an emergency. A typical American cannot pay for the funeral that negative freedom hastens.

Matters are still worse than this. It is not enough to remove the wealth of those top few hundred families in order to correct the math of national freedom. We actually have to count that wealth *against* the national welfare, because its concentration leads to practices and policies that leave almost everyone less mobile and less free. The tiny group of "have yachts" are more politically coherent and powerful than the enormous mass of "have-nots," and they will act to keep it that way.

As the French philosopher d'Holbach noted more than two centuries ago, and as contemporary research confirms, the consumption patterns of the very wealthy act to weaken the sway of everyone else, the 99.99 percent. Oligarchs spend wealth to protect wealth, which brings only detriments to other citizens (except to the handful of accountants, lawyers, and lobbyists they employ). This behavior warps the system into their service. It cuts off revenue that would fund public services that would allow tens of millions of Americans to create better lives. It spreads stagnation and undoes the American Dream.

Oligarchs do not just have the biggest piece of the pie. They often have the pie cutter. And when they do, it does not matter much if the pie gets bigger. Very important redistributive policies were passed by Congress in the early 2020s. But the first two years of the Biden administration was the very laudable exception, not the rule.

In the twenty-first century, federal and state governments have generally been outmatched by American oligarchs and their hirelings. Tax evasion and fraud have become the norm. The wealthy lobbied against policies meant to support a middle class. Monopolies blocked competition, and big firms stopped unionization. Inequality is not merely a set of numbers but a distressing experience. People who see unfairness from the beginning of life are discouraged and demobilized.

As oligarchy intruded, even talking about mobility became difficult. As more educated and articulate people were instrumentalized to serve wealth, those who tried to ask the *why* questions were mocked by the burgeoning chorus. Everything had to be the way it was because rich people paid others to say so. Without history and the humanities, ridiculed inside and outside the academy for decades, American minds were less able to conjure up defenses. It all seems normal until it seems intolerable.

The Tsar Bell in Russia is so heavy that it has never been rung. If a bell is always silent, is it really a bell? If the weight of inequality is so great that we cannot even speak about it, are we really free people? The language itself warps and cracks. In conditions of extreme inequality, truths are not only ignored but considered awkward or shameful. As the French thinker Raymond Aron noted, "At a certain level of inequality, there is no longer human communication." In the *Republic* and the *Laws*, Plato maintained that it was impossible for the wealthy to be just to others. He has Socrates speak of a "city of the rich" and a "city of the poor." Two different modes of existence make a single society impossible.

In conditions of extreme inequality, the word *freedom,* which should belong to everyone, attaches instead to abstractions that suit oligarchs. When we speak of "free markets" instead of "free people," we are in trouble. In American oligarchy, "free speech" all too often means the privilege of the very wealthy to transmit anonymous propaganda and to fund electoral campaigns. In such a situation, we the people will have little to say.

## ETERNITY POLITICS

There are many values, and we all need a chance to realize our own combinations of them. Any attempt to select just one at the expense of all the others will end in tyranny. The politics of inevitability acknowledged only a single value: entrepreneurship. To be sure, entrepreneurship is a very good thing. But no value is enough in itself, and no value alone generates all the others.

Left on its own, untempered by other values, entrepreneurship becomes (and became) an argument for wars of profit and private prisons, for the impotence of government, and for the nonexistence of communities. It becomes an excuse for blaming others for their poverty. Treating entrepreneurship as the only value actually hinders entrepreneurship, by creating monopolies that prevent competition; by weakening the public services that young people need to gain skills; and by littering minds with exculpatory nonsense about how the status quo is the only alternative, the end of history, and so on.

A single value and a single future will collapse into a *politics of eternity*, in which values and the future vanish entirely. Fake cheerfulness and real determinism give way to nostalgia and resentment. This happened in the USSR and in Russia, then in the United States.

Freedom needs the fourth dimension—time, an open future. The politics of inevitability reduced the future to a single possibility. When there is only one vision of the future, the moral muscles grow limp. If there are no alternatives, why imagine them? Once political imagination fades, the alternatives seem to be the official future or none at all. When the promise of the politics of inevitability is broken, we despair. Its parting curse is thus the politics of eternity. One future becomes none.

The future has vanished: social mobility is lost, we are disoriented by crises. And so we need a still more reassuring story, one that is invulnerable to our fears or that turns them against another people. Politics can be safely located in legend. Time loops back to a mythical moment when the tribe was great. What was lost since then is the fault of some other group. *We are innocent. They are guilty.*

The politics of inevitability wore away at factuality in the 1990s and 2000s by insisting that all data fit into a larger story of a rosy future. Many Americans got used to a "narrative" to which the facts must bow. The politics of eternity takes the next step, denying factuality as such. Eternity politicians say (with some justification) that inevitability politicians selected the truths they liked; they then move on (with no justification) to the indefensible position that truth is just personal preference.

Politicians of inevitability are fake economists who lull us to sleep with the idea that larger forces will always bring us back to equilibrium. Politicians of eternity are real entertainers who assuage our sense of loss with an appealing tale about the past. They gain our confidence by circling us back to a mythical era when we as a nation were (supposedly) innocent. These time-looping con artists nudge us away from democracy and toward their own feeling that they should rule forever and never be sent to prison (a motive especially apparent in the case of Trump and also Benjamin Netanyahu). Deprived of historical knowledge and of the habit of ethical thinking by the politics of inevitability, we are easy marks. Rising authoritarians succeed in this century not by proposing futures but by making any conversation about them seem pointless or absurd.

Vladimir Putin was the most important politician of eternity. His Russia drew directly from Brezhnev's 1970s, a time of nostalgia for the victory of 1945. Putin and his generation were raised with the idea that the supposed innocence of an older generation justified any action by a younger one. He looped back to Brezhnev's 1970s, and from the 1970s to an imagined 1945, and then to a baptism a thousand years before that, which supposedly joined Russia with Ukraine forever and made Russians eternally innocent. Russia was always the victim and always the victor. Russians had the right to determine whether or not Ukraine and Ukrainians existed; anyone who denied that right was an enemy. A Russian fascist tradition that spoke in just this way was discovered and celebrated.

And so Ukraine could be invaded, cities leveled, millions of people forced into flight, hundreds of thousands killed, on the logic that this was somehow a replay of the Second World War or a restoration of the tenth century. Russia was innocent, all was permitted. The full-scale invasion of 2022 demonstrated how the atavistic whining of the wealthiest fossil oligarch, Putin himself, could direct the world's attention away from the future—and draw resources away from where they were needed most. Putin's genocidal undertaking was supported by the wealthiest digital oligarch, Elon Musk.

Americans, as this suggests, did not have to look to Russia for a politics of eternity. Our own materialists, the Silicon Valley ones, have followed the same trajectory as the Soviet and post-Soviet elite: they no longer promise a brighter future but instead tell us that the present is as good as it gets. Musk and others wax nostalgic for the racial purity of an imagined past. Donald Trump offered a time when America was "great." Like Putin's invasions of Ukraine in 2014 and 2022, Trump's attempted coup of 2020–21 was an effort to stop time, to keep a democracy from moving forward.

Eternity politics comes down to the idea that some single person should rule forever, usually to preserve personal wealth and avoid responsibility for crimes.

## ECOLOGICAL WAR

When the future is lost, so are we. Political tomfoolery does not actually stop time. The fourth dimension still has rules, even if we ignore them. Time moves forward, even when we fail to keep pace, as in the 2010s. The law of necessity does not take pity on us when we abandon the law of freedom. On the contrary: as we choose to be less free, we also abandon our power to change the world around us. And then the future, a spurned lover, comes for us, breathing vengeance.

Both the politics of inevitability and the politics of eternity lack contact with the most basic elements of reality: physics, chemistry, biology; the earth, its atmosphere, life. The politics of inevitability molded inconvenient facts into a story of progress. The one true inevitability was overlooked: the more carbon dioxide we emit, the more sunlight is trapped, and the warmer Earth becomes. The science of global warming was well established by the 1980s. Dissidents warned about it, from Sakharov to Havel. Most of the human-made carbon dioxide now in the atmosphere has been emitted *since* communism came to an end in Europe in 1989.

Inevitability politicians and their cheerleaders rationalized this, and everything else. The climate may be warming, they said, but the problem will generate its own solution. It will all somehow turn out fine. Wealth inequality may be increasing, but that's just a side effect of general prosperity. We may be leading shorter, sadder lives in front of screens, but somehow that just proves our laudable autonomy. The cheerleaders wrote books to spread rationalization memes: we are getting smarter (we're not); it's not as bad as the newspapers portray (it's worse); in the end, maybe all this is just a simulation (it's not), so we are not responsible (we are) and shouldn't worry since we don't really exist (we do).

After politicians of inevitability bent the facts, politicians of eternity broke them. Politicians of inevitability understated the problem of climate change. Today politicians of eternity deny that climate change matters, or they deny the underlying science or science as such—because, after all, there is no truth. The only true eternity they can bring is extinction.

The politics of eternity gives way to a *politics of catastrophe*. Oligarchs fiddle, the world burns. A Trump mocks science; a Putin invades Ukraine with an army funded by fossil fuels; a Musk opens Twitter to a flood of lies about both Russian fascism and global warming.

By turning away from the future and denying science, eternity politicians bring climate calamity closer to the present. Then when the droughts and the fires and the storms and the floods affect our daily lives, eternity politicians blame those who are harmed. They shift attention from the greenhouse effect, which they have caused, to climate refugees, their victims.

At that moment, the politics of eternity becomes the politics of catastrophe. The politics of inevitability proposes a single positive future; the politics of eternity does away with the future; the politics of catastrophe summons a negative future ever closer. It fills the ever-shorter remaining time with undifferentiated fear. We are not striding forward into multiple futures as free people; instead, the bleakness comes to embrace us.

Vladimir Putin is a product of the politics of inevitability, in that Western leaders understand him as a technocrat tamed by money. An outstanding eternity politician, he leads the vanguard of catastrophe. He established a myth of Russian innocence. He worried about a future in which there would not be enough Russians. He then sent his armies to invade Ukraine and to deport to Russia women and children deemed assimilable, among a series of other genocidal policies. The horror of the war in Ukraine foreshadows the politics of catastrophe generally.

The fear of catastrophe takes two forms: for some, that of an ecological disaster that is indeed all around us but could be resolved by political and technical means; for others (such as Putin), that of a demographic crisis that can be solved only by insisting upon racial superiority. These are, so to speak, the objective and subjective catastrophes. When the objective catastrophe comes, those who have chosen the subjective one will be ready to blame, harm, and kill other people (as Russia under Putin is doing).

That is a familiar historical pattern. Our future, if we proceed through the politics of catastrophe, looks ever more like Hitler's dark fantasy of ecological war. The fourth and fifth dimensions are abandoned, and so we struggle for space in a crowded third. Russia's invasion of Ukraine has this feel, with its kidnapped children, eugenic deportations, fascist propaganda, and atavistic racism. *Time has run out,* is the message. *Land must be seized and colonized, and whoever says otherwise is just getting in the way of collective survival and must be eliminated.*

We know the way back toward freedom: a reclamation of the future. We must restore social mobility and prevent the coming catastrophe.

Both can be done, but only through the conscious activity of sovereign, unpredictable people. Fear is not enough. It will not get us where we need to go. From the most basic facts we can build a scaffolding of hope. We need to ground ourselves in history and science to take a turn toward a better future. It is all within our reach.

## RESPONSIBILITY POLITICS

In the time warps of inevitability, eternity, and catastrophe, we lose history. We lose knowledge of the past and the sense of time's flow.

In the politics of inevitability, the facts about the past are just dispensable details since we see a general trend and a happy end. In the politics of eternity, the past is a morality play of innocence and guilt. In the politics of catastrophe, the approaching disaster enervates the present and occludes the past. Then the oligarchs appear, naked in their power, perfect in their petulance, fighting wars of racial competition and global famine.

History is a foundation of mobility and thus of freedom. We need history to slip free of the time warps and find our way to a more reassuring sense of time. When we think historically, we see structures inherited from the past, plausible choices in the present, and multiple possibilities for the future.

Mobility depends on a sense of the future, which depends on a sense of the past. The same holds for freedom itself. We draw values from the past, consider them in the present, and apply them toward some future that we wish to realize. The practice of considering and combining values is impossible without a sense of time past and time to come.

Nothing is entirely new. Everything has some instructive connection to past events. Nor is anything really eternal or inevitable. If we have the references, we remember that past catastrophes have been survived, overcome, and even exploited. Then the present seems less shocking, and the future more open. The possibilities are more numerous than they seem, and some of them are good. Indeed, some of them are wonderful. The future could be far better than we can presently imagine.

History defends us against the politics of inevitability by reminding us of the multitude of possibilities at every point. History undoes the politics of eternity by teaching us to learn responsibility from the past rather than resentment from the present. Confronting catastrophe, as we do today, we need to extend time, first backward and then forward, stretching our minds, extending ourselves. Indeed, to see our way forward, we will have to look back.

More than anything else, Václav Havel wrote of "the world" and "the earth" and of responsibility to it. "Living in truth" could make sense in politics only when it was an attitude toward nature and the universe, not just ourselves. As the future crashes in, we can panic and blame others. Those predictable reactions make us part of the mob and the catastrophe. Or we can, as free people, take responsibility, look deep into Earth's past, and save our world.

# Factuality

## LIVING TRUTH

We get leverage on liberty when we understand the facts of our existence. If we know something about child development, we can raise children to be sovereign. If we understand social media, we can avoid being predictified. If we know the history of Nazism, we can recognize the politics of ecological collapse. If we have some grasp of natural history, we can imagine structures that would open the future. Confident about the big truths of science, we can resist the apostles of negative freedom and their bogus certainties.

Negative freedom is the fantasy that the problem is entirely beyond us, and that we can become free simply by removing an obstacle. We have confronted a few forms of negative freedom: just eliminate property (Marx); just eliminate the Jews (Hitler); just eliminate the imperialists (anti-colonialists); just eliminate government (Americans). Negative freedom presents itself as revolutionary, but the revolution it demands ignores the terrain that matters: the way we think about ourselves and the way we evaluate the world. Our contemporary American version of negative freedom is presented as the hard truth, but it fails entirely to deal with how the world actually works. It does not assimilate the most essential knowledge: biology, chemistry, and physics; birth, death, aging; the earth we live on; our place in the universe; our power to consider that place.

Life, liberty, and the pursuit of happiness. A right to life begins with knowledge: what life is; how life works; how life is possible on this earth. If we neglect that knowledge, we cease to be. We are vulnerable to nature and to those who wish to manipulate and harm us. Yet if we gain and apply knowledge about the energy of life, we can not only avoid the worst but ensure the best. Our universe neither makes us free nor prevents us from being free. It leaves open a realm of what should be, a law of freedom that allows us our endless combinations of virtues. Its constraints become our capacities if we understand them and apply our knowledge with a purpose.

Negative freedom is enmeshed in lying. That we need no government is a false account of us and the world, defended by people who falsify the world. Because burning fossil fuels will make life impossible, those who thereby profit spread lies that lead us all toward death. Conversely, the sources of energy that will also allow us to live will allow us to do so freely and more honestly. Alternatives such as solar energy and fusion are hard to centralize and therefore do not favor oligarchy. They are consonant with what we understand about life on Earth and so do not require a deadly net of propaganda. If we can break the oligarchical lying now, a better future awaits.

## SUNS

The right to life comes before the right to liberty on Jefferson's list, and for good reason. We must understand life in order to enjoy liberty. When we know where the regularities of the universe halt, and where our own inspiration begins, we can navigate the borderland in between. We have to respect *what is*, peel away from it, transform it, and create something we think *should be*.

The more we know about the facts of the universe, the better equipped we are to change it by realizing values. And we know an extraordinary amount. For some ancient thinkers, Earth was the universe's center. In the *Iliad,* Achilles returns to battle with a shield newly forged for him by Hephaestus, the god of the smithy. The shield is embossed with the doings of the whole human world. People are at the center, with moon and sun off to the side.

The Founders of the United States knew better. Living more than two millennia after the *Iliad* was set down, they were children of modern astronomy and physics. They understood that Earth orbits the sun. In ancient Greece, Aristarchus had rightly proposed heliocentrism, but Aristotle rejected his view. The geocentrism then canonized by Ptolemy prevailed for more than fifteen hundred years. Copernicus revived Aristarchus's hypothesis and began the overthrow of the Ptolemaic (geocentric) view in 1543. Kepler defended the Copernican heliocentric view in 1596, Galileo a bit later. In 1687, about half a century before the Founders were born, about a century before the revolution they made, Newton explained the orbits of the planets via gravity. Jefferson was interested in the discovery of the planet Uranus and observed an eclipse.

We are not at the center of everything. We are special thanks not to location but to vocation. It is not where we are, but what we do, that counts. And to *do,* we have to *know.* The Founders knew more about the universe than the ancients; we know more than the Founders. The Founders had an idea of gravity but did not know that the sun is made of plasma. They owned farms (and often slaves) but did not know how plants mediate solar energy for us. Jefferson was an acknowledged authority on fossils, which he called "bones," but he mistook the claws of extinct ground sloths for those of living lions, and he thought Earth was only six thousand years old.

It is not reasonable to expect those who came before us to be ideal. Only tyrants present their predecessors as icons, inert and perfect. The best that free people can hope for is a legacy of self-correction. The Founders were wise enough to expect us to know more than they did. They inscribed into the Constitution an institution (a patent office) to promote the "Progress of Science and useful arts." They believed that scientific advances could improve political life. John Adams applied an analogy from physical equilibrium to defend the political checks and balances of the Constitution. Jefferson delighted in "the tranquil pursuit of science" and half jested in letters that he preferred agronomy to politics. Benjamin Franklin tried to understand electricity.

We know, as the Founders and the ancients did not, that humans are not the culmination of creation on a young Earth. If the history of life on Earth were a book of five thousand pages, we would appear on the last one. The giant ground sloths that Jefferson mistook for lions had inhabited the Americas for tens of millions of years, a time span unimaginable to the Founders. Yet that too is only a small fraction of the history of life on Earth. They and other giant mammals—such as mammoths, mastodons, and giant rhinoceroses—followed the dinosaurs; and even the dinosaurs, in the grand scheme of things, are quite young, having gone extinct only sixty-six million years ago. Trilobites, the prize fossil of Clinton County in my youth, were around for a quarter-billion years before going extinct about a quarter-billion years ago. This gets us back half a billion years—which is only about an eighth of the way to the beginning.

Fossil fuels are evidence of comparably ancient organisms. We say "fossil fuels" all the time without ever quite hearing the connection between our daily burn and the ancient past. Coal, natural gas, and oil are chemically transformed remnants of life from hundreds of millions of years ago. Since about the time of the American Revolution, humans have dug up fossil fuels and consumed the energy left by past life. We have thereby generated and mastered electricity but also changed the climate. As we physically consume the remnants of former life, we put in doubt life's future.

We are a species that extinguishes others. Most of the larger mammals of the Americas, including the mastodons and the ground sloths, came to an end after humans crossed over from Asia about twenty thousand years ago. The more recent arrival of humans from Europe about five hundred years ago has coincided with about five hundred further extinctions. Humans can also create the conditions of our own extinction.

Unlike other species, we can be aware of our power and our peril and choose to endure. To do so, we must dare to know the world around us and the world within us, to know what is possible and how we hold ourselves back. Today we know enough to supply energy to ourselves without burning fossil fuels. Doing so would make the future more secure and the present more open to freedom.

## FUSION

We will not be free, nor will we survive, if we ignore the limits of our Earth or deny the rules of our universe. Freedom and survival depend on recognizing constraints and turning them in our favor.

As we work out what we know about life, we grow into a broader understanding of it and enable a more expansive notion of liberty. Unlike ancient thinkers, and unlike the Founders of the United States, we know that our universe is a play of matter and energy, back and forth. Life is a special form of that play. We are a special form of life, capable of the dignity of knowledge.

Our freedom is not something outside the universe or against the universe but a way we learn to work with the universe, and therefore something we add to the universe. If we start with what the universe is, we can find our way to ourselves.

The fundamentals are not difficult. Almost all the visible matter of the universe is simple: atoms of hydrogen and atoms of helium, found in stars. About three-quarters of the visible matter in the universe is hydrogen, and about one-quarter is helium. All the other substances, taken together, make up a tiny fraction.

An atom is the smallest unit of matter that exhibits specific qualities. It is (usually) made of three kinds of subatomic particle: protons, neutrons, and electrons. Each atom has a central core, or nucleus, made of protons (with a positive charge) and neutrons (with no charge). Around the nucleus are layers, or shells, that hold electrons (with a negative charge, usually balancing the protons).

Each electron is fundamentally identical to every other electron; each proton is fundamentally identical to every other proton; each neutron is fundamentally identical to every other neutron. Uniformity also defines the still-smaller particles, the quarks, that make up protons and neutrons. The neutron is always composed of two down quarks and one up quark, the proton of two up quarks and one down quark.

Atoms with different numbers of protons are different substances, known as *elements,* that exhibit different qualities. Hydrogen and helium are the simplest elements. Hydrogen has a single proton, a single electron, and usually zero neutrons; helium has two protons and usually two neutrons. The difference between hydrogen and helium is the beginning of a variation among substances. Both are gases at room temperature; you are breathing a very small amount of each right now. Whereas helium is inert, hydrogen will bond with other elements. Both are lighter than air, but hydrogen is more flammable than helium. This is why blimps are filled with helium.

Gravity acts on all the mass in the universe in the same way, yet it also initiates this basic diversity. First gravity brings hydrogen clouds together. If the cloud becomes large enough, gravity can overcome the electrostatic repulsion of the hydrogen atoms, getting them into close enough range for the strong nuclear force to apply and to begin their fusion into helium. And so a star is formed, and the process continues.

Such fusion also brings into being elements that are more massive than helium. When stars die, they expand and then contract; and in doing so fuse more massive and more chemically complex elements, with more protons and neutrons. The building blocks of your body, molecules of carbon (six protons) and oxygen (eight), were created in this way by fusion inside a prior generation star. Our human bodies are archives of the universe, records of the life and death of stars.

Elements, different one from another, create another level of diversity by combining with one another. The matter we touch, see, hear, and smell includes *compounds,* materials constituted of two or more elements, bonding together according to simple rules. The electron or electrons of an atom find orbits in layers around its nucleus. These shells have a certain number of slots where electrons can fit. Two atoms bond when an electron occupies a slot in a shell in both of them. When atoms of two different elements bond, they form a molecule that exhibits new qualities.

On Earth we witness the results of such transformations, known as chemical changes, all the time. Indeed, we are one such result. Consider water. Our own bodies are mostly water. Earlier forms of life from which we evolved lived underwater. Closer ancestors brought water to shore inside their bodies. Water is a compound of two hydrogen atoms and one oxygen atom. At room temperature, hydrogen and oxygen are both gases, but the water they form together is a liquid, with extraordinary qualities. When water freezes, it floats, which allows life to continue under the surface. Without that particularity, our kind of life would not have evolved.

Fusion inside stars initiates the variety of the universe, creating all the elements beyond hydrogen and helium (and trace amounts of lithium), which in turn combine to form compounds.

Fusion also generates the energy needed to animate matter in the forms that we call life. No matter how you are getting the light and heat you need to live and read, its ultimate source is the fusion reactions in our sun (or previous generation stars). The energy produced by fusion reactions in the sun's core slowly diffuses to its surface. After thousands of years, packets of energy called photons radiate outward from the sun, lighting and heating Earth. Fusion is therefore the original source of almost all the energy needed by life on Earth. If we could harness it directly, a new kind of freedom would present itself.

Physics offers us hidden gifts. In a universe where a restraint can become a possibility, freedom and survival might be around an unexpected corner, the result of a clever gambit that we initiate ourselves.

## LIVING HARMONIES

"In the struggle between you and the world," says Kafka, "take the side of the world." Freedom is not negative, not a matter of our breaking what is around us. Freedom is not us against the world but us within the world, knowing it and changing it. Freedom involves turning restraints into possibilities, a habit that can save our species. Our kind of life arose within a set of restraints that began with fusion inside stars confined by gravity.

Photons bounce around the sun's core for a long time before finding their way to the solar surface, whence they scatter into the universe at the speed of light. From the perspective of the sun, Earth is a tiny dot, ninety-three million miles away. A tiny proportion of the energy radiated by the sun reaches our planet, bringing heat and light. It is enough for us. If you are reading by sunlight, the photons that allow you to distinguish the letters from the page took eight minutes to reach you—but they arose in the sun's core thousands of years before this alphabet was invented, perhaps at around the time humans began to use symbols to write in Asia or were killing the giant mammals of North America.

Our bodies are attuned to radiation borne by photons: what we see as light, the colors between indigo and red, and the lower frequency, infrared, that we feel on our skin as heat. This experience of energy allows us to know and name the world. One morning I edited this chapter by a lake at the edge of a forest; I could anticipate when there would be enough light to work, and when the lake's surface would be warm enough for a swim. A paragraph or two was written in the time it took for photons to leave the surface of the sun and reach my retinas. But every event in human history that allowed me to think about freedom took place between when those protons were formed in the sun's core and when they reached its surface.

We can use light to see and infrared rays to stay warm. But we do not power our bodies directly from the sun. The leaves of plants extract carbon dioxide from the air and absorb solar energy, then juggle elements to create molecules rich in chemical energy. In photosynthesis, solar fusion energy contributes to the chemical energy of our life, in the form of matter that we can eat and exploit. If we eat other animals, we gain energy from their molecules, too.

Photosynthesis co-creates an atmosphere that enables our kind of life. Carbon dioxide traps infrared radiation (heat) from the sun in the atmosphere: the greenhouse effect. By extracting carbon dioxide, plants keep Earth from becoming too hot. Plants release oxygen, the element that our bodies need to transform the matter we eat into energy. Oxygen enters our lungs when we inhale, and it is passed by our blood to little power generators (mitochondria) in each of our cells. Our blood floods our brain with oxygen so that we can live and think—and ask what it means to live and think and ask what is right and good. In this way, what starts in the core of stars ends as grace in the core of us.

In some sense, we know all this, at least in a general way. But we have to *know that we know it,* be alive to our knowledge of it, to live in truth. When we become aware of the living harmonies that begin with gravity, we can find ways to liberate ourselves.

## TINY STARS

Endorsing Jefferson's right to life means applying what we know. We have to apply our knowledge of the sun to Earth. Solar fusion has been going on for about 4.5 billion years, photosynthesis for about 3.5 billion. We have existed among the opportunities they create as a species for less than a million years, as literate civilizations for about five thousand, and as industrial cultures changing the atmosphere for about two hundred.

Humans have stripped a third of the trees from Earth's surface. We have learned to dominate our fellow creatures. We humans alone outweigh all the wild land mammals taken together by a factor of twenty; our livestock weighs thirty times as much as the mammals beyond the fences. The dominion extends into the past. We take our energy by stripping open the earth and burning the remains of former life. In consuming that past, we also consume the future.

Steam engines, which burned coal (fossilized plants), were the beginning of an industrial revolution that followed the American Revolution by a few decades. The Industrial Age brought new forms of pain and inequality but also the spread of capacities that could enable ever larger numbers of people to be free. The Founders knew about steam engines, but they had no notion that burning fossil fuels would change the climate so as to threaten technological civilization and indeed human life.

Since the Founders' time, humans, and above all Americans, have undone the global climate that arose from a certain balance of fusion and photosynthesis—one that held when our ancestors evolved in Africa a million or so years ago and still held when Jefferson wrote of life, liberty, and the pursuit of happiness. We have known about it for fifty years or more. What will we do? We have about twenty years to find a new balance between fusion and photosynthesis that will allow us to keep on living.

Like the basic science of life, the basic technology of survival is not complicated. The elegant ways to find a sustainable new equilibrium are to plant trees, build fusion power plants, and use solar and wind and other renewables along the way. We are close to knowing how to generate usable fusion safely on Earth, using deuterium (a form of hydrogen) from seawater as the fuel. Guided fusion reactions promise cheap and limitless energy without climate change. (As we run short on time, we will likely also need other measures, such as carbon capture and advanced fission reactors.)

Shockingly, global investment in fusion is less than 1 percent of global subsidies for fossil fuels, which as I write amount to about $7 trillion a year. This balance sheet is a suicide note. It is perhaps the strangest thing about us. Fusion is the sort of transformative technology promised to the twenty-first century by the twentieth. We will need it to reach the twenty-second.

The remains of former life, the fossils we have used as fuels, should stay in the ground. Respect for the deep past would enable a more prolonged future. If we built fusion power plants, we would be imitating solar energy by lighting tiny stars on Earth. Accompanied by other renewables, that would be a graceful solution, bringing both freedom and survival.

If we act to bring fusion to Earth, we will be applying some of our knowledge of the universe and thereby changing it. The universe is already a bit different, since we have built fusion devices on Earth that generate more energy than they consume. A universe in which a self-aware life-form uses fusion to thrive is a different universe than one in which the spark of life in freedom is allowed to die.

## EXTINCTION SPIRAL

Hitler told a lie about nature. The Earth's surface was a realm of deadly competition, he said; races had to fight for land and food to survive; Germany, in murdering Jews, was only allowing nature to take its proper course.

This vision, aside from its inherent horror, was based upon untruth. In *Mein Kampf,* Hitler denied the efficacy of agricultural technologies such as irrigation and fertilizer. To make endless racial struggle seem inevitable, he had to discredit scientific solutions. Like the renewable energy technologies of the early twenty-first century, the agricultural technologies of the early twentieth century were in full development and were going to work. Germany without the war would soon have been able to feed itself. Indeed, after the war, it could and did, as the result of science and cooperation, not racism and conquest.

Our lie about nature is that there is no global warming, or that if there is global warming, there is no technological solution. Unlike Hitler, some of the fossil oligarchs who sponsor this lie are motivated by the desire for profit. They finance propaganda instructing us that hydrocarbons are safe and that renewables are risky. Some of them share Hitler's view of life as conflict: they imagine that when the catastrophe comes, their money will allow them to escape, or that their race will be spared.

In Hitler's Germany, the ecological fiction worked together with a political fiction. If life was a race war, then a racial party should control the state, and democracy should be undone. In our own politics, in a less strident way, an ecological lie also works together with a political fiction. In the United States, the political party that denies (or ignores) global warming also suppresses votes. Breaking democracy also breaks the ecosphere.

The slower we are to react to global warming, the more dire will be the consequences, and the greater the temptation will be to blame those who suffer. Then the ecological lie returns the favor and reinforces the electoral lie: politics, in catastrophic times, becomes a matter of punishing the weak rather than preventing the disasters brought by the strong. That is what our extinction spiral will look like.

Technology can help. But it must be the right type of technology, enabling us to shift from three dimensions into four and five, rather than driving us into two dimensions or one, a flat screen or a party line.

Artificial intelligence will really be such when it answers our frivolous queries by pointing out that we are burning the planet and should stop. An actual AI would remind us that (by Google's own count) we put about two thousand tons of carbon dioxide into the atmosphere every day with our Web searches alone—and that every query to the programs now termed "artificial intelligence" burns about ten times as much as every Web search. We do not see the grim coal-powered air-conditioned server farms that we activate with our internet traffic, and so do not think of our screen-staring as globe-warming and Earth-destroying. Yet it is. We think of clicks as magic tricks, but each one burns a bit of the past and a bit of the future.

The sheer amount of time we spend before screens distracts our attention from the drastic changes in the physical world around us. Climate change (like social media) is a nemesis called forth by our flaws: the hesitation to know the world as it is; the misunderstanding of freedom as negative; the inequality of wealth; the racism. In the United States, those who deny climate change are disproportionately white males. Most likely, what such people really mean is that they trust that others will suffer first. They might well be right. Poor and Black people are more likely to live near factories and hazardous waste sites, which means that flooding can kill them faster than others.

The interaction of American racism and climate change is not a speculation about the future. It is the timeline we are on. Consider the fateful election of 2000. Al Gore won it by a close margin—close enough, unfortunately, that the Supreme Court was able to deny him the presidency by halting the vote count in Florida. One reason the election was so close was that mass incarceration had already removed four million Americans from the voter rolls, including *more than one in five* Black men in Florida (and felonies in Florida were a very expansive category). Without the associated disenfranchisement, Gore would have been president, the Iraq war would not have happened, we would not have borrowed money from China to fight it, and global warming would have been addressed. In that world, we would all be freer; we missed it by confusing liberation with punishment in the 1970s, 1980s, and 1990s.

We will not be able to indulge our sadopopulism for much longer. Given the physics of global warming, the sadopopulist urge to watch others suffer first will bring about mass death. Waiting for the poorer or the darker people to be flooded out means putting in the air the carbon dioxide that will make your own family's lives impossible.

My lifetime is a half-century of failure. We have known for my entire life that climate change threatens the survival of the species. I was born a few weeks after the Apollo mission put a man on the moon. Had we treated climate change with the same seriousness as lunar exploration, we would have solved it long ago—and likely generated spin-offs that would have accelerated space travel.

We did otherwise. We displaced fears and entrenched errors. Two striking American domestic policies of my lifetime are the promotion of oligarchs and the incarceration of African Americans. The two work together. As we have created an American carceral state, we have weakened the structures that once gave American families a better chance to raise their children in freedom.

## SIGNIFICANT ROUGHNESS

We have named the first three forms of freedom: sovereignty, unpredictability, and mobility. Factuality is the fourth. To get purchase on the world, we have to test ourselves and our convictions. Truthfulness is not an archaism or an eccentricity but a necessity for life and a source of freedom. The science of global warming is an example of a general truth. We may not want to hear about it; but if we ignore it, we are less free.

Without factuality, every form of freedom is menaced. We cannot know how brains develop and so cannot educate for sovereignty. We cannot know how algorithms work, so cannot confront the problems of social media. We do not know how few people have how much money, nor see the barriers to mobility that keep us unfree. Without facts, we cannot measure the change in climate.

When we are open to facts, they help us to be unpredictable and therefore free. Facts are not what we expect or want. They do not fit our prejudices but knock holes in them. They challenge what people around us think. Facts temper our minds to resist the machine's power to predictify us. Goethe, the greatest of German writers, spoke of "significant roughness": as we pass through life, we take hits from bruising truths, which keeps us fit and unruly.

We cannot enable freedom without institutions, which we cannot build without some shared sense of reality. Values will vary from person to person. And so it must be facts that anchor conversation about which structures we decide to build together. If we have different values, we will nevertheless sometimes have a shared interest in action. But if we have different facts, concord is impossible. We can disagree about how best to get clean water. But if we disagree as to whether lead is poisonous, we won't get far.

Facts enable sovereignty by allowing people to decide for themselves, without relying on authorities. Facts are needed both for court rulings and for elections. Facts enable self-defense against the wealthy and the powerful. Since they can be known in common, they can enable an individual to seek allies and, along with them, justice. If it is agreed that facts are no different from opinions, the free person has no ground on which to make a stand. If facts do not count, what James Madison called "clamor and combinations" will always win, which means that tyrants and oligarchs will always win. When facts are respected, each of us is entitled at least to a hearing and has a shield against the hail of static. Even when we fail, there is dignity in trying.

In Tomas Venclova's poem "The Shield of Achilles," truth is the barrier to nonexistence after a cataclysm:

> Whole cities disappear. In nature's stead,
> A white shield, counterweight to non-existence.

In W. H. Auden's very different "Shield of Achilles," it is absence of truth that brings the disaster:

> That girls are raped, that two boys knife a third,
> Were axioms to him, who'd never heard
> Of any world where promises were kept,
> Or one could weep because another wept.

## PARTY LINE

The communist big lie was that the party was always right. It was a kind of meta-lie, a lie about all the other lies. It demanded the capacity to adapt to anything, especially to contradiction.

The communist party line was reversed with vertiginous rapidity. In the Soviet Union in the 1920s, landowning peasants were the party's ally in building a revolution; then in the 1930s they became the detritus of a useless past. Heroes of the 1917 revolution were executed as its traitors twenty years later, then posthumously rehabilitated twenty years after that. In 1933 fascism was just one more form of capitalism; in 1935 it was an enemy requiring alliances with non-communists; in 1939 it was a bulwark against British capitalist imperialism (as the USSR allied with Nazi Germany); and in 1941 fascism was the great enemy (after Hitler betrayed Stalin). After 1945 the West Germans were fascists but the East Germans were somehow not; during the Cold War a fascist was simply the chosen enemy.

In George Orwell's *1984,* the backdrop is a world war. The protagonist's homeland, Oceania, suddenly changes from being allied *with* Eastasia *against* Eurasia to being allied *with* Eurasia *against* Eastasia. No one was supposed to take notice. Orwell was recalling the traumatic acrobatics of a Stalinist line that built collective conformity from wrecked consciences. Stalinism revealed the human ability to have faith in an entity whose utterances had no fixed content, followed no rules of evidence, and were often mutually contradictory. People were capable of altering their views completely, *and* of acting as though they had never changed, *and* of preparing to change them again in the near future. Orwell invented a name for it: *doublethink.*

Stalinism might seem like the exotic faith of a distant past. But in twenty-first-century Russia, too, people can follow a changing line: *Yesterday a war against our brothers the Ukrainians was unthinkable; today a war against our enemies the Ukrainians is inevitable.*

Dissidents rejected the big lie and valorized local everyday truths. Their central labor in the communist bloc was the chronicle, the list of specific details about human suffering and injustice. Throughout the communist world, those in opposition labored to record the names of those sent to psychiatric prison or to the Gulag. Then they themselves were sent to psychiatric prison or to the Gulag.

These courageous people understood that facts were a condition of freedom, and that the facts would not record themselves. Facts need us, and we need them.

## PERFECT VICTIMS

For the Nazis, it was not that the party was always right, but that the Jews were always wrong. The Jews were the source of capitalism, communism, Christianity, law, the state, modern physics, technological solutions to scarcity—anything that got in the way of the racial struggle. In this grand fiction, Jews hindered the German race by seducing the women, corrupting the men, kidnapping the babies, and infecting the mind.

If Germans had failed in the past, this too was the Jews' fault. Jews were held responsible for defeat in the First World War. Germany would have won, went the legend, had its brave soldiers not been "stabbed in the back." This fiction made another world war more likely. It perpetuated a misanalysis of the previous one, which was that Germany could win a war on two fronts with Americans involved. It also defined the victims of any war as (non-Jewish) Germans, with the Jews as the aggressors. From this it followed that anything that Germans ever did to Jews would be self-defense. When Germany began to lose the Second World War, such reasoning became a justification for the extermination of the Jews.

Stated as propositions like these, a big lie can seem absurd: but it is precisely the lie's titanic scope, as Hitler himself said, that makes it successful. In *Mein Kampf,* Hitler explained the public relations strategy that others have since followed: tell a lie so enormous that your followers cannot imagine that you would deceive them on such a scale. Because of the lie's very grandeur, people are psychically overinvested when they accept it, and they cannot get out without pain. A big lie is an untruth that is too big to fail.

A big lie enables drastic crimes that, once committed, reinforce its hold on minds. We can sometimes accept that we have been fooled, and we can sometimes accept that we have killed; but we cannot accept that we have murdered for a lie. Once we have killed, it must have been in the service of something true. Once Germans began to kill Jews, they needed the Nazi big lie about an international Jewish conspiracy more than before. Once the Germans began to lose the war, they needed the lie still more. When the Allied bombs came down on Germany, many Germans really did think it was a Jewish attack. Only the final defeat of Nazi Germany slowed down this particular big lie.

A big lie is more than the absence of truth and the presence of deception. It has the power to shape how minds and therefore societies work. It turns people away from others' *Leib* and the little truths around them. It provides an interpretive scheme for all facts and values, allowing us to live without the effort of declaring and accommodating. When a lie is big enough, it confirms the power of the Leader, who becomes the arbiter of reality. A big lie enters into institutions, magnifying its own force. It creates enemies, those who do not wish to follow the new article of spontaneous faith, or those who are too slow to do so.

A big lie can bring down a whole country. The twentieth century should have been Germany's century, but Germans got caught in a story. The twenty-first century could be America's, but Americans . . .

## AMERICA'S END

Americans do not have to reach back in time, nor across the Atlantic, to find a leader who tells a big lie to a public energized by contradiction and conspiracy.

Americans live in a country where a sitting president gave advance warning that he would declare victory even if he lost an election. Having lost decisively in November 2020, Donald Trump proceeded to declare victory with Hitlerian boldness, speaking of "a historical landslide." He repeated claims of fraud that he knew to be false, and he urged his followers to support him in overthrowing representative government. Thousands obliged by invading the Capitol on January 6, 2021.

A major television network, Fox, lent credence to his lie, even though the television hosts knew that they were repeating an untruth. They were worried that the stock price of their company might otherwise fall. This chain of events should give pause to anyone who believes that unregulated capitalism is consistent with democracy. When push came to shove, capitalism was consistent, in the case of one very important company, with a coup and with the propagation of the associated big lie.

In the aftermath of the failure of Trump's coup attempt, some Americans held three contradictory propositions to be true: (1) the Capitol was not really stormed; (2) the Capitol was stormed by right-wing allies of Trump to keep him in power, and this was good; (3) the Capitol was stormed by left-wing agitators who wanted to harm Trump's reputation, and this was bad.

Trump's big lie recalled both the fascist and the communist inheritance. It was like a communist party line in that people were meant to follow it despite all the evidence. They were to believe the manifestly contradictory, as in the communist tradition. But their belief practices were enabled by an underlying prejudice, as in Nazi practice. Racism was a foundation of Donald Trump's big lie and coup attempt. Neither made sense without the implicit understanding that Black people were not really people and that Black votes were not really votes.

In 1965 the Voting Rights Act empowered the federal government to enforce the Fifteenth Amendment to the Constitution, according to which people cannot be denied the vote on grounds of race. Since then, racial lying has taken on less blatant forms. One is the belief that elections in which Black people vote are tainted. It then seems right and proper to exclude Blacks from voting and to conflate their votes with fraud. Trump questioned vote counts in Philadelphia, Atlanta, and Detroit because big cities are home to Black people.

Trump's big lie threatens everyone's right to vote, by creating the conditions under which an imperfect democracy can fail. It has already led to one violent coup attempt, which was a rehearsal for the next one. Though insurrectionists are forbidden from holding office by the Constitution, Trump purports to be campaigning for president. By doing so while affirming that elections do not work, he makes plain that his aim is simply to seize power.

To the big lie is now added the promise of revenge against all who did not accept it. Like any big lie, Trump's demands violence to overcome the stubbornness of the facts and of those who believe in them. Trump's big lie thus becomes the pretext for a permanent state of exception, which in practice means dictatorship. The president who led an insurrection promises, should he return to power, to use the Insurrection Act to crush opposition. Trump has committed to making the federal government one giant safe space for his fiction, firing civil servants and replacing them with lie loyalists. Government by bootlick bureaucracy cannot work.

The big lie has already created media safe spaces, where it is repeated over and over again. It filtered a political party into the true believers, the cynics, and the fools—and as Havel and Orwell both reminded us, there need not be any actual true believers among the powerful for a big lie to persist. The big lie justifies legislation to hinder American democracy. American states pass memory laws to whitewash the history of voter suppression, laws that are part of an old racist tradition.

The big lie entered into American institutions in the first weeks of 2021, when "fraud" (voting while Black) was invoked as a justification to make it still harder for nonwhite people to vote, and to take the process of counting votes away from those who are qualified. Candidates for state attorney general ran for and won office on the big lie, opening the possibility of fraudulent counts and coup plotting in the future. Trump's lying was the smoke screen behind extralegal recounts, a tool that can be used to generate uncertainty and to prevent an election from being completed on time. Such legal maneuvers to subvert voting are traditional ways to bring down a democracy: votes are managed rather than counted, and so power no longer rests with the people.

## ELECTING DICTATORS

To repeat Trump's big lie of 2020–21 is to promise to steal an election. Politicians who do so are announcing that they plan to seek power without winning. Any presidential candidate who runs on the big lie is aiming not to achieve a victory in the sense of getting the most votes, but to attain power by getting close enough to engineer a coup. This makes voters accomplices in a coup attempt. Such voters know, or half know, that the purpose of their votes is not to win an election but to gain for their candidate some plausibility. To vote for a big liar is to vote for a regime change.

In the American system, this can work, and quickly. Americans have no actual voting system. Elections are run by states and administered by counties. State legislatures, often themselves extremely unrepresentative (as in Ohio now), already suppress voting, devise absurdly discriminatory districts, and build prisons that shift representation to supporters of their own party. Some state legislatures have even tried to give themselves the power to overturn actual vote counts.

If some combination of these efforts succeeds, the less popular party might control both the House of Representatives and the Senate. Then the unrepresentative Congress could appoint a defeated presidential candidate. Americans believe in the Constitution, but the Constitution is interpreted by a Supreme Court that has acted to weaken American democracy. At some conjuncture, it could lose its authority, perhaps at the precise moment when it appoints (for a second time, after 2000) a losing candidate as president.

Factuality is a form of freedom. Factuality means telling the truth about the coup attempt of 2020–21. It means living in truth, rather than taking comfort from a big lie.

## MISSING REPORTERS

Like the other forms of freedom, factuality takes work. We might like to imagine that the truth emerges from controversy, or that a "free market of ideas" will always bring us what we need to know. But it does not. Fox brought a big lie into American society. Or take the example of free-marketeer Elon Musk's purchase of Twitter. As money shapes the platform, tweets promoting climate denialism and Russian fascism fill everyone's feeds. On Facebook, fake news reliably outcompetes real news.

Freedom is positive, a struggle and an act of creation. Factuality depends on people who are ready to hear the truth and are ready to seek it. This requirement is not at all as straightforward as it appears. We can live a lie. We can be fooled. We can pose as people who doubt everything, and yet believe the most outrageous lies. Those who wish to fool you will tell you that you know right from wrong, by which they mean that you are about to believe what they say. Social media serve up what we are prone to accept, which is not the same thing as the truth.

Facts do not arise on their own, and they are not necessarily believed. People tend to endorse conspiracy theories when they doubt the efficacy of their own actions. It follows that, in the words of Peter Pomerantsev, we must "build an environment where facts matter."

Like freedom in general, freedom of speech cannot be negative. It cannot be a matter of stripping people of all education and protections and setting them loose as atomized individuals in a jungle of money, power, and spectacle. Freedom of speech is positive, in the sense that it depends on protecting those who take risks, encouraging others to listen, and indeed maintaining all the other forms of freedom.

Historical references can help—without them I would not have been able to affix the term *big lie* to Trump in the first place, back in 2020. Reporters can sometimes name and undo a big lie. But these are last-ditch efforts, defensive struggles. Big lies function in an environment that is already denuded of the little truths. Individuals can seek and heed the little truths, but there is a structural issue here that no individual can resolve. No one person can find out the truth about every matter essential for a life.

The truth about your school board and your local politicians is not something that you will likely get by your own efforts—not to mention the truth about campaign finance, bank bailouts, or foreign wars. The labor has to be social, in the sense that communities make fact-finding possible and attractive for individuals. Factuality requires institutions, above all investigative reporting. Ultimately, to resist the few big lies, we will need to produce millions of little truths.

The peak year for newspaper subscriptions in the United States was 1984, when I was a freshman and sophomore in high school and sometimes covered a friend's paper route. My hometown, Centerville, Ohio, had a biweekly newspaper, with some reporting. You could read about the city council, the township trustees, or the zoning board—or follow your own Little League baseball team in the standings. Dayton, the local metropolis where I worked as a teenager, had two newspapers (admittedly owned by the same family) until 1986. Each had a section for metropolitan reporting. The headlines were often about local rather than national matters. The unpredictability of local politics was there for me to discover.

Driving southeast to visit my grandparents on their farms, after I got my driver's license in 1986, I could buy a different newspaper in each county seat, and sometimes I did. My paternal grandparents took their local paper as well as the *Cincinnati Enquirer* on Sundays. My maternal grandmother's collection of mastodon and mammoth tusks was written up in 1976 (under the memorable headline "Lady Collects Old Tusks of Forgotten Mammoths") by *The Western Star*, a weekly newspaper published in Warren County, the next county west from her Clinton County.

*The Western Star* was so titled because Ohio was once the West. Founded in 1807, about a year after my mother's ancestors settled, *The Western Star* was the oldest American newspaper beyond the original thirteen colonies that continuously published under its original name. In the 1970s, at a time when *The Western Star* had the reportorial resources to chronicle a minor paleontological caper the next county over, no one would have thought that it could cease to exist. And yet it did, after almost two centuries in print. In the early 2000s, *The Western Star* became an advertising glossy, then ceased publication entirely in 2013. The same thing has happened all over America. Local newspapers disappear or are bought by hedge funds and continue as digitalized shells without local coverage or local color.

To be sure, local newspapers had their failings. They could be swayed or captured by local elites. But reporting was at least possible. Journalism could be a vocation to seek the truth about one's own community. People could know a reporter personally. Young people growing up now in Warren County, Ohio, do not know what it was like to have access to local news. Not only will they miss curiosities about farm women and their fossils, they will never read an investigative report about (for example) the prisons in their county. Reality fades, even physical reality, when we have no one to help us concentrate on what is right in front of our faces.

The internet can be regarded as an infrastructure for information; but that very word now means a digital signal rather than a human fact. An information highway full of deliberate fiction is no more useful than a regular highway full of robot automobiles programmed to crash into one another. Granted, young people can google whatever comes to their minds. But can a search engine get them to the unpredictable edges of their own lives? Can it get them to the surprises one finds in a local newspaper? Now that you know that a reporter covered my grandmother's fossil collection, you are likely more confident that there really was a mastodon tusk on the porch in 1976, and rightly so. (There still is.) If you find the article, you can see the white porch I ran through on that summer's day. You can check this through a search engine, though not easily—and only because a reporter was present in the first place.

And what the reporter brought was not just facts but values, for example, wonder, admiration, respect for science, attention to local color. The reporter was there, her *Leib* was on that porch, and she left a small trace. It is not just the facts that go missing when reporting ceases, but also our sense of the diversity of the country, down to the level of its counties, its farms, its porches, its grandmothers. That human richness is also a fact, but a fact of the sort that no machine will find for us.

Today such reporting is gone. How then will future internet searches work? You can check the weather online from almost anywhere, but what you find depends on a few government-funded weather services. Were they not to exist, the search technology would be useless. Now that there is no local reporting in most of the country, we face a similar situation. The internet runs ever faster circles around ever scarcer knowledge. A search engine can fill your screen with stuff, but it cannot help you appreciate and navigate the quirks and curiosities around you. Nor can it tell you what you really need to know.

The internet cannot report. It can only repeat. And as AI (or rather "AI") enters the picture, it will not even repeat what people once reported—it will invent what people want to hear.

## TRUTH'S HORIZON

The decline of American local journalism was hastened after 2008 by the financial crisis. We should have bailed out the newspapers then: the cost of doing so would have been invisible compared to the cost of rescuing the banks. Since 2010, social media have soaked up most of the advertising revenue that once supported newspapers. Beginning in 2017, a sitting American president began to regularly call the press "the true enemy of the people." In 2020 Americans were confused about a pandemic, in part because they lacked the local reporters who could tell them about unexpected illnesses and full hospitals, or publish interviews with local doctors or nurses (who were often bound by gag orders, an aspect of commercial medicine). The collapse of American reporting accompanied and accelerated other major social changes of the twenty-first century: the Covid pandemic, climate change, oligarchy, and opioid addiction.

The end of local factuality, of home truths, brings national discord. As a sense of local reality dissolves, Americans cede their opinions to faraway people on talk radio or cable television, then to placeless algorithms. In the absence of shared local knowledge, human anxieties and fears have to be processed as national politics, ideological conflict, or social media spats. When we no longer have any reporters, we say that we distrust "the media," but all the while we cling to the mechanized bits of it that are attuned to how we already feel. Once we substitute Facebook for local newspapers, as people in Warren County and Clinton County have done—as much of America has done—we drift toward a spectral world of "us and them."

During the 2016 electoral campaign, huge numbers of Americans believed the pure inventions of Russian propagandists that they found in their social media feeds. In the aftermath of the 2020 election, many Americans preferred their feelings about the election to its actual outcome. They had no personal knowledge of fraud. They had lost the idea that local news would check such abuses, because they had no local news. Lacking everyday institutions of factuality, all they had to go on were impulses amplified by social media. Perhaps some were at a point in their lives where they were vulnerable to a conspiracy theory that explained everything. It "felt" true that Trump had won.

As Lord Acton put it, "There is no error so monstrous that it fails to find defenders among the ablest men." Social media efficiently unite monstrous errors with their defenders. A shared belief in Trump's big lie created a sense of "us," of belonging to a tribe, a feeling that Fox and Facebook affirmed. I was struck by this at the time: people were convinced by their own feelings and said so openly. It was hard to talk about what happened without being treated as part of the conspiracy, without becoming the "them" in an "us and them." This binarism is native to our fear response, and the brain hacks bring it forward.

If our concept of freedom is negative, then the truth seems frustrating, just one more barrier to our impulses. If we lose track of the difference between "it is true" and "it feels right," we are not free; forces greater than us will hack our brains to make it feel right.

The pursuit of truth is the first bulwark in a defense of the self. Believing a lie means serving a master, living or digital. That is a plausible end station for us: deluded and unfree, living and dying in a tedious alternative reality.

Our eternity politicians tempt us in this direction. Since no one knows what truth is, runs their ploy, there is no point knowing anything. Searching for facts risks hurting your feelings, and you don't want that. This version of fascism is, weirdly, a safe space. You are fine the way you are; you have no need to learn. Reporters are enemies, since they might challenge you. Historians are to be ignored—they rob you of your tribal certainties. Best to pass laws that force teachers to avoid the essential subjects of American history.

Truth is a human value. The value is in the hunt. To say that there are no facts because we can't define truth is like saying that there are no families because we can't define love. Without facts, we are led leaderless. James Baldwin called truth "freedom which cannot be legislated, fulfillment which cannot be charted." Leszek Kołakowski spoke of a "horizon of truth." The horizon is to be chased. It is a pursuit worthy of free people.

## FLOWING FOUNTAIN

The playwright Euripides lived at the height of classical Greek culture. More than two thousand years ago, he realized that democracy depends on truthful, risky speech. Amid all the blather we now hear about freedom of expression, it is easy to forget its purpose: to create the circumstances in which facts ennoble the individual and challenge the powerful. We protect truthful, risky speech because tyranny is born of lies.

The hazards of speaking freely are very real. Around the world, people are imprisoned and murdered for what they say. In Assad's Syria, opponents of the regime were tortured and killed in horrifying numbers. In Lukashenko's Belarus, people who protested his rigged election have been hunted down and imprisoned by the thousands. In Xi's China, the suppression of vocal dissent has become a kind of science. In Putin's Russia, people are arrested simply for holding up blank pieces of paper. Vladimir Kara-Murza was sentenced to twenty-five years in prison for speaking the simple truth about the Russian invasion of Ukraine.

Volodymyr Vakulenko, a Ukrainian author of children's books, kept a handwritten diary of the first few weeks of the Russian occupation of his village in northeastern Ukraine. The single father of an autistic son, he described with love and humor how his child learned to react to the sound of bombings. Because Vakulenko was a Ukrainian writer, he was targeted for execution by Russian authorities. After his first arrest, he buried the diary. After his second arrest, he was murdered, and his body was thrown into a pit.

One of his colleagues, the Ukrainian novelist Victoria Amelina, learned of the diary's existence and was determined to find and publish it. She dug it out of the ground and wrote a foreword about the duty to preserve the words of Ukrainian writers, so many of whom had been murdered in the last century. A writer lives on, she wrote, as long as that writer is read. It was one of her last texts. Later that month she was murdered in a Russian rocket attack. Victoria Amelina and Volodymyr Vakulenko were free speakers. They needed protection.

Russian war propagandists begin from the premise that nothing is true. If nothing is true, then there is no dignity in speech and no reason to protect it. If there is no truth, then our utterances are no different from any other sound; our mouths, minds, and bodies are objects among other objects, in no way special. We are just *Körper* among other *Körper*, and the contest for dominance in a conversation space is no different from, say, the contest of boulders in an avalanche. It is just about size and power.

Freedom is positive, and so is freedom of speech: it makes no sense without the affirmation of truth as a virtue, and the creation of institutions to protect people seeking it. It is the truth seekers' freedom, their capacity to take risks with their bodies, that reminds us what the protection is for.

Freedom of speech requires free human speakers, as free as possible and as many as possible. Such people are sovereign, capable of judgment on their own; they are mobile, able to see and take risks; they are unpredictable, and so they can accept that facts challenge beliefs. They are facing danger for the rest of us and helping us to see the state of the world.

Reporters are an avant-garde. They declare freedom for us every day. We should be accommodating them and their work. The celebrated Austrian reporter Hugo Portisch said that "journalism is the freest profession," adding the important qualification: "in a free, democratic world." Freedom of speech requires institutions that no single free speaker can create. Reporters are the heroes of our time, and heroes are to be defended, not just commended. If we protect those who take risks, then we protect everyone else. If we make their careers safe and appealing, we build a land of the free.

Freedom of speech means a right to facts. Defending that right means sharing the facts about which people can speak. Only humans go into the world to discover the new and unpredictable. The mass delivery of plagiarism and fiction can be done by machines. Reporting cannot. Machines have no *Leib* and no values. Truth and risk mean nothing to them. They are not speakers, and they cannot be free. They cannot do the investigating; we need more human reporters to investigate the machines (and everything else).

Freedom of speech is not a firehose of digital information. Freedom of speech is a "fair-flowing fountain," to borrow a phrase from Euripides. Its justification is of quality, not quantity. The qualities are truth and risk.


## POWERFUL LIES

If the American nation endures, it must be a land of the free. For this, we will need free speakers.

Not all rhetoric about "free speech" is meant to protect free speakers. Oligarchs claim to be "canceled" (Putin) while they are invading countries, or crown themselves "free speech absolutists" (Musk) while using their platforms to censor. If freedom of speech is treated as negative freedom, as removing barriers for those who already control countries and information spaces, free speakers will not have much of a chance. As Simone Weil put it, those who "most deserve to express themselves" will not in fact have the freedom to do so.

It is worth being very attentive when oligarchs talk about free speech. The issue is not just that they are insincere or hypocritical. It is that they seek to traduce freedom of speech by making it seem senseless. Oligarchs pretend to be the victims, even when they own social media platforms or are presidents of countries. We are meant to conclude that freedom of speech is just the removal of any remaining impediments to the caprice of those who already control conversations. Debating the latest instance of oligarchical whining, we forget that the purpose of freedom of speech is to speak truth to power.

We need the freedom of speech to defend freedom in general, but this does not at all mean that everyone who refers to "free speech" is defending freedom. We will need laws to protect the freedom of speech, but that does not mean that its purpose will be captured in every legal formulation. A right to free speech, formulated in law, will always incidentally protect much that does not really need protecting. After all, the lies of the powerful are never in danger; nor are the bromides that everyone wants to hear. Whether or not speech is legally protected, the flood tide of propaganda and platitudes flows unhindered.

Freedom is positive, not negative. If there is no speaker, no person, then no question of freedom arises. Actual human expression is a minuscule part of the internet. Often what we hear or read does not come from a person but from institutions, such as corporations. In those cases, there is often no one person who would stand behind, say, a given advertising slogan. A wealthy individual who wishes to broadcast heinous disinformation about voting, or to lie about the climate, hides behind a web of organizations. Negative freedom is summoned as the justification: there should be no barriers to the cultural power of lying billionaires. But it is senseless to claim that freedom of speech protects such delegated deception. There is no truth, no person, no risk.

When "free speech" is invoked, here are the questions that can help ascertain whether it is a con: Where is the *Leib*? Where is the truth? What is the risk to the *Leib* taken by that person in telling that truth? If there is no *Leib,* no truth, no risk, then the concept of freedom of speech is being debased.

## MURDEROUS ORDERS

If I tell you to stop someone from voting, am I exercising freedom of speech? Certainly not. What about an armed policeman who stands in front of a voting booth and asks certain people what they are doing? An even clearer case—that is not freedom of speech. If an American president seeks to overturn an election and a regime, that is not an exercise of the freedom of speech. To point this out is not to deny Trump's right to speak freely, which is not in danger.

If I tell you to shoot someone, am I unaccountable because I was only exercising freedom of speech? If Putin sends hundreds of thousands of people to commit hundreds of thousands of murders, are his orders free speech? Obviously not.

When a dictator denies the existence of a nation, this is genocidal hate speech, a form of action that must be resisted. In an imperialist essay published in 2021, Putin argued that events that occurred in the tenth century "pre-determined" the unity of Ukraine and Russia. This statement is grotesque as history, since the only human creativity it allows, in the course of a thousand years and hundreds of millions of lives, is that of the tyrant to retrospectively and arbitrarily choose his own genealogy of power.

To claim otherwise, said Putin, to speak of actual history, of the centuries of human actions and choices, was "Russophobia." Russian officials and propagandists repeated that lie, even as Russians invaded Ukraine, deported millions of people, destroyed Mariupol and killed about one hundred thousand of its residents, tortured half the population of the city of Kherson, murdered local elites and buried them in mass graves, and sought not only to freeze out the whole country by destroying the power grid but to blackmail Africa and the Middle East by cutting off supplies of food.

Invited in 2023 to speak about this at the United Nations Security Council, I pointed out that the notion that Ukrainians were "Russophobes" was part of the Russian state's campaign to destroy them. The claims that Ukrainians were vermin, beasts, Nazis, and so on were made by a media monopoly controlled by an oligarchic dictatorship. There was no person, no truth, and no risk. The lies were told not only to preserve power but to allow that power to commit genocide.

When I said this, the Russian ambassador had no response. He simply threatened to find some other way of dealing with me. That was a sign that I was speaking freely.

## FREE SPEAKERS

Some Americans seem to think that defending freedom of speech just means saying the words *free speech* over and over, like an incantation. Too often, our free speech "debates" involve practiced provocateurs yelling "Free speech!" right after saying something they know to be untrue and obnoxious—and right before hustling back behind the tinted windows of limousines for the next gig paid for by the discreet oligarch. These everyday trivializations of an important idea demand that we think carefully about how we speak of this fundamental right. If it becomes one more cliché, losing its sense and meaning, the thing itself will wither.

The very phrase *free speech,* though we say it all the time, gets us on the wrong track. It suggests that speech is what is oppressed and what is to be liberated. That is incorrect. There is no speech without a *Leib,* without a person. Speech is not oppressed. *People who speak* are oppressed. Speech cannot be liberated. *People* must be liberated so that they can speak. Freedom of speech means nothing without free speakers. Only people can take risks. Only people can be free.

Freedom of speech for people means safe circumstances in which to express oneself, and an opportunity to learn, so as to have something to say—which means access to journalism, access to science, access to education. The declaration of the First Amendment that the government shall "make no law . . . abridging the freedom of speech" is meaningless without the accommodations needed to create free speakers.

How then to establish the structures that produce free speakers? Affirming truth, though necessary, is not enough. Even generating facts, though indispensable, is not enough. We do not have the natural capacity to distinguish truth from lies, or even an inborn preference for facts over fiction. We need the forms of freedom—sovereignty, unpredictability, mobility—to become free speakers and good listeners. Getting at the truth requires determined and cooperative work. Factuality, in other words, depends on solidarity.

# Solidarity

## JUST PEOPLE

Freedom is the value of values, but it does not stand alone. Nor can a free person. The practical recognition of these philosophical truths is *solidarity*, the fifth form of freedom.

We need the salve of solidarity in the hard logic of life. Young people can become sovereign and unpredictable thanks to the care of others. The time needed to care for them can be organized only by common effort. As young people grow older, they need to be able to move: out of school, out of the house, into futures that they can imagine and shape. Even rebellion should be nurtured. Their mobility begins with their own initiative but also requires the work of previous generations.

Solidarity is not just a pleasant cloud of good intentions. It is a necessary component of a working project of social mobility. In the absence of solidarity, such a project will turn against itself and toward racism, sadopopulism, the politics of eternity, postimperial immobility. If the goal is not opportunity for all, some will be satisfied when others are still more immobile. The sad facts of American history bring this home.

Solidarity closes a circle. None of the things that we need to become free, including knowledge, can we produce by ourselves. The most fundamental truths, the ones about ourselves that allow us to see the world, we must owe to others—as both Stein and Weil argued. To be free, each of us needs the truth, but factuality requires institutions as well as risk-takers. If freedom is the value of life, one of its forms is the self-conscious labor of making freedom possible for others. Solidarity is the guiding light of a land of the free.

Solidarity is the mark of a just person. Our values differ, as they should and must. Freedom is the value of values, because it is what allows that difference to reside in us and in the world we make around us. Each of us has the right to a freedom that allows us to learn, choose, and combine values. We are not the same, but in the most essential sense, we are equal.

## TESTIFYING

Like freedom in general, freedom of speech requires declarations made by individuals and accommodations made by some people to others. These individual capacities to declare and accommodate are sovereignty; their application in society is solidarity. Without solidarity, without protection of free speakers and without the support of institutions that enable listening, freedom of speech (like freedom itself) becomes an empty slogan. Without solidarity, freedom of speech becomes a parody of itself, used by its oligarchical enemies as a slogan to enforce their own dominance and to undermine freedom as such.

One powerful image of a free speaker is that of the courageous witness to suffering. And this is quite right. In my experience, though, people who take courageous stands have friends in the background. Those who testify about atrocities have support. And for testimony to be recorded and archived, a surprisingly large number of people have to cooperate. The effectiveness of a historical witness depends on the quiet work of many others. This is true even when, or especially when, the witness is no longer alive. Victoria Amelina sought and found Volodymyr Vakulenko's diary after he was murdered. When she was murdered in turn, she left behind a book about women researching war crimes. That testimony remains.

Making sense of even the most horrific events requires methods. Survivor testimony is now important to our understanding of the Holocaust, for example, but it was not so in the 1980s, when my grandmother reminded me of "all of those Jewish people." Jewish voices were often dismissed as irrational or superfluous. Without an organized effort, these voices would never have entered into history. They persist and resonate thanks to the work of institutions. The people at the origins of those institutions—such as the Holocaust Survivors Film Project in New Haven (founded in 1978) and its successor the Fortunoff Video Archive for Holocaust Testimonies at Yale—were motivated by values. When Victoria Amelina investigated war crimes, she was working with a Ukrainian group called Truth Hounds. In writing her book about women investigating atrocities, she had support from a group called Documenting Ukraine.

A world or a country in which we are entirely alone with our experiences is not a place of freedom. This is true in all cases, not just the extreme ones. The farmer and the vet tech and the waiter all have a story, but that story has to be heard by someone else and brought together with other circumstances. Thousands of people can be poisoned by the water supply in Flint, Michigan, and say so; but if they are Black or poor, if they have few local reporters, or if their town is run by an unelected emergency manager, the basic truth of this most fundamental matter will not break through for more than a year. We cannot be free unless our truths can be greeted by others, which means that we and they must share a common human understanding that there is such a thing as truth, that someone else's bodily experience has a dignity that I can understand even if the experience was not mine.

In Ukraine, one can feel overwhelmed by the sheer scope of Russian war crimes and the different kinds of evidence needed to understand and record them. One day, for example, I talked to farmers who had to rig tractors to clear their fields of mines. Then I visited a

Ukrainian port that Russia had closed with missiles. From there I went to a café to write about it all, only to find that it had been destroyed by a Russian rocket. There is a pattern here, an attempt to crush a people by destroying agriculture and demoralizing cities, but it takes more than one person to bring that fact to life.

Taking a risk to be a witness for truth affirms the meaning of the freedom of speech, as Euripides understood, as John Lewis understood, as Victoria Amelina understood. The truth does not exist without the risk, and we will need examples that show us how to take risks for truth. We will also need the laws, institutions, and norms that keep those risks as low as possible. No individual can do everything that is necessary to make all of us free. To "organize the service of truth," as Havel put it, requires solidarity.

## CIVIL RIGHTS

A vote records an important truth about an individual. The procedure of voting is applied solidarity.

It might seem that voting is a purely individual right. All I must do is enter the voting booth and express my preferences. If I think about the matter at all, I can imagine that every other citizen faces the same constraints and obligations that I do, and that they will be able to vote. But what if this is not the case? What if the voting booth is part of a larger landscape of discrimination?

The history of voting is one of inequality. And this inequality is not always so simple as some people having the vote and others not. Some votes can count for more than others. All citizens might have a formally equal right to vote, but some can nevertheless find it substantially harder to vote than others. An "emergency" can be invoked that deprives people of the right to elect leaders. All these problems apply to the United States today. Americans who do not live in this truth are consolidating an injustice.

Martin Luther King, Jr., wrote in 1963, "We have waited more than 340 years" (since the arrival of the first slave ship) for rights. For an interval after the Civil War, African Americans did enjoy the right to vote in the American South. After the withdrawal of federal troops from the South in 1877, however, state governments disenfranchised Black people. So long as much of the South was run by authoritarian white supremacist regimes, the United States could hardly be considered a democracy.

The Freedom Riders of 1961 appealed to solidarity as well as to mobility. They spoke of rounding out the logic of freedom. John Lewis, who was one of them, helped organize the March on Washington for Jobs and Freedom in 1963. Lewis called for protesting "until the revolution of 1776 is complete." The recognition that all people were created equal had to be extended to every person.

The civil rights movement was about the vote. Its success was the passage of the Voting Rights Act of 1965, which (until mutilated by the Supreme Court in 2013) forbade measures that impeded African Americans from voting. Its example of applied solidarity was important throughout the world.

## CIVIL SOCIETY

The east European dissidents of the 1970s and 1980s spoke of "civil society." In a one-party communist system in which voting had been a meaningless ritual for everyone for decades, they needed another vector of solidarity. By "civil society" they meant the freedom of people interested in the same things or committed to the same causes to meet and act together.

Late communism was supposed to be "rational," in that people would get their consumer goods if they did not stand out and would be punished if they spoke of alternatives to the status quo. Life was only about *how* we seek pleasure and avoid pain, not about *why* we live and what we should do. It was on this logic that dissidents were sentenced to psychiatric prison: to have an ethical sense or a political imagination was supposedly a sign of irrationality and thus of illness.

Civil society opposed such an understanding of rationality. We are not objects to be schematically manipulated, but subjects with improbable, personal values who should be allowed to find one another to better fulfill those commitments. People's authentic interests were understood to be unpredictable and therefore to lead to unpredictable relationships, like that of Havel and the rock musicians, or Michnik and the workers, or even Havel and Michnik themselves, meeting on that mountaintop.

Isolation is an essential part of the "rational" behaviorist program for politics. Communists stayed in power by keeping people apart. All relationships were about power, which was to flow downward from the politburo to the people. When late communism worked, citizens co-created a public atmosphere of lies and half-lies, not believing in the ideology but pretending to believe. Havel worried that such habitual, half-conscious mendacity would stifle the unpredictable zones of life where people's authentic interests might intersect. It was hard for people to find spontaneous human connections when they felt that they had to demonstrate conformism to get through the day. What they cared about came to seem shameful and secret. For the dissidents, civil society meant horizontal relationships, established on the basis of what people happened to really love.

The great success of civil society in eastern Europe was the Polish labor movement Solidarity. In 1980, Polish workers struck not only for economic goals but for human rights under the wise motto "No freedom without solidarity!" The workers forced the communist regime to accept their demands, and their union soon had ten million members. So long as Solidarity was legal in communist Poland, rates of alcohol consumption and rates of suicide were low. Though Solidarity was suppressed in 1981, its veterans formed eastern Europe's first post-communist government in 1989.

In 1989, thanks to civil society, Poland led the way from communism. Freedom, after all, would require more than just the absence of Soviet violence. It would also require a positive sense of a new political order. Adam Michnik, freed from prison, put the union slogan on the masthead of a newspaper: "No freedom without solidarity!" A few months later, Havel was elected president of Czechoslovakia. In "The Power of the Powerless," Havel recognized the practical need for solidarity as a step toward liberation. If unfreedom was a collective project, wrote Havel, then freedom was as well. He evoked "the powerful realization that freedom is indivisible."

The philosopher Charles Taylor, a friend of the Solidarity movement, made the case about solidarity and freedom this way: "The free individual who affirms himself as such already has an obligation to complete, restore, or sustain the society within which this identity is possible." If freedom is a right, maintained the philosopher Joseph Raz, then it is also a duty. Freedom cannot be selfish. To declare oneself free is to promise to act such that others can be free. We must imagine a society of free people and try to build it. Morally, logically, and politically, there is no freedom without solidarity.

Freedom requires its forms: sovereignty, unpredictability, mobility, and factuality. If I claim them for myself, then I must do so for everyone. They can only be brought to life as a common project. It is logically incoherent, morally obtuse, and politically ineffective to claim freedom only for oneself. That is choosing the isolation that tyrants would have chosen for us. They use the word *freedom* quite often; without solidarity, we will be fooled, and we will fool ourselves. Solidarity is a high and vital form of freedom. It makes of freedom justice.

## PRACTICAL POLITICS

In late communist eastern Europe, civil society was understood not as politics but as "anti-politics." It was not seen in the 1970s and 1980s as the program for government that is advocated here, for the simple reason that the dissidents had given up on influencing communist regimes directly. They knew that they could not begin from *freedom from,* since the aspiration to make the state smaller or remove barriers was senseless. They had to begin from *freedom to,* in the sense of affirming values.

Philosophically, though, the notion of civil society can be extracted from that historical limitation. It legitimates a certain kind of government, one that would create the conditions for us to become free and to acknowledge and engage with the commitments of others. For civil society to work, it has to be seen not as anti-politics but as politics: as a politics of freedom. Rather than ignoring government, it informs government.

That is not, however, how matters looked in eastern Europe after 1989. Negative freedom prevailed. The advocates of a "free market" mocked solidarity and confidently proclaimed that capitalism would do the work of freedom. The wealth and prestige of the United States and Great Britain were more decisive at the time than any argument. But the job of liberating people cannot be delegated to the market, contrary to what many of us believed in 1989. The market did raise average living standards in eastern Europe (though not in the United States), but it did not create civil society or solidarity.

The politics of inevitability pushed the dissidents to the margin, often with their own connivance, and made their ideas seem naïve. All the discussions were suddenly about *how* to get to a single possible future after a "transition." All the *why* of the 1970s and 1980s seemed embarrassing. I remember some of the best thinkers of the communist period, such as Martin Šimečka, confessing that their previous commitments now seemed senseless. They were persuaded that their historical role had been played out: now the politics of inevitability would take over. Such judgments were mistaken: the rhetorics of responsibility, solidarity, and factuality that were developed to analyze and resist late communism also applied to early capitalism. In democratic conditions, they are not less but more relevant. They can be used for critique but also for creation.

In the twenty-first century, the new democracies of eastern Europe began to drift into the politics of eternity, and some of them began to fail. Russia was the early and dramatic example of a regime that discredited its own tradition of civil society and reasserted the traditional "vertical" of power. Russia's regime survives in the 2020s thanks to the extraction and export of fossil fuels and the spectacle created by wars in Syria and Ukraine. Its propaganda mocks all values, telling people that they are on their own. Its elites escape as best they can, sending their assets and their children to Europe.

## BUBBLE MEN

The opposite of solidarity is escapism: I flee the scene with stuffed pockets while everyone else suffers from my selfish choices. On a negative account of freedom, escapism will seem acceptable or even laudable. In negative freedom, the cowards—the Putins, the Trumps, the Musks—are the heroes.

Escapism makes freedom impossible. When the very privileged believe that they and their families can elude the tragedy unfolding around them, they will obstruct the national work needed to create the forms of freedom. Having chosen escape, they will deride those who work in solidarity for freedom. Their money will draw others into the snide chorus. Wealth preservation distorts politics for everyone who is not wealthy—in the demanding circumstances of the twenty-first century, fatally and finally. The attempt by the monied few to monopolize the future closes it down for everyone else.

Under the politics of inevitability, we were not meant to notice that wealth was concentrating in very few hands; if we did, we were instructed that class war waged by the oligarchs against the rest was a necessary step on the path to a brighter future. (One billionaire, Warren Buffett, did try to clarify: "There's class warfare, all right. But it's my class, the rich class, that's making war, and winning.") Under the politics of eternity, as the oligarchs emerge from the shadows, we are meant to think of a glorious past when we were innocent, while the very wealthy colonize the future with their deadly frivolities. In catastrophic times, oligarchs divert resources from the human struggle to live free and direct them toward the dumb delusion that a chosen few can flee.

Escapism is the absolutely predictable oligarchic posture during catastrophic times. The rest of us have to endure the oligarchs' moronic fantasies—Ukraine is Russia, immortality is possible, space travel will save us, life might be a simulation—as time runs out on our hopes for dignity and survival as a species. A poignant element of our tragedy is its profound stupidity. There are things so idiotic that you need $10 billion to believe them.

Digital oligarchs distract us with promises of a high-tech future while pinning us with brain hacks to the untenable present. Elon Musk dreams of space while his company promotes lies about global warming, thereby weakening support for the technologies we would need for space travel. Fossil oligarchs summon climate extinction while preparing exits for themselves. Vladimir Putin's narcissistic invasion of Ukraine offers a preview of the end of the world. The leading American fossil oligarch is Charles Koch, global warming's best friend. His name means "man cook." God has a revealing sense of humor.

## MORTALITY

One form of oligarchical escape is from time: the dream of some that they will live forever. They won't. God also has a sense of irony: the surname of a prominent death escapist, Ray Kurzweil, means "a little while."

The fantasy of immortality is for the few. It is a rejection of solidarity. As such, it is not just selfish but dangerous for freedom. Forever is the wrong time scale. Freedom requires a sense of time that extends into the future, through one life and into the next generation or two. With that kind of range, we can think of values and of the world, of the *why* as well as the *how*. The finitude of our time on Earth gives shape to life. If we believe that we can live forever, we lose all contact with virtue and thus with freedom. On an infinite time scale, *why* transforms itself back into *how*: how to stay alive, minute after stressful minute.

An immortal being could not be free. No choice would be meaningful, because all could be deferred. Life itself would become the only value, sadistically affirmed by the background mortality of others. Anxiety about accidental death and assassination would fill the mind, dissolving any capacity to think of anything (or anyone) else. One notices this tendency in the company of people who are trying to live forever. Knowing that we are mortal is what allows us to take risks, even little ones such as leaving the house to get coffee or pick up a kid from school. If we really had everything to lose at every moment, we would curl up in a ball.

To be sure, life is good and life in liberty is better. Everyone has a right to life, though, not just the very wealthy. In the twenty-first century, the life expectancy of Americans has *decreased* relative to that of other prosperous countries. Men in the United States can expect lives that are eight years shorter than those of Japanese men. Eight years is a long time to be unnecessarily dead.

American millennials worry about climate change and biodiversity, and rightly so. But even absent an extinction event, it is possible that they will live shorter lives than their parents or even their grandparents. Much of the risk of early death comes from disadvantaged childhoods, and thus from the absence of social mobility and from the unequal distribution of wealth. These violations of the right to life are a result of oligarchy.

Wealthy Americans who want to lengthen life have options ready to hand. They can invest in hygiene and vaccinations (as the Gates Foundation does) or in small nonprofits that improve the quality of life (as MacKenzie Scott does). The simplest way for the wealthy to extend the lives of their fellow Americans would be to pay their fair share of taxes. Most don't; a good government, one legitimated by freedom, would ensure that they did. Giving 330 million Americans five more years of freedom is a nicer prospect than giving three billionaires a million years of anxiety. It also has the virtue of being possible.

## VENUS

Another oligarchical escape is to outer space. A search is on for Earth-like planets in the galaxy. The study of exoplanets is fascinating and highly deserving of support. Yet it is not clear that any other planet, no matter how good it might look from a distance, could actually sustain us. Earth is our home not only because of the physical characteristics that we might detect on another planet from afar, but also thanks to its particular and intimate interaction with life. Earth provided the conditions for very simple life some four billion years ago, and ever since then, life has been remaking our planet. As the evolutionary biologist Olivia Judson has written, many of the aspects of nature that we take for granted, such as the composition of the atmosphere, the color of the sky, and the variety of minerals, depend, in fact, on life. Our existence on Earth is historical, and no other planet has Earth's history.

Our private pioneers of space exploration are absolutely right that only ideas that seem crazily ambitious now will have a meaningful payoff later. But that triumph, when it comes, will not be the rescue of *Homo sapiens*. In order to get to outer space, we will have to thrive and prosper here for another several decades.

In our own solar system, the escapists favor Mars. There are excellent reasons to explore Mars, but the red planet will not rescue us from climate change or any other immediate threat. The time scale of human survival or extinction, roughly between now and 2040, is simply too short. In any event, the technical problems involved in settling Mars are far greater than those involved in resolving climate change.

And they overlap. If we want to explore space, we will need fusion-powered rockets—which means that we would *first* have to master fusion power here on Earth. But if we had fusion power on Earth, we could supply ourselves with endless clean energy, reverse global warming, and remove any need to leave our planet. Regardless of whether we want to stay or go, it is fusion power that deserves our immediate attention.

In discussions of escaping to space, no one ever mentions Venus, our nearest neighbor, the planet most similar to Earth. Venus is a depressing exhibit of the greenhouse effect, the physical phenomenon that our escapist oligarchs are bringing about, directly if they are fossil oligarchs, indirectly if they are digital oligarchs. Venus's atmosphere of carbon dioxide traps the sun's heat, making its surface unthinkably hot. Our activities in general, and those of our oligarchs in particular, are making Earth more like Venus. So we are supposed to look away.

It will be far easier to stop the greenhouse effect on Earth than to find and settle a suitable exoplanet, or to terraform Mars. Space exploration is a worthy goal, but it is far harder than, and no substitute for, keeping our own planet habitable. The logical sequence is simple: fusion reactors, renewable energy, freedom on Earth; then fusion rockets, exploration, and discovery in space.

Even if this sequence somehow did not hold, it is implausible that we could establish order in the universe if we cannot do so on our home planet.

## VOID

Incidentally, why is it that we, rather than someone else, seem to be doing all the searching for life beyond the home planet? Given that we inhabit a planet that is suitable for life, why has no one else *found us*? Why does no one even seem to be looking?

There must have been other civilizations in our galaxy. But to communicate with us, they would have had to reach the stage of digital technology. At that point, they were, we might surmise, undone by their own creations, their own social media, their own surveillance, their own artificial intelligence, their own nemesis.

It is our moment here on Earth that suggests such a hypothesis. Since 2010, when social media took over the internet, the hyped new technologies—think cryptocurrency, self-driving cars, the metaverse, the whole gig economy—have generally turned out to be scams. Social media are not high technology in any meaningful sense: they are mid-twentieth-century behaviorist manipulation done at scale. They hinder scientific thought. Elon Musk's version of Twitter is anti-evidence and pro-conspiracy, proposing a new dark age of charismatic leadership and magical thinking. The idea of technology itself has to be rescued from the cycle of propaganda-driven investment scams.

To reach the stars, we will have to look away from our phones. We can get to other planets only with fusion rockets. We will develop fusion rockets only when we have fusion power. We will have fusion power only if we try to address climate change. We will address climate change only if people believe that it is happening. People will believe that it is happening only if social media are reformed. Musk owns a platform that instructs us that climate change is a hoax. That makes space travel much less likely.

Let us turn our technology upward and outward, away from the psychological exploitation of vulnerable minds and toward construction and exploration. Let us first build solar panels and windmills and fusion power plants and use them to save Earth from the greenhouse effect, then resolve the remaining technical problems of space exploration.

If we can survive on this planet, we might have the time and capacity to explore other planets. We should explore them only after we can ensure life and freedom on this one. We owe as much to ourselves—and to anyone else we might encounter along the way.

## SUBJECTS

Our least ambitious forays into space might have taught us the most. Thanks to satellites, we are now able to draw the contours of prehistoric cities that did not leave behind large temples or fortresses (for example, Nebelivka, in today's Ukraine).

Because what remains for us from early Near Eastern civilizations are walls and idols of stone, we tend to imagine progress as ever lower barriers and ever less paganism. From a terrifying regime of exploitation and human sacrifice, humanity moves forward, the walls recede, and the gods are tamed. But those appearances might well be deceptive. Cities as old as those of ancient Egypt and Mesopotamia were designed in concentric circles, like the rings of a tree, with no visible sign of organized worship or hierarchy. Although it would be a mistake to draw too firm conclusions, we should keep our minds open. Progress is more than the removal of some previous evil, and freedom is more than the reduction of repression. The notion of a horrifying past might just be nothing more than an excuse for an untenable present.

Positive freedom leads us back to one another. Were freedom just negative, the mere absence of barriers, I could think of you as just one more barrier. Since it is positive, a presence of virtues I affirm in a world I shape, I see you doing the same. Positive freedom leads us to treat one another as actors in history. If freedom is something we must build together, then each of us has a stake in the other. If virtues are real but clash, then we have to declare our own as well as accommodate those of others. If freedom is about the future, we must work together to keep it open.

Getting this wrong is not just a philosophical but an existential mistake. If we accept the erroneous tradition of negative freedom, we will end up turning against one another. We will have trouble seeing the other as a person, a *Leib,* an equal. Unable to see others, people who have fallen for negative freedom will have trouble seeing even *themselves* (and the harm they are doing to themselves). If we think of freedom only as a liberation from unwanted barriers, we will fail to create the right structures. If we start with the idea of freedom as "inside and outside," we will end up with a fascism of "us and them."

What "inside and outside" and "us and them" have in common is the starting point that we are the good, or that the good is within us. Good and evil are divided peremptorily and perfectly. Good is us; we are good. No need, then, to consider what the good things might be, or seek the help of others in finding them.

American defenders of negative freedom are in the habit of arguing that Nazi Germany and the Soviet Union were results of positive
freedom. Any attempt to "intervene in the economy," goes the argument, must lead to totalitarianism. This view has been repeated inces-
santly since the 1940s, and it is familiar to the point of being common
sense. But it is the purest propaganda, entirely contrary to history.
Hitler and Stalin, leaders of revolutionary parties bent on violence,
would have been baffled to learn that they came to power as a result of
kindergarten or pensions. They did not.

Positive freedom saves not only freedom but also the market from
the free marketeers. Stalinism and Nazism had a chance precisely
because defenders of negative freedom had no challengers in the
1920s, and capitalism collapsed into the Great Depression as a result.
Negative freedom in our American sense—the demolition of government services—generates fear and anxiety, making extreme politics
more likely. The welfare state reduces the human anxiety and political
risks inherent in the boom-and-bust cycle of markets. It thereby makes
extreme politics of the Nazi and Soviet variety less likely, by depriving
them of their undergirding of loneliness and anxiety.

## OBJECTS

In the twenty-first century, which we share with the algorithms, the
idea of negative freedom can lead us to still more profound perversity. When we settle for negative freedom today, we end up siding
with the nonhuman against the human. This may sound strange, but
it is where this American misunderstanding of freedom has led us.
When we think of freedom as negative, we think only of the barrier,
not of the person. And then we begin to think of people themselves
as the barrier.

There is, after all, nothing especially human about avoiding barriers. Pathogens are good at it, and so is malware. If we think of freedom as negative, we wake up one day as the champions of both kinds

of viruses, of alien bits of DNA and unknown computer code. They must be allowed to penetrate our mouths, invade our retinas, go everywhere. In practice, among the most unquestioned American rights are those of photons to flow from computer displays to optic nerves to deliver targeted advertising, of electrons to move among banks to allow tax evasion, and of carbon dioxide molecules to heat the air and doom the species.

The problem is one not of technology but of worldview. Following the logic of negative freedom, we concern ourselves with an abstraction (the economy) rather than the bodies of people. Instead of free people, we find ourselves speaking of a "free market." The people *become* the barriers, to be removed—or penetrated. The myth of the free market instructs us that *things* should be free to circulate without hindrance.

When the word *freedom* is conceded to the economy, it follows that the market has rights. Such rights will be enforced *against* people, who are expected to experience the market's rights as duties. On this logic, people have a duty *not* to concern themselves with how things are bought and sold, or with how money is moved, or with monopolies, or wage slavery, or pollution, or carbon dioxide emissions.

The ideology of the free market demands that we extend the law of necessity deep into our lives and minds. It is bad enough to submit to the law of necessity, to the world as it is. It is much worse when we choose to extend the law of necessity by inventing new laws to which we then submit.

## HAND

Markets are indispensable, and they help us do many things well. But it is up to people to decide which things those are and under which parameters markets best serve freedom. In important areas, such as health care, the market provides a poor service. If the body is a site of profit, it is not a site of health. We need to understand our bodies, and treating them as commodities makes this much harder to do. The leading source of health information in the United States now is direct-to-consumer drug advertising.

Birth is the most important moment of our lives, but obstetrics is hard to make profitable, and so mothers and babies die who ought to have lived. Infant and maternal mortality is higher in the United States than in any other rich country—and the trend is in the wrong direction. Prevention is the most important part of health care, but it is hard to make money from keeping people well, so we let it go. We are an aging population, and preventive therapies—geroscience—can aid well-being and freedom. It is not clear, though, whether they will make money. Certain kinds of illnesses are more profitable than others. Death is profitable when efficiently managed, when families are drained of wealth during the last days of a loved one's life. Commercial medicine profits first by depriving our lives of years, and then by adding to them a few days.

And so Americans live shorter, sicker lives while spending far more money on health care than others in comparably rich countries. Without a positive idea of freedom, without some concept of the *Leib*, we do not see how strange this is. Being unable to see a doctor or afford medication when we are sick is not a mark of freedom. Nor is being dead.

When Americans enter a hospital, their first encounter is often with a financial officer. This verification of insurance reminds the sick that money comes before the body. It suggests that there is no *Leib*, only a *Körper*, an object from which money might be made.

After the patient is admitted, nurses visit the patient, their bodies blocked by a large computer caddy on wheels. During the interaction, the machine is interposed physically between the patient and the nurse, making actual communication problematic. If and when a physician appears, that interaction too will likely be hindered by a machine. Doctors are constrained by their digital masters to describe their encounters with patients in a standard matrix of billable categories. Their eyes and fingers search for the right window on the screen. Whole visits pass without any eye contact between doctor and patient.

As medicine has been mechanized, American life expectancy has fallen relative to comparable countries. Failure then becomes part of the narrative. The ideology of the "free market" tells us that there is no alternative to commercial medicine, so avoidable pain and death must be part of some larger and happier story. This sadistic con exploits a religious resignation, one that I have heard countless times: "things happen for a reason." It is heartbreaking to hear Americans invoke a higher "reason" after their loved ones have died unnecessarily as a result of commercial medicine. That people on our own continent—in Canada and Costa Rica—live longer and healthier lives than we somehow never gets mentioned.

When I was very sick and hospitalized, I wanted the visible hand of a doctor, not the "invisible hand" of the "free market." Those who speak of a "free market" have the notion that its "invisible hand" will decide for us, like a parent for a child. This is a lullaby of submission, one more fantasy that the universe will tell us what is good and necessary. When the invisible hand slaps us down, we are supposed to understand that our pain served some higher goal. This empty rationalization simply places the economy where the church stood for medieval theologians and where the monarchy stood for early modern absolutists: an abstraction before which we kneel.

## EFFICIENCY

Freedom requires care with words. When we are not careful, we drift along with familiar solecisms until we founder on the shores of cliché. In conceding a word, we concede a concept, and in conceding a concept, we give up the thing itself. A key example is the concession of the word *free* before we even begin, as in *free market*.

A different example is our embrace of *efficiency,* a nonvalue that poses as the highest value. The word resets the conversation. It places *why* out of bounds, offering an endless *how*. Efficiency talk distracts us from thinking about purposes and hastens us instead toward a calculation regarding how quickly something is being done. Commercial medicine, for example, is efficient in extracting money from the sick. And that is how hospitals are judged by those who own them. Accepting profit as the goal, however, means forgetting about life and health.

Efficiency talk is dismissive of virtues, which are presented as hindrances to getting things done. Efficiency mavens sneer at values as "irrational," a waste of time. Accepting this means supplanting the manifold commitments of people with the hidden purposes of those who hold power. Those who deploy efficiency jargon are actually demanding that you work for *their* purposes, which you are to accept as a matter of course. In this way, efficiency talk generates submission: we do not choose our ends, but race to realize those of others.

History confirms that efficiency talk can lead a people away from freedom. Efficiency was the argument for shifting American manufacturing to China in the 1980s and 1990s. The result was the decline of freedom in the United States, and the rise of China as the superpower of oppression. In repressive conditions, workers in China make our cell phones and much else. They are instruments in a political project that has no purpose beyond the pleasure of their rulers, who (for example) find it efficient to sell the organs of murdered political dissenters and the hair of ethnic minorities imprisoned in concentration camps. Today's China, with its communist ideology and capitalist practice, is about efficiency.

There is nothing new about dehumanizing efficiency jargon. Efficiency was an argument for American slavery in the nineteenth century and for Nazi and Soviet concentration camps in the twentieth. Julius Margolin, in his memoir of five years in the Gulag, defined it as a place where no one could ask *why?* "Here there is no why," said an Auschwitz camp guard to Primo Levi.

In the Warsaw Ghetto, Jews labored until the food they consumed was regarded as more valuable than the labor that could be extracted from them. Then they were sent to Treblinka to be gassed. The clearing of the ghetto was timed according to efficiency.

If efficiency is the only measure, then values evaporate and solidarity is impossible. *Leib* becomes *Körper,* to be used and cast away.

## LIBERTARIAN UNFREEDOM

Deniers of climate change and oligarchical escapists often call themselves "libertarians." If libertarianism means that liberty is the value of values, then this is a libertarian book. As generally formulated in the United States, however, libertarianism is an ideology of submission to the nonexistent "free market," based on contradictions and lies.

According to the libertarians, the "free market" defends freedom. If the market does not defend something, it follows, that thing is not freedom. If the market does not protect a certain right, then we are expected to concede that it is not a right.

When libertarians argue that markets defend freedom, they really mean that humans have a duty to defend markets. In a "free market," freedom is defined as the right of things to move around unhindered by humans, who are defined as barriers, or as entities with duties toward things. Human beings must be denied the freedom to change how capitalism works, and that denial must be labeled "freedom." Thus in a "free market," politics begins from Orwellian oppression.

The "free market" only exists as a slogan covering senseless contradictions and justifying political bullying. There is no such thing as a "free market" in the world, nor can there be. Capitalism minus norms and laws is murderous conquest. If someone invades your country, seizes your house, enslaves your children, and puts your kidneys up for sale, that is the magic of the unregulated market at work.

Markets cannot be free. Only people can be free. Freedom is a human value. It can be recognized and pursued only by humans. There is no substitute for freedom, no way to delegate it. The moment we delegate freedom, to the market or anything else, it becomes submission. When people surrender the word *free,* freedom vanishes from their lives.

Libertarianism is incompatible with every form of freedom. American libertarianism forbids us from raising the question of how people become free, and it therefore impedes sovereignty. By treating freedom just as a matter of the impulses of individuals, the ideology stops us from thinking about the structures that we need to create sovereign individuals. Libertarians oppose the parental leave and the public schools needed to create free young people (including entrepreneurs), and the labor unions and the health insurance we need to allow workers to enjoy mobility.

Libertarianism requires us to be predictable. The ideology of the "free market" reduces us to robots following simple algorithms. What are we to value in life? Who knows. What are you to do in daily life? Follow your impulses and buy something. What should the government do? Nothing. To always have the same answer means falling into our most probable states.

In practice, the "free market" is directed against social mobility. By categorizing redistribution, welfare states, and political action in general as forbidden "interventions" in the economy, libertarianism guarantees the triumph of giant corporations and the concentration of wealth. This makes social advance ever more difficult. Though libertarians pose as defenders of freedom, they create societies in which young people have nowhere to go.

Libertarians champion "rationality" even as they spread the anti-science propaganda of fossil oligarchs. In so doing, they oppose factuality. By opposing state policy that would alter present energy markets, libertarianism also guarantees a future of lethal climate change.

Most fundamental to libertarianism is its opposition to solidarity. It counsels us to act selfishly at all times, consoling us with the thought that this behavior will lead to the good of everyone. Competition can be a very good thing, as a practice within rules girded by norms. Yet even Adam Smith, the most famous of all thinkers about the market, understood that competition functions on the basis of virtues that it does not itself generate. Freedom comes from us, not from markets; and without freedom that comes from us, markets will work poorly. Libertarianism makes us pessimists about those virtues, persuades us that we cannot be good on purpose. But we can be.

We are free within a borderland of the unpredictable, a human zone between *what is* and *what should be*. When ideologies claim that there is no difference between the two, or that the difference is being closed by some higher power, they are denying our zone of freedom. Like the ideology of "scientific socialism," the ideology of the "free market" claims that *what is* can become *what should be* thanks to some larger economic logic.

*Restore private property, or remove it, and all will be well.* In both cases, the rhetoric begins as a fantasy of revolution—*free the market! unite the proletariat!*—and ends with the odious assurance that nothing is really true and nothing really matters and so there is no alternative to the status quo.

## OLIGARCH HYPOCRISY

There is no need to explain why certain very wealthy people endorse the fantasy of a "free market": for them, the game is wealth preservation, and libertarianism provides the rules. The state collects taxes, and therefore they must delegitimate the state. The way to do so is to claim that the state is ineffective at everything it does. The notion that freedom is state inaction makes sense only for the tiny minority who can protect their families without a representative government.

Libertarian digital oligarchs claim they owe no taxes because they made their money themselves. This is ridiculous. The infrastructure that made their companies possible was paid for by taxes and built by government. Had there been no antitrust legislation, the transistor would never have become the basis for Silicon Valley, which would not now exist. American tax dollars paid for the development of the computer, the internet, and the World Wide Web. The iPhone was dependent on public sector research. Taxes fund the Silicon Valley start-ups of the people who then propose the "free market" for the rest of us. Digital oligarchs spread their libertarian schtick on jaunts around the world funded by the travel budgets of government contractors.

With comparable hypocrisy, some of our fossil oligarchs also declare the libertarian right not to pay taxes. But their fortunes, too, depend on government. Fossil fuel extraction depends on grotesquely large government subsidies, including the use of federal land. Native Americans were violently driven from the land by military or police campaigns—state power—so that private companies could extract fossil fuels. This unambiguous and coercive government intervention is at the origins of the fossil oligarchy. Libertarians claim to believe in property rights. Were they sincere, libertarians would be at the forefront of those arguing for reparations for Native Americans. Why are they not? Because libertarianism is a sham.

Wealthy libertarians favor the state interventions that allowed them to generate their wealth; they just oppose government action that might enable others to do the same. Our fossil oligarch libertarians (Charles Koch is the leading example) claim to oppose bureaucracy. Yet they themselves constitute the pro-global-warming bureaucracy, as well as the pro-electoral-subversion bureaucracy. They claim to favor small government, but by spending money on elections, they make the government larger, by glomming their corporations on to it. The Koch Foundation was behind the *Citizens United* case, which opened elections to unlimited corporate-backed political advertising under the palpably ludicrous logic that companies are people and that money is speech. As a result, the country took a giant step toward oligarchy, and Americans are now less free.

## CYBORG POLITICS

For those who are not wealthy, the free-market fantasy is seductive for a different reason: it lifts the burden of responsibility that comes with freedom. We can dream that the "free market" will make all decisions for us. Our one and only decision is to concede our freedom to it.

Once we join the libertarian cult, we do not have to take the trouble to evaluate the world. We are soothed by the notion that our impulses are automatically translated into the general good. We use our minds to rationalize, to justify whatever the markets give us, a habit that is submissive in the extreme. If a problem such as global warming looms on the horizon, we imagine that the "free market" will somehow automatically address it—a delusion that is suicidal.

To be sure, elegant answers have their charm. It is tempting to submit to a single value, to relinquish the aspiration to be free. The extreme solutions calm us by removing any occasion for thought: large state and tiny market (Stalinists), or large market and tiny state (libertarians). When we give ourselves over to these total solutions, we are pacified, no longer wrestling with the world. We have an answer for everything, like a simple computer program. We have retreated from the borderland of the unpredictable into the safe space of automatic replies.

Havel defined ideology as a "bridge of excuses between the system and the individual." Libertarianism is exactly that: a bridge of excuses, a substitute for thinking. When we accept that freedom is negative and call the market "free," we spurn our responsibility to decide what sort of market and what sort of government we want.

Libertarians and our digital nemesis are natural partners because both encourage yielding to impulse, and both promote binary reactions. Libertarianism propagates a mindless binarism: "free market" good, government bad. The use of this binary algorithm transforms libertarians into human automata—lobbyists for objects.

The process also works in the other direction: people who spend time on social media tend to become libertarians. Their politics take on a weird, cyborg form. Libertarians are the earnest defenders of the right of photons to bring advertisements to your eyes, and of the right of carbon dioxide to pollute our skies. They take a firm stand for the electrons used to transfer wealth away from tax authorities and into tax shelters. In so doing, they spread unfreedom and death.

## DEATH CULT

Like Marxism, libertarianism functions as both science and religion. It assures us that economics is both pure knowledge and a cult of the immaculate "free market." The notion that one's own selfish acts join with those of others to create a mystical harmony is a religious view in its content (and most likely in its origin).

Libertarianism, although some of its advocates believe themselves to be secular people, rests on faith and reveals itself in guilt. Americans are taught to feel bad for tainting capitalism. The "free market" is presented as a sacred space wherein people are not to "intervene." Capitalism had no virgin birth. The market has no purity, mythical or otherwise. It is a social arrangement subject to change by free people.

It is normal to feel guilt or shame when we mistreat others, ignore their declarations, or fail to accommodate them. A corresponding sense of responsibility can lead us toward solidarity with others and thus more freedom for us all.

Yet feeling guilt about the market makes no sense. In fact, it is a trap. Normal human guilt follows the unpredictable course of personal choices and commitments. Market guilt follows the predictable course of a story told by the powerful: of a "free market" that may not be violated. Because such guilt is predictable, it is subject to manipulation by the authors of the fiction. The American sense that we do wrong when we violate the pristine market is a gift to our oppressors. Such a feeling makes it harder for us to feel responsibility toward people.

Markets should work for us, not the other way around. Properly managed, they can indeed create some of the conditions that allow people to be free. They work depending on the rules. These rules should be informed by values, not by spurious notions of purity. When the rules are right, many of our cares are lifted.

Free people will do what makes sense for them, without shame. When the market fails, to react by changing course is normal. When markets constrain freedom, we work together to alter them. When we need new institutions, we build them. Facing a challenge such as a depression or a financial crisis, we intervene. Facing a species-threatening calamity such as global warming, we come together to intervene again. Solidarity helps us to see all of this.

# NOTALITARIANS

A free person sees the world in color, as through a kaleidoscope. There is no one right answer but countless combinations, which we learn to imagine and make. Believers in an ideology have only black and white, others and themselves, a single truth.

A value left alone perverts itself and opens a void. This happens in politics, as well as in our minds and bodies. Holding on to just one value, we never practice and never attain grace.

If we believe in only one good thing, then every choice seems easy—for a time. What happens, though, when we cease to believe? Then we have nothing to fall back on: no other values, and no practice considering values. We have grown accustomed to discrediting all other values for the sake of the one. And so when we lose that one value, absolute clarity gives way to total cynicism. A world of black and white blurs into gray.

In prison, Adam Michnik wrote that the most dangerous people were the ones who believed in one truth or in zero truths. Totalitarianism is religious science, or scientific religion. Notalitarianism is bottomlessly agnostic about both values and facts. Totalitarians give us one truth that seems to hold everything together. They merge *what is* with *what ought to be,* making both meaningless, leaving the power to custodians who explain why the rest are creatures of *how*. When the one truth slips away, notalitarians arrive to give us the one truth that there are no truths.

Freedom begins with the recognition of the difference between the *is* and the *ought*. Free people operate in the space between, in a borderland of unpredictability. Totalitarianism claims to close the gap between *what is* and *what should be* permanently and for everyone. A notalitarian shrugs and says that the problem does not exist: Who knows what (if anything) exists, and who knows what (if anything) should be? Totalitarianism takes all the oxygen from the room; notalitarianism fills the space with laughing gas.

Totalitarianism and notalitarianism both draw us into a politics of "us and them." In totalitarianism, we believe our group understands the single good. Notalitarianism invites us to prefer our feelings to those of others, which leads us to raise our tribe above other tribes, with no need to give reasons. Since there are no truths and no values, we need not explain our sense of "us and them." Having a "them" means never having to find the courage to be "us." We never have to confront our fears with commitments.

Totalitarians and notalitarians are self-righteous. If we accept a single value, we feel that we are always right, because we think we are saying the right things with the right people. If we believe that nothing is of value, we also feel that we are always right, since it is impossible to be wrong. Since nothing (in the notalitarian mode) really matters, all that is sure are our feelings, on which we are the only authorities, and which we authentically express. Feeling is not only first, as the poet E. E. Cummings said: it is first and last, alpha and omega, everything. When a billionaire emerges who rules from impulse, notalitarians embrace their fickle *Führer*.

Notalitarianism is seductively snide. Believing in nothing is presented as intelligence. Facts are all contested, and so they are no better than opinions, which are no better than emotions—so forget the reporters, historians, and scientists. Those who express values are dismissed as fools. Everything is excused, because anyone's excuse is as good as anyone else's. Let the liars lie and the truth perish. Let the oligarchs try to escape and enjoy watching everyone else suffer. Let the world end with a smirk.


## LAKE AND FOREST

It is easy to espouse one value or to disavow them all. Believing in just one thing, like believing in nothing at all, enables us to scorn other people and reject their values. And this is very satisfying. But freedom is not scorn and rejection. It is choice and affirmation. It is not a shove off a cliff but a climb up a mountain. Negative freedom objectifies. Positive freedom—true freedom—humanizes.

Freedom is hard, so we are tempted by simple algorithms that stand in for thinking and keep us from acting. The simplest is to defer any evaluation and to stay clear of the world of values. Let someone else make decisions for us. Let God tell us what is right. Let the members of the politburo or the prophets of the "free market" tell us what is right. Let the Leader, the tribe, the television, the internet tell us what is right.

Ideology produces algorithms of helplessness for us. "Scientific socialism" placed responsibility elsewhere. Does something seem to be going terribly wrong? Has your agricultural policy starved millions of people? Did your alliance with Hitler precede and enable the invasion of your country by Nazi Germany? That was just the price of progress. And there was no alternative. Faith in the "free market" functions much the same way, sometimes exactly the same way. Financial markets have collapsed? Monopolies have coalesced? The billionaires have collected all the new wealth generated in your country since the day you were born? Birth pangs of a new age. There is nothing you can do.

The special American national algorithm is the *false tragedy of choice*. This conviction leads us to constrict the world of values and make ourselves less free. It has cut lanes so deep into common sense that it takes work even to see it.

The false tragedy begins with the acceptance that choices must be made between values. So far, so good. But rather than encouraging you to realize as many values as you can, the false tragedy demands a *final* disposition whenever tension between values appears. In making a choice now, you must nullify *forever* the value you cannot realize. After the unchosen value has been banished, you are to be congratulated on your hardheaded realism: manly nod, downturned lips. And so the realm of values shrinks, as does the range of future choices.

If we think that opting for one value means obliterating another, we retreat step by step from the borderland of the unpredictable.

Rather than using our minds to seek ever new combinations, or ever new values, we persuade ourselves that the easy answer was correct, that only one value really matters. As we concede our right to practice and choose, we try to persuade others to do the same. Freedom then winds down.

Americans' false tragic choice is between entrepreneurship and social justice. But we can sometimes have both, as much of American history shows. It is always right to try for both, since both are good things, and indeed work well together. Without a baseline of fairness, especially for children, there will not be much entrepreneurship. The people who will innovate in the future require care now. The better our public schools, the more start-up stars we will educate. The more we enforce opportunity with antitrust laws, the more room we create for founders of small businesses. The greater their access to health care, the more people are free to try something new. "There is no incompatibility," as the economist Hayek rightly says, "between the state's providing greater security in this way and the preservation of individual freedom."

The false tragedy of choice is where our recognition of the *Leib* fails, where solidarity is blocked, where we live our lies. It works in politics insofar as white people think of themselves as the entrepreneurs, and of Black people as those who take advantage of any program designed for social mobility.

Seeing through the false tragedy of choice moves us toward an idea of freedom that does not depend on exploiting others. If we understand that solidarity is a form of freedom, we will resist the urge to make a quick, dismissive decision. Freedom does not mean denying others good things because of some remorseless logic; it means thinking of ways to hold values, and thus individual people, together.

The first trick in reconciling values is to avoid the trapdoors: submission, totalitarianism, notalitarianism, the false tragedy of choice. We must not give up on a value just because we cannot realize it right now. In another conjuncture, at a later time, with greater wisdom or in better circumstances, or perhaps just after a good night's sleep, we might find a way to combine values. What seems like an irresolvable clash might just be a matter of choosing one value now and another later. Sometimes we simply need to find the viewpoint from which a fulfillment of two or more values can be seen.

Over the course of a life, or the history of a nation, we can find ways to bring values together. As we practice freedom, we climb higher and see new vistas. Simone Weil, musing about "contradictory virtues in the souls of saints," envisioned a winding elevation: "If I am walking up the flank of a mountain, I might first see a lake, and then, after a few steps, a forest. I have to choose between the lake and the forest. If I want to see both the lake and the forest, I have to climb higher."

# Conclusion
## Government

### AWAKENING

I am writing this conclusion in the back seat of a friend's car, looking down on the coast of the Black Sea. I am in the Kherson region of Ukraine, the target of one of the three prongs of the Russian invasion in 2022.

To my southwest is Snake Island, the reputed site of the tomb of Achilles, taken in this war by Russia, then reclaimed by Ukraine. Greek myth records Achilles fighting Amazons—Scythian horsewomen. Though the first encounter of Greece and Scythia was indeed hostile, Scythians of the Black Sea coast and the steppe fed Athens during its time of glory. The lands of what is now southern Ukraine nourished the philosophers who appear on these pages: Socrates, Plato, Aristotle. Greek democracy, famously defended by Pericles, was part of a larger political synthesis with Scythia, whose leaders on this coast merged the two cultures. Euripides placed Iphigenia, the most interesting figure in Greek drama, on Crimea. She led a cult of Artemis that had to be brought to Greek lands so that women could better understand passages in life.

In nearby burial sites, archaeologists have found the Scythian and Greek grave goods of rulers attached to both cultures, and the weapons and armor of women warriors. Men and women died last year, I am thinking now, as we exit for gas, so that people could move freely on this land, as I am doing now. Perhaps some future archaeologist will marvel at the gender diversity of the Ukrainian army, just as we marvel at the Scythians. Russians have stolen the Scythian gold and much else from the region's museums, any object that might connect Ukraine to histories known to others. Russia's attempt to destroy this nation runs from the past to the future, from Ukraine's culture to its agriculture.

It is a very hot September day. A gas station on one side of the highway is a black ruin, while across the asphalt another functions normally. De-miners move slowly through one field as the adjacent one burns. A field ignited during this hottest summer in history poses a problem for people of goodwill. The firemen cannot enter before the de-miners, but the de-miners cannot enter before the firemen. Cooperation is needed because of the menace of climate change but is thwarted by the malice of Russia's hydrocarbon fascism.

The sunflowers are struggling in this heat, even on the fields where the mines have been cleared. The region's farmers export wheat and sunflowers (or their oil) and sell watermelons locally. In normal times, the Ukrainian black earth, extending from this coast northward, can feed about half a billion people. The fertile soil usually nourishes much of Africa and Asia. Hunger, though, has been a weapon in this war. Russia has hindered this supply of food by destroying a major dam, bombing the ports, and mining the fields. I slept through air raid sirens last night in Odesa; the missile was headed for the port at Izmail. I wanted to begin writing this conclusion yesterday, but the place I had chosen to work had been hit by a rocket.

The fields are calming in their familiarity and inviting in their difference, a more colorful Midwest spilling out into a saltwater sea—one that in childhood I knew from the stories of Iphigenia and Prometheus. We sometimes had a row or two of sunflowers, but I had never before walked between fields and been able to see only sunflowers and blue sky. I met farmers earlier today who had de-mined fields with improvised equipment and got some of their crops in. The farm machinery was mostly familiar, although I had to be told that some burned-out chassis were once John Deere tractors. One farmer had a Ukrainian trident mounted where I would have expected a weathervane.

They have been tough and ingenious, these farmers, and they have also had help. It took an army (supported by Ukrainian civil society) to de-occupy this land. The bunkers and trenches are still here to be seen. An international foundation provided some of the combine harvesters. The farmers had laborers, all of whom had stories, some very traumatic, of Russian occupation. As we sit and eat slices of watermelon, one of them calls the occupiers "rashysty," a Ukrainian neologism that means "Russian fascists" and is a play on words in several languages. This reminds me that these farmlands, once steppe, are precisely where Indo-European languages began. Ancient Greek, Shakespeare's English, the Ukrainian we are speaking now, indeed the languages spoken by almost half of the people alive today—all have their origin right here.

The farmers give us gifts of watermelons. They fill the trunk; some are now riding next to me in the back seat. My friends and I will take them back to Kyiv and give them away as gifts. As much of the Kherson region was de-occupied in late 2022, watermelons became a sign of joy, of the unity of the country. During this horrible war, when almost everyone in Ukraine seems to be grieving, people here seem all the more attached to small gestures of solidarity, all the more open to saying what actually matters, to enunciating the small virtues of everyday life, which are no less real than the mines in the fields.

Ukrainian resistance reminds us that freedom cannot be entrusted to impersonal forces, or to wealthy people or powerful corporations that tell us that there are no alternatives and that there is nothing we can do. We can learn something about which structures are best, and some are certainly better than others. But we can build them only with the help of values. "We rely not upon management or trickery," as Pericles said in his funeral oration for Athenian soldiers who had perished in the Peloponnesian War, "but upon our own hearts and hands."

## GEOMETRY

The sun shines on a field in Kherson oblast; a watermelon grows, I eat it, I write some paragraphs in a car. Smoke rises from the ground in the distance. The sun shines on a farm in Clinton County, Ohio; the corn rises; I pull a cord and ring a bell. Wisps of cloud flee overhead. Our stories are a play on time, back and forth; I need my improbable past for my unpredictable future. My past began before me, and my future continues after me.

Our universe is a play of matter and energy, back and forth. Life is a special form of that play. We are a special form of life, capable of freedom because we are capable of seeing our own purposes and realizing them. In the Christian Gospels (Luke 17:21), the "kingdom of God" is within us. Eighteen hundred years after Luke, Enlightenment skeptics rightly said that virtues cannot be extracted from the world around us. The world of what *ought to be,* the fifth dimension, has its own rules. We can make them work for us, and for the world, but first we have to understand them.

We have encountered, but not quite yet listed, five rules of the geometry of the fifth dimension. The first rule is difference: the world of *what is* (the first four dimensions) and *what ought to be* (the fifth) are distinct. They can be brought together only through us, through our bodies. The second is plurality. In the realm of *what should be* are many virtues, not one. The third rule is intransitivity. The various goods are good for various reasons. The virtues are not reducible to one another. They cannot be ranked. It is not that honesty is better than loyalty; they are simply different.

The fourth rule is tension. We cannot just pull all the virtues from the fifth dimension into our four of time and space. In practice, the virtues compete with one another. I might like to be punctual, but I should also be patient. I might wish to be a person of integrity, but sometimes I should compromise. We might value skepticism, yet we have faith. Love is blind, but it takes discernment to know what not to see. That leads us to the fifth rule: combinability. People can bring together virtues in creative ways and sometimes create new ones.

Imperfection enables freedom. The world of values (not only Stein but also Weil and Kołakowski used this phrase) is flawed. It cannot be made perfect, but it can be improved. The rocket attack that destroyed the café also hit the main cathedral in Odesa, leaving glass all around. Seeing the world of values is like watching the sun's rays scatter through the jagged colors of a broken stained-glass window. The light is thrown in many directions, and the rays cross one another. The result is beautiful but strange and a bit different every time. At some point, we realize that we can pick up the fragments and make our own patterns.

We do not have Eden, a place where all the light comes together, where all good things are united. Nor is there a single truth of which all the facts are mere parts. And that is why we have a chance at freedom. A fascist philosopher repeatedly cited by Vladimir Putin, Ivan Ilyin, was haunted by imperfection and called on Russia to overcome it with violence. If there were only one truth and all facts were just elements of it, then some leader or some machine could claim to have calculated the future for us. If there were only one value and all others were just fragments of it, then some leader or some machine could dictate for us the right course of action. But this cannot be done.

The space between *what is* and *what ought to be* is where we roam as free people, extending the borderland of the unpredictable. We decide which values to affirm, in what combination, for what reasons, and at what time. Then we try again. With practice, we attain our own human form of grace.

There is no escape from judgment, the choice of values. We can add our own rules to those of the fifth dimension, but we remain subject to its peculiar geometry. There will be tensions among the rules we choose, just as there are clashes among virtues. No rule can be final, since there is no way to rank all the virtues. We always have to judge the circumstances in order to decide which rules might apply. In an essay titled "The Priest and the Jester," Kołakowski argued that it is right to make rules and also right to mock them. For Confucius, one rule of propriety was not to overdo it. Gillian Welch sings in "Miss Ohio" that "you want to do right, but not right now."

We cannot wish away the rules of the fifth dimension, any more than we can wish away gravity or entropy. It is when we accept the tensions and clashes, and navigate courageously among them, that we become free people and help others to become so. Simone Weil wrote that our task was to see the clash among virtues for what it is, and to make it as easy for one another to handle as we can. This purpose is served by the forms of freedom. They are the justification of government, and the outlines of a good one.

## INDIVIDUALS

Freedom never just means government leaving us alone; nor does it mean our leaving government alone. The forms of freedom must be daily practice. The forms of freedom legitimate government and guide individuals.

Consider sovereignty, the first form of freedom. Children need support to gain the capacities that will allow them to flourish in freedom. This is generational political work, which cannot be done without government and without individuals guiding that government.

That said, there is much else that individuals can do. We can all find settings where learning about others will help us to understand ourselves. Support a school. Help raise a child who is not yours. Volunteer. Read aloud at a library. Coach a team. Vote for candidates who favor parental leave.

The same holds for unpredictability, the second form of freedom. It also demands structures. We can be free only if we reimagine and restructure social media. No individual can alter the shape of the companies that mine our brains. This has to be a matter for policy.

Yet we can all do something ourselves. We need to affirm our own combinations of values rather than conform. We should not obey in advance. Our personal choices and our common labor set an example.

We can also work to keep ourselves unpredictable by meeting people and buying (or borrowing) books. Better than raging against the machine is reading against the machine. Search engines make you more mechanical; library shelves make you less so. Staring at screens makes you easier to handle; listening to people makes you less so.

We all need mobility, a trajectory of our own. To move in life, we need structures awaiting us as we mature. No individual can build the infrastructure of possibility alone; we need government to build the architecture of the American Dream, whether it be autonomous and affordable public universities or functional public roads. Whether government in fact does so will depend on individuals. Free adults will have to support the institutions that helped them, with their voices, votes, and time.

Factuality too requires institutions, such as local reporting, and this in turn demands policy. Yet it also requires ethical commitment, and this is the work of individuals. We can say that we believe in truth. We can treat facts as a worthy pursuit. We can recognize reporters as the heroes of our time. Paying for newspaper subscriptions is a start. Too often, we profit from the reporting of others without rewarding them. Subscribe to media that offer investigative reporting, and post to social media items that are reported by a human. Support campaigns to tax social media companies in order to fund local reporting.

Without solidarity, we fail to see others' travails as like our own, and so we lose the ability to see ourselves. Choosing a way to express solidarity makes us freer—and helps us to resist frustration and demoralization. Deliberate in organized settings. Pick a civil society organization to join, and another (if you can afford it) to support financially. Try to listen. Remember that neighbors might have had worse luck. Help others vote. Listen to those whose families' historical experiences are very different from your own.

Find organizations that allow you to help others. If you have the means, pay off someone else's medical debt. Support a project in a war-torn country that empowers those affected. (Documenting Ukraine is one I helped establish while writing this book.) If you can, show solidarity by taking care of Earth. Global warming and pollution generally affect the poor first. Eat less meat, plant a tree, insulate your home, get solar panels, use and agitate for public transportation.

As climate change makes Earth less habitable and accelerates and exacerbates conflict, the fifth dimension becomes harder to find. Make a point of mentioning climate change every day. Americans know that it is real, but we are deterred from speaking about it by an entirely artificial controversy. Do not vote for a party that denies climate change. People who lie about the end of the world will keep lying until the world ends.

## DIVISIONS

You were not born free. But neither were you born to be a vessel of lies. Your destiny is neither subjugation nor automation. You can evaluate, transform, and take responsibility. Declare yourself free. Then accommodate yourself to tender virtues and bruising facts, to friends and neighbors, to fellow citizens, but not to expectations or algorithms. Life can be much better than it seems to us now, as individuals and as citizens. We can become free.

Our political divisions draw us away from freedom as principle, making it harder to get to freedom as practice. They have been hardened by the collapse of local news, the rise of oligarchy, and the reach of social media. The algorithms push us toward mindless controversy and away from mindful discussion of priorities. The repetition of mechanized clichés makes our political discussion endlessly stale. The mechanization has to be addressed by government policy, but the human misunderstandings are for us to resolve.

Some conservatives proclaim that they want freedom but that sadly it must be traded for security. This is almost never true. In general, we need freedom for security, and security for freedom. Others proclaim freedom as the highest value but have trouble saying what this means. Right-wing characterizations of freedom tend to be negative, which is a dead end. If we take negative freedom to the extreme, we just reach oligarchic chaos. This then intersects with the fascist idea that we need a Leader who is above the law and should be allowed to stage coups.

Certainly, the state can be oppressive. But the actual alternatives are better government and worse government. We can and should be very creative about the justification and shape of government. But the choice of no government means groundless faith (real or fake) that some larger force will organize matters for us. It just brings bad government, tyranny by the ruthless and the rich. Annulling government in the circumstances of the twenty-first century means humiliation and extinction by climate change.

Americans on the Left make a different mistake: they fail to acknowledge freedom as the value of values, preferring equality. Recognition of our equal dignity is, to be sure, necessary for any discussion of freedom. But equality is a beginning rather than an end. There is no tragic choice between freedom and equality. They work together. The forms of freedom, all five of them, create the conditions for less inequality in practice. Without the virtues kept alive by free people, equality loses all substance in politics. Stripping it away from freedom makes it meaningless. We can all be equally miserable, equally zombified, or equally dead.

It is freedom that enables us to choose and combine values, including those thought to be progressive. Although the Left often concedes the language of freedom to the Right, people on the Left do propose policies that would further freedom. They just usually fail to make their case in those terms.

What seems to be a permanent clash between Left and Right reveals an unspoken (and as-yet-unspeakable) American consensus: freedom is indeed the value of values, as some on the Right claim; yet to live free, we need the structures that many on the Left support.

It would be naïve, of course, to deny that some Americans want to be tyrants. We have seen an all-too-predictable coup attempt by a man concerned about preserving his money and staying out of prison. Some of our hydrocarbon barons and our Silicon Valley supermen think they should be running the world. And many Americans do like submitting to a person or an entity that provides lies for all occasions. That is why freedom is a struggle.

Freedom might bring sense to politics. If the Right can accept that a concept needs structures, and the Left that structures need a concept, then freedom could become the basis of a broad agreement about the structure of government in the United States. In the meantime, free people can overcome at least some political divides by applying their own values and moving beyond what seem like the inevitable binaries.

It will take a bit of reflection, some acknowledgment of others, and perhaps a smile. Leszek Kołakowski proposed that we should all become conservative-liberal-socialists. I see his lopsided smile in my mind's eye as I recall his provocative formulation, but the idea is a serious one. To regard freedom as central is liberal. The conviction that freedom is about virtues is conservative. The belief that structures gird values is socialist. These three approaches to politics are perfectly justified and complementary. They do not succeed in isolation. If they work at all, they work together.

Though it might seem heresy to say it, to be a democrat is to be a republican, and to be a republican is to be a democrat.


## DEMOCRATS

We link the words *democracy* and *freedom,* and rightly so. Freedom is the value of values, and the case for democracy must begin with it. Democracy is the system toward which the forms of freedom lead, the best resolution of freedom as a principle.

"We the people" will be sovereign in government only when individual persons are sovereign in their lives. Only the unpredictable voter (in the unrigged district in the unmonetized election) gets the attention of the candidate. A person who is socially mobile will believe that better futures are possible and will vote for the candidate who offers one. A person who expresses solidarity will care about the votes of others; a person who cares about factuality will count the ballots. Democracy remains the best available way to address differences in value commitments.

Just as the forms of freedom favor democracy, democracy favors the forms of freedom. Democracy marks sovereignty by establishing the vote as a political coming-of-age. It opens avenues for unpredictable action, since no one knows in advance who will run for office (you could) or who will win a fair election. It promises mobility, since votes can bring policies that change how life is lived. Democracy leaves behind a trail of facts, a record of people ruling themselves. And it expresses solidarity: when the rules are right, all Americans have a voice. The rich and powerful can organize in secrecy; the people as a whole cannot and generally don't want to.

Freedom requires a sense of past and future, and democracy produces political time. Democracy invites deliberation, insisting that we take the time we need to declare and accommodate values. Its enemies are always in a hurry to make us angry or efficient or both. We need a sense of an open future, which democracy provides. Democracy divides time into foreseeable intervals, from election to election. It creates a sense of durability, since elections are a procedure for creating a new government on a regular basis, something that other regime types lack. Democracy hinders aspiring tyrants from staying in power until death. Democracy ensconces us in the greater history of our own country: our own choices are part of a deeper past and, we may hope, a brighter future.

Democracy is not only a procedure but an awakening. It is fifth-dimensional politics, just as freedom is fifth-dimensional life. It does not arise on its own. It needs us and our values. Democracy is a verb disguised as a noun. Its supporters must believe in it and improve it.

## VOTERS

A democracy has the quality of being "responsive to all of its citizens," says the political theorist Robert Dahl. This is not America, not yet. Applying the principles that the American Founders elucidated until they are made consistent, we should seek an ever more extensive understanding of what liberty demands: not negative but positive freedom, not for the few but for everyone.

It is impossible to base a voting system on the principle of government getting out of the way. The closure of voting booths is a sign of an ailing democracy, not a healthy one. Only positive freedom makes sense: people apply their values in the world thanks to institutions justified by their capacity to help. Freedom is positive in the sense that it arises from us; it is positive in the sense that it affirms values; and it is positive in the sense that it informs politics. All that begins with knowledge of others, which leads to knowledge of ourselves. Only by taking a hard look at our history can we see the failures in American voting and make them right. Democracy is self-correction.

A democracy will depend upon laws that enable participation. But not all laws do so. Some laws have been (and remain) deliberate instruments of disenfranchisement. Women were excluded from the vote in the United States until the 1920s, and Black people in the South until the 1960s (after a brief interval in the 1860s and 1870s). African Americans and Native Americans today face entrenched difficulties in voting. American laws also allow the very richest to avoid paying taxes and to influence elections (and then policy) by spending money. Such laws disenfranchise all nonbillionaires by granting to the few electoral power not enjoyed by the many. A country with oligarchical elections and voter suppression is not a land of the free. A democratic America would establish an equal right to vote for all citizens at all times.

Citizens who happen to live in Washington, D.C., which is more populous than Wyoming or Vermont, are not allowed to elect representatives to Congress. Citizens who live in Puerto Rico, which is more populous than twenty-one of the fifty states, cannot vote for president. They elect a resident commissioner to Congress, but that official has no vote. Americans should not be denied representation by the accident of where they were born, or where they find a job, or where they fall in love. Puerto Rico and Washington, D.C., should be states.

Fifty-two is a nice number: about the number of weeks in a year, the exact number of cards in a deck, and precisely four times the number of original colonies. For each stripe there could be exactly four stars. It would be an elegant flag.

A right to vote involves a declaration (I vote) as well as an accommodation (we make voting easy for one another). Arbitrary laws place the burden on some people to prove who they are, or they establish tests that allow officials to halt a vote. Voting stations are routinely closed so that some people must wait hours while others walk right in. Memory laws are passed, so that children never learn that such practices continue a racist tradition. This is a way to block us from knowing one another and thereby to keep us unfree. It hinders the generational labor we all need for freedom. There is no excuse for any of this, and much shame.

Too many people in the current fifty states do not vote. About 90 percent of Canadians are registered to vote; America should do no worse. Canada has a Register of Future Electors that prepares young people to become voters: Why should America not have something similar? It would affirm every form of freedom: the sovereignty that young people attain; the unpredictability that they can manifest; the mobility that they will want; the factuality of one vote per person; the solidarity of a common tradition.

Voting should not be denied to any citizen, including people who have been convicted of crimes. Denying incarcerated and formerly incarcerated people the vote is a moral hazard, since it tempts politicians to imprison people who might vote against them. That has been American practice for forty years. Hence our system selects for politicians who think about how best to prevent citizens from voting. A democracy cannot be formed from people whose first thought is how to disable it.

Our own first thoughts, if we wish to be free ourselves, have to be for the predicaments of others. If we can empathize with the *Leib* of others, we can have a *demos,* a people, and then we can have a democracy. Only by imagining bodies in voting booths, or waiting to vote in long lines, or intimidated from voting, can we see the problems that must be resolved.

Voter suppression reflects the racism of the past and projects racism into the future. Since both its perpetrators and its victims know that its purpose is white supremacy, it confirms tribalism and reproduces a politics of pain. Doing nothing to halt voter suppression means complicity in white supremacy. If white Americans do not care that others' votes are at risk, they take for granted that the country belongs to them as a tribe or a mob and thereby partake in the decline of democracy.

If you are white, this might seem like a strong formulation. A simple test can verify its fairness. The philosopher John Rawls invented a reality check called the "veil of ignorance." It asks you to bracket what you know about your place in society behind this "veil," so as to look at the world more objectively and make better policy. The philosopher Charles Mills noted that we must know some basic facts about a given society in order to know what knowledge about ourselves is relevant. One of these is race. So let's imagine that you know that Black people are hindered from voting. And now let's place you behind a veil of ignorance, such that you don't know the American social fact of your own race. How would you think about voting laws then?

If you knew that you might open your eyes and be an African American, would you care more about voter suppression? If the answer is yes, and it surely is, that means that being white has desensitized you to a basic question of freedom. Happily, as free people we can change our minds and live in truth.

If some are denied the right to vote, the ever-present risk is that the vote will become meaningless for all. Those who can vote will tend to regard it as a privilege rather than a right and see its denial to others as confirmation of that privilege. Rulers can then take advantage of that sensibility to push the system to a point where voting is a mere ritual. To declare for democracy, then, is to make the accommodations necessary for every citizen to participate in government. Everyone who speaks of "democracy" is logically committed to the proposition that all adult citizens have the right to vote.

A large representative democracy works only when people are in fact represented. Democracy is rule by the people, so nonhuman entities (algorithms, corporations, and foundations) should neither vote nor pay for political campaigns. No American should count for more than any other American. Campaigns should be transparently and publicly financed. Candidates should be publicly funded; voter registration should be automatic; voting stations should be plentiful; ballots should be paper; gerrymandering should be outlawed. These formulations might sound radical; in other democracies, they are commonsensical ground rules.

Voting is not some technical matter to be left to the whims of pettifogging administrators and self-interested partisans. It is an action, par excellence, in which we can gain sovereignty by imagining the position of others. When voting works as it should, it expresses the forms of freedom: we are sovereign, and so we know what we are doing; we are unpredictable, and so others do not know what we will do; we are mobile in that our vote can change the future; we endorse factuality when we vote on the basis of what we know; we show solidarity in our understanding that each vote counts equally. We declare with our own votes, and we accommodate ourselves to the final count.

In a land of the free, we would take pride in how many of us vote, and how easily. Election day would be a national holiday in our republic, to celebrate our vote and to ensure it.


## REPUBLICANS

Americans sometimes say that their country is a republic, meaning that it need not be a democracy. This makes no sense. Both words commit us to the same principle: we should rule ourselves.

In the ancient cases, the practice of "rule by the people" (democracy) or the definition of government as a "common matter" or "the people's issue" (republic) meant assemblies of citizens. In the American system, voting (democracy) is meant to create a government that is representative of the common good (a republic). As Thomas Jefferson wrote to James Madison, the "avowed object" of democracy is "the nourishment of the republican principles of our constitution."

Americans who describe the system as a republic rather than a democracy are citing Madison, who was comparing the American representative system to ancient assemblies. He was *not* saying that a republic excludes while a democracy includes. He had in mind representation as a means of inclusion: whereas the chaos of ancient democracies prevented the people from ruling, voting would enable orderly government. Madison thought that an electoral democracy would allow the meaningful participation of a far greater number of people than was possible in older forms of democracy. In this he was absolutely right.

Having a republic means paying attention to that greater public. It asks us to pursue our own freedom by knowing the situation of others and by creating the appropriate institutions for knowing the preferences of all. Those who care about a republic would never hinder democratic practice. They would simplify representation rather than complicate it. They would make our present system work better than its iterations in previous centuries, just as Madison wanted the American system to work better than Greek and Roman assemblies.

Representation has to be more complex than assembly, since it must involve elections. Many Americans, including some who sit on the Supreme Court, fetishize the administrative difficulties created around voting, supporting bureaucracy over representation. Getting law and practice behind voter suppression is simply a way to exclude people without having to say that they are not equal to others. Disingenuous racism is still racism. It is wrong to make others less free for bad reasons. And it is also wrong, and damaging, to live inside a lie.

The Supreme Court has ruled that spending money on election campaigns is freedom of speech, and it has acted to make it easy to spend private money (and hard to spend public money) on campaigns.

The ideological basis of these decisions was a very explicit libertarianism, which is a belief system at odds with freedom. It is farcical to imagine that an election can be considered from the premise that the distribution of wealth at any given moment is somehow sanctified, and from the norm that the only unnatural action is to limit the power of the wealthy in any way.

These Court rulings begin from artificially limited situations that frame the question of free expression and elections in a catastrophically narrow way. If one were seriously concerned about freedom of speech during electoral campaigns, one would ask first of all whether the least protected—the dissenters, the poor, the traditionally disenfranchised—have a platform to make risky statements and are protected after they make them. One would ask whether everyone finds it equally easy to vote, to campaign, to run for office. In ruling on the cases as it has, the Court frames freedom of speech as the question of whether a given wealthy person or entity has been harmed by not being able to spend money on elections. This makes a mockery of freedom of speech before the deliberation even begins. To frame freedom of speech as the wealthy person's right not to have to run against publicly financed opponents goes beyond mockery to insult.

If we do not immediately see this oligarchical nonsense for what it is, this is perhaps because we have been trained to think of freedom of speech as negative, as only a matter of preventing the government from doing something, rather than as positive, as protecting human beings who take risks by speaking truth to power and as creating settings in which people can listen to one another.

The freedom of expression of the very wealthy would not be threatened by holding fair elections in which they have the same right to run for office and to vote as everyone else. No supporter of a republic can accept the absurd notion that a central concern in elections is conferring explicit and additional political privileges upon those already dominant in society thanks to their wealth. Two thousand five hundred years of recorded political thought and political practice reveal the basic fallacy. The point of freedom of speech is to challenge accumulated power, which means accumulated wealth. Associating freedom of speech with spending private money on elections is therefore perverse in the extreme.

Wealth inequality is always a problem for a republic; privileging wealth in elections is a direct endorsement of oligarchy. It puts the power and prestige of the existing government behind the oligarchical transition, laundering money by dirtying democracy. Confusing money with speech summons the oligarchs to appear with a brazen message but without personal responsibility. Representation should be connected to public rather than private interests. That is, after all, what *republic* means.

## HISTORIANS

The American Founders were amateur historians of the Greeks and the Romans; it helps us to be amateur historians of the Founders.

Classical Greece generated the useful conceptual contrast between democracy and oligarchy. In the fifth century B.C., Athens was a democracy and Sparta was an oligarchy. When Sparta defeated Athens, it imposed its own system. Athenians then realized that their own inequality was part of the problem. The ancients understood that great differences in wealth threatened democracy, and that the very rich could use propaganda to bring it down—perhaps siding with oligarchs from other countries as they did so.

The history and language of ancient Rome brings the equally useful contrast between republic and empire. In Roman history, a republic was the opposite of an empire; in an empire, there was no common good, and inequality was openly avowed. The founding of an empire was the abolition of a republic, and the founding of a republic was the abolition of an empire. The American Founders contended with this ancient past as they tried to establish a better democracy and a better republic. It is one of the most appealing things about them.

We have to do the same: learn from the past if we identify with it. This does not mean feeling ashamed. Pride is part of patriotism, and

Americans have very good reason to be proud. It does mean listening to people who have other attitudes to the past. Only by knowing others can we build the institutions that are right for everyone. It is incongruous, in any event, to take pride without taking responsibility. Schools must teach the hard parts of American history—those censored by cowards as "divisive concepts." People who are taught to fear "divisive concepts" cannot be sovereign, since they will lack the terms of engagement needed to learn from others. A nation built on fear of conversation will be too fragile and porous for solidarity. The toughness needed to face the past is the same toughness needed to face the future.

Sovereign people know the risks. If we identify with mobs and overlook the people in our lives, our republic is in trouble. If we worship oligarchs who identify with oligarchs abroad, we are in trouble. Republics die from wealth inequality. At the time when the United States was established, the most notable republic was the Polish-Lithuanian one, which had existed at that point for more than two hundred years. Thanks to enormous inequality of wealth, native oligarchs and then foreign empires captured its parliament. Like the Athenians before them, the wiser Poles then realized that oligarchs in one country have more in common with oligarchs in another country than with their own people.

This history is forgotten today, but for the Founders, the partition of Poland was a process unfolding before their eyes. Some of its political refugees came to fight for the American Revolution, in the hopes that a sound republic could be established here. The American struggle against Britain might well have failed without them. Tadeusz Kościuszko, a military engineer, was an indispensable officer on the American side. It is difficult to see how the revolutionary Continental Army, which he served without pay, would have maintained itself without his skills and devotion. When Kościuszko was finally compensated with an estate, well after the war, he asked his friend Thomas Jefferson to sell it to manumit and educate slaves (including Jefferson's).

It helps to know such historical details, which sometimes help us to see ourselves. Like the Founders, we must critique in order to create, and we must know some history in order to critique. We have to be at least as thoughtful about the eighteenth century, about that rebellion of 1776, as the Founders were about ancient Athens and Rome. The language of democracies, oligarchies, republics, and empires that the Founders inherited from antiquity remains applicable. Like American democracy, an American republic is an aspiration. My incarcerated student Maurice was right to say that "freedom is the process of grappling with the past."

We can excuse Jefferson for his flaws, idealize the eighteenth century, and miss our chance. Or we can take Jefferson's ideas seriously, seeing what he did not. We can develop his rights to "life, liberty, and the pursuit of happiness" further. We can have positive freedom for everyone, in a democratic republic that allows good government. The future could be so much better than the present.

## CHILDREN

If you are reading one vignette of this book every day, more than a million American children have been born since you turned the first page. I finished this book in 2023, and perhaps you are reading it in 2026—the American semiquincentennial, halfway to the half-millennium. If so, five times as many American children were born in the interval between my writing and your reading than there were total people living in all thirteen colonies in 1776.

Every single one of those children of the 2020s is just as much an American as Jefferson or Franklin or Washington. And in a sense they are more important, for their lives, in freedom or unfreedom, are America's future. If we want a land of the free, we will have to imagine those children and their predicament. A legitimate American government would be grounded in freedom, which means (can only mean) one that creates the right conditions for the people still to come.

This does not mean toasting the younger generation and remarking lightly that it will save the rest of us. It won't, and can't, without the help of older generations and sound policy. Even if the United States becomes a perfect democratic republic in the 2030s, the interests of the millions of children born in the 2020s will not be directly represented by their vote until the 2040s. By that time, our choices will already have decided the fate of their world.

Let us assume that we get this right. Then let's imagine their perspective, decades hence, looking back from a land of the free. In 2076, at America's tercentennial, children born in 2026 will be in the prime of life. How will that prior half century appear to them, in retrospect, looking back from 2076 to 2026? What must happen in the 2020s for them to live in a land of the free in 2076?

In the short term, Ukraine must win its war against Russia. If its allies fail it, tyrants will be encouraged around the world, and other such wars will follow. In 2024 and 2028, America will need presidents and presidential candidates who believe in counting votes rather than starting coups. If we can get through the 2020s on those terms, we have a chance to spend the next half century in a self-correcting democratic republic.

We will have to set aside imperial immobility and sadopopulism, and address racism and wealth inequality. That will require us to rethink freedom, confront the past, and reconsider the meaning of *democracy* and *republic*. Climate disaster will have to be mitigated—no child born in the 2020s will lead a life of freedom unless we do that. To become a land of the free by the tercentennial, Americans must get through five decades without the politics of catastrophe—and without the catastrophe itself.

We still treat the interests of the fossil oligarchs as more important than the freedom and security of everyone else. We still dig up the remains of ancient life and burn them. We are still consuming the energy left behind by hundreds of millions of years of life, and in doing so we are accelerating the end of our own kind of life. We need solar panels, wind power, and miniature stars: fusion reactions on Earth. Fusion could create essentially unlimited energy without greenhouse gas emissions. A country that could reach the moon in eight

years in the 1960s should be able to attain fusion in twenty years starting in the 2020s.

The energy market is a social creation. It can be altered. Diverting
a fraction of today's gigantic hydrocarbon subsidies to fusion, solar,
and wind could clear our skies—and our minds. All American subsidies of oil and gas drilling, including access to federal land, should
cease.

The transition to sustainable energy can be hastened by requiring
firms to pay for emitting carbon dioxide. Proceeds would go to a public trust, a "Tercentennial Trust," which would pay every American
adult $2,076 every Fourth of July. Reducing the threat of catastrophe
affirms our right to life. Halting the politics of catastrophe favors the
cause of liberty. Doing it this way will bring some happiness to American families every year on Independence Day.

## SOVEREIGNS

So much for catastrophe. What about capabilities, the form of freedom
we have called sovereignty? What must we provide to children born in
the 2020s so that they will live in a land of the free in the 2070s? Three
new rights would complement Jefferson's traditional ones: the right
to vote, the right to one's mind, and the right to health care.

One way to endorse sovereignty is to claim a right to vote. This
involves all the measures already discussed, as well as automatically
registering young people to vote as part of their public education. It
would likely also make sense to lower the voting age to sixteen. Let's
please not pretend that teenagers are less competent than their grandparents, or any worse at navigating modern media. They have much
longer to live in the American republic and an incentive to make that
republic livable.

Applying what we know about the brain and social media, we must
care for young minds. A second way to strengthen sovereignty is to
claim a right to one's mind: *habeas mentem*. It is a venerable idea that
freedom begins from the control of one's own body: *habeas corpus*. In

the twenty-first century, taking freedom seriously means redoubling concern for our embodied minds, and attending to sovereignty and unpredictability as forms of freedom. Creating a mind that can evaluate the world and make unpredictable choices requires the tender attention of many other minds.

A third way to support sovereignty is a right to health care. No more American babies should be born into a country where medical attention is uncertain. To be rushed out of the hospital only hours after birth, the typical American experience for newborn and mother, is an ill omen. Uneven coverage by private insurance and unreliable care in private hospitals build fear into parents' lives and illness into their children's.

## PARENTS

Universal access to health care is possible, desirable in itself, and necessary for a future in freedom. Jefferson spoke of rights to life and to the pursuit of happiness as well as to liberty. Nothing hinders the pursuit of happiness more than ill health, as Jefferson understood. And, of course, better health care means longer lives. But the case for a right to health care is fundamentally about liberty.

If we were all insured, we would be less fearful—and so we would be freer in our lives and choices and less vulnerable to tyrants. People would no longer be pinned to bad jobs for fear of losing insurance coverage. Americans would all be more unpredictable, sovereign, and mobile. Policies can support these forms of freedom; they will arise and endure only with factuality and solidarity. In addition to health care, all American children would have access to clean air, food, and shelter. The creeping privatization of water has made us less mobile and less free. Potable and available tap water keeps us going.

We live in only one direction in time, from birth to childhood to adulthood to old age. Children need families and caretakers, and those families and caretakers need time. This can be supplied only by sound policy: maternity leave, paternity leave, predictable work scheduling, paid sick days, public childcare, and vacations. I have lived with children in countries that have these policies, which lend the gentle hint of freedom to the roughness of the everyday. Families need calm to navigate life's passages, and thus they need public school, health care, and retirement pensions. When such institutions are in place, social mobility replaces daily fear, and a land of the free can prosper and endure.

If we do not establish the forms of freedom around children, then child-rearing oppresses everyone. Fear opens the way to unfreedom, and much of the fear in our country has to do with children. You cannot be a better parent than the structures around you permit you to be. Few American parents can devote the time, attention, and resources to their children that they would like. And the work of having children is greater when anxiety is the norm. In a land of the free, all of this would have to change for the better.

## MOVERS

As for the children themselves, they are eventually going to need to break away from their families and find work. As we learned during the years of social immobility under Covid regimes, frozen lives are incompatible with freedom. Young Americans need a renewed American Dream.

Freedom begins with the body and with the recognition of the bodies of others. Many Americans require spaces that are designed for those who cannot walk. Once we understand that freedom is mobility and mobility is physical, we have an argument for designing buildings and public spaces for everyone. Regardless of physical ability, we know that people feel better and more at home where there are parks, trees, and green spaces in cities. We need the trees so that we can survive climate change; we also need them to help us get through the day.

Whether people in the future are free will depend on how they can move within and between cities. Four out of five Americans now live in cities, and soon it will be nine out of ten. We should think not of smart cities but of enabling and empowering cities, designed to encourage movement, encounters, and protest. Americans should be using public transportation within and between cities, which is generally unavailable in the United States.

I grew up at the intersection of a road called "Centerville Station," but the eponymous rail station itself no longer existed. A few miles north was "Feedwire Road," which referred to an interurban railway network that had once served the Dayton area, including Centerville. Local rail had vanished by the time I was a boy, and travel by any means but the automobile was unthinkable. The last train departed Dayton in 1979; ten years later, as communism came to an end in Europe, Dayton's beautiful Union Station was closed.

The United States must invest in rails. Not every line needs to be profitable for the system as a whole to energize the economy. Cars can help people to feel free, but people should not be forced to use them. Automobiles warm the atmosphere, but they also (in the present regulatory climate) reproduce inequality. Predatory lending prevents people from buying simple automobiles, and it leaves them in the end with no car and much debt. Making it harder for people to move makes it harder for them to live and indeed to work.

## WORKERS

And yet we do work, and we will continue to do so. The robots had their chance to take all the jobs during the pandemic, and they did not. If young people in the twenty-first century are going to chase the American Dream, the labor market they enter will have to be designed around humans and their freedom. Rather than pronouncing the incantatory phrase "free market," we should arrange the market in such a way as to enable mobility for people. Markets follow rules, and rules can be changed. Right now, for example, American companies get a tax break for buying robots but not for training people. This should be reversed.

Russia reveals the extreme of immobility and wealth inequality. The Tsar Bell is still on the ground. Markets fail when monopolies arise, and our markets are already hugely distorted. The failure ruins the lives of people seeking work. Young people should not be banished into a sticky matrix of economic monocultures. If the purpose of the market is freedom, then some American companies are just far too big. Despite some promising legislation in the early 2020s, the problems here are very deep.

Monopolies make a mockery of entrepreneurship, rewarding property owners and shareholders rather than people who start businesses and take risks. Friedrich Hayek rightly insisted that the government break up monopolies, which he said were no better than Soviet central planning. The United States has the appropriate laws on the books (the Clayton and Sherman acts). Federal agencies and judges need only enforce them as written. The Founders understood that monopolies were incompatible with democracy. That is a lesson not to be forgotten, lest we invite new kinds of empire over ourselves.

To arrange the market to enable freedom, we will have to restructure financial timekeeping. We treat a company's quarterly returns as the measure of its success. This hinders good choices, gives robots advantages over people, and inflates inequality. The quarterly report is just an accounting convention. Changing the way companies report would encourage them to think more broadly about customers and workers.

Social mobility requires cooperative labor. Freedom includes the right to organize. Union membership girds solidarity. It also supports factuality, since dealing with unions keeps managers and companies (and reporters) honest. Labor unions exemplify civil society and defend civil rights. Without them, a labor market stagnates, and social mobility slows. Labor unions, historically, have been one of the few sites where interracial coalitions form. They can be relied upon to support democracy. And labor organizing, because it involves human contact, can weaken the myths that algorithms tend to spread.

## PRISONERS

If the purpose of the market is freedom, money should not be made by detaining human bodies. When the government pays companies to imprison, it creates a lobby for locking people up. Private prisons, private jails, private detention centers, and private concentration camps should all be banned. Private contractors should not be employed for any policy of coercion, including border enforcement, and certainly not for the control of demonstrations.

It is wrong to incentivize incarceration. More deeply, it is wrong to confuse punishment with freedom. When Václav Havel was elected president of Czechoslovakia in 1990, his first impulse was to release prisoners who had been sentenced by the communist regime. He had reason to believe that there had been systemic injustice.

When communism came to an end in eastern Europe, roughly the same percentage of the Czechoslovak population was behind bars as the American. The American percentage kept increasing. Even as we proclaimed the inevitability of freedom, more and more Americans lost it, in a basic sense. Even as Americans deplored ethnic cleansing in Yugoslavia, few noticed the escalating racial imprisonment at home. A search of *The New York Times* in the 1990s reveals that the phrase "ethnic cleansing" appears 1,928 times, and "mass incarceration" only 132.

To be sure, Americans committed crimes. But that was not the cause of mass incarceration. Crime rates, violent crime rates, and murder rates all peaked in 1991, the year the Soviet Union collapsed. Then they began to decline. But there was no freedom dividend: The number of American prisoners almost doubled in the 1990s.

Rates of incarceration correlate not with local crime statistics but rather with poverty and with the population of African Americans. Mass incarceration affects Black people more than others, and we will not resolve the problem without confronting the larger question of how other Americans regard (or disregard) Black bodies. We need solidarity to get to mobility.

Granted, other countries are more repressive in other ways. But that is hardly the right standard for a land of the free. That relativizing habit of mind arises from negative freedom: things are less bad here than somewhere else; therefore, things are basically all right; therefore, we are free. We have to see freedom as positive, as beginning from virtues, as shared among people, and as built into institutions. A premise of a land of the free cannot be mass incarceration.

The numbers are shocking. About 1.7 million Americans are now in prison, roughly as many as live in West Virginia. It is as though we have an entire state imprisoned. No land that cages so many humans looks free from the outside, or feels free from the inside.

No more prisons should be built or planned. Planning prisons is planning incarceration and disenfranchisement. The goal should be to have fewer prisons over time, with fewer people in them. People should no longer be packed into cells meant for single occupants. Everything we know about the body tells us that this punishment is cruel and unusual. We should abandon any notion of a war on drugs. Sentences should be shorter. Prisons should be allowed to invest in programs that we know to be rehabilitative, such as trauma education, university coursework, library, theater, and art.

The creation of capabilities belongs to freedom, as Edith Stein said. Prehabilitation is much better than rehabilitation, for everyone. Young people should be given a chance at a life in freedom. Keeping people out of prison is a matter of giving them, as children, chances to develop the capacities for freedom, and the opportunity, as young adults, to enter the labor market. Freedom is better than crime, for all concerned, especially the (potential) victims. It is also far less expensive. Investing in young people costs far less than incarcerating them as teenagers and young adults.

Of course, people should take responsibility for their actions. Yet before we take that position, we have to check ourselves for self-righteousness. Sometimes the impulse can be racial: *People like me take responsibility, people like them do not.* Given that the business fraud and coup plotter Donald Trump is today's poster child of American whiteness, white people should perhaps reflect upon his lifetime of utter irresponsibility when experiencing such "us and them" reactions. Impunity is the opposite of responsibility.

Only a free person can be responsible. And no one can become free by themselves. The structures that enable freedom are moral but also political. It follows that we are *all* responsible for creating the conditions that make it possible for others to become free. No doubt people will commit crimes and be sentenced to prison. But before we self-righteously speak of the responsibility of others for their actions, we must be sure we have done whatever we can to allow young people to grow up free.

The sign at the gates of Nazi concentration camps read *Arbeit macht frei,* "Work will make you free." In other words, if you take responsibility for yourself, all will be well. In the Gulag, prisoners were subjected to a regime of individual responsibility. They had to obey exacting rules and meet demanding work quotas. When they failed, they were denied food rations or were placed in harsher confinement. We have no trouble seeing the sadism of such hypertrophic responsibility. The application of the principle of individual responsibility in conditions where the individual cannot take responsibility is tyrannical.

Obviously, U.S. prisons are not Nazi or Soviet camps. But these historical examples alert us to the attitude that we must avoid: sadistic responsibility talk that makes us complicit in tyranny. When we speak of responsibility without having created the conditions for freedom, we diminish both concepts. Americans do tend to leave people in impossible situations, categorize their failure as their individual responsibility, then punish them further. Babies are not responsible when their parents are poor; kids are not responsible when their schools are bad. The very existence of the carceral state becomes a silent excuse not to create a welfare state. To see the pain of others as confirmation of one's own superiority is to be irresponsible—complicit in sadopopulism and tyranny.

Freedom has to begin with an attitude of recognition, of empathy for the *Leib*. Nothing can generate this attitude for us. We must cultivate it in ourselves.

## DISTRIBUTIONS

One of my incarcerated students, Justin, took his writing assignments to friends who were not in the class, then turned in their responses to me. One of his friends wrote that before his imprisonment, he had never been far from the housing project where he grew up. For him, the cell inside was an unsurprising continuation of the immobility that gripped everyone he knew on the outside. I wanted to reject this as literary hyperbole, but as I read on, I knew that I couldn't.

Prison is an extreme case that reveals a larger reality. Social mobility will remain out of reach as long as wealth and income are so unevenly distributed. James Madison took for granted the "silent operation of laws" that would "reduce extreme wealth to mediocrity" and "raise extreme indigence towards comfort." Thomas Jefferson dreamed of nothing less than economic equality: "Can any condition of society be more desirable than this?"

The United States moved in that direction, during the decades of the American Dream, from the 1930s to the 1970s. But after four decades of normalizing oligarchy, we now face inequalities that are simply grotesque—inconsistent with a good government, with democracy, with a republic. Steady movement away from today's absurd distribution of wealth would break deadlocks, create hope, and ease minds. Barbara Jordan was right that "the American dream need not forever be deferred." (She was referring to "Harlem," a poem by Langston Hughes.)

Law serves tyranny when it favors a minuscule minority of oligarchs. If America is to become a land of the free, it must apply law to its titanic inequalities of wealth and income. The enforcement of existing laws would be a very good start. Americans lose about *$1 trillion* every year to tax fraud and evasion by the very wealthy. Offshore tax evaders should be given a year to come onshore or be prosecuted. Known practices that serve oligarchical escapism should be banned. These include mirror trades, anonymous real estate transactions, and limited partnerships that hide true owners and beneficiaries.

The United States should tax consumption as well as income. Income tax rates should be set to reflect how much a payment affects a person's lifestyle: this is solidarity. During the Eisenhower years, the top income tax rate was 91 percent. A top rate of 75 percent would suit. In such a system, *most* Americans would likely pay *less* tax. The tax code of 1980, before policies of inequality torpedoed the American Dream, is a useful reference. Wealth taxes (on assets without deferral) would improve the lives of hundreds of millions without altering the lives of the few thousand who would pay them. If very wealthy Americans paid taxes, we could give ourselves the chance to become a land of the free. The people in question would notice no difference in their material lives. And everyone else would find life more vibrant and more secure.

For thousands of years, political thinkers have understood the consequences of extreme inequality. It is hard to find defenders of freedom who believe that a few people should dominate the economy. Lord Acton, the great conservative British thinker, believed that governments had to redistribute wealth. Extreme differences in economic power, he thought, would make people dependent, freedom of speech meaningless, and the very idea of liberty a mockery. Thomas Paine, the author of the revolutionary pamphlet *Common Sense,* was of a similar mind. A government that served freedom, he thought, would eliminate poverty. John Stuart Mill, the most important liberal in the Anglo-Saxon tradition, took for granted that state action would rectify durable inequalities. Mark Twain had a Black man make all the relevant points in his short story "Corn-Pone Opinions." Isaiah Berlin, the outstanding liberal of the twentieth century, believed in the welfare state. Friedrich Hayek, an economist admired by conservatives, believed that everyone should have a secure minimum income.

Martin Luther King, Jr., the leader of the civil rights movement, was of the same view. He was organizing against poverty when he was assassinated.

Most of what is proposed in this chapter would cost little, or would even save money (smaller prisons, single-payer health insurance). Yet the argument about costs is, in an important sense, beside the point. The American budgetary problem is not that the government spends too much but that wealthy people do not pay their taxes. Allowing people to hoard wealth—and bend government to enable their hoarding—is not only wrong in the sense of contrary to freedom, it is also very inefficient.

Even were that not the case: freedom comes first. Budgets reflect choices, choices reflect values, and values are the domain of free people. We cannot get to freedom without breaking the bad mental habits and without attending to the basic physical needs.

## MINDS

A touchscreen is no prison wall, but we are surrounded and surveilled and nudged and controlled. We have consented to a grim behavioralist grid of stimulation. We are being predictified.

Social media have to be reformed by common action, through good government. Even so, good individual decisions about our bodies are a start. We should assert our own unpredictability against and beyond the digital world. This will help us to become the kinds of citizens who will choose the right policies.

Our minds are best served when our bodies can be in motion. We should give our *Leib* pride of place. Seven hours a day of screen time, the American average, is just too much. That is about as much as we sleep. It is almost half of our waking hours.

If you can, do some physical exercise every day before you reach for your phone. This alone can alter how free life seems, how unpredictably a day plays out, how the eye meets the pixel when the time comes. If you reside in a place with more than one room, avoid having screens on tables where people eat, or in rooms where people sleep. At night, charge your devices as far away from you as possible, in a place where you cannot see them, such as a drawer. The last thing you touch before you go to sleep should not have a microprocessor. When you are not at work, try to spend no more than an hour per day in front of a screen.

Try to write and post one paper letter each month to someone you care about. Don't rage against the machine; page against the machine. Read books in physical form. Keep a couple by your bed and a list of those you have read.

If this sounds radical or strange, remember that not so very long ago no one had a smartphone, and people then were freer, more intelligent, and more physically fit. Keep in mind, as well, that the people who run Silicon Valley take drastic measures to prevent their own products from making addicts of their children. They set timers to cut the power on their routers, for example, and contractually oblige babysitters not to show screens to their children. They want the best for their families. Like drug dealers, they don't push product in their own home.

"The system is based on lies," thought Havel. "It works only as long as people are willing to live within the lie." When you are online, live in truth. Make sure you know your own purposes before you open your computer and close the screen when you have fulfilled them. Resist the impulses you feel when your eyes are on pixels. They are not really yours; they are engineered through you. When you act on them, you leave a record of your predictability. Take a breath; be pleasant and reasonable. Try not to respond directly to stimuli; instead, try to change the game or direct people's attention to their offline capacities. You cannot overcome the dreariness, but you can create an oasis that other humans will find. Lots of people do a beautiful job of this on X, Instagram, and Telegram; look for a good example. Our power to resist the fiction industrial complex is limited but real.

When you are in the real world, don't forget to speak to people. Make small talk, find common subjects. Every moment of eye contact is two bodies that are safe from screens and available for the flicker of an unpredictable encounter. If you must be in the fake world, direct its symbols to energize others for action in the real world. The most productive examples of communication through social media involve people urging public action. We can see the significance of this in the reaction of tyrants. The Chinese government is most consistent in censoring people who use the internet to encourage their fellow citizens to demonstrate in public. As this confirms, the most dangerous truths are "discussion preparatory to action" (Pericles), the ones that get people off the couch.

We can behave better or worse as individuals, but we cannot reform the internet without the right principles and their application as policy. We have to start from the premise that freedom is positive. It was repressive, in this domain, to keep government out; because government did too little, the internet brought unelected and unchosen manipulators into our homes, lives, and minds. We must begin with the *Leib,* the knowledge we gain when we see the defensive flaccidity of others and realize that the same has happened to us. A digital policy that liberates our bodies can begin with our minds, since that is what we have to lose. Americans should all have a reasonable chance to develop and to protect their minds, a right to *habeas mentem*. In twenty-first-century America, a right to *habeas mentem* would suggest a public mandate, a private one, and a charter for fair transparency.

The public mandate is access to public school. Human children need human schools. They should learn to express themselves before things are expressed through them. Our digital oligarchs usually attended schools without screens, and they insist on the same for their children. Americans nevertheless spend more than $10 billion every year to put screens in schools so that oligarchs can profit from stunting the education of nonoligarchical children. We should pay teachers and librarians instead. (Those librarians must be able to shelve books in peace, without having to look over their shoulders for self-righteous censors or fear denunciations from angry parents.) If there is a screen in front of a child at school, it should be for the purpose of learning to code. The Online Privacy Protection Act of 2000 should be modified so that youths ages thirteen to eighteen are no longer treated as adults.

The machine has to be a tool for the pupil, not the other way around. Students need math and physics for self-defense against oligarchy. They need history for a sense of structure and possibility, and arts and humanities to develop values. Art is what shakes up the everyday and exposes the present moment for us, enabling us to make the unexpected connections from the past to the future. A lyric in a song, a peal of a bell, or a bit of stained glass can open a channel and change a person's world. Students need books in the library that will surprise and challenge them. Every grade of every American school should publish a newspaper, based on reporting.

This mandate includes a thriving system of public universities, accessible to all. Students should not leave university with debts that block their mobility and constrain their lives. To be public means to be constructed in a way that serves the larger value of freedom of speech. Like the institution of journalism, the institution of the autonomous public university helps young Americans grow up to become free speakers.

A campaign against freedom of speech is directed against universities in the name of "free speech" itself. The plan is to destroy both the universities and the freedom. Colleges and universities teach what students will not learn elsewhere and at other times in life, and that is all to the good. Students learn, and students question. Universities enable young people, who we hope are already sovereign and unpredictable, to embrace mobility: in space, in time, in values. Aside from the instruction they receive, they enjoy years, at a critical moment in life, when they can say what they think. This is a precious chance for them to become free speakers, and for many of them it will be the last one. For this very reason, universities are attacked by tyrants and their satraps.

I was expected to work in school and during college, and six years passed between my doctoral degree and my first (and thus far only) job with health insurance. I worked a variety of jobs, from telemarketing to construction, and I can say with confidence that the degree of freedom of speech that prevails on a campus is incomparably greater than on other worksites. Students have the chance to develop opinions and reconsider values. Autonomous public universities thus serve the forms of freedom. For them to remain autonomous and public, they must be self-governing. Placing universities under the direction of political commissars would disable them and leave young people less free.

The private mandate is the teaching of professional ethics to software engineers and computer programmers and the establishment of bodies (such as exist in other professions) to sanction violations. Machines have no values. Neither freedom nor any other value will be present in computer programs unless humans put it there. Today this realm operates largely without ethics. Coaches on a playing field have ethics, but the authors of our docility do not; judges of written laws have ethics, but makers of the unpublished rules of social media do not; therapists have ethics, but influencers do not. To be sure, corporations sometimes do good things: Microsoft, Amazon, and Google did important work to defend Ukraine from cyberwar. But a better internet will depend on people who think better about the freedom of others and who understand their work as a profession with ethics and rules.

After the public mandate and the private mandate, Americans would benefit from a charter of fair transparency, which begins from the premise that machines serve minds, not the other way around, and that a person should be able to judge whether this is the case. The overall relationship between mind and machine can be established only by a collective effort, which is to say by policy.

A charter for fair transparency would be based on three principles: (1) things should be transparent to us; (2) we should not be transparent to things; and (3) we should not be oppressed by data we cannot see.

From the principle that *things should be transparent to us* flow five good practices. (1) Social media must ask whether users want investigative reporting in their feeds and open an appropriate algorithmic pathway. (2) Social media must ask whether users want opinions that challenge their own and open an appropriate algorithmic pathway. (3) Social media must issue corrections to users who have viewed false material that was presented to them as news. (4) Every statement and advertisement on social media must be traceable to a human being. (5) All code should be accessible, at a glance and a click, its purpose described in an intelligible English summary.

From the principle that *we should not be transparent to things* flow the next five good practices. (6) We should have to opt into (and not opt out of) the sharing of our data. The default setting on all software should be zero data retention and zero data transfer to third-party sites. (7) Data arising from an action should be communicated only for its plain purpose rather than stored or sold. (8) Every data harvest that does occur should be compensated and listed in a register. (9) Intimate data regarding health, location, and the like should never be stored or transferred. (10) Software must offer privacy settings that are accessible, uncomplicated, and durable (rather than having to be constantly reaffirmed).

The third principle is that *we should not suffer from data inequalities*. From it flow the final five good practices. (11) We should have the right to see which private entities know what about us and to correct their mistakes. (12) Algorithmic screening of job and school applicants must generate a legible record of the reason for rejection. (13) Public health data that arises from the testing of our bodies must be accessible to us. (14) Nongovernmental organizations should be authorized, at our request, to help us make sense of our data profiles. (15) When we lack traditional documentation, we should be allowed to use known data flows to establish our identity.

It takes a while for a new right such as *habeas mentem* to be established. In the meantime, our choices matter all the more.

## LISTENERS

Declaring for freedom means declaring for freedom of speech. Declaring for freedom of speech means taking the side of the facts. Taking the side of the facts means supporting the institutions that give them a home.

A declaration is balanced by an accommodation. A free speaker is taking a risk. Those who take risks need solidarity, in the form of protection of the freedom of speech. A country of free speakers requires the institutions that regulate these risks and thereby make factuality possible.

Free speakers are necessary, but so are receptive listeners. We need the calm capacity to pay attention. People who live within big lies do so because they feel isolated and powerless. They do not believe that they make a difference in the world, so they accept that a conspiracy governs everything. In a vicious cycle, unfreedom advances lies, which makes people still less free. We need a virtuous cycle of freedom and courage.

A good government would take specific steps to protect investigation and encourage its reception. The legal scholar Zechariah Chafee, a leading interpreter of the First Amendment, knew that freedom of speech required that we take "affirmative steps to improve the methods by which discussion is carried out." Around the world, the better democracies do just this. The Norwegian constitution, for one, requires the state to create favorable conditions for discussion.

Americans, when asked, say that journalists should monitor governments and companies on the basis of verified facts. This declaration should be accommodated but is not. If there are not enough journalists to do what we want, then we are less free. Americans also say, when asked, that they prefer that their views be challenged online. Since we lack the option to support actual reporting on social media, we are less free. Given that Americans spend about two hundred billion hours a year on social media, this is a consequential violation of rights.

Historically speaking, it is normal to regulate new media so that rights can be formulated, acknowledged, and respected. It is precisely these conventions that create the forms that we then take for granted, such as, for example, the book. We protect freedom of speech not only when we resist censorship or express horror at book burnings, but also when we make expression possible with norms about plagiarism and copyright. Yet the institution of copyright did not arise automatically after the invention of the printing press. It was made by people, justified by values, and enforced by the state. This lesson must be applied to social media. We will be freer when we have a setting on our platforms that promotes local journalists in our feeds. They should be supported in the precise sense of getting paid for their valuable work.

We cannot get free of the internet, but we can assert human values upon it. It is not freedom to be continuously nudged in the direction of prejudices and vulnerabilities shared by a class of people we neither see nor choose. It is freedom to make an evaluation and realize it. The brain hacks push us toward alienation and powerlessness. This is not neutral: it drives us away from factuality and thus from freedom. If social media are impossible to avoid, then they must be altered to enable liberty.

Freedom of speech is not the surging emotion of a given moment. Emotions and moments are easily managed by oligarchs and machines. Freedom of speech is grander than that and rests on the foundations of humility and risk.

## NEWS

Americans say that they want "significant roughness": fresh and renewed factuality. The people who supply facts on a daily basis are investigative journalists. Some of the most important reporters cover local news. Candidates for local office lie—how to check? They raise money—from whom? Local governments spend money—on what? Firms pollute—where? In most of the counties in the United States, no one has any idea about any of these things, because reporters no longer cover any of these beats. Most of American territory is a news desert, and a news desert is no land of the free. We need home truths, both for their own sake and as preparation for the larger ones. A vacuum of local factuality draws in the big lies and the conspiracy theories.

As Simone Weil wrote, discovering and receiving the truth takes work, whereas producing and believing the false is effortless. Facts are indispensable; they have costs; and people aspiring to freedom will bear them. Americans talk all day long about the news but pay almost no one to report it. Most of what passes as "news" is repetition, speculation, and spin. Investigative journalists do heroic, indispensable work. But they are far too few. Specialists in public relations now outnumber journalists by about six to one. Let us imagine a country where the ratio was even.

James Madison, envisioning the future of America, hoped for a "circulation of newspapers through the entire body of the people." That once existed. When George Orwell wrote his novel *1984* (in the year 1948), there were about ten million more newspaper subscriptions in the United States than there were households. Today our reality approaches the society described in the novel: we all look at screens, and Americans in most parts of the country have no access to any human reporting about the world around them. Every American county should have a local news source with local reporting by local reporters. News deserts should be replaced with news fountains.

So long as our minds are ensnared by negative freedom, we will see no solution to any of this. If we believe that government is there to be hobbled, we will discern no policies that would enable freedom, even when they are close at hand.

The purpose of government is to establish the forms of freedom. Factuality is needed for all the rest, and factuality requires policy. Freedom of speech is hard national work. Investigation, local newspapers, and newsstands should all be subsidized. Public schools should teach reporting through field trips and live conversations. A news ombudsperson in every American county could record local meetings and the relevant documentation, all to be uploaded on a national Wiki system. College graduates should be offered a year of public service to serve as local correspondents.

Local news is a public service. It can be very easily justified in purely economic terms, as a brake on corruption and waste. But the larger point is that we all need knowledge about what is happening right around us. The resources are at hand. Internet firms make tremendous profits by distributing reporting for which they do not pay, while drawing advertising revenues away from the people who are doing the actual work. These costs could be corrected; or, as the economists say, the externalities could be internalized. Targeted advertising should be taxed to support local reporting.

Factuality is an indispensable form of freedom. As we lose it, life seems ever more chaotic, the past harder to remember, the future less assured. But factuality can be attained. We have the tools. We can be free speakers, and we can be free people.

## RINGS

Right before I rang that bell on the farm, I was sitting on a swing that hung from a limb of a maple tree. Its branches covered the first few rows of a cornfield. An old sycamore on the other side of the gravel lane shaded the farmhouse. The valleys marking the boundaries of the farm were still wooded. We kids explored the woods and the creeks, as our parents and grandparents had before us.

Trees ring, though in a different way than bells. Each ring of a tree records a year of growth, persistence, and survival. Tree rings convey a smooth accommodation to the challenges of the seasons, grading time by growing in space. The old sycamore has a ring for every year the house has stood. When a tree dies, the rings can tell us about the past, just as air bubbles in melting glaciers can, just as arrowheads can, just as fossils can. These little signs from other lives can help us to situate ourselves and to see our moment for what it is.

My little declaration of freedom in 1976 was loud and clear. It was mine, but it was not made by me alone. The idea to ring the bell was that of an older cousin, who often set an example. She kept us in an orderly line, a convention that allowed each of us to do what we wished when the time came. My cousins and I were all on a farm, a human landscape that we children had done nothing to create. Someone else had laid down the country roads and the gravel lane. Someone else had planted the trees. Sycamores grow by creeks; the one that shades the farmhouse was replanted, probably in 1825. Someone else, my maternal grandfather, had hung the bell.

It rang, over the decades, to bring people together. It once called children to the one-room schoolhouse on the corner of the two roads where my mother's family settled. My mother's father's father, my great-grandfather, attended that school. When the school was torn down, the bell was moved to another farm, where my mother's father was raised. There it was a farmyard bell, calling the men in the fields back for dinner. When my grandfather retired from farming, he moved the bell to the farm he took over as an adult, the one I knew as a child. It has been ringing continuously far longer than the Liberty Bell ever did, for well over a century now. Perhaps bells ought to be small.

As a boy, I had only a very broad sense of these debts. I knew that the sycamore was as old as the house. I knew who tilled the soil: my grandfather. He called his acres "Arrowhead Farms," after the flint relics that he found in his fields. He kept them in wooden cases lined with red felt. He occasionally took them on tour, wearing a bolo tie with a blue stone.

Someone else provided me with food, drink, shelter, language, a past. I did not find out for myself about cracked bells and underground railroads. Books were laid before me; stories were told to me. Though freedom is a quality of a single life, it is the work of generations. The bell is an object of sentiment for me, but it is in my life and on these pages only because it was also an object of sentiment for my grandfather, and that was only true because it had called farmers to work and children to school. Only an individual can be free, but only a community can make individuals. And yet for a community to do this, generation upon generation, its practices must be examined in light of the demands of freedom.

On Easter Sunday 1988, I was standing in the shade of the sycamore tree with my friend Danny Gubits. I was waxing on, looking down the hill toward the road, about all that my grandfather had achieved unaided. Danny corrected me: "He had the color of his skin." I remember the first flush of resistance, the warm blood in my face, my desire to describe an America where skin color did not matter, at least on a farm. And then I saw the absurdity of that and conceded the point.

The history of the land did not begin with the arrival of my maternal ancestors in 1806, or with the Declaration of Independence in 1776, or with the arrival of the first slave ship in 1619. Who left the arrowheads turned up each year by my grandfather's plow? The mastodon tusk hanging in the porch implied a still longer timeline. Who had hunted those giant mammals down? And what about the far older fossils that my grandmother had found and labeled? We cannot reason our way to freedom without the past, including the deep past.

We are born at a certain moment, which we neither control nor know in advance, and which we cannot even begin to grasp until much later in life. And yet we can, with experience, learn to place ourselves in longer histories, to think in time. We cannot be free until we have a certain sovereignty over ourselves, which requires us to understand that the present moment is not the only one, and that its impulse is not the only thing we have. We live freely in a moment insofar as we can get beyond it and see ourselves in it.

Freedom rings like a bell, startling and declarative. When I pulled the cord, I was doing something of my own, something loud and true. But I was calling to others using an instrument forged and preserved by others. I had just leapt from a swing hung from the shading limb of a tree, a small comrade of its equilibrium. Freedom also rings like a tree, transforming the unliving into the living, grading and growing, aging and adapting, recording and renewing.

## GRASP

That summer day on the farm, six-year-old me made a little choice. I could have kept swinging on the swing, using my energy and my kid's understanding of physics just to have fun. Instead, I jumped off the swing, trotted away from the tree, and took my place in line to ring the bell.

When my turn came, I inhaled and held my breath while pulling the rope, then exhaled as I released. Leaning back and gripping the rope, I used a bit of my own energy, which I owed to plants and to the sun. My ultimate debt was to gravity, since solar gravity created the fusion that allowed the plants to grow and me to thrive. A more immediate debt: in leaning back, I borrowed Earth's gravity, turning it to my own purposes. I had practiced ringing the bell like that; doing so came naturally. We are free to do what we can do, when we know why we are doing it.

The rope in my hands tugged the top of the bell, even as its clapper, hanging freely on the inside, remained still. An object in motion tends to stay in motion; an object at rest tends to remain at rest. The lip of the moving bell struck the clapper. The vibrating iron compressed nearby air, pushing out waves at the speed of sound. They reached the ears of everyone on the farm, and all knew what the sound meant: time to gather and eat. And because our minds are more than survival guides, some of us thought of something else: freedom.

It might seem that everything that happened when the bell rang is predictable, subject to description as science. Waves of one kind of energy became waves of another kind of energy. Through the mediation of different kinds of matter (solar plasma, photosynthetic plant cells, human mitochondria), electromagnetic energy (or light waves) became kinetic energy (or sound waves). The sun shone, corn grew, I ate it, I acted. Photons from the local star excited electrons in leaves, setting off chemical changes that supplied a young *Homo sapiens* with the energy needed to pull a rope and make one bit of iron strike another.

As I hope I have shown, that is not everything. A universe with electromagnetic energy is not the same as a universe with eyes that see via light waves. A universe with kinetic energy is not the same as a universe with ears that hear via sound waves. A universe with physical regularities is not the same as one where beings, such as a human child, apprehend them and turn them to their own purposes. A universe shaped by gravity is not the same as a universe whose creatures can mindfully hang bells with a thought to their purpose. A universe where levers work is not the same as a world where a boy makes a lever of himself. A *Körper* is not the same as a *Leib*. Gravity can become grace. I had my own six-year-old's grasp of physics, and I had more than that: an incipient idea of freedom.

What I lacked was an understanding of what freedom might mean for everyone. I did not feel, hands grasping the rope, that the world was against me. What I needed to understand was all the cooperation that it took to get me to a state of freedom. What I have argued for in this book, and perhaps you have come along with me, is that we can all get to a better state, together.

## INCLUSION

It is pleasant for me to think on my childhood, but I must liberate myself from its errors. The bicentennial, one of my fondest memories, drew me toward the time warps. It readied my mind for a politics of inevitability, in which all would be well simply because an empire (or something else) had been removed. It prepared me for a politics of eternity, in which any challenge to the righteousness of my place or actions would be met with a reference to a perfect past commemorated in round numbers.

James Madison praised Americans for building their new republic without "blind veneration of antiquity." That is the attitude we should apply to the Founders themselves. Emulating them means transcending them. They were historical actors, not memory pets. They took a risk in declaring independence. Seventy-six years later, Frederick

Douglass reminded Americans of that. "There was a time," he said, "when to pronounce against England, and in favor of the cause of the colonies, tried men's souls. They who did so were accounted in their day, plotters of mischief, agitators and rebels, dangerous men."

It is perverse to celebrate a past fight for freedom while accepting tyranny in the present. Each epoch demands a courage specific to its challenges. Speaking in 1852, Douglass was addressing slavery, into which he himself was born: "What, to the American slave, is your Fourth of July? I answer: a day that reveals to him, more than all other days in the year, the gross injustice and cruelty to which he is the constant victim."

Two hundred years after the Founders signed the Declaration of Independence, some cousins rang a bell on a farm in Clinton County, Ohio. My younger brother, who was five, was also in the line. My youngest brother, who was three, had to be helped to pull the rope. It is fine to celebrate prosperity and the American Dream. I love the recollection and the family and the farm, and I would not have become myself or written this book without them. But we will not get to that future by misunderstanding the past or drowning it in myths of innocence.

My brothers and I were children of the 1970s. Our lives have been quite different, and I don't speak for them; but I am struck, looking back, that we just barely grasped the brass ring, dodging the difficulties that came early in the next century: an idiotic war in 2003, a financial crisis in 2008, growing inequality throughout. Among the large extended family that met on the farm in the 1970s and 1980s, the younger cousins have had a harder time of it than the older ones. Timing matters, and my brothers and I were favored by the fortune of earlier generations.

Social mobility has been tougher for most Americans since my childhood, but in different ways for different people. When I was born in 1969, about 80,000 Black men were in prison. By 1990, when I watched the Reds win their third World Series in my lifetime, the figure had more than quadrupled, to about 360,000. In the early 2020s, when I began to play softball with my daughter, nearly 700,000 African American men were incarcerated. There are more people with life sentences today than there were total people in prison when I was born, and almost half of these lifers are Black men. I can speak of the different trajectories of my brothers and cousins, but no one of that generation, sixteen cousins in all on both sides of my family, has been incarcerated or shot. Nearly half a century after the story I tell, everyone who stood in that line to ring the bell is still alive. I might take that for granted, but I shouldn't. Among the African American families in Dayton, Ohio, or in New Haven, Connecticut, the count often looks sadly different.

Seeing such inequalities is a matter not just of fairness but of freedom for everyone. Whites drawn into racial politics obstruct liberatory policies. As my incarcerated student Alpha put it, "You guys are oppressing yourselves with your own oppression." Freedom begins with virtues, with ideas of what is good. The moment we accept that the status quo is justified, we find ourselves in the dead land of negative freedom, defensive and helpless. It hurts to say that something is wrong and that I bear some responsibility; but without that bit of courage, freedom never begins.

I can declare my own sense of America, but only if I am ready to accommodate others' stories. I can tell my own story of the Fourth of July, but it helps me to know that Alpha's family saw it as a holiday that belongs to others. When I imagine his family barbecue on the balcony of an apartment in a housing project, I see myself and my own memories with greater clarity. Others' reckonings with freedom begin elsewhere, which must be acknowledged: not only as a matter of respect, but also as a matter of logic. Evan, another incarcerated African American student, wrote that "freedom is a farce in America until 'we' includes me." He's right.

I must accommodate any virtues I assert from my own experiences to virtues that begin elsewhere. My hope is that this will lead to a richer notion of liberty, to more creative policy, and to more freedom for everyone.

## CHANCE

In 1976 the child I was leapt from a swing, waited in a line, and rang a bell. Unpredictable memories brought me back to that moment, just as an unpredictable life since then has made me free. I was full of futures then and have realized some of them, including this book. I will not be marking 2076, the American tercentennial. But with luck and labor, my children will see our country's fourth century begin.

Of a winter's day on that same Ohio farm, my five-year-old son let a gloved hand graze across the bell's pull, then watched with patient fascination as the rope swayed back and forth, ever more slowly, until it returned to its initial motionless equilibrium. Then he tramped off, in little blue boots, to search for fossils and arrowheads in snow-dusted fields. He found something else: a small stone worked by human hands into a cube, marked with counters on each side: an ancient game piece.

We did not make the facts about the universe that guide a die when cast. We cannot undo the law of necessity. But there is also a law of freedom, a mysterious complicity, that we can practice until we attain grace. What we cannot change we can understand and turn to our purposes. Someone very long ago, taking a hand to chance, chose to make that die, someone who was practiced at making things. Someone at a much later time found it, someone who was practiced at seeing.

Of a summer day on that same Ohio farm, my son, now eleven, took turns ringing the bell with a friend who is Black. The bell rings as it always has; its flaw, that second awkward peal, set off a chain of involuntary memories. My son is not a white kid the way I was. He confronts adults in his friend's defense. He has a chance at freedom that I didn't have, or that I failed to take. He likes Afrofuturism because of the Black Panther movies, whose aesthetic is the work of someone whom I remember as a girl in Ohio.

Through her images, Hannah Beachler will touch more minds than anyone else who graduated from our high school. This is perhaps not what anyone would have predicted, but unpredictability is the soul of freedom.

As I try to bring this book to a close, my daughter sits across the table from me at Claire's, an eatery in downtown New Haven. Softball practice is over, and we are supposed to be doing homework. A little plate empty of cupcake is at her right hand, a book about Greek myths at her left, the same collection I once found in a public school library as a kid. It abounds in flawed heroes, limited gods, and metamorphoses that join childhood wonder to adult dilemmas.

My daughter can throw a ball hard, like her father, like her paternal grandfather, like her paternal great-grandfather, whose bats and gloves I held in my hands, and in whose last pickup truck, a 1992 Dodge Dakota, we drove to this vegetarian restaurant. This evening we'll watch some tapes of the 1975 World Series, which I want my daughter to see.

The Reds lost game one. They came back, though. They won the series on Joe Morgan's single in the last inning of the last game. He was the best player of his time, and his hit won the best World Series of all time. He kept his eye on the ball, the lump of physics became his, the law of necessity became the law of freedom. I am trying to get my daughter to practice more.

Like other kids her age, she has spent much of her conscious life in a pandemic, with tyrants in power in countries she cares about. She has learned that her dad can hover at the edge of death, that good writers can be in prison, that friends can text from bomb shelters. She knows that serving as a flower girl for a bride precedes welcoming a refugee with a baby. This is the way things are, but not how things must be.

She takes it in, as does my son, our world of restraints and opportunities, along with the sports and the books and the solidarity and the truth my wife and I and others try to share with them. My children are, I hope, sovereign and, I am sure, unpredictable, as they start to think of where they will go in life.

My kids have a chance. We all do. This world could be ever so much better.

As I look at my daughter's smiling face, I think of what I can leave behind: an idea about freedom. Our problem is not the world; our problem is us. And so we can solve it. We can be free, if we see what freedom is. We can see creativity in the past, possibility in the present, liberty in the future. We can recognize one another, create a good government, and make our own luck.

"We live in a world," says Simone Weil, "where people can expect miracles only from themselves." We can seize our chance. It is our last one, but it is a good one.

# Appendix

## POSITIVE AND NEGATIVE FREEDOM

|  | Positive freedom | Negative freedom |
|---|---|---|
| Freedom | value of values | absence of barriers |
| Preposition | freedom to | freedom from |
| Question | why? | how? |
| Attitude | creative | certain |
| Source | people in the world | external forces |
| Task | becoming individuals | removing barriers |
| Government | must be made for freedom | must be dismantled for freedom |
| Speech | truth and risk | impulse and impunity |
| Body | *Leib* | *Körper* |
| Others | bodies, individuals, possibilities | barriers, problems, commodities |
| Beginning | bloody birth | abstract adulthood |
| Virtues | real, plural, and challenging | irrelevant, single, or private |
| Truth | horizon, connector | opinion, barrier |
| Thought | reasonability | rationality |
| Science | engagement with the world | one opinion among others |
| Internet | politics | nature |
| Markets | one useful institution among others | source of freedom |
| Oligarchy | impedes freedom | side effect of freedom |
| Racism | historical, requires reflection | personal, irrelevant to freedom |
| Communism | important warning | too much government |
| Fascism | present danger | too much government |
| Totalitarianism | error of single value or truth | too much government |

# Acknowledgments

"It is time to cease dreaming of liberty," wrote Simone Weil, "and to decide instead to conceive it." I first conceived of this book as a sort of dense philosophical poem, with every claim tersely ordered. A brush with death attached me unduly to this rigid form.

Early readers such as Leora Tanenbaum (who was my very first editor in college) and Susan Ferber (who edited a revised version of my dissertation) told me that I had failed. So I started again. As I opened again to life, a somewhat different sort of life than before, my solitary reckoning became a book of encounters. The formulation of my medical experience as a rights argument (in chapters 1 and 5) was influenced by Sara Silverstein's scholarship. The physician friend present during my illness was Njeri Thande.

Once I had a new text, I realized that I would feel dishonest if I did not present my arguments about freedom to incarcerated Americans. I thank Zelda Roland and her colleague Vanessa Estimé for their work with the Yale Prison Education Initiative. Under its auspices (and as adjunct faculty at the University of New Haven), I taught a seminar on the philosophy of freedom inside MacDougall-Walker Correctional Institution in Suffield, Connecticut, in spring 2022 and workshopped the manuscript there in spring 2023. I gained from my incarcerated students perspectives on the United States and an education in political thought. I mention a few of them in the text by first name; each of them made a contribution to this book. My incarcerated student Kyle made an important point about the conclusion.

Russia invaded Ukraine right before the prison teaching began. The atrocity of Russian occupation was met not only by the resistance of Ukrainian civil society but also by an elevated discussion of freedom. I brought the manuscript with me to wartime Ukraine three times and revised it there. Two of my journeys to de-occupied zones (the ones mentioned in the preface) were in the company of the journalist Nataliya Gumeniuk, to whom I also owe insights about positive freedom. In Kyiv I was able to discuss the main ideas at the PEN Club thanks to Volodymyr Yermolenko, who also commented on the manuscript. A draft of this book was workshopped at the Ukrainian Catholic University in Lviv, where Taras Dobko, Myroslav Marynovych, Iryna Sklokina, and Volodymyr Sklokin commented on some key passages and Yaroslav Hrytsak offered important words of support. The Recovery Project arranged for me to visit rehabilitating soldiers in Kyiv.

In summer 2023, colleagues and friends, many having made the difficult trip from wartime Ukraine, commented on a draft of this book at a seminar in Krasnogruda, Poland. My friends at the Borderland Foundation there facilitate encounters through music, art, and theater. Their persistence and creativity have lent this project a certain optimism. I thought about freedom during summers there, in the warmth of the hospitality of Krzysztof Czyżewski and Małgorzata Czyżewska. Writers I read regularly in Krasnogruda (Czesław Miłosz and Józef Czapski) led me to Simone Weil. I was earlier able to give a Tony Judt memorial lecture in Krasnogruda, recalling the late historian friend with whom I first worked out some of the ideas presented here.

During a chance conversation in New Haven, Daniel Judt made an important point about early American definitions of freedom that led me to restructure the introduction. Daniel also planned a public discussion about his father between myself and Ta-Nehisi Coates at the

New York Public Library. That exchange, which took place two days after Russia invaded Ukraine, broached issues of race and colonialism that I address here. The occasion was a new edition of *Ill Fares the Land,* a book of Tony's that arose while I was working with him on *Thinking the Twentieth Century.* Such conversations raised and smoothed my own subject, like a river pushing rocks.

The encounters that made this book possible include those with teachers who are no longer with us. In addition to Tony, I would like to mention Isaiah Berlin and Leszek Kołakowski. I recall Leszek for his wisdom and humor, even as I draw a different politics from a pluralism similar to his. I remember Sir Isaiah for his generosity and sense of intellectual adventure, even though I disagree with his famous text on freedom.

Those two thinkers and their books hovered over my graduate studies at Oxford. My doctoral supervisors were Timothy Garton Ash and the late Jerzy Jedlicki, the first of whom was a historian of the suppressed Solidarity movement, and the second of whom was interned when martial law was imposed in Poland in 1981. Both of them helped me think my way toward chapter 5. Jerzy's story of childhood survival in the Holocaust was important for the particular case I make for "normality" in chapter 2.

Since 1996, Vienna has been one of my intellectual homes. The Institute for Human Sciences, founded by the late Krzysztof Michalski and later led by Shalini Randeria and by Misha Glenny, has provided a perfect setting for intellectual friendship. Ivan Krastev, my colleague there, has been an important interlocutor. I thank Katherina Hasewend and Katherine Younger for their work at the institute. As the Russo-Ukrainian war began, we extended the institute's long-standing cooperation with Ukrainian scholars by establishing Documenting Ukraine, a program that has allowed us to support hundreds of colleagues. This engagement allowed me to keep thinking about freedom. If you would like to support Ukrainians documenting the war, please go to www.iwm.at/documenting-ukraine/donors.

I am grateful for Volodymyr Zelens'kyi's willingness to speak to me about Václav Havel and Andrei Sakharov, about dissidence and resistance, and about the argument of this book. At the beginning of a long conversation, he asked me what I wanted to talk about. When I replied "the philosophy of freedom," he spread his arms wide and exclaimed, "So let's talk about that!" Valeryi Zaluznhnyi and about fifty Ukrainian soldiers kindly took the time to speak to me, as did a few hundred Ukrainians who had experienced Russian occupation or who work in civil society or government. Long ago, Volodymyr Dibrova, Oxana Shevel, and Roman Szporluk introduced me to Ukrainian studies. Halyna Hryn and Lidia Stefanowska taught me the language.

Encounters include people we know, people we once knew, people we do not know, and people we could not have known. The Institute for Human Sciences was founded in part as an archive for the papers of Jan Patočka, a Czech philosopher who figures on these pages. Klaus Nellen is the hero of that story. Václav Havel, whom I knew only slightly, owed much to Patočka, who died after police interrogation in 1977. Ludger Hagedorn discussed Patočka with me. Havel and Patočka figure here as students of unpredictability. My reading of them, and chapter 2 in general, owes a huge amount to Roger Penrose, a dominant thinker of my youth whom I have never met.

This book brought me back, somewhat unpredictably, to Czech thinkers and the Czech language. I owe my period of sustained contact with Czech culture to Milada Vachudová (*fille et mère*). Ivan Havel allowed me to attend his seminars in Prague. Paul Wilson kindly commented on the parts of the manuscript touching upon his experiences with the Plastic People of the Universe and Czechoslovak dissidence. Milan Babik hosted a beautiful conference on Václav Havel. Kieran Williams read the entire manuscript, and Pavel Barša commented on the first two chapters. Roger McNamee was kind enough to comment on my predictability argument in chapter 3 as well as on the rest of the manuscript.

I owe a debt to the librarians of Yale's Sterling Memorial Library, who made it very easy to access whatever tradition I needed. Within Yale's extraordinary library system, Stephen Naron directs the Fortunoff Video Archive of Holocaust Testimonies, where I serve as faculty adviser. His inclusive view of Holocaust studies has led to projects that have informed this work. My citation of the podcast version of testimony of Leon Bass in chapter 3 is a small example of his outreach.

Marci Shore, an authority on the history of philosophy, offered critical comments and steady good sense. Edith Stein is a major figure in Marci's forthcoming history of phenomenology, and my approach to Stein's life and work owes much to Marci's seminars and lectures. Much the same is true for Leszek Kołakowski and Václav Havel, figures from whom I draw a few ideas here, but who emerge in all their biographical and intellectual richness in Marci's book. Without Dan Shore's opera *Freedom Ride* and my meeting with Raymond Arsenault on a stage in Boston, chapter 3 on mobility would have been incomplete. Ideas about social mobility I gathered long ago from Thomas W. Simons, Jr., were also important to that chapter, as was a conversation with Byron Auguste.

Amanda Cook, whom I happened to meet for the first time right after graduating from college, edited this book. Amanda applied herself to this manuscript with tact and daring, and changed it very much for the better. Tina Bennett, who was my friend in graduate school and is my agent now, generously commented on drafts. Tim Duggan, a champion of earlier books, was an early interlocutor on this one. Detlef Felken, a devoted editor for fifteen years, read drafts of this book with great insight. He has been an enthusiastic supporter of my work, and I send him every good wish upon his retirement from Beck.

Olivia Judson inspired me with the arguments of her ongoing work in natural history, which I had the privilege of reading in draft. Stuart Rachels read the entire manuscript with care and spurred an involuntary memory. Andrzej Waśkiewicz, like Olivia and Stuart a friend from graduate school, commented on the entire manuscript and supplied references to political theory. I also entrusted versions of the text to Laura Donna, Daniel Fedorowycz, Peter Loewen, Leah Mirakhor, and Angel Nwadibia. In addition to the lecture at LMU München that I describe in chapter 1 and the workshops mentioned here, I presented arguments from this book remotely to Stanford University, the College of William and Mary, and the Lviv Book Forum.

Jason Stanley of Yale's philosophy department read this manuscript, twice co-taught a class with me on mass incarceration, and introduced me to thinkers I needed to know. At a Yale Law School gathering, I appreciated Daniel Markovits's remark that I was replacing rationality with unpredictability as the central category of freedom. Patrick McCormick, a student at Yale Law School, offered me important references. Yale undergraduates Isabel Kalb and David Rosenbloom helped me with research. A two-year project by Yale graduate Daniel Edison kept me close to Leszek Kołakowski. Yale history department faculty and staff have kept my spirits up over the years. Brenda Torres assisted me during the writing and publication. I thank Jim Levinsohn, the dean of Yale's Jackson School, for his support of my academic and public work.

Debts can be intellectual and personal at the same time. I hope that, even in the oblique form of acknowledgments, the importance of friendships emerges. My children and my parents are both subjects and inspirations here. I was not particularly good at being parented, nor am I now particularly good at parenting, but the double encounter informs this book. Though one of its theses is that the difficulty of child-rearing requires a reworking of our concept of freedom, I hope the moments of simple joy with families shine through. My brothers, Philip Snyder and Michael Snyder, and my mother and father, Christine Hadley Snyder and E. E. Snyder, commented on this book as I neared completion. In their cases, as in all others, generosity need not signify accord.

The happiness list in chapter 1 is borrowed with modifications from one by Władysław Tatarkiewicz, which I found by accident in a library. By his own account, Tatarkiewicz became a philosopher after a chance encounter in a train station. I have had some lucky breaks as well, too many to acknowledge here. My idea of freedom involves creating the conditions for good fortune for as many people as possible. And then, within the expansive frontiers of a shared borderland of the unpredictable, we thrill to the elevating grace of the individual.

# Notes

## PREFACE

x **But is that, even that, liberation?:** I started thinking about this subject thanks to Dan Stone, *The Liberation of the Camps: The End of the Holocaust and Its Aftermath* (New Haven: Yale University Press, 2015); review at *AJS Review* 40, no. 1 (2016): 206–9.

xi **Children need places to play:** Rutger Bregman, *Humankind: A Hopeful History,* trans. Elizabeth Manton and Erica Moore (New York: Little, Brown, 2020), 279.

xii **what philosophers call "negative freedom":** The most famous treatment of positive and negative freedom is Isaiah Berlin, "Two Concepts of Liberty," a lecture delivered in 1958, reprinted in *The Proper Study of Mankind* (London: Chatto & Windus, 1997), 191–242. As the argument develops, I will specify what I mean by negative and positive liberty. Berlin skews the argument from the beginning by assuming that freedom is "freedom from" (193) and identifying positive freedom as authority (194). There might be two concepts of liberty, as Berlin says, but I think the clear distinction between them owes more to his essay than to the history of ideas. Philosophically speaking, as Charles Taylor and others have shown, the two collapse together. Any notion of negative liberty is empty without some idea of positive liberty. I believe that Berlin's distinction, furthermore, was unproductive for his own arguments. In the essay (219), he identifies positive freedom with guidance toward a single human nature. I agree that the assumption of such a single human nature is mistaken and dangerous, but will disagree that this has anything to do with positive freedom. His own idea of pluralism, as I will try to show, must in fact lead to a notion of freedom as positive. Even if freedom is the absence of interference, as Berlin says when describing negative liberty, this is only undesirable because of the (multiple) positive aims and purposes of the individual. As Berlin rightly says, those aims must and will contradict each other; freedom then becomes the capacity or state in which we can consider and adjudge and affirm them in practice. From this it follows that we would strive to create such a state, also in politics. Freedom is positive in three senses: it is positive because it is a presence in a person and among people rather than an absence in the world; it is positive in that it depends upon the affirmation of virtues; and it is positive because it requires thoughtful political action.

xiii **"Stone Walls do not":** Richard Lovelace, "To Althea, from Prison" (1642).

xiii **became a torture facility:** The memoir of one inmate is Stanislav Aseyev, *The Torture Camp on Paradise Street* (Cambridge, Mass.: Ukrainian Research Institute, 2022).

xiii **Auschwitz had been:** See Debórah Dwork and Robert Jan van Pelt, *Auschwitz* (New York: Norton, 1996); Sybille Steinbacher, *Auschwitz* (Munich: Beck, 2004).

xiii **Koselsk, a Soviet POW camp:** For documentation of the Soviet mass executions remembered as the Katyn massacre, see Anna M. Cienciała, Nataliia S. Lebedeva, and Wojciech Materski, eds., *Katyn: A Crime Without Punishment* (New Haven: Yale University Press, 2007). For the notebooks taken from the pockets of murdered men, see *Pamiętniki znalezione w Katyniu* (Paris: Éditions Spotkania, 1989). On the widows, see Andrzej Spanily, ed., *Pisane miłością* (Gdynia: Rymsza, 2003), vol. 3. On the memory cultures, see Alexander Etkind et al., *Remembering Katyn* (London: Polity, 2012).

xiii **The Brothers Karamazov:** The twentieth-century novel that for me most invokes Dostoevsky as student of character is Der Nister's *The Family Mashber*, set in his hometown of Berdychev, Ukraine, in the 1870s. Der Nister was arrested in Stalin's anti-Semitic purge in 1949 and died in a prison hospital in 1950. Vasily Grossman was also born in Berdychev, where his mother was murdered in the Holocaust. His novels *Life and Fate* and *Everything Flows* have shaped what I was able to do as a historian; their register of empathy has no doubt influenced my argument here.

xv **"*they* talk about the country":** Y. F. Mebrahtu, lecture at the Swedish Academy, March 22, 2023.

xv **bringing it to life:** See Charles Taylor, "What's Wrong with Negative Liberty," in *Philosophy and the Human Sciences: Philosophical Papers* (1979; reprint Cambridge: Cambridge University Press, 1985), 2:211–29, esp. 2:212, 216–17, 225, 227.

xviii **Freedom justifies government:** Compare Hannah Arendt: "Freedom is the sense (*Sinn*) of politics" and Charles Taylor: "The basic point of politics is freedom." I mean that freedom provides an ethical justification for a certain kind of government, as well as guidance as to how such a government would be designed.

## INTRODUCTION: FREEDOM

2 **George Washington's birthday:** Kenneth Morgan, "George Washington and the Problem of Slavery," *Journal of American Studies* 34, no. 2 (2000): 279–301.

4 **He started work:** Stuart W. Leslie, *Boss Kettering* (New York: Columbia University Press, 1983).

5 **the Soviet Union always seemed close:** I cannot discuss Soviet history in any depth.

Beautifully rich is Karl Schlögel, *The Soviet Century*, trans. Rodney Livingstone (Princeton: Princeton University Press, 2023); originally published in German in 2018.

5    **the people who suffered directly:** See Odd Arne Westad, *The Global Cold War: Third World Interventions and the Making of Our Times* (Cambridge: Cambridge University Press, 2005).

6    **danger doesn't come from afar:** A book that opened the way later for this sort of reflection was Christopher Browning, *Ordinary Men* (New York: HarperCollins, 1992). See also Karl Schneider, *Auswärts eingesetzt: Bremer Polizeibataillone und der Holocaust* (Essen: Klartext Verlag, 2011).

6    **not so very long before:** On knowledge of the Holocaust, see Frank Bajohr and Dieter Pohl, *Der Holocaust als offenes Geheimnis* (Munich: Beck, 2006); Richard Breitman and Allan J. Lichtman, *FDR and the Jews* (Cambridge, Mass.: Harvard University Press, 2013); Peter Fritzsche, "The Holocaust and the Knowledge of Murder," *Journal of Modern History* 80, no. 3 (2008): 594–613.

6    **than it later became:** Raul Hilberg's synthesis, first published in 1961, anticipated most of the subsequent debates in the field. It was not widely read. *The Destruction of the European Jews*, 3 vols. (New Haven: Yale University Press, 2003).

7    **how easily a partially democratic system:** On the German case, see Gary King et al., "Ordinary Voting Behavior in the Extraordinary Election of Adolf Hitler," *Journal of Economic History* 68, no. 4 (2008): 951–96; Benjamin Carter Hett, *The Death of Democracy* (New York: Holt, 2018); Richard J. Evans, *The Coming of the Third Reich* (New York: Penguin, 2003).

7    **how quickly big lies:** My account of the return of fascism in the 2010s is *Road to Unfreedom* (New York: Crown, 2018). A classic intellectual history is Zeev Sternhell, *Les anti-Lumières* (Paris: Gallimard, 2010); a phenomenology is Jason Stanley, *How Fascism Works* (New York: Random House, 2020); a theory is George Mosse, *The Fascist Revolution* (New York: Howard Fertig, 1999); a typology is Stanley Payne, *Fascism* (Madison: University of Wisconsin Press, 1980); a useful study is Philippe Burrin, *Fascisme, nazisme, autoritarisme* (Paris: Seuil, 2000); a helpful reminder is Sarah Churchwell, "American Fascism: It Has Happened Here," *New York Review of Books,* June 22, 2020.

10   **sentenced to Siberian exile:** Janet M. Hartley, *Siberia* (New Haven: Yale University Press, 2014), 115.

10   **made all the handcuffs:** See "250,000 Handcuffs Sought During Coup," *Los Angeles Times,* August 25, 1991.

11   **reading at night:** I was reading Walter Benjamin's *Arcades Project* for Mary Gluck's graduate seminar on Marxism.

12   **Marx and Engels:** Between Marx and Lenin is Friedrich Engels; see especially his *Anti-Dühring* (1878; New York: International Publishers, 1972). I cannot tell the story of the Second International here, although this is necessary to explain Leninism adequately (and helpful for current debates). Lenin was a good organizer, an excellent debater, and a supreme tactician, and his tactics were defensible interpretations of things Marx wrote. Philosophically, however, he was incompetent; in his metaphysics and metahistory, he managed to combine the worst

of Marx with the worst of Engels. This is an example of how ideas matter in history. On the tradition, see James Joll, *The Second International* (London: Weidenfeld & Nicolson, 1955); Leszek Kołakowski, *Main Currents of Marxism,* vol. 2: *The Golden Age,* trans. P. S. Falla (Oxford: Oxford University Press, 1978); Gary P. Steenson, *After Marx, Before Lenin* (Pittsburgh: University of Pittsburgh Press, 1991). My contribution was *Nationalism, Marxism, and Modern Central Europe: A Biography of Kazimierz Kelles-Krauz* (1997; reprint New York: Oxford University Press, 2017).

12    **in Vienna in April 1992:** The proceedings of that conference, including my paper, can be found in John Williamson, ed., *Economic Consequences of Soviet Disintegration* (Washington, D.C.: Institute for International Economics, 1993).

12    **what must follow:** See, for example, "Text of Bush's Address to Nation on Gorbachev's Resignation," *New York Times* (hereafter *NYT*), December 26, 1991.

13    **overthrowing democratically elected rulers:** On the related subject of influencing foreign elections, see David Shimer, *Rigged: America, Russia, and One Hundred Years of Covert Electoral Interference* (New York: Knopf, 2020).

13    **civil rights movement:** See Mary L. Dudziak, "Desegregation as a Cold War Imperative," *Stanford Law Review* 41, no. 1 (1988): 61–120. On Americans in the civil rights movement sincerely convinced of Soviet racial equality, see Glenda Gilmore, *Defying Dixie: The Radical Roots of Civil Rights, 1919–1950* (New York: Norton, 2008).

13    **gave way to verities:** On the politics of inevitability, as I will describe it in chapter 3, consult Isaiah Berlin's essay "Historical Inevitability," in *The Proper Study of Mankind* (London: Chatto & Windus, 1997), 119–90. It was delivered as a lecture in 1953.

14    **no need to know the past:** J. R. R. Tolkien, whom I read as a kid, correctly despised the view of history as "allegory," the sense that something that happened had to happen because of rules or repetitions. Instead he advocated seeing history as "applicability," as having a capacity for patterns and possibilities. Foreword to the 1954 edition of *The Fellowship of the Ring.*

14    **racial violence in Los Angeles:** The Los Angeles police had classified 47 percent of local Black men and male teenagers as members or affiliates of gangs. Elizabeth Hinton, *America on Fire: The Untold History of Police Violence and Black Rebellion Since the 1960s* (New York: Liveright, 2021), 240.

14    **each challenge seemed technical:** Daniel Markovits, *The Meritocracy Trap* (New York: Penguin, 2019).

15    **the attackers "hate freedom":** President George W. Bush, "Authorization for the Use of Military Force," September 18, 2001.

15    **an adventure in negative freedom:** My view at the time was the same as my view now; see "War Is Peace," *Prospect,* November 21, 2004.

15    **terror and wars:** David Satter, *The Less You Know, the Better You Sleep* (New Haven: Yale University Press, 2016); Krystyna Kurczab-Redlich, *Wowa, Wolodia, Wladimir* (Warsaw: W.A.B., 2016), 334–46, 368. The wars included cyberwars: Hannes Grassegger and Mikael Krogerus, "Weaken from Within," *New Republic,* November 2, 2017; Marcel Van Herpen, *Putin's Propaganda Machine*

(Lanham, Md.: Rowman & Littlefield, 2016); John Markoff, "Before the Gun-fire, Cyberattacks," *NYT,* August 12, 2008; Irakli Lomidze, *Cyber Attacks Against Georgia* (Ministry of Justice of Georgia: Data Exchange Agency, 2011).

15    **rationality would bring democracy:** An attentive view was Michel Eltchaninoff, *Dans la tête de Vladimir Poutine* (Arles: Actes Sud, 2015).

16    **a new politics:** On Russian oligarchy, see Karen Dawisha, *Putin's Kleptocracy* (New York: Simon & Schuster, 2014); also Anders Åslund and Andrew Kuchins, *The Russia Balance Sheet* (Washington, D.C.: Peterson Institute, 2009). For an interesting moment of reflection, see Karl Schlögel, *Entscheidung in Kiew* (Munich: Carl Hanser Verlag, 2015), 78.

16    **they were also gays:** An early study of Russian antigay propaganda was Tatiana Riabova and Oleg Riabov, "The Decline of Gayropa? How Russia Intends to Save the World," *Eurozine,* February 5, 2014. For explicit official Russian state-ments regarding a gay international conspiracy, see Vladimir Yakunin, "Novyi mirovoi klass vyzov dlya chelovechenstva," *Narodnyi Sobor,* November 28, 2012.

17    **presidential candidate won:** For the case that Russian intervention made the dif-ference in the 2016 presidential election, see Kathleen Hall Jamieson, *Cyberwar* (New York: Oxford University Press, 2018). For important background, see Edward Lucas, *Cyberphobia* (New York: Bloomsbury, 2015).

17    **with Russian assistance:** Russian assistance was thoroughly documented in the Mueller Report (*Report on the Investigation into Russian Interference in the 2016 Presidential Election,* May 2019). But its existence was also clear at the time. See Snyder, *Road to Unfreedom,* chap. 6, for further primary sources. For some of what we knew in 2016 and 2017: Timothy Snyder, "Trump's Putin Fantasy," *New York Review Daily,* April 19, 2016; Franklin Foer, "Putin's Puppet," *Slate,* July 4, 2016; "How Vladimir Putin Is Using Donald Trump," *Newsweek,* August 29, 2016; Craig Timberg, "A Russian Journalist Explains How the Kremlin Instructed Him," *New Yorker,* November 22, 2017; Julia Ioffe, "What Russian Journalists Un-covered," *Atlantic,* December 30, 2017; Zachary Cohen, "Russian Politician: US Spies Slept While Russia Elected Trump," CNN, September 12, 2017; "Fabrika trollei," RBK, October 17, 2017; Andrew Higgins, "Maybe Private Russian Hack-ers Meddled in Election, Putin Says," *NYT,* June 1, 2017; Elizabeth Dwoskin et al., "Google Uncovers Russian-Bought Ads," *NYT,* October 9, 2017; Mike Isaac and Daisuke Wakabayashi, "Russian Influence Reached 126 Million Through Facebook Alone," *NYT,* October 30, 2017; Casey Michel, "How the Russians Pretended to Be Texans," *Washington Post,* October 17, 2017. On Trump's Rus-sian financial backing, see Craig Unger, "Trump's Russian Laundromat," *New Republic,* July 13, 2017; Natasha Bertrand, "The Trump Organization," *Busi-ness Insider,* November 23, 2017; Shaun Walker, "Trump in Moscow," *Guardian,* September 18, 2017; Jo Becker, Adam Goldman, and Matt Apuzzo, "Russian Dirt on Clinton? 'I Love It,' Donald Trump Jr. Said," *NYT,* July 11, 2017.

17    **wealthy through undertaxed inheritance:** Why is it that people who claim to have achieved everything by themselves, thanks to their own talent and effort, leave money to their children?

17    **comfortable denying everything:** The record of Trump's lying just at the beginning of his term was staggering: "Fact Checking," *NYT,* April 27, 2017; "Fact Checker," *Washington Post,* October 10, 2017.

17    **Despite a constitutional ban:** This is section 3 of the Fourteenth Amendment. See William Baude and Michael Stokes Paulsen, "The Sweep and Force of Section Three," *University of Pennsylvania Law Review* 172, no. 3 (February 2024): 605–745.

17    **why we do it:** Consider Charles Taylor, who wrote that freedom involves separating ourselves from some of our desires "as not reflecting who we are or want to be."

18    **defending a history thesis:** Ilia Chedoluma, "Інтелектуальна біографія Михайла Рудницького (1889–1975)," Ukrainian Catholic University, 2022.

18    **colleague leading the class:** This was Jeffrey Sonnenfeld, who records the details in an email of March 29, 2023.

20    **Free will is character:** In Kant's practical reason, we define our ends, and we thereby mold our will.

## SOVEREIGNTY

21    **"Do we not":** Edith Stein, *Einführung in die Philosophie* (Freiburg: Herder, 1991), 194.

21    **word she used:** Edith Stein, *Zum Problem der Einfühlung* (Halle: Buchdruckerei des Waisenhauses, 1917), chap. 3.

22    **"There can be a *Körper*":** Stein, *Zum Problem der Einfühlung,* 50–53.

22    **a "zero point":** Stein, *Zum Problem der Einfühlung,* 61–64.

22    **that we are liberated:** Stein, *Zum Problem der Einfühlung,* 77–79.

22    **phenomena come into view:** Stein, *Zum Problem der Einfühlung,* 77.

23    **source of a politics of freedom:** The beginning of a politics of fascism is elsewhere, in the arbitrary definition of the enemy. See Carl Schmitt, *The Concept of the Political,* trans. George Schwab (Chicago: University of Chicago Press, 2007), 25–28; also Schmitt, "Eröffnung," *Das Judentum in der Rechtswissenschaft,* vol. 1: *Die deutsche Rechtswissenschaft im Kampf gegen den jüdischen Geist* (Berlin: Deutscher Rechtsverlag, 1936), 14–18; Schmitt, "Neue Leitsätze für die Rechtspraxis," in Herlinde Pauer-Studer and Julian Find, eds., *Rechtfertigungen des Unrechts* (Berlin: Suhrkamp, 2014), 513–16.

23    **see ourselves as *Leib*:** The German plural form is *Leiber,* which I am avoiding to minimize confusion.

24    **"We have seen deeds":** Edith Stein to Pius XI, April 12, 1933, in Susanne Batzdorff, *Aunt Edith: The Jewish Heritage of a Catholic Saint* (Springfield, Ill.: Templegate, 2003), 226–27.

24    **the Heldenplatz, where a huge crowd:** The classic artistic rendering is Thomas Bernhard's play *Heldenplatz* (1988; reprint Frankfurt: Suhrkamp, 1995). A good summary of the pogrom mood is Martin Pollack, "Des is a Hetz und kost net viel," *Der Standard,* March 2, 2013. See generally Gerhard Botz, *Nationalsozialismus in Wien* (Vienna: Mandelbaum, 2008).

24 **Jews murdered at Auschwitz:** See Götz Aly and Susanne Heim, *Vordenker der Vernichtung* (Hamburg: Hoffmann und Campe, 1991); Götz Aly and Christian Gerlach, *Das letze Kapitel: Der Mord an den ungarischen Juden 1944–1945* (Frankfurt: Fischer-Taschenbuch Verlag, 2004).

25 *Körper* **we concentrate in a camp:** On the objectification of the body in the Soviet camp system, see Golfo Alexopoulos, *Illness and Inhumanity in the Gulag* (New Haven: Yale University Press, 2017). On the German camp system, see Nikolaus Wachsmann, *KL: History of the Nazi Concentration Camps* (New York: Farrar, Straus & Giroux, 2015).

25 **publishing the work of a friend:** Adolf Reinach, *Gesammelte Schriften, Herausgegeben von seinen Schülern* (Halle: Niemeyer, 1921).

25 **Edmund Husserl, their supervisor:** This was a frustrating labor. One suspects that Husserl would be a better-known figure today if he had paid attention to Stein's revisions.

26 **"We have to admit":** Stein, *Zum Problem der Einfühlung*, 55.

26 **Facing a law of necessity:** The argument that people recognize themselves as mutually recognizing one another goes back to Hegel's *Phenomenology of Spirit*. Stein adds specific language of the body, and the point that mutual recognition means objective knowledge about self and world, and we are working forward from there.

27 **an act of love:** Simone Weil, *La pesanteur et la grâce* (Paris: Plon, 1947), 122. This book consists of excerpts from notes written before May 1942.

27 **"the same combination of nature":** Simone Weil, *Cahiers 1* (Paris: Plon, 1951).

27 **"To love a stranger":** Weil, *La pesanteur et la grâce*, 121. Leviticus 19:34: "But the stranger that dwelleth with you shall be unto you as one born among you, and thou shalt love him as thyself; for ye were strangers in the land of Egypt: I am the Lord your God."

28 **"a source of mystery":** Simone Weil, *Réflexions sur les causes de la liberté et de l'oppression sociale* (Paris: Gallimard, 1951), 63. The book was written in 1934.

28 **"thought to enter into direct contact":** Weil is following Hegel here.

28 **a poor athlete by nature:** Françoise Meltzer, "The Hands of Simone Weil," *Critical Inquiry* 27, no. 4 (2001): 611–28.

29 **The Reds brought together:** Of the starting "great eight" (pitchers rotate), two were white, three were Black, and three hailed from the Caribbean or South America. See James Pilcher, "Diversity Meant Wins for Big Red Machine," *Cincinnati Enquirer*, June 21, 2015; Adrian Burgos, "El Profe: Tony Pérez's Lonely Road to Cooperstown," *La Vida Baseball*, May 14, 2018; Bobby Nightengale, " 'The best player I ever saw': Cincinnati Reds Hall of Famer Joe Morgan Dies at 77," *Cincinnati Enquirer*, October 12, 2020.

31 **Americans are fifteenth:** These rankings will change a bit from year to year. See Freedom House, the World Happiness Report, and the World Health Organization for current figures.

31 **thought about baseball:** I also listened, when I was a bit better, to Lucinda Williams's album *Car Wheels on a Gravel Road*. When I was young, I might be lying on a platform in the back of a van, or even in the open bed of a pickup

truck, when the vehicle reached my paternal grandparents' farm. The very distinctive squeeze of tires on gravel told me that we were home.

32    **give a lecture in Munich:** Timothy Snyder, "Can the United States Be a Free Country? Present Risks and Future Challenges" (video), Munich History Lecture, December 3, 2019, https://lisa.gerda-henkel-stiftung.de/mhl_timothysnyder.

33    **another was commercial medicine:** I borrow this term from Andrija Štampar via Sara Silverstein. See George Vincent, Diary, entry for July 18, 1926, RG 12, Rockefeller Foundation Archives. We like to think we have health care that incidentally involves some wealth transfer; we actually have wealth transfer that incidentally involves some health care. See Peter Bach, "Changing the Drug Pricing Game" (video), TEDMED, November 2017, no. 687810.

34    **I was eventually diagnosed:** My diary entry for December 30, 2019: "They said exhaustion. Flu? Give you some fluids. Wanted me out? Today they say sepsis."

34    **Having nearly died:** I wrote a book about the experience: *Our Malady: Lessons in Liberty from a Hospital Diary* (New York: Crown, 2020).

36    **Simone Weil as loneliness:** Weil, *La pesanteur et la grâce,* 76. In his 1964 novel *Mein Name sei Gantenbein,* Max Frisch defines hell as living through a story in which everything is already known.

36    **right to liberty:** As the argument develops in the next chapter, we will see the difference between the pursuit of happiness (on the basis of what is regarded as good) and the provision and denial of pleasure (which can be an instrument of unfreedom).

37    **The Founders bemoaned:** George Washington to James Madison, October 14, 1793; Washington to Jefferson, October 11, 1793.

37    **government action must work against:** See Jonathan M. Metzl, *Dying of Whiteness* (New York: Basic Books, 2019).

37    **like plantation owners:** Loïc Wacquant links the peculiar institutions in his essay "From Slavery to Mass Incarceration," *New Left Review* 13 (January–February 2002): 41–60.

39    **called this** *habitude***:** Simone Weil, *Oeuvres complètes,* vol. 1: *Premiers écrits philosophiques* (Paris: Gallimard, 1988), 275–77.

40    **"an intention permeating the whole":** Stein, *Zum Problem der Einfühlung,* 64.

40    **"little lump of physics":** Roger Angell, "The Interior Stadium," *New Yorker,* February 20, 1971. I read it in the beautiful assemblage of paintings and essays published as *This Great Game* (New York: Prentice Hall, 1971).

40    **"Nature resists," says Simone Weil:** Weil, *Réflexions sur les causes de la liberté,* 38.

40    **"the world of values":** Stein, *Zum Problem der Einfühlung,* chap. 4.

41    **"law of necessity":** Stein, *Zum Problem der Einfühlung,* chap. 3.

41    **"a double law":** Simone Weil, *On Science, Necessity, and the Love of God,* trans. and ed. Richard Rees (Oxford: Oxford University Press, 1968), 12.

42    **called themselves Borderlanders:** See Krzysztof Czyżewski, *Toward Xenopolis: Visions from the Borderland,* ed. Mayhill Fowler (Rochester, N.Y.: Rochester University Press, 2022).

42    **Each new capacity:** See Penelope Eckert and Sally McConnell-Ginet, "Commu-

nities of Practice," in Kira Hall, Mary Bucholtz, and Birch Moonwomon, eds., *Locating Power* (Berkeley, Calif.: Berkeley Women and Language Group, 1992), 93.

42    **shot and gassed to death:** Sara Bender, *The Jews of Białystok During World War II and the Holocaust,* trans. Yaffa Murciano (Waltham, Mass.: Brandeis University Press, 2008).

43    **"The past and the future":** Weil, *La pesanteur et la grâce,* 65.

43    **a "fortress" of resources:** See Alvin Gouldner, "Stalinism: A Study of Internal Colonialism," *Telos,* no. 34 (Winter 1977–78): 5–48; Lynne Viola, "Die Selbst-kolonisierung der Sowjetunion und der Gulag der 1930er Jahre," *Transit,* no. 38 (Winter 2009): 34–56. I develop this theme in *Bloodlands.* For a broad reflection see Alexander Etkind, *Internal Colonization* (London: Polity, 2011).

43    ***Lebensraum,* living space:** On German occupation policies, see Karel C. Berkhoff, *Harvest of Despair: Life and Death in Ukraine Under Nazi Rule* (Cambridge, Mass.: Harvard University Press, 2004); Wendy Lower, *Nazi Empire-Building and the Holocaust in Ukraine* (Chapel Hill: University of North Carolina Press, 2005). Hitler's attitude to Ukraine is a theme of my *Black Earth: The Holocaust as History and Warning* (New York: Crown, 2015).

43    **these colonial fantasies:** There is also a Polish colonial tradition, but it was re-thought in the second half of the twentieth century. See Jerzy Giedroyc, *Auto-biografia na cztery ręce,* ed. Krzysztof Pomian (Warsaw: Czytelnik, 1996). This is a theme of my *Reconstruction of Nations* (New Haven: Yale University Press, 2002).

43    **Russian television today:** Documented in Julia Davis, *In Their Own Words: How Russian Propagandists Reveal Putin's Intentions* (New York: Ibidem Press, 2024). See also Timothy Snyder, "The War in Ukraine Is a Colonial War," *New Yorker,* April 28, 2022.

44    **At a rehabilitation facility:** Some of the conversations from this encounter are reflected in Nataliya Gumenyuk, "Yes, Tiredness Is Ravaging the Ukrainian Sol-diers I Meet. But They Never Think of Giving Up," *Guardian,* December 15, 2023.

44    **left a safe job:** His story was told in "While I Was Crawling, 4 Mines Exploded and I Lost My Left Limbs," *Chosun* (South Korea), December 7, 2023.

44    **We worked together:** Yedida Kanfer was responsible for transcribing the conver-sations.

45    **Together we achieved:** Tony Judt with Timothy Snyder, *Thinking the Twentieth Century* (New York: Penguin, 2012).

46    **I got white-guy handshakes:** After reading a revised version of this text, my stu-dent named Alpha gave me what he jokingly called a "white-guy hug." Code-switching happens in body language as well as in spoken language. The latter is something I confront and think about in Ukraine and in my own country, but it would take another book to consider how the practice relates to power. I will just say that doing one kind of code-switching in English can make you aware of other kinds of code-switching, and that noting code-switching in another lan-guage (for example, Ukrainian-Russian) can make you more aware of what is happening in your own. For an attempt to redirect philosophy of language away

from information and toward attunement, see David Beaver and Jason Stanley, *The Politics of Language* (Princeton: Princeton University Press, 2023).

46    **"have to see the body of others"**: Lisa Guenther makes a series of related points, for example: "We need everyday corporeal relations with others in order to be ourselves, not just because we define our particular social and psychological identities in relation to one another, but also because we have a constitutive desire for the bodily presence of others." *Solitary Confinement: Social Death and Its Afterlives* (Duluth: University of Minnesota Press, 2013), 213. I don't claim to be an expert in this tradition, but it seems to me that Guenther is reacting to Merleau-Ponty, who in his turn drew from Stein's notion of the *Leib,* which became for him *le corps vécu.* See Margaretha Hackermeier, *Einfühlung und Leiblichkeit als Voraussetzung für intersubjektive Konstitution* (Hamburg: Dr. Kovacs Verlag, 2008).

46    **"imprisoned in my own self"**: Stein, *Zum Problem der Einfühlung,* 72.

46    **"The constitution of the foreign individual"**: Stein, *Zum Problem der Einfüh-lung,* 99.

48    **out of the question**: Edith Stein to Roman Ingarden, February 9, 1917, in Edith Stein, *Self-Portrait in Letters,* trans. Josephine Koeppel (Washington, D.C.: ICS Publications, 1993), 9.

48    **as a breadbasket**: See Frank Golczewski, *Deutsche und Ukrainer, 1914–1939* (Paderborn: Ferdinand Schöning, 2010); Peter Borowsky, *Deutsche Ukrainepoli-tik 1918* (Lübeck: Matthiesen Verlag, 1970); Gerald Feldman, *German Imperial-ism 1914–1918* (New York: John Wiley & Sons, 1972).

48    **Confronted with their wounded bodies**: Edith Stein's German hauteur colored her own reflectiveness, which is nonetheless real. "When we discovered," she recalled, "one of our [German] compatriots in a transport, we German nurses were jubilant. But once we had had him for a few days, we usually became very subdued. These countrymen of ours [German soldiers] were demanding and critical; they could upset the entire ward if anything did not suit them. Those from the 'barbaric nations' were humble and grateful. I pitied them so, these poor Slovaks and Ruthenians [Ukrainians], dragged out of their quiet villages and sent into battle. What did they know about the history of the German Reich and of the Hapsburg monarchy? Now they lay there suffering without knowing what for." *Life in a Jewish Family,* ed. L. Gelber and Romaeus Leuven, trans. Josephine Koeppel (Washington, D.C.: ICS Publications, 1986), 333.

50    **pools with cement**: Hinton, *America on Fire,* 50.

50    **larger political reaction**: Vesna Weaver, "Frontlash: Race and the Development of Punitive Crime Policy," *Studies in American Political Development* 21 (Fall 2007): 230–65.

51    **we define ourselves**: It is worth keeping in mind Rudiger Safranski's remark that "a person is defined by not permitting himself or herself to be defined." *Zeit: Was sie mit uns macht und was wir aus ihr machen* (Munich: Hanser, 2015), 47.

51    **inspired German racial laws**: James Q. Whitman, *Hitler's American Model: The United States and the Making of Nazi Race Law* (Princeton: Princeton Univer-sity Press, 2017).

52 **If we begin from magical maturity:** Although John Stuart Mill does support education, this critique applies to his most popular work: *On Liberty* (1859; reprint Indianapolis: Hackett, 1978). But it is a problem for the entirety of major traditions.

52 **the sovereignty of the state:** An important Russian thinker, Vladislav Surkov, maintains that the sovereignty of the state means the sovereignty not of all people but of one person, the dictator. Vladislav Surkov, *Texts 97–10,* trans. Scott Rose (Moscow: Europe, 2010). Citing Ilyin: Vladislav Surkov, "Suverenitet–ieto politicheskii sinonim konkurentosposobnosti," in *Teksti 97–07* (Moscow: 2008); Vladislav Surkov, "Russkaya politicheskaya kultura: Vzglyad iz utopii," *Russ.ru,* June 7, 2015.

53 **legal theorist Carl Schmitt:** For Schmitt's sovereign, see Carl Schmitt, *Politische Theologie: Vier Kapitel zur Lehre von der Souveränität* (1922; reprint Berlin: Duncker & Humblot, 2004), 13. See also Jean-Pierre Faye, "Carl Schmitt, Göring, et l'État total," in Yves Charles Zarka, ed., *Carl Schmitt ou le mythe du politique* (Paris: Presses Universitaires de France, 2009), 161–82; Czesław Madajczyk, "Legal Conceptions in the Third Reich and Its Conquests," *Michael: On the History of Jews in the Diaspora* 13 (1993): 131–59. A helpful introduction to Schmitt's thinking in English is *Writings on War,* trans. and ed. Timothy Nunan (Cambridge: Polity Press, 2011).

53 **Adolf Hitler taking advantage:** See Yves Charles Zarka, *Un détail nazi dans la pensée de Carl Schmitt: La justification des lois de Nuremberg du 15 septembre 1935* (Paris: Presses Universitaires de France, 2005); Raphael Gross, *Carl Schmitt and the Jews: The "Jewish Question," the Holocaust, and German Legal Theory,* trans. Joel Golb (Madison: University of Wisconsin Press, 2007); Mark Edele and Michael Geyer, "States of Exception," in Michael Geyer and Sheila Fitzpatrick, eds., *Beyond Totalitarianism: Stalinism and Nazism Compared* (Cambridge: Cambridge University Press, 2009), 345–95; Stephen G. Wheatcroft, "Agency and Terror: Evdokimov and Mass Killing in Stalin's Great Terror," *Australian Journal of Politics and History* 53, no. 1 (2007): 20–43.

53 **the social contract:** I am focused here on a tradition that begins with Hobbes and continues with Locke. There are of course other powerful descriptions of state sovereignty, for example those associated with Plato and Bodin. I don't believe that any of them handle either the empirical problem (the state is already there) or the ethical problem (how to legitimate it via freedom).

54 **a life in freedom:** Ernst Bloch, considering inequality in his first book, claimed that "we know the inscription on the gravestones of most children before they are even born." *Geist der Utopie* (1918; reprint Berlin: Suhrkamp, 2018), 411. Getting to sovereignty enables getting to unpredictability and mobility.

54 **We are born undeveloped:** For a summary of this research, see Center for the Developing Child, "InBrief: The Science of Early Childhood Development," Harvard University, 2007.

54 **Humans evolved to be patient:** See Sarah Blaffer Hrdy, *Mothers and Others: The Evolutionary Origins of Mutual Understanding* (Cambridge, Mass.: Harvard University Press, 2011); Bernd Heinrich, *Why We Run: A Natural History* (New York: HarperCollins, 2001).

55 **the right structures must *already* be in place:** Compare Joseph Raz: "Autonomy is possible only if various collective goods are available." *The Morality of Freedom* (Oxford: Oxford University Press, 1986), 247.

55 **Stein pointed out:** It seems to me that Edith Stein's patient demolition of some of Heidegger's basic concepts deserves a broader readership than it has received. Here is a suggestion: "*Dasein* is for him emptied to the point of being a sequence from nothing to nothing. And yet, it is rather the fullness that first really makes it understandable why the human being is 'about its being.' This being is not only a temporal extension and therefore constantly 'ahead of itself'; the human being always requires being given new gifts of being in order to be able to express what the moment simultaneously gives her and takes away." "Martin Heidegger's Existential Philosophy," trans. Mette Lebech, *Maynooth Philosophical Papers,* no. 4 (2007): 80. See also Ken Casey, "Do We Die Alone? Edith Stein's Critique of Martin Heidegger," KenCasey99.wordpress.com, June 2, 2012.

55 **"being toward death":** *Sein-zum-Tode* is about living life authentically through an immanent awareness of death. My interior critique: beginning from birth better generates the sense of time as possibility that Heidegger himself seems to have in mind (in *Sein und Zeit,* 1927). My exterior critique: competing, absolute virtues and their affirmation give a sense to life that, while in some sense constrained by death, does not lean hard on it.

55 **"being toward life":** Marci Shore played with a number of Heideggerian ideas when pregnant, for example, literalizing *Geworfenheit,* or "thrownness," as involving birth itself (a baby is "caught"—what then?). As far as I know, no one has yet tried to write such a book, but there are other examples of reorienting Heidegger toward birth, or at least of thinking about his concepts about birth. See Lisa Guenther, "Being-from-Others: Reading Heidegger After Cavarero," *Hypatia* 23, no. 1 (2008): 99–118.

55 **"Beginning, before it becomes":** Hannah Arendt, *The Origins of Totalitarianism* (New York: Harcourt, Brace, 1951), 477.

56 **As children, they themselves:** From the age of about eighteen months, children from richer families are using language differently. Noted in David Denby, *Lit Up* (New York: Picador, 2018), 116.

56 **negative childhood experiences:** For an introduction to this research, see Center on the Developing Child, "InBrief: The Impact of Early Adversity on Children's Development," Harvard University, 2007; also Christina Bethell et al., "Positive Childhood Experiences and Adult Mental and Relational Health in a Statewide Sample," *JAMA Pediatrics* 173, no. 11 (November 2019); V. J. Felitti et al., "Relationship of Childhood Abuse and Household Dysfunction to Many of the Leading Causes of Death in Adults," *American Journal of Preventive Medicine* 14, no. 4 (May 1998): 245–58.

56 **"the one thing that man possesses":** Weil, *Réflexions sur les causes de la liberté,* 71.

56 **Our knowledge of early childhood development:** For a helpful set of articles, see "Advancing Early Childhood Development: From Science to Scale" (series), *Lancet* 389 (October 2016).

56 **good at recognizing faces:** Faraz Farzin, Chuan Hou, and Anthony M. Norcia,

"Piecing It Together: Infants' Neural Responses to Face and Object Structure," *Journal of Vision* 12, no. 13 (December 2012): 6.

56 **someone else's speech:** Elizabeth Bates, Luigia Camaioni, and Virginia Volterra, "The Acquisition of Performatives Prior to Speech," *Merrill-Palmer Quarterly of Behavior and Development* 21, no. 3 (July 1975): 205–26.

56 **It takes caring people:** The point is not to make parents individually confront the neurology of child-rearing. It is to account for this knowledge in creating general conditions that make parenting more fruitful. See Joyve Leyson, "Upbringing and Neuroscience," in Malte Brinkmann, Johannes Türstig, and Martin Weber-Spanknebel, eds., *Leib–Leiblichkeit–Embodiment* (Berlin: Springer, 2019), 259–62.

57 **Positive emotions broaden the range:** Barbara Fredrickson, "The Broaden-and-Build Theory of Positive Emotions," *Philosophical Transactions of the Royal Society of London, Biological Sciences* 359, no. 1449 (September 29, 2004).

57 **We can learn to govern ourselves:** See Clyde Hertzman, "The Lifelong Impact of Childhood Experiences: A Population Health Perspective," *Daedalus* 123, no. 4 (1994): 167–80.

57 **Abundant research indicates:** See the consensus recommendations in World Health Organization, "Improving Early Childhood Development: WHO Guideline," WHO.int, March 5, 2020, 11 and passim.

57 **unstructured play; and choices about things:** Rutger Bregman, *Humankind: A Hopeful History,* trans. Elizabeth Manton and Erica Moore (New York: Little, Brown, 2020), 279–96.

57 **Motherhood belongs to freedom:** I was brought to this conclusion by Heather Boushey, *Finding Time: The Economics of Work-Life Conflict* (Cambridge, Mass.: Harvard University Press, 2016).

58 **Adults lend to children:** Luce Irigaray made a similar argument, using the conceit of breath: we live in the womb thanks to a mother's breathing, but we can never breathe for her or pay her back in kind. *L'oubli de l'air chez Martin Heidegger* (Paris: Éditions de Minuit, 1983), 10, 31–35, 42–43.

58 **"a loan that must be constantly renewed":** Weil, *La pesanteur et la grâce,* 80.

58 **make it impossible:** This can be bad faith rather than a misapprehension, as the novels and essays of Margaret Atwood remind us.

59 **each maternity ward:** True, Plato did not write of maternity wards. But the problem that new things might arise is one of his philosophy, not of my account of it.

60 **and expand it:** For Leszek Kołakowski, it was important that new virtues could be created, for if all good things had already been done, we could not be free. He developed this thought in a speech of December 3, 1965, first published in *Życie Literackie,* no. 50 (1965): 34–35, then reprinted in *Marzec 1968 w dokumentach MSW* 1 (Warsaw: IPN, 2008), 266–68.

60 **describe the cave:** Plato, *Republic,* bk. 7.

60 **a "release," a liberation:** At the end of *The Apology.*

60 **Socrates says that "such captives":** Plato, *Republic,* bk. 7.

61 **between certain shadows:** Let us accept Plato's demanding construction of the cave experiment, in which people would sit for years looking at a wall and see only the

shadows of "carved objects," and never notice the bodies of the people who are actually carrying those objects back and forth. Plato does away with the problem of the bodies of the puppeteers by putting them behind a low wall. They are holding the objects above the wall and somehow never exposing their hands and arms.

61      **presence of other bodies:** I perform a similar but far more extended analysis upon the Turing Test, with attention to gender, in "And We Dream as Electric Sheep," *Eurozine*, May 6, 2019. I write in this book less on gender than I wish I had done, but would like to refer readers to that essay, which extends and complements *On Freedom* in some areas.

62      **Plato tells us:** In the *Theaetetus.*


## UNPREDICTABILITY

63      **texts that captivated me:** I will be drawing on Havel's 1975 play *Audience*; his 1975 open letter to Czechoslovak communist party leader Gustav Husák; and his 1978 essay "The Power of the Powerless." I am not seeking to provide an overall account of Havel's thought: for that, see David Donaher and Kieran Williams, eds., *Václav Havel's Meanings* (Prague: Karolinum, 2024); David Danaher, *Reading Václav Havel* (Toronto: University of Toronto Press, 2015); James Pontuso, *Václav Havel: Civic Responsibility in the Modern Age* (New York: Rowman & Littlefield, 2004); Delia Popescu, *Political Action in Václav Havel's Thought* (New York: Lexington Books, 2011); Daniel Brennan, *The Political Thought of Václav Havel* (Leiden: Brill, 2017). For critique, see Pavel Barša, *Cesty k emancipaci* (Prague: Academia, 2015). As in the case of Isaiah Berlin, I will be arguing that Havel's ideas, taken seriously, point in a different political direction than the one generally accepted.

64      **a two-character play:** An English version of *Audience* can be found in Václav Havel, *Three Vaněk Plays,* trans. Jan Novák (London: Faber & Faber, 1990).

64      **period known as "normalization":** The locus classicus on the early years is Kieran Williams, *The Prague Spring and Its Aftermath* (New York: Cambridge University Press, 1997).

64      **"Everything is shit":** Václav Havel, *Hry* (Prague: Lidové Noviny, 1991), 230.

65      **"the gradual erosion":** Václav Havel, "Dear Dr. Husák," in Jan Vladislav, ed., *Václav Havel or Living in Truth* (London: Faber & Faber, 1987). This text is an open letter, sent in April 1975.

65      **a Bohemian in every sense:** Mary Gluck's emphasis on awareness of commercial life and public charisma is consistent with what I mean here. See her *Popular Bohemia: Modernism and Urban Culture in Nineteenth-Century Paris* (Cambridge, Mass.: Harvard University Press, 2008).

65      **moment of contact:** See Václav Havel and Adam Michnik, *An Uncanny Era: Conversations Between Václav Havel and Adam Michnik,* ed. Elżbieta Matynia (New Haven: Yale University Press, 2014). See also Robert Pirro, "Václav Havel and the Political Uses of Tragedy," *Political Theory* 30, no. 2 (2002): 228–58.

66      **"the most probable states":** Václav Havel, "Power of the Powerless," in *The Power*

*of the Powerless* (1985; reprint London: Vintage Classics, 2018), 17. This essay was written and published in samizdat in 1978.

68    **Second Law of Thermodynamics:** In 1969 Jaroslav Putik had already used the phrase "some kind of thermodynamic law" to describe normalization. See Jonathan Bolton, *Worlds of Dissent: Charter 77, the Plastic People of the Universe, and Czech Culture Under Communism* (Cambridge, Mass.: Harvard University Press, 2012), 72.

68    **"Life rebels against all uniformity":** Havel, "Dear Dr. Husák."

68    **"illuminates its surroundings":** Havel, "Power of the Powerless," 36.

69    **phrase of Havel's:** Evgeny Zamiatyn's novel *We*, completed in 1921, the paradigmatic digital dystopia, provides the formulation "the new, the improbable, the unpredictable" (128).

69    **Communists on television dramas:** I learned this from Paulina Bren, *The Greengrocer and His TV* (Ithaca, N.Y.: Cornell University Press, 2010). See also Martin Štoll, *Television and Totalitarianism in Czechoslovakia* (New York: Bloomsbury, 2018); Ellen Mickiewicz, *Split Signals: Television and Politics in the Soviet Union* (New York: Oxford University Press, 1990).

69    **less on "hitting" than on "sitting":** "Government's an affair of sitting, not hitting." Aldous Huxley, *Brave New World* (1932; reprint New York: HarperCollins, 2006), 46.

69    **"our machines are disturbingly lively":** Donna Haraway, "A Manifesto for Cyborgs: Science, Technology, and Socialist Feminism in the 1980s," *Australian Feminist Studies* 2, no. 4 (1985): 5.

70    **least interesting features:** See Nicholas Carr, *The Shallows* (New York: Norton, 2011).

70    **Havel anticipated just such a digital future:** A very precise forecast of digital addiction is to be found in David Foster Wallace, *Infinite Jest* (New York: Little, Brown, 1996).

70    **an example of the "death principle":** Havel, "Dear Dr. Husák."

70    **then invited us:** An uncanny fictional unification of late communism with digital manipulation of the body is Jerzy Sosnowski, *Apogryf Agłai* (Warsaw: W.A.B., 2001).

70    **living in a computer simulation ourselves:** There is more to be said. At some point I hope to have the opportunity to comment on David J. Chalmers, *Reality+: Virtual Worlds and the Problems of Philosophy* (New York: Norton, 2022), a book that is brilliantly of its moment.

71    **"hidden life of society":** Havel, "Dear Dr. Husák."

71    **"The freedom to play rock music":** Havel, "Power of the Powerless," 54.

71    **Jan Patočka, a noted philosopher:** In what follows, I don't even scratch the surface of Patočka's life and work. Marci Shore's forthcoming history of phenomenology in central and eastern Europe delivers the connections.

71    **he called young musicians "our cosmonauts":** Jan Patočka, "On the Matters of the Plastic People of the Universe and DG 307," *Labyrinth* 19, no. 1 (September 2017): 25.

72    **wished to export predictability:** For personal histories of the late Soviet Union, see Katja Petrowskaja, *Vielleicht Esther* (Berlin: Suhrkamp, 2014).

72    **The dream of a communist future:** On the general setting, see Alec Nove, "Marxism and 'Really Existing Socialism,'" in *Studies in Economics and Russia* (London: Palgrave Macmillan, 1990), 171–221; Alfred B. Evans, "Developed Socialism in Soviet Ideology," *Soviet Studies* 29, no. 23 (1977): 409–28. For a case study, see Amir Weiner, *Making Sense of War* (Princeton: Princeton University Press, 2001), and for background, David Brandenberger, *National Bolshevism: Stalinist Mass Culture and the Formation of Modern Russian National Identity, 1931–1956* (Cambridge, Mass.: Harvard University Press, 2002).

72    **Helsinki Final Act, signed in 1975:** Michael Cotey Morgan, *The Final Act: The Helsinki Accords and the Transformation of the Cold War* (Princeton: Princeton University Press, 2018).

73    **to report on conditions:** Abraham Brumberg, "Dissent in Russia," *Foreign Affairs* 52, no. 4 (1974): 781–98; Emma Gilligan, *Defending Human Rights in Russia* (New York: Routledge, 2004).

74    **It arose from the "race music":** Paul Linden, "Race, Hegemony, and the Birth of Rock & Roll," *Journal of the Music & Entertainment Industry Educators Association* 12, no. 1 (2012).

74    **postwar American music:** Russian fascists and Soviet Stalinists held the same view of jazz. See Ivan Ilyin, "Iskusstvo," in D. K. Burlaka, ed., *I.A. Il'in–pro et contra* (St. Petersburg: Izd-vo Russkogo khristianskogo gumanitarnogo in-ta, 2004), 485–86; Maxim Gorkii, "O muzyke tol'stikh," *Pravda,* April 18, 1928. On jazz as anti-communist, see Leopold Tyrmand, *Dziennik 1954* (London: Polonia Book Fund, 1980).

74    **One of these bands:** For the simplicity of the argument I am developing about the unfolding of chance and agency, I focus on the Plastics as exemplary of a larger scene of rock, folk, and later jazz music. See Bolton, *Worlds of Dissent,* chap. 4.

74    **The Plastics started covering:** See Tony Mitchell, "Mixing Pop and Politics: Rock Music in Czechoslovakia Before and After the Velvet Revolution," *Popular Music* 11, no. 2 (1992): 187–203.

74    **of a Jewish family:** Jon Stratton, "Jews, Punk and the Holocaust: From the Velvet Underground to the Ramones: The Jewish-American Story," *Popular Music* 24, no. 1 (2005): 79–105.

74    **pop artist Andy Warhol:** Joan Acocella, "Untangling Andy Warhol," *New Yorker,* June 1, 2020.

74    **the old Habsburg monarchy:** The contemporary locus classicus is Pieter M. Judson, *The Habsburg Monarchy* (Cambridge, Mass.: Harvard University Press, 2016). In the vast literature on Habsburg nationality, some points of orientation are István Deák, *Beyond Nationalism* (New York: Oxford University Press, 1990); Jeremy King, *Budweisers into Czechs and Germans* (Princeton: Princeton University Press, 2002); Keely Stauter-Halsted, *The Nation in the Village* (Ithaca, N.Y.: Cornell University Press, 2001); Iryna Vushko, *Lost Fatherland: Europeans Between Empire and Nation-States, 1867–1939* (New Haven: Yale University Press, 2024).

74    **performed by his band:** "Plastic People" is track 1 of *Absolutely Free,* Verve
      Records, 1967. It is discussed in Bolton, *Worlds of Dissent.* See also Lily E.
      Hirsch, *Insulting Music* (London: Palgrave, 2022), 75–85.

75    **by the Kingsmen:** Richard Williams, "A Rock 'n' Roll Classic," *Independent,*
      June 26, 1993.

75    **by Richard Berry:** Jon Pareles, "Richard Berry, Songwriter of 'Louie Louie,' Dies
      at 61," *NYT,* January 25, 1997.

75    **lifted directly from Touzet's composition:** On this genealogy, see Christopher
      Doll, "A Tale of Two Louies: Interpreting an 'Archetypal American Musical
      Icon,'" *Indiana Theory Review* 29, no. 2 (2011): 71–103; Roberto Avant-Mier,
      *Rock the Nation: Latin/o Identities and the Latin Rock Diaspora* (London:
      Bloomsbury, 2010).

75    **therefore a butterfly:** Helpful to me in making the transition to academic history
      was John Lewis Gaddis, *The Landscape of History* (Oxford: Oxford University
      Press, 2002). That book followed his important article on positivism, predict-
      ability, and Cold War: "International Relations Theory and the End of the Cold
      War," *International Security* 17, no. 3 (1992–93): 5–58.

75    **we always carry with us:** This is a point Krzysztof Michalski and Václav Havel
      ("Power of the Powerless," 117) liked to stress. On Patočka's thought, see James
      Dodd, *The Heresies of Jan Patočka* (Evanston, Ill.: Northwestern University
      Press, 2023).

75    **"the only real help":** Patočka, "On the Matters," 25.

76    **Havel did not like:** Havel, "Power of the Powerless," 74–77.

76    **to a Polish peasant:** Timothy Garton Ash, *The Polish Revolution: Solidarity,* 3rd
      ed. (New Haven: Yale University Press, 2002). This book was originally pub-
      lished in 1984.

76    **self-presentation was modest:** I found something similar in my research on rescue
      during the Holocaust. People who did in fact rescue Jews tended to describe their
      actions as normal, although they differed radically from the sociological normality
      around them. I discuss this in the last chapter and the conclusion of *Black Earth.*
      For similar conclusions, see Nechama Tec, *Christian Rescues of Jews in Nazi-
      Occupied Poland* (New York: Oxford University Press, 1986), 154; Samuel P.
      Oliner, *Altruistic Personality* (New York: Touchstone, 1992), 6; Ewa Fogelman,
      *Conscience and Courage* (New York: Anchor Books, 1994), 6, 73, 140, 260.

76    **normal Ukrainian life:** Myroslav Marynovych, *The Universe Behind Barbed
      Wire: Memoirs of a Ukrainian Soviet Dissident,* trans. Zoya Hayuk (Rochester,
      N.Y.: Rochester University Press, 2021).

77    **"an embargo on normal human aspirations":** Marynovych, *Universe,* 233.

77    **Workers' Defense Committee:** The classic chronicle by a participant is Jan Józef
      Lipski, *KOR: A History of the Workers' Defense Committee in Poland 1976–
      1981,* trans. Olga Amsterdamska and Gene M. Moore (Berkeley: University of
      California Press, 2022); originally published in Polish in 1983.

77    **The dissidents made no grand claims:** For a more sophisticated historical sum-
      mary, see Marci Shore, "A Pre-History of Post-Truth, East and West," *Eurozine,*
      September 1, 2017.

77    **"as if they were free"**: Adam Michnik, *Letters from Prison and Other Essays* (Berkeley: University of California Press, 1985).

78    **contended that "spiritual maturity"**: Rowan Williams, "The Spirit in the Desert: Self Discovery," posted August 21, 2015, www.youtube.com/watch?v =jLwDIs3pkrg, at 7:20. See also his *Silence and Honey Cakes: The Wisdom of the Desert* (Oxford: Lion Books, 2003).

79    **This is the dead end:** This claim can be contested in two ways, at least. One is to maintain that 1968 had some progressive consequences (I agree). David Edgar, *The Radical Legacy of 1986 Is Under Attack, Guardian,* May 10, 2018. Another is to argue, as Christian Laval has done, that the argument for a neoliberal connection is completely false and that its very existence in the culture is nothing more than further evidence of the hegemony of neoliberalism. This might be too clever. Christian Laval, "May '68: Paving the Way for the Triumph of Neo-liberalism?," *Le Deleuziana,* no. 8 (2018). There were of course other tendencies entirely. See Jacob Collins, *The Anthropological Turn: French Political Thought After 1968* (Philadelphia: University of Pennsylvania Press, 2020).

80    **looked for older mentors:** For Michnik personally, very important was Antoni Słonimski, a poet who first made his name in the interwar period. See Marci Shore, *Caviar and Ashes: A Warsaw Generation's Life and Death in Marxism* (New Haven: Yale University Press, 2006).

80    **"world of values"**: Leszek Kołakowski, "Pochwała niekonsekwencji," *Twórczość,* no. 9 (1958): 92, reprinted in Zbigniew Mentzel, ed., *Pochwała niekonsekwencji. Pisma rozproszone z lat 1955–1968* (London: Puls, 1989), 2:158.

80    **Any single virtue has an absolute claim:** Antoine de Saint-Exupéry has a nice moment of this in *Vol de nuit,* after the disappearance of a pilot: "This woman was also speaking in the name of an absolute world, of its duties and its rights." *Vol de nuit* (Paris: Gallimard, 1931), 88.

80    **cannot be told without virtue:** James Madison rightly thought that it was "chimerical" to think about liberty without virtue. Virginia Ratifying Convention, June 20, 1788.

81    **we are doing right:** Aristotle, *Nicomachean Ethics,* bk. 3, chap. 5.

81    **"the reality of evil"**: Leszek Kołakowski, "Warum brauchen wir Kant?," *Merkur,* nos. 9/10 (1981): 917, published the same year in Polish as "Kant a zagrożenie cywilizacji." Simone Weil puts it this way: "In every situation, whatever we do, we do evil, intolerable evil." Weil, *La pesanteur et la grâce,* 167.

81    **pluralism means not relativism:** See Isaiah Berlin, *The Crooked Timber of Humanity* (Princeton: Princeton University Press, 1990), 11 and passim.

81    **a commitment to creative courage:** A good example was Józef Czapski, about whom I hope to write at greater length: "I always tried to choose what seemed like the lesser evil and I struggled as hard as I could to reduce that evil." Czapski to Ludwik Hering, October 28, 1948. His thinking anticipated and influenced a number of the east European dissidents. Czapski was influenced by Weil, who wrote of "the least bad idols."

81    **"There can be good judgement"**: Thomas Nagel, *Mortal Questions* (Cambridge: Cambridge University Press, 1979), 135.

81    **"Do your best"**: Hannah Beachler, speech on winning Best Production Design
      for *Black Panther* (video), https://www.youtube.com/watch?v=LpBvXKLCvyg,
      at 4:09; Emily Shapiro, "Hannah Beachler's Emotional Speech During Historic
      Oscars Production Design Win: 'My Best Is Good Enough,'" ABC News, Feb-
      ruary 24, 2019. Compare to Leon Bass's recollections, cited in chapter 3. In the
      2000 song "Optimistic," Radiohead also assures that "the best you can is good
      enough," but I'm less sure what they meant.

81    **invent new virtues**: Leszek Kołakowski, "Etyka bez kodeksu," *Twórczość*, no. 7
      (1962): 85, reprinted in Kołakowski, *Kultura i fetysze* (1967; reprint Warsaw:
      PWN, 2000), 158. Hannah Arendt, Isaiah Berlin, Friedrich Nietzsche, and Sim-
      one Weil also held the view that the highest human achievement was the cre-
      ation of virtues.

81    **They emerge when we do things**: In the words that Thomas Bernhard heard from
      his grandfather: "Ever more mosaic stones in the great picture of the world!"
      *Ein Kind* (1981; reprint Munich: dtv, 2016), 77.

82    **"all of our Łódź family"**: Tamara Kołakowska, *Było . . . Wspomnienia z młodości*
      (Cracow: Znak, 2021), 85. For the history of the Łódź ghetto, see Andrea Löw,
      *Juden im Getto Litzmannstadt* (Göttingen: Wallstein Verlag, 2006). A valuable
      historical novel is Steve Sem-Sandberg, *The Emperor of Lies* (London: Faber &
      Faber, 2011). On the aftermath, see Shimon Redlich, *Life in Transit: Jews in
      Postwar Łódź* (Boston: Academic Studies Press, 2010).

82    **"My existence is realized"**: Kołakowski, "Etyka bez kodeksu," 173.

82    **one of Kołakowski's subjects**: Leszek Kołakowski, *Main Currents of Marxism,*
      trans. P. S. Falla, 3 vols. (Oxford: Oxford University Press, 1978).

83    **a Polish social thinker**: Andrzej Waśkiewicz has since written a series of books
      on social and political thought, including *Paradoksy idei reprezentacji politycz-
      nej* (Warsaw: Scholar, 2012).

83    **my laptop was stolen**: I told the story for History News Network in 2005, https://
      historynewsnetwork.org/article/160270.

84    **the CEOs quickly drafted**: Jeffrey Sonnenfeld, who convened this meeting, re-
      called what happen then and thereafter in an email of March 29, 2023.

84    **has no clear purpose**: Martin Burckhardt, *Philosophie der Maschine* (Berlin:
      Matthes & Seitz, 2018), 31. Compare Giorgio Agamben, *The Open: Man and
      Animal* (Stanford, Calif.: Stanford University Press, 2004), chap. 8.

84    **they are disengaging us**: My long treatment of computer, mind, and body is *Und
      wie elektrische Schafe träumen wir: Humanität, Sexualität, Digitalität* (Vienna:
      Passagen, 2020), which arose as the essay "And We Dream as Electric Sheep: On
      Humanity, Sexuality and Digitality," published with notes in *Eurozine,* May 6,
      2019, and without notes as "What Turing Told Us About the Digital Threat to a
      Human Future," *New York Review of Books,* May 6, 2019. It elaborates a num-
      ber of ideas raised here and extends the gender dimension of the argument in
      chapter 2.

86    **a Polish scenographer**: My biography of Henryk Józewski is *Sketches from a
      Secret War: A Polish Artist's Mission to Liberate Soviet Ukraine* (New Haven:
      Yale University Press, 2006). Excerpts from his own rather mystical memoir

appear in Henryk Józewski, "Zamiast pamiętnika," *Zeszyty Historyczne,* no. 59 (1982): 3–163.

86    **unpredictable sort of life:** My biography of Wilhelm von Habsburg is *The Red Prince: The Secret Lives of a Habsburg Archduke* (New York: Basic Books, 2008).

87    **that Russia would invade:** Timothy Snyder, "Don't Let Putin Grab Ukraine," *NYT,* February 3, 2014.

87    **The rule of law and human dignity:** On the Maidan, see Marci Shore, *The Ukrainian Night: An Intimate History of Revolution,* rev. ed. (New Haven: Yale University Press, 2024).

87    **civil society organizations:** Snyder, *Road to Unfreedom,* chaps. 3 and 4.

87    **for a conference:** For further information about *Ukraine: Thinking Together,* see https://www.iwm.at/event/ukraine-thinking-together.

87    **Colleagues and I:** The call was from Leon Wieseltier and Frank Foer; some of the organizers were Tania Zhurzenko, Vasyl Cherepanyn, Oksana Forostyna, Katherine Younger, and Klaus Nellen.

88    **got his skull broken:** Sally McGrane, "The Abuse of Ukraine's Best-Known Poet," *New Yorker,* March 8, 2014.

88    **Bohdan was murdered:** Alison Smale, "Lviv, in Western Ukraine, Mourns One of Its Own Killed in Kiev," *NYT,* February 23, 2014; Ukrainian Catholic University Foundation, "UCU Scholarship in Memory of Hero Bohdan Solchanyk Endowed," UKUFoundation.org, December 10, 2020.

89    **speaking from experience:** The wartime experience that Yevhenii Monastyrskyi has written about in philosophical terms is that of an internal refugee: "We, Internally Displaced Persons," *apofenie,* November 29, 2023. The title refers to Hannah Arendt's "We Refugees" of 1943.

89    **"unnatural space peopled":** James Davis III, "Law, Prison, and Double-Double Consciousness: A Phenomenological View of the Black Prisoner's Experience," *Yale Law Journal* 128 (2018–19).

89    **complained of solitary confinement:** Austin Reed, *The Life and Adventures of a Haunted Convict,* ed. Caleb Smith (New York: Modern Library, 2017). This work was composed around 1858.

89    **our need for encounter:** Lisa Guenther, *Solitary Confinement: Social Death and Its Afterlives* (Duluth: University of Minnesota Press, 2013), 213. This is a very basic summary of one of a series of arguments she has made in confrontation with Levinas, Merleau-Ponty, and Heidegger.

90    **all the dopamine hits:** Former Facebook employees tell us that this was the goal. Amy B. Wang, "Former Facebook VP Says Social Media Is Destroying Society with 'Dopamine-Driven Feedback Loops,'" *Washington Post,* December 12, 2017; Jaron Lanier, *Ten Arguments for Deleting Your Social Media Accounts Right Away* (London: Bodley Head, 2018), 8.

90    **changed the world:** For example, we are now living in a world in which a girl has killed herself because a nonexistent boy broke up with her (https://www.megan meierfoundation.org/).

91    **mechanically amplified prejudices:** Virginia Eubanks, *Automating Inequality: How*

*High-Tech Tools Profile, Police, and Punish the Poor* (New York: Macmillan, 2018), 172. On this example, see Snyder, *Road to Unfreedom,* chaps. 4 and 5.

91 **exactly the same Russian institutions:** I tell the story of the new tyranny of the 2010s in *Road to Unfreedom.* Readers interested in primary sources should please consult that book. For a quick philosophical summary, see Michiko Kakutani, *The Death of Truth* (New York: Tim Duggan Books, 2018), chapters 7–8.

91 **liked Black criminals:** See for example, Ryan Grenoble, "Here Are Some of the Ads Russia Paid to Promote on Facebook," *HuffPost,* November 1, 2017; Cecilia Kang, "Russia-Financed Ad Linked Clinton and Satan," *NYT,* November 2, 2017; Ben Collins et al., "Russia Recruited YouTubers," *Daily Beast,* October 8, 2017; April Glaser, "Russian Trolls Are Still Co-Opting Black Organizers' Events," *Technology,* November 7, 2017. See also Sara Wachtel-Boettcher, *Technically Wrong* (New York: Norton, 2017).

91 **Internet Research Agency:** See the sources on Trump and 2016 cited in the introduction; Snyder, *Road to Unfreedom,* chap. 6; and Craig Silverman and Jeff Gao, "Infamous Russian Troll Farm Appears to Be Source of Anti-Ukraine Propaganda," *ProPublica,* March 11, 2022.

91 **Prigozhin also directed:** Nathaniel Reynolds, *Putin's Not-so-Secret Mercenaries: Patronage, Geopolitics, and the Wagner Group* (New York: Carnegie Endowment for International Peace, 2019).

91 **The agglomeration of data:** On how the most sensitive data is quantified, see Mathilde Loire, "Que deviennent les données des applications pour le suivi des règles?," *Le Monde,* August 24, 2017; Sam Schechner and Mark Secada, "You Give Apps Sensitive Personal Information. Then They Tell Facebook," *Wall Street Journal,* February 22, 2019.

91 **Chinese authorities judge you:** Lotus Roan, "When the Winner Takes It All," Issues Paper, Australian Strategic Policy Institute, 2018; Randolph Kluver, "The Architecture of Control: A Chinese Strategy for e-Governance," *Journal of Public Policy* 25, no. 1 (2005): 75–97.

92 **Your qualities are turned back:** Zbigniew Herbert had a poem about (and entitled) "The Interrogation of the Angel." Herbert, *Wiersze zebrane,* ed. R. Krynicki (Cracow: Wydawnictwo a5, 2008), 331–32.

92 **give sleep away:** See Michael Finkel, "While We Sleep, Our Mind Goes on an Amazing Journey," *National Geographic,* August 2018.

92 **"quantity of creative genius":** Weil, *La pesanteur et la grâce,* 192.

92 **Much is wrong with IQ tests:** James Robert Flynn, *What Is Intelligence?* (New York: Cambridge University Press, 2009).

92 **Reverse Flynn Effect:** James Flynn himself blames the rise of the internet and the decline of traditional reading. See also Bernt Bratsberg and Ole Rogeberg, "Flynn Effect and Its Reversal Are Both Environmentally Caused," *Proceedings of the National Academy of Sciences of the United States of America* 115, no. 26 (2018): 6674–78.

93 **sense of the continuity:** Marcel Proust, *Du côté de chez Swann* (Paris: Grasset, 1913). Consider also Józef Czapski, *Lost Time: Lectures on Proust in a Soviet*

*Prison Camp,* trans. Eric Karpeles (New York: New York Review Books, 2018). This book was published in the original French in 1948.

93    **Our minds flutter:** Sheri Madigan et al., "Association Between Screen Time and Children's Performance on a Developmental Screening Test," *JAMA Pediatrics* 173, no. 3 (2019): 244–50; Seungyeon Lee et al., "The Effects of Cell Phone Use and Emotion-Regulation Style on College Students' Learning," *Applied Cognitive Psychology* 31, no. 3 (June 2017): 360–66.

93    **we do not remember:** Adrian F. Ward et al., "Brain Drain: The Mere Presence of One's Own Smartphone Reduces Available Cognitive Capacity," *Journal of the Association of Consumer Research* 2, no. 2 (2017).

93    **How do we regain time?:** When I was recovering from serious illness in the hospital and unable to sleep, I listened to music that helped me to remember my life.

96    **gives way to increasing fear:** As I wrote these endnotes, a colleague's lecture was changed into a moderated conversation while he was en route to the site.

97    **No notion of means-ends rationality:** When I speak of rationality in this book, I have in mind either means-ends rationality or the word *rationality* as it is used in libertarian and other propaganda, in the sense of rationalization. For a list of definitions of *rationality,* see Susanna Siegel, *The Rationality of Perception* (Oxford: Oxford University Press, 2017), 15–16.

97    **like satellite servers:** In Yevgeny Zamiatyn's novel *We,* to be "perfect" is to be "machine-equal." *We* was an inspiration both for *Brave New World* and for *1984.*

98    *why* **creatures into** *how* **creatures:** Frantz Fanon, *Black Skin, White Masks,* trans. Richard Phillcox (New York: Grove Press, 2008), esp. chaps. 1 and 5; originally published in French in 1952.

98    **therefore as instruments:** As my cousin Emma Jane Mitchell's work reminded me, this is the link between colonial and disability discourses.

98    **our mechanical colonizers:** Compare Massimo Cacciari, *Europe and Empire: On the Political Forms of Globalization,* trans. Massimo Verdicchio (New York: Fordham University Press, 2016), 114.

98    **have no agency:** Compare Lanier, *Ten Arguments,* 33: "relentless, robotic, ultimately meaningless behavior modification in the service of unseen manipulators and uncaring algorithms."

98    **"capitalism will be succeeded":** Simone Weil, *Réflexions sur les causes de la liberté et de l'oppression sociale* (Paris: Gallimard, 1955). Henry David Thoreau worried that we had become the tools of our tools. On concentration and attention in his time, see Caleb Smith, *Thoreau's Axe* (New Haven: Yale University Press, 2023).

98    **In "surveillance capitalism":** Shoshana Zuboff, *The Age of Surveillance Capitalism: The Fight for a Human Future at the New Frontier of Power* (New York: PublicAffairs, 2020).

98    **rationality means constant monitoring:** For a similar line of thought, consult Joseph Raz, *The Morality of Freedom* (Oxford: Oxford University Press, 1986), 357.

98    **rationalize the past:** In his novel *Stiller,* Max Frisch presents a Switzerland where people believe that freedom is something that they possess, rather than a prob-

lem to be confronted. This leads them to rationalize the present rather than think about the future.

99    **"utility becomes something"**: Simone Weil, *On Science, Necessity, and the Love of God,* trans. and ed. Richard Rees (Oxford: Oxford University Press, 1968), ix.

100    **"calculus of the nervous system"**: Cited in Burckhardt, *Philosophie der Maschine,* 241.

101    **exploits brain hacks**: See Roger McNamee, *Zucked* (New York: Penguin, 2019), 9 and passim.

101    **continues every time**: Gail B. Peterson, "A Day of Great Illumination: B. F. Skinner's Discovery of Shaping," *Journal of the Experimental Analysis of Behavior* 82, no. 3 (2004): 317–28.

101    **The first brain hack is *experimental isolation***: For a brief introduction, see Tristan Harris, "How Technology Is Hijacking Your Mind," *Medium,* May 18, 2016.

101    **an artificial loneliness**: "If we are alone too long," says Maupassant, "we populate the world with phantoms."

102    **intermittently reinforce others**: See Alexandra Rutherford, *Beyond the Box: B. F. Skinner's Technology of Behaviour from Laboratory to Life, 1950s–1970s* (Toronto: University of Toronto Press, 2009).

102    **what you fear**: Lanier, *Ten Arguments,* 18.

102    **indifferent to motives**: Here and above I am learning from Guenther, *Solitary Confinement,* 111–20.

102    **seemed to understand**: I learned this from Peter Godfrey-Smith's delightful *Other Minds: The Octopus, the Sea, and the Deep Origins of Consciousness* (New York: HarperCollins, 2014). See also Ashley Ward, *The Social Lives of Animals* (New York: Basic Books, 2022); Roger T. Hanlon and John B. Messenger, *Cephalopod Behaviour* (Cambridge: Cambridge University Press, 2018).

103    **only familiar pyrite baubles**: The connecting figure here is Ayn Rand, who was a Bolshevik *à rebours.*

103    **"warning to the West"**: Havel, "Power of the Powerless," 35–36.

103    **Our collective unreasonability**: Herman Melville puts it nicely in his story "Bartleby the Scrivener": "The constant friction of illiberal minds wears out at last the best resolves of the more generous."

103    **One form this unreasonability takes**: For this and succeeding brain hacks, see Lee McIntyre, *Post-Truth* (Cambridge, Mass.: MIT Press, 2018), 42ff.

104    **nudges us along**: See Roman Bornstein, "Ingérence numérique, mode d'emploi," *Le Débat,* no. 208 (2020–21): 42–55.

104    **"What we need is warm silence"**: Simone Weil, *La personne et le sacré* (Paris: Payot & Rivages, 2017), 45. This book was composed in 1942–43.

104    **some of the apparent people**: On this phenomenon in political campaigns, see Onur Varol et al., "Online Human-Bot Interactions: Detection," *Proceedings of the Eleventh International AAAI Conference on Web and Social Media,* March 27, 2017; Alessandro Bessit and Emilio Ferrara, "Social Bots Distort the 2016 U.S. Presidential Election Online Discussion," *First Monday* 21, no. 11 (November 7, 2016); Marco T. Bastos and Dan Mercea, "The Brexit Botnet and User-Generated Hyperpartisan News," *Social Science Computer Review* 37, no. 1

(2017); Selina Wang, "Twitter Is Crawling with Bots," *Bloomberg,* October 13, 2017; Severin Carrell, "Russian Cyber-Activists 'Tried to Discredit Scottish Independence Vote,'" *Guardian,* December 13, 2017; Carole Cadwalladr, "The Great British Brexit Robbery: How Our Democracy Was Hijacked," *Guardian,* May 7, 2017.

104    **the biggest Facebook group:** Francis Agustin, "Troll Farms Peddling Misinformation," *Business Insider,* September 19, 2021.

104    **our emotions hollow:** The debate about "Can machines think?" took a turn with Alan Turing, "Computational Machinery and Intelligence," *Mind* 236 (1950): 433–66, question at 433. See Roger Penrose, *The Emperor's New Mind* (New York, Oxford University Press, 1989), 6–7 and passim. In my essay "And We Dream as Electric Sheep," I argue that the Turing test has to be reconsidered in light of the presence of the *Leib.*

104    **must be correct:** Eubanks, *Automating Inequality,* 172. I learned the term *math-washed* from Eubanks.

104    **bodies of other people:** Animals are almost as important as people in Philip K. Dick, *Do Androids Dream of Electric Sheep?* (1966; reprint London: Penguin, 2007). Although I do not develop the theme here, this makes sense. Humans can also feel empathy toward nonhuman creatures (although we need not). We can eat as much meat as we do only because we are physically distanced from the animals whose bodies we consume. See also Agamben, *The Open.*

104    **begin to harden:** They amplify the Dunning-Kruger effect.

104    **until we feel attacked:** Carol Tavris and Elliot Aronson, *Mistakes Were Made (But Not by Me)* (London: Pinter & Martin, 2015), 83.

105    **stole the election:** On digital politics in 2016, see Yuriy Gorodnichenko, Tho Pham, and Oleksandr Talavera, "Social Media, Sentiment and Public Opinions: Evidence from #Brexit and #USElection," National Bureau of Economic Research, Working Paper no. 2463 (2018).

105    **You have exposed your buttons:** This includes our racism. See Sofiya Umoja Noble, *Algorithms of Oppression* (New York: NYU Press, 2017), 36, 115, 124, and passim.

105    **without being a thinker:** I have the notion of "thinking without a thinker" from Burckhardt, *Philosophie der Maschine,* 17 and passim.

105    **without there being a conspiracy theorist:** Lanier, *Ten Arguments,* 108–9.

105    **claim that Hillary Clinton kidnaps children:** I tell the story in *Road to Unfreedom.* See also Marc Fisher, John Woodrow Cox, and Peter Hermann "Pizzagate: From Rumor, to Hashtag, to Gunfire in D.C.," *Washington Post,* December 6, 2016; Mary Papenfuss, "Russian Trolls Linked Clinton to 'Satanic Ritual,'" *HuffPost,* December 1, 2017. The director of the Internet Research Agency, Yevgeny Progozhin, was later a major actor in a war that did, in fact, involve kidnapping children.

105    **Putin says Ukraine does not exist:** Putin made these claims for over a decade and continues to make them. Telling for me was Vladimir Putin, "Rossiia: natsional'nyi vopros," *Nezavisimaia Gazeta,* January 23, 2012. See also Vladimir Putin, "Novyy integratsionnyy proyekt dlya Yevrazii," *Izvestiia,* October 3, 2011.

105 **Trump says that he won:** Jim Rutenberg and Kate Conger, "Elon Musk Is Spreading Election Misinformation, but X's Fact Checkers Are Long Gone," *NYT,* January 25, 2024.

106 **As we expose our vulnerabilities:** For empirical examples from 2016, see Massimo Calabresi, "Hacking Democracy," *Time,* May 29, 2017; Nicholas Confessore and Daisuke Wakabayashi, "How Russia Harvested American Rage," *NYT,* October 9, 2017; David Pierson, "Russia Tried and Failed to Harvest Social Discord in America. Then It Discovered Social Media," *Los Angeles Times,* February 22, 2018; Rebecca Shabad, "Russian Facebook Ad Showed Black Woman," CBS, October 3, 2017.

106 **As we come to feel more lonely:** The argument about loneliness goes back to Hannah Arendt and (I think) to Hegel, who defined freedom as being "at home" *(bei sich selbst zu sein).* See Arendt, *Origins of Totalitarianism,* 352 and passim. Loneliness makes us less free in other ways: see Vivek Murthy, "Our Epidemic of Loneliness and Isolation," U.S. Surgeon General's Advisory, 2023.

106 **citizens' beliefs and fears:** For example, in 2016, likely Trump voters were exposed to pro-Clinton messages on fake American Muslim sites. Russian pro-Trump propaganda associated refugees with rape.

106 **calls people "vermin":** Marianne LeVine, "Trump Calls Political Enemies 'Vermin,' Echoing Dictators Hitler, Mussolini," *Washington Post,* November 13, 2023; Caleb Ecarma, "Detention Camps, 'Vermin' Rivals, and a Government Purge," *Vanity Fair,* November 13, 2023.

106 **ready for violence:** Robert Pape, "Deep, Divisive, Disturbing and Continuing: New Survey Shows Mainstream Support for Violence to Restore Trump Remains Strong," Chicago Project on Security and Threats, January 2, 2022.

106 **storm the Capitol:** *Final Report of the Select Committee to Investigate the January 6th Attack on the United States Capitol,* December 22, 2022.

107 **not to make love:** See Kate Julian, "Why Are Young People Having So Little Sex?," *Atlantic,* December 2018. In Philip K. Dick's *Do Androids Dream of Electric Sheep,* Rachel tells Decker at a tender moment: "Don't pause and be philosophical, because from a philosophical standpoint it's dreary."

107 **locate our political fantasies:** See Alice Marwick and Rebecca Lewis, "Media Manipulation and Disinformation Online," Data & Society Research Institute, 2017; Tamsin Shaw, "Invisible Manipulators of Your Mind," *New York Review of Books,* April 20, 2017; Paul Lewis, "Our Minds Can Be Hijacked," *Guardian,* October 6, 2017.

107 **our capacities to see diversity:** In *The Left Hand of Darkness,* Ursula K. Le Guin wrote that "to oppose something is to maintain it."

107 **Our fear is there:** The machine does not have to understand racism to magnify and exploit it. Compare Jennifer Saul, "Dog Whistles, Political Manipulation, and Philosophy of Language," in Daniel Fogal, Daniel W. Harris, and Matt Moss, eds., *New Work on Speech Acts* (Oxford: Oxford University Press, 2018), 360–83.

108 **we become the chatbots:** Arundhati Roy, lecture at Swedish Academy, March 22, 2023.

108    **"he who is deceived"**: Mikhail Bakhtin, in his 1943 diary, quoted in Leonidas
       Donskis, *Modernity in Crisis: A Dialogue on the Culture of Belonging* (New
       York: Palgrave Macmillan, 2015), 133.

108    **give our recruiter an alibi**: See Lee McIntyre, *Post-Truth* (Cambridge, Mass.:
       MIT Press, 2018), 42.

108    **This is *cognitive dissonance***: An accessible introduction is Tavris and Aronson,
       *Mistakes Were Made,* 22 and passim.

108    **"living automata, which some mysterious hand"**: Lev Shestov, *All Things Are
       Possible* (London: Martin Secker, 1920).

109    **ancient Greek poems**: On classical reflections, see Burckhardt, *Philosophie der
       Maschine,* and Adrienne Mayor, *Gods and Robots: Myths, Machines, and
       Ancient Dreams of Technology* (Princeton: Princeton University Press, 2018).

110    **George Orwell saw vocabulary**: Peter Bieri also warned of "mindless habits of
       speech" in his *Wie wollen wir leben* (Salzburg: Rezidenz, 2011).

110    **in his novel *1984***: George Orwell, *1984* (London: Secker & Warburg, 1949).

110    **their bodies are always observed**: Michel Schneider might be right, however, that
       our situation is more one of "Big Mother" than "Big Brother." Schneider, *Big
       Mother: Psychopathologie de la vie politique* (Paris: Jacob, 2005).

110    **their language is famished**: Victor Klemperer, *The Language of the Third Reich,*
       trans. Martin Brady (London: Continuum, 2006), 10–17 and passim.

110    **firefighters burn books**: Ray Bradbury, *Fahrenheit 451* (New York: Ballantine,
       1953).

110    **only by knowing ourselves**: Compare Simone Weil, "L'Iliade ou le poème de la
       force," which she published in *Les Cahiers du Sud* under a masculine pseudonym
       in 1940 and 1941. This text was very influential during the war upon people who
       did not know she was its author, such as Czesław Miłosz. I discovered it in Ber-
       nard Knox and Simone Weil, *L'Iliade: Poème du XXIe siècle* (Paris: Arlea, 2006).

110    **notion of nemesis**: See Rachel Bespaloff's chapter on Hector in her *De l'Iliade*
       (Paris: Les Belles Lettres, 2022), originally published in 1943. This essay was
       published in English translation alongside Weil's by the *New York Review of
       Books* in 2005.

110    **After the *Iliad* was finally published**: The edition I read is *Chapman's Homer:
       The Iliad,* trans. George Chapman, ed. Allardyce Nicoll (1611; reprint Prince-
       ton: Princeton University Press, 1998).

## MOBILITY

113    **debate team with a patient coach**: This was Ralph Bender: https://www.youtube
       .com/watch?v=gd_PEwwzSK0.

114    **enabling me to write**: Bruce Chatwin asks whether we are so easily distracted
       because we do not move enough. *The Songlines* (London: Penguin, 1987), 161.

114    **Those who require more assistance**: Eva Feder Kittay, "Centering Justice on
       Dependency and Recovering Freedom," *Hypatia* 20, no. 1 (2015): 286. See also
       David Mitchell with Sharon L. Snyder, *The Biopolitics of Disability* (Ann
       Arbor: University of Michigan Press, 2015).

115 geroscience—preventive treatment: Cassandra Willyard, "Aging Without Ill-ness," *Science News,* January 13, 2024, 22–26.

116 challenge of maturity: "Freedom as an inner capacity of man is identical with the capacity to begin, just as freedom as a political reality is identified with a space of movement between men." Arendt, *Origins of Totalitarianism,* 477.

116 Irene Morgan came of age: On her life and trial, see "Irene Morgan Kirkaldy (1917–2007)," Archives of Maryland.

116 illegal, in theory: Robert L. Carter, "The Implications of the Irene Morgan Decision Review Note," *Lawyers Guild Review* 6 (1946): 599–601.

116 Nothing much changed: Joseph R. Palmore, "The Not-So-Strange Career of Interstate Jim Crow," *Virginia Law Review* 83, no. 8 (1997): 1773–817.

117 *liberation* was not the word: The inmates, according to the nurse, "couldn't be liberated. What they needed was medical care, lots of it and as soon as possi-ble." Dan Stone, *The Liberation of the Camps: The End of the Holocaust and Its Aftermath* (New Haven: Yale University Press, 2015), 74.

117 "Racism is at the root": Leon Bass, in podcast episode 2, Fortunoff Video Archive for Holocaust Testimonies, https://fortunoff.library.yale.edu/podcast/leon-bass/.

118 Woodard tried to return: Richard Gergel, *Unexampled Courage: The Blinding of Sgt. Isaac Woodard and the Awakening of President Harry S. Truman and Judge J. Waties Waring* (New York: Farrar, Straus & Giroux, 2019).

119 their own "hate bus": These and other details above are drawn from Raymond Arsenault, *Freedom Riders: 1961 and the Struggle for Racial Justice* (Oxford: Oxford University Press, 2007). A photo of the hate bus can be found at http://images.google.com/hosted/life/1dcba96f781e9302.html. On the American Nazi Party, see Frederick J. Simonelli, *American Fuehrer: George Lincoln Rockwell and the American Nazi Party* (Champaign: University of Illinois Press, 1999).

120 join the ranks of the Free French: Fanon was from Martinique, but in his book he discusses the experience of African soldiers. See Eric T. Jennings, *Free French Africa in World War Two* (Cambridge: Cambridge University Press, 2015).

120 "sense of always looking at oneself": W. E. B. Du Bois, *The Souls of Black Folk* (1903; reprint Oxford: Oxford World's Classics, 2007), 8.

120 "I was coming into the world": Fanon, *Black Skin, White Masks,* 89.

121 to be a good German: Peter Longerich, *Politik der Vernichtung* (Munich: Piper, 1998), or *Holocaust* (New York: Oxford University Press, 2010). See also Thomas Kühne, *Belonging and Genocide* (New Haven: Yale University Press, 2010).

121 Hitler identified Jews: My summary of Hitler's worldview can be found in *Black Earth.* It works with the available primary sources, which include Adolf Hitler, *Hitler and His Generals: Military Conferences 1942–1945,* ed. David M. Glantz, trans. Roland Winter, Krista Smith, and Mary Beth Friedrich (New York: Enigma Books, 2003); Hitler, *Hitler's Second Book: The Unpublished Sequel to Mein Kampf,* ed. Gerhard L. Weinberg, trans. Krista Smith (New York: Enigma Books, 2010), dictated 1928, German edition 1961; Hitler, *Hitler's Table Talk 1941–1944: His Private Conversations,* trans. Norman Cameron and R. H. Stevens (New York: Enigma Books, 2000); Hitler, *Mein Kampf* (1925–26; reprint Munich:

Zentralverlag der NSDAP, 1939); Hitler, *Sämtliche Aufzeichnungen, 1905–1924,* ed. Eberhard Jäckel and Axel Kuhn (Stuttgart: Deutsche Verlags-Anstalt, 1980); Hitler, *Staatsmänner und Diplomaten bei Hitler,* part 2: *Vertrauliche Aufzeichnungen über die Unterredungen mit Vertretern des Auslandes 1942–1944,* ed. Andreas Hillgruber (Frankfurt: Bernard & Graefe, 1970). On time, compare Johann Chapoutot, "L'historicité nazie: Temps de la nature et abolition de l'histoire," *Vingtième siècle,* no. 117 (2013): 43–55.

121 **no fourth dimension:** Reinhart Koselleck, *Futures Past,* trans. Keith Tribe (Cambridge, Mass.: MIT Press, 1985).

121 **so that nature could be redeemed:** Hitler, *Mein Kampf,* 69, 287; Hitler, *Sämtliche Aufzeichnungen,* 462–63.

122 **was a "Jewish swindle":** Hitler, *Mein Kampf,* 282–83. The role of food in Hitler's practice has been appreciated since Christian Gerlach, *Krieg, Ernährung, Völkermord: Forschungen zur deutschen Vernichtungspolitik im Zweiten Weltkrieg* (Hamburg: Hamburger Edition, 1998).

122 **The idea was to dominate:** See Timothy Snyder, "The Causes of the Holocaust," *Contemporary European History* 21, no. 2 (2012): 149–68.

123 **Marx's analysis of capitalism:** Often it was his running political commentary, informed by that analysis, that was most on target. See Karl Marx, *The Eighteenth Brumaire of Louis Bonaparte* (New York: International Publishers, 1987); originally published in German in 1852.

123 **Stalin had to plan an industrialization:** I narrate this in greater detail in *Bloodlands,* chap. 1. See also Hiroaki Kuromiya, *Stalin* (Harlow: Pearson Longman, 2005).

123 **for about a generation:** This can be nuanced, of course. See Sheila Fitzpatrick, *Education and Social Mobility in the Soviet Union, 1921–1934* (Cambridge: Cambridge University Press, 1979).

123 **concentration camps of the Gulag:** See Oleg V. Khlevniuk, *The History of the Gulag* (New Haven: Yale University Press, 2004); Lynna Viola, *The Unknown Gulag: The Lost World of Stalin's Special Settlements* (New York: Oxford University Press, 2007); Anne Applebaum, *Gulag: A History* (New York: Doubleday, 2003).

123 **about four million people were starved:** Barbara Falk, *Sowjetische Städte in der Hungersnot 1932/33* (Cologne: Böhlau Verlag, 2005); Jan Jacek Bruski, *Hołodomor 1932–1933* (Warsaw: PISM, 2008). I devote chapter 1 of *Bloodlands* to this starvation campaign. The current state of the art in English is Anne Applebaum, *Red Famine: Stalin's War on Ukraine* (New York: Doubleday, 2017); abundant research is now available in Ukrainian.

124 **provided the example:** Hua-Yu Li, *Mao and the Economic Stalinization of China, 1948–1953* (New York: Rowman & Littlefield, 2006); Frank Dikötter, Dikötter, *Mao's Great Famine* (London: Bloomsbury, 2010).

124 **killing at least forty million people:** Dikötter, *Mao's Great Famine.*

124 **colonization of India and Africa:** On various continuities from overseas colonialism, see Magnus Brechtken, *"Madagaskar für die Juden": Antisemitische Idee und politische Praxis 1885–1945* (Munich: R. Oldenbourg Verlag, 1997); Peter

Black, "Askaris in the 'Wild East': The Deployment of Auxiliaries and the Implementation of Nazi Racial Policy in Lublin District," in Charles W. Ingrao and Franz A. J. Szabo, eds., *The Germans and the* East (West Lafayette, Ind.: Purdue University Press, 2008), 277–309; Willeke Hannah Sandler, *Empire in the Heimat* (New York: Oxford University Press, 2018); Jürgen Zimmerer, *Von Windhuk nach Auschwitz* (LIT Verlag, 2011); Lora Wildenthal, *German Women for Empire, 1884–1945* (Durham, N.C.: Duke University Press, 2001).

124     **Stalin believed that the USSR should exploit:** See Timothy Snyder and Ray Brandon, eds., *Stalin and Europe: Imitation and Domination, 1928–1953* (New York: Oxford University Press, 2014).

124     **drew inspiration from the imperial mobility:** See Hitler, *Hitler's Second Book;* Klaus P. Fischer, *Hitler and America* (Philadelphia: University of Pennsylvania Press, 2011).

125     **France had just ceded to Britain:** Ute Planert and James Retallack, eds., *Decades of Reconstruction* (Cambridge: Cambridge University Press, 2017), part 1.

126     **new postcolonial regimes:** Enlightening here is Kamel Daoud, *Meursault, contre-enquête* (Paris: Barzakh Editions, 2013).

126     **just over a decade:** See Eric Foner, *Reconstruction: America's Unfinished Revolution* (New York: HarperCollins, 2014).

127     **no change in the system:** A helpful recent history is Ulrike von Hirschhausen and Jörn Leonhard, *Empires: Eine globale Geschichte, 1780–1920* (Munich: Beck, 2023).

127     **destroying young republics:** On postwar wars, see Robert Gerwarth, *The Vanquished: Why the First World War Failed to End, 1917–1923* (London: Allen Lane, 2016). On the weakness of the liberal democratic position, see Mark Mazower, *Dark Continent: Europe's Twentieth Century* (New York: Vintage, 2000).

127     **a colonial war for Ukraine:** In the last couple of decades, the significance of the Eastern Front has been newly appreciated. A turning point was Norman Davies, "The Misunderstood Victory in Europe," *New York Review of Books*, May 25, 1995, 8–17.

127     **supported by American economic power:** Adam Tooze, *The Wages of Destruction: The Making and Breaking of the Nazi Economy* (New York: Viking, 2007).

128     **France could not return:** Simone Weil anticipated this chain of events: "Le sang coule en Tunisie," March 25, 1937, in *Oeuvres complètes*, vol. 2, *Écrits historiques et politiques*, bk. 3 (Paris: Gallimard, 1988), 131.

128     **east European replicate regimes:** On communization, see Anne Applebaum, *Iron Curtain: The Crushing of Eastern Europe 1944–1956* (New York: Doubleday, 2012); Bradley Abrams, "The Second World War and the East European Revolution," *East European Politics and Societies* 16, no. 3 (2003): 623–64; Jan T. Gross, "The Social Consequences of War: Preliminaries for the Study of the Imposition of Communist Regimes in East Central Europe," *East European Politics and Societies* 3, no. 2 (1989): 198–214; T. V. Volokitina et al., eds., *Sovetskii faktor v Vostochnoi Evrope 1944–1953* (Moscow: Sibirskii khronograf, 1997); O. N. Ken and A. I. Rupasov, eds., *Politbiuro Ts.K. VKP(b) i otnosheniia SSSR s zapadnymi sosednimi gosudarstvami* (St. Petersburg: Evropeiskii

Dom, 2001); Wolfgang Müller, *Die Sowjetische Besatzung in Österreich 1945–1955 und ihre politische Mission* (Vienna: Böhlau Verlag, 2005).

128    **forced to retreat from Afghanistan:** I am simplifying a complex war. See Artemy Kalinovsky, *A Long Goodbye: The Soviet Withdrawal from Afghanistan* (Cambridge, Mass.: Harvard University Press, 2011).

129    **The anti-colonial struggle *in* Europe:** Important in reframing the war as imperial was Mark Mazower, *Hitler's Empire: How the Nazis Ruled Europe* (London: Allen Lane, 2008).

129    **mistakes of the 1930s:** See Eugen Weber, *The Hollow Years: France in the 1930s* (New York: Norton, 1996).

130    **European economic cooperation:** See Alan Milward, *The European Rescue of the Nation-State* (Berkeley: University of California Press, 1992); Harold James, *Europe Reborn: A History, 1914–2000* (Harlow: Pearson, 2003).

130    **That created an idea of mobility:** Charles Maier, "The Politics of Productivity: Foundations of American International Economic Policy After World War II," *International Organization* 31, no. 4 (1977): 607–33.

130    **The new *social mobility*:** See Tony Judt, *Postwar* (New York: Penguin, 2005), esp. chaps. 7 and 8. What Andrew Moravcsik calls the "choice for Europe" has to be seen against the impossibility of choosing empire; *The Choice for Europe* (Ithaca, N.Y.: Cornell University Press, 1998). What Kieran Klaus Patel calls "Project Europe" has to be seen alongside the failing imperial project; *Project Europe: A History* (Cambridge: Cambridge University Press, 2020). Helpful here is Patrick Weil, *How to Be French,* trans. Catherine Porter (Durham, N.C.: Duke University Press, 2008).

130    **most of them driven:** For a summary of the expulsions, see *Bloodlands.*

130    **Expelled Germans who arrived:** On the West German politics, see Pertti Ahonen, *After the Expulsions* (Oxford: Oxford University Press, 2003). In communist Poland, there was dramatic physical and social mobility, but it did not continue, nor was it anchored in comparable political institutions. See Krystyna Kersten, "Forced Migration and the Transformation of Polish Society in the Postwar Period," in Philip Ther and Ana Siljak, eds., *Redrawing Nations: Ethnic Cleansing in East-Central Europe, 1944–1948* (Lanham, Md.: Rowman & Littlefield, 2001), 75–86. See also Philipp Ther, *Deutsche und polnische Vertriebene* (Göttingen: Vandenhoeck & Ruprecht, 1998).

130    **Europeans suppressed (and forgot):** See Mark Mazower, "An International Civilization? Europe, Internationalism, and the Crisis of the Mid-Twentieth Century," *International Affairs* 82, no. 3 (2006): 553–66.

131    **extract their cash:** Vanessa Ogle, "The End of Empire and the Rise of Tax Havens," *New Statesman,* December 18, 2020; Ogle, "Archipelago Capitalism: Tax Havens, Offshore Money, and the State, 1950s–1970s," *American Historical Review* 122, no. 5 (2017): 1431–58.

131    **Through the 1970s:** On this and what came next, see Chrystia Freeland, *Plutocrats* (New York: Penguin, 2012), 13 and passim.

132    **stuck in the estate:** On the durability of these practices, see Orel Beilinson,

"Tomorrow Belongs to Me: Coming of Age in the Other Europe, 1813–1914," doctoral dissertation, Yale University, 2023.

132     **American policies of social mobility were reversed:** John O'Connor, "U.S. Social Welfare Policy: The Reagan Record and Legacy," *Journal of Social Policy* 1, no. 1 (1998): 37–61.

132     **The neglect of antitrust law:** See David Schultz, "Justice Brandeis' Dilemma Revisited: The Privileged Position of Corporate Power in American Democracy," *University of St. Thomas Law Journal*, no. 1, article 6 (February 2023).

132     **burdens on everyone else:** Thomas Piketty, Emmanuel Saez, and Gabriel Zucman, "Distributional National Accounts: Methods and Estimates for the United States," *Quarterly Journal of Economics* 133, no. 2 (May 2018): 553–609.

132     **Canadians on average lived:** These figures will vary from year to year. See end-of-year 2021 data compared in Shameek Rakshit et al., "How Does U.S. Life Expectancy Compare to Other Countries?," *KFF Health Tracker,* October 10, 2023.

133     **postcolonial tax havens:** For estimates of the scale, see Deborah Hardoon, Sophia Ayele, and Ricardo Fuentes-Nieva, *An Economy for the 1%,* Oxfam, January 18, 2016; James Henry in "Interview: World's Super-Rich Hide $21 Trillion Offshore," Radio Free Europe/Radio Liberty, July 28, 2012.

133     **millions of Americans:** The growing literature on the origins and form of the American carceral system includes Regina Kunzel, *Criminal Intimacy: Prison and the Uneven History of Modern American Sexuality* (Chicago: University of Chicago Press, 2008); Caleb Smith, *The Prison in the American Imagination* (New Haven: Yale University Press, 2011).

133     **were disproportionately Black:** By 2010, 450 of 100,000 white Americans were imprisoned, compared to 2,306 of 100,000 Black Americans. See Leah Sakala, "Breaking Down Mass Incarceration in the 2010 Census," Prison Policy Initiative, May 28, 2014; or "U.S. Incarceration Rates by Race and Ethnicity, 2010" (graph), at: https://www.prisonpolicy.org/graphs/raceinc.html. Then see Thomas P. Bonczar, "Prevalence of Imprisonment in the U.S. Population, 1974–2001," U.S. Department of Justice, Bureau of Justice Statistics, Special Report no. NCJ197976, August 2003.

133     **known as prison gerrymandering:** Jason P. Kelly, "The Strategic Use of Prisons in Partisan Gerrymandering," *Legislative Studies Quarterly* 3, no. 1 (2012): 117–34; Michael Skocpol, "The Emerging Constitutional Law of Prison Gerrymandering." *Stanford Law Review* 69, no. 5 (2017): 1473–539.

134     **state of Ohio:** Taylor Schneider, "Unveiling the Distorted Democracy: The Troubling Reality of Prison Gerrymandering," ACLU Ohio, September 18, 2023.

135     **"little zone" . . . "big zone":** This formulation can be found throughout the Gulag memoir literature, including Myroslav Marynovych, *The Universe Behind Barbed Wire: Memoirs of a Ukrainian Soviet Dissident,* trans. Zoya Hayuk (Rochester, N.Y.: Rochester University Press, 2021). See also Nanci Adler, "Life in the 'Big Zone': The Fate of Returnees in the Aftermath of Stalinist Repression," *Europe-Asia Studies* 51, no. 1 (1999): 5–19.

135     **earn a degree:** All but one of the students who were awarded a degree at the

prison's first graduation ceremony on June 9, 2023, had taken my class. Video from Fox 61 here: https://www.youtube.com/watch?v=cw-OoV0aZ1g; collection of news coverage here: https://www.yaleprisoneducationinitiative.org/single -post/celebrating-our-first-graduates.

135    **worked against the welfare state:** See Robert C. Lieberman, *Shifting the Color Line: Race and the American Welfare State* (Cambridge, Mass.: Harvard University Press, 1998); Jill Quadagno, *The Color of Welfare: How Racism Undermined the War on Poverty* (New York: Oxford University Press, 1994).

135    **white politicians had designed:** For the history of race and the New Deal, see Ira Katznelson, *Fear Itself: The New Deal and the Origins of Our Time* (New York: Liveright, 2013), and Katznelson, *When Affirmative Action Was White: An Untold History of Racial Inequality in Twentieth-Century America* (New York: Norton, 2005).

136    **mutated into new forms:** Keeanga-Yamahtta Taylor, *Race for Profit: How Banks and the Real Estate Industry Undermined Black Homeownership* (Chapel Hill: University of North Carolina Press, 2019); Kevin F. Gotham, "Racialization and the State: The Housing Act of 1934 and the Creation of the Federal Housing Administration," *Sociological Perspectives* 32, no. 2 (2000): 291–317.

136    **the Wagner Act excluded:** See Eileen Boris and Jennifer Klein, *Caring for America: Home Health Workers in the Shadow of the Welfare State* (Oxford: Oxford University Press, 2012); and Jennifer Klein, *For All These Rights: Business, Labor, and the Shaping of America's Public-Private Welfare State* (Princeton: Princeton University Press, 2003).

136    **Unions did become:** Andrew W. Martin and Marc Dixon, "Changing to Win? Threat, Resistance, and the Role of Unions in Strikes, 1984–2002," *American Journal of Sociology* 116, no. 1 (2010): 93–129.

136    **In a sad symphony:** See Mark Peffley, Jon Hurwitz, and Paul M. Sniderman, "Racial Stereotypes and Whites' Political Views of Blacks in the Context of Welfare and Crime," *American Journal of Political Science* 41, no. 1 (1997): 30–60.

136    **The American idea that we must choose:** Consider the research summarized by Paul Butler: "If white people are informed that a policy has an adverse impact on blacks, it actually increases their support for it." *Chokehold: Policing Black Men* (New York: New Press, 2017), 71.

136    **The image of work-shy:** A crucial text here was Frederick L. Hoffman, *The Race Traits and Tendencies of the American Negro* (New York: Macmillan, 1896).

137    **Seduced by a sense of ethnic honor:** Khalil Gibran Muhammad extends this story across the century, emphasizing that the patterns I describe in the 1980s have a longer tradition. *The Condemnation of Blackness: Race, Crime, and the Making of Modern Urban America* (Cambridge, Mass.: Harvard University Press, 2019), chap. 2, esp. 41, 47, 51, 76, 85. See also Matthew Ward, "The Legacy of Slavery and Contemporary Racial Disparities in Arrest Rates," *Sociology of Race and Ethnicity* 8, no. 4 (2022): 534–52.

137    **someone else, someone Black:** See the judgments of and statistics provided by a former prosecutor in Butler, *Chokehold,* 63 and passim.

138    **In 1968 Richard Nixon:** Elizabeth Hinton, *From the War on Poverty to the War on Crime* (Cambridge, Mass.: Harvard University Press, 2016).

138    **a stereotype that white kids:** This generational experience stands behind Jason Stanley's *How Propaganda Works* (Princeton: Princeton University Press, 2015).

138    **"It is as if, sometime around 1980":** Richard Rorty, *Achieving Our Country: Leftist Thought in Twentieth-Century America* (Cambridge, Mass.: Harvard University Press, 1998), 86.

139    **Told that the system was working:** Two books by Jacob Hacker and Paul Pierson address related issues: see *Let Them Eat Tweets* (New York: Norton, 2020) and *Winner-Take-All Politics* (New York: Simon & Schuster, 2010).

139    **suicide and addiction:** Anne Case and Angus Deaton, "Rising Morbidity and Mortality in Midlife Among White Non-Hispanic Americans in the 21st Century," *Proceedings of the National Academy of Sciences* 112, no. 49 (November 2, 2015); Debbie Weingarten, "Why Are America's Farmers Killing Themselves in Record Numbers?," *Guardian,* December 6, 2017; Sam Quinones, *Dreamland: The True Tale of America's Opiate Epidemic* (London: Bloomsbury Press, 2016); Nora A. Volkow and A. Thomas McLellan, "Opioid Abuse in Chronic Pain: Misconceptions and Mitigation Strategies," *New England Journal of Medicine* 374 (March 31, 2016).

139    **not simply personal tragedy:** J. H. Wasfy, Charles Stewart III, and Vijeta Bhambhani, "County Community Health Associations of Net Voting Shift in the 2016 U.S. Presidential Election," *PLOS One* 12, no. 10 (2017); Shannon M. Monnat, "Deaths of Despair and Support for Trump in the 2016 Presidential Election," Pennsylvania State University, Research Brief, December 4, 2016; John Lynch et al., "Is Inequality a Determinant of Population Health?," *Milbank Quarterly* 82, no. 1 (2004): 62, 81.

140    **ESPN's best commentator:** Kirk Herbstreit's on-air commentary on race, after the murder of George Floyd: "The Black community is hurting. If you've listened, you've heard the words 'empathy' and 'compassion' over the last few months. How do you listen to these stories and not feel pain and not want to help? You know what I mean? It's like . . . wearing a hoodie and putting your hands at 10-2 . . . Oh God, I better look out. I'm wearing Nike gear, like what? What are we talking about? You can't relate to that if you're white, but you can listen and you can try to help because this is not okay. It's just not. We gotta do better, man. We gotta, like, lock arm-in-arm and be together." I was proud and impressed. And I also thought: We get to cry in public and it makes us good people, but it's not so simple for our Black colleagues.

142    **No matter what he wore:** As Susanna Siegel argues, how we see is influenced by prior rationalizations. *The Rationality of Perception* (Oxford: Oxford University Press, 2017), 22 and passim.

142    **the way Fanon described:** "The black man's first action is a reaction." Fanon, *White Skin, Black Masks,* 19.

143    **murdered the Jews of Odesa:** Jean Ancel, *The History of the Holocaust in Romania,* trans. Yaffah Murciano (Lincoln: University of Nebraska Press, 2011).

143 **murdered the Jews of Kherson and Dnipro:** See Dieter Pohl, "Schauplatz Ukraine: Der Massenmord an den Juden im Militärverwaltungsgebiet und im Reichskommissariat 1941–1943," in Norbert Frei, Sybille Steinbacher, and Bernd C. Wagner, eds., *Ausbeutung, Vernichtung, Öffentlichkeit* (Munich: K.G. Saur, 2000), 135–79; Dieter Pohl, "Ukrainische Hilfskräfte beim Mord an den Juden," in Gerhard Paul, ed., *Die Täter der Shoah* (Göttingen: Wallstein Verlag, 2002); see also Andrej Angrick, *Besatzungspolitik und Massenmord: Die Einsatzgruppe D in der südlichen Sowjetunion 1941–1943* (Hamburg: Hamburger Edition, 2003).

143 **his father's grotesque predicament:** This and other details from Georgi Arbatov, *The System: An Insider's Life in Soviet Politics* (New York: Crown, 1992).

144 **The Great Terror of 1937–38:** On the Soviet mass murder policies of 1937–38, see Rolf Binner and Marc Junge, "Wie der Terror 'Gross' wurde," *Cahiers du monde russe* 42, nos. 2–4 (2001): 557–614; Nicolas Werth, *La terreur et le désarroi* (Paris: Perrin, 2007); Paul R. Gregory, *Terror by Quota* (New Haven: Yale University Press, 2009); Terry Martin, "The Origins of Soviet Ethnic Cleansing," *Journal of Modern History* 70, no. 4 (1998): 813–61; N. V. Petrov and A. B. Roginsksii, "'Pol'skaia operatsiia' NKVD 1937–1938 gg.," in A. Ie. Gurianov, ed., *Repressii protiv poliakov i pol'skikh grazhdan* (Moscow: Zven'ia, 1997), 22–43. I try to synthesize in *Bloodlands,* chaps. 2 and 3.

144 **Stalin's alliance with Hitler:** See Roger Moorhouse, *The Devils' Alliance: Hitler's Pact with Stalin, 1939–1941* (London: Bodley Head, 2014); Gerd Koenen, *Der Russland-Komplex* (Munich: Beck, 2005); Sławomir Dębski. *Między Berlinem a Moskwą* (Warsaw: PISM, 2003); John Lukacs, *The Last European War* (New Haven: Yale University Press, 2001). I try to synthesize in *Bloodlands,* chap. 4.

144 **to make careers:** Jan Tomasz Gross, *Revolution from Abroad* (Princeton: Princeton University Press, 1988).

144 **murdered Soviet Jews:** A chain of important sources: Yitzhak Arad, Shmuel Krakowski, and Shmuel Spector, eds., *The Einsatzgruppen Reports* (New York: Holocaust Library, 1989); Joshua Rubenstein and Ilya Altman, eds., *The Unknown Black Book* (Bloomington: Indiana University Press, 2008); Yitzhak Arad, *The Holocaust in the Soviet Union* (Lincoln: University of Nebraska Press, 2009); Yuri Radchenko, "Accomplices to Extermination: Municipal Government and the Holocaust in Kharkiv," *Holocaust and Genocide Studies* 27, no. 3 (2013): 443–63; Leonid Rein, "Local Collaboration in the Execution of the 'Final Solution' in Nazi-Occupied Belorussia," *Holocaust and Genocide Studies* 20, no. 3 (2006): 381–409. I treat the "Holocaust by bullets" in the occupied Soviet Union in detail in *Black Earth*.

145 **Soviet leaders kept dying on him:** See Peter Baker, "How Reagan and Bush Overcame Skepticism to Collaborate with Gorbachev," *NYT,* September 1, 2022.

146 **led by Boris Yeltsin:** For an excellent biography, see Timothy J. Colton, *Yeltsin: A Life* (New York: Basic Books, 2008).

146 **reactionaries tried to remove him:** On Gorbachev's difficulties, see Chris Miller, *The Struggle to Save the Soviet Economy: Mikhail Gorbachev and the Collapse of the USSR* (Chapel Hill: University of North Carolina Press, 2016). The locus classicus on the national question is Terry Martin, *The Affirmative Action*

*Empire: Nations and Nationalism in the Soviet Union, 1923–1939* (Ithaca, N.Y.: Cornell University Press, 2001). On the relationship between 1989 and 1991, see Mark Kramer, "The Collapse of East European Communism and the Repercussions Within the Soviet Union," *Journal of Cold War Studies* 5, no. 4 (2003); 6, no. 4 (2004); 7, no. 1 (2005).

147 **After Poland joined the European Union:** Jarosław Kundera, "Poland in the European Union. The Economic Effects of Ten Years of Membership," *Rivista di studi politici internazionali* 81, no. 3 (2014): 377–96.

148 **a trick that might be called** *sadopopulism*: I discuss sadopopulism at greater length in *Road to Unfreedom,* chap. 6.

148 **offering relative degrees of pain:** See comparable arguments in Fintan O'Toole, *The Politics of Pain: Postwar England and the Rise of Nationalism* (New York: Liveright, 2019).

149 **Sadopopulism normalizes oligarchy:** The oligarchical appeal of sadopopulism, at least in some cases, can be traced to a reading of René Girard, *The Scapegoat,* trans. Yvonne Frecerro (Baltimore: Johns Hopkins Press, 1989), esp. chap. 3.

149 **three time warps:** I have developed these ideas of inevitability, eternity, and catastrophe in my books and lectures since November 2016 and the publication of *On Tyranny,* but the notion of time warps is not mine. See Hans Ulrich Gumbrecht, *After 1945: Latency as Origin of the Present* (Stanford: Stanford University Press, 2013); Chapoutot, "L'historicité nazie."

149 **supposedly brings the world as it should be:** Nathan J. Kelly and Peter K. Enns, "Inequality and the Dynamics of Public Opinion," *American Journal of Political Science* 54, no. 4 (2010): 855–70.

149 **Facts about the present:** On inequality globally, see Paul Collier, *The Bottom Billion: Why the Poorest Countries Are Failing and What Can Be Done About It* (Oxford: Oxford University Press, 2007).

150 **The American prison population:** See reports by the Sentencing Project, or this graph: www.sentencingproject.org/research/.

151 **labor unions were besieged:** On the relationship between deunionization and inequality, see Bruce Western and Jake Rosenfeld, "Unions, Norms, and the Rise in U.S. Wage Inequality," *American Sociological Review* 76, no. 4 (2011): 513–37. The conclusion here is that deunionization accounts for between one-fifth and one-third of the increase in inequality. On wages, see Paul Mason, *Post-Capitalism* (New York: Farrar, Straus & Giroux, 2015).

151 **about a fifty-fifty chance:** Raj Chetty et al., "The Fading American Dream: Trends in Absolute Income Mobility Since 1940," *Science* 356 (April 24, 2017): 398–406.

151 **fraction of the population:** Emmanuel Saez and Gabriel Zucman, "Wealth Inequality in the United States Since 1913: Evidence from Capitalized Income Tax Data," National Bureau of Economic Research, Working Paper no. 20265 (October 2014), 1, 23; Piketty, Saez, and Zucman, "Distributional Accounts," 1, 17, 19.

151 **nor even 1 of 1,000:** If we stay with 1 of 1,000, we find that this group controls four times as much wealth as 50 percent of the U.S. population. See "Distribution of Household Wealth in the U.S. since 1989," updated regularly by the Board of Governors of the Federal Reserve System.

152 **a lower effective tax rate:** Greg Sargent, "The Massive Triumph of the Rich," *Washington Post*, December 9, 2019.

153 **in an emergency:** According to Bankrate's 2023 annual emergency savings report, only 48 percent could do so. See also Jonathan Morduch and Rachel Schneider, *The Financial Diaries: How American Families Cope in a World of Uncertainty* (Princeton: Princeton University Press, 2017).

153 **the consumption patterns of the very wealthy:** Paul Henri Thiry, Baron d'Holbach, *Système de la nature* (Paris: Chez l'éditeur, 1770), 250–57; see also Andrzej Waśkiewicz, *Ludzie-rzeczy-ludzie. O porządkach społecznych, w których rzeczy łączą, a nie dzielą* (Warsaw: Universitas, 2020).

153 **lobbyists they employ:** A shamefully direct case is that of former politicians paid by hydrocarbon interests. Rick Noack, "He Used to Rule Germany," *Washington Post*, August 12, 2017; Erik Kirschbaum, "Putin's Apologist?," Reuters, March 27, 2014.

153 **This behavior warps the system:** See Freeland, *Plutocrats*, 236 and passim.

154 **discouraged and demobilized:** See Benjamin Newman, Christopher Johnston, and Patrick Lown, "False Consciousness or Class Awareness?," *American Journal of Political Science* 59, no. 2 (2014): 326–40; Melissa Schettini Kearney, "Income Inequality in the United States," testimony before the Joint Economic Committee of the United States Congress, January 16, 2014. See also John Freeman, ed., *Tales of Two Americas* (New York: Penguin, 2017).

154 **"At a certain level of inequality":** Raymond Aron, *Dix-huit leçons sur la société industrielle* (Paris: Gallimard, 1962), 50. Benjamin Constant noted that the poor are judged by people hostile to them, and the rich by their peers and allies. *Principes de politique* (1806), chap. 17.

155 **A single value and a single future:** On the first page of the preface to her greatest work, Hannah Arendt takes as her premise that "Progress and Doom are two sides of the same medal." *Origins of Totalitarianism*, xi, also 144.

155 **give way to nostalgia:** Americans believe that America was great when they were young. See Robbie J. Taylor, Cassandra G. Burton-Wood, and Maryanne Garry, "America Was Great When Nationally Relevant Events Occurred and When Americans Were Young," *Journal of Applied Memory and Cognition* 6, no. 4 (2017): 425–33.

156 **most important politician of eternity:** I sketch this out in "Vladimir Putin's Politics of Eternity," *Guardian*, March 16, 2018. For explicit confirmation from the Russian side, see Vladislav Surkov, "Dolgoe gosudarstvo Putina," *Nezavisimaya Gazeta*, February 14, 2019.

156 **A Russian fascist tradition:** See citations of Ilyin in the conclusion; also Charles Clover, *Black Wind, White Snow* (New Haven: Yale University Press, 2016), esp. 214–23; also Alexander Sergeevich Titov, "Lev Gumilev, Ethnogenesis and Eurasianism" (Ph.D. diss., University College London, 2005); Andreas Umland, "Post-Soviet 'Uncivil Society' and the Rise of Aleksandr Dugin" (Ph.D. diss., University of Cambridge, 2007).

157 **the wealthiest digital oligarch:** Simone Weil foresaw ninety years ago the "oppo-

sition" between "those who dispose of the machine, and those who are disposed of by the machine." Weil, *Réflexions sur les causes de la liberté*.

157    **as we choose to be less free:** Jared Diamond, *Collapse: How Societies Choose to Fail or Succeed* (New York: Penguin, 2005).

158    **The science of global warming:** Joseph Majkut, "John Chafee's 1986 Climate Hearings," Niskanen Center, June 15, 2016; Wolfgang Behrenger, *A Cultural History of Climate* (New York: Polity, 2010); Spencer R. Weart, *The Discovery of Global Warming* (Cambridge, Mass.: Harvard University Press, 2003).

158    **from Sakharov to Havel:** Andrei Sakharov in a manifesto translated by the *New York Times* in 1968 under the title "Progress, Coexistence, and Intellectual Freedom"; Václav Havel in a lecture at George Washington University in 1993 that was published in the *New York Review of Books* as "The Post-Communist Nightmare," May 27, 1993.

158    **Most of the human-made carbon dioxide:** Our World in Data, "Cumulative $CO_2$ Emissions by World Region, 1751–2017."

158    **understated the problem of climate change:** Meanwhile it had long been established within the relevant milieux as a major problem of national security. See Gordon R. Sullivan et al., "National Security and the Threat of Climate Change" (Alexandra: CNA Corporation, 2007); U.S. Department of the Navy, Vice Chief of Naval Operations, "Navy Climate Change Roadmap," May 21, 2010; U.S. Department of Defense, *Quadrennial Defense Review Report,* February 2010.

158    **opens Twitter to a flood of lies:** David Klepper, "Climate Misinformation 'Rocket Boosters' on Musk's Twitter," AP, January 19, 2023.

159    **summons a negative future ever closer:** Jacques Sémelin helpfully reminds us that politics never stops. *Purifier et détruire: Usages politiques des massacres et génocides* (Paris: Seuil, 2005).

159    **the bleakness comes to embrace us:** See David Wallace-Wells, *The Uninhabitable Earth* (New York: Tim Duggan Books, 2019).

159    **a myth of Russian innocence:** On Ilyin, see the conclusion. See also Dina Khapaeva, "La Russie gothique de Poutine," *Libération,* October 23, 2014. On Christian fascism, see Vladimir Tismaneanu, "Romania's Mystical Revolutionaries," in Edith Kurzweil, ed., *A Partisan Century* (New York: Columbia University Press, 1996), 383–92.

159    **Hitler's dark fantasy of ecological war:** I spell this out in the conclusion to *Black Earth*. See also Snyder, "Hitler's World May Not Be So Far Away," *Guardian,* September 16, 2015.

160    **just dispensable details:** In his story "Sputnik Sweetheart," Haruki Murakami remarks that "In an incomplete way of being such as ours, the superfluous also has its place." *Sputnik Sweetheart,* trans. Philip Gabriel (New York: Knopf Doubleday, 2002).

160    **a morality play of innocence and guilt:** Using another term ("anti-history"), Jill Lepore makes a similar argument in *The Whites of Their Eyes* (Princeton: Princeton University Press, 2010), 5, 8, 15, 64, 125. See also Masha Gessen, *The Future Is History* (New York: Riverside Books, 2017); Shaun Walker, *The Long*

*Hangover: Putin's New Russia and the Ghosts of the Past* (Oxford: Oxford University Press, 2018).

161 **History undoes the politics of eternity:** Compare Hannah Arendt: "The last century has produced an abundance of ideologies that pretend to be keys to history but are actually nothing but desperate efforts to escape responsibility." *Origins of Totalitarianism,* 9.

161 **"the world" and "the earth":** Kieran Williams, "Václav Havel's Word to the Class of 2017," *Medium,* June 2, 2017.

## FACTUALITY

163 **manipulate and harm us:** In *Leviathan* (1651), Thomas Hobbes says that it is "ignorance of causes" that makes some people dependent on others.

164 **authority on fossils:** Thomas Jefferson, *Notes on the State of Virginia* (Philadelphia: Mathew Carey, 1794); Keith Thomson, "Jefferson's Old Bones," *American Scientist* 99, no. 3 (2011): 200.

165 **humans are not the culmination:** On the implications of geological time for human self-conception, see Stephen Jay Gould, *Time's Arrow, Time's Cycle* (Cambridge, Mass.: Harvard University Press, 1987). See also Rebecca Woods, "Telling Time with Mammoths," *Journal for the History of Knowledge* 4 (November 2023).

166 **dignity of knowledge:** A point I take from David Denby, *Lit Up* (New York: Picador, 2018).

169 **"In the struggle between you and the world":** Franz Kafka, *Nachgelassene Schriften und Fragmente,* vol. 2 (Frankfurt am Main: Fischer, 1992). Compare Paul North, *The Yield: Kafka's Atheological Reformation* (Stanford, Calif.: Stanford University Press, 2015).

171 **generate usable fusion:** Jason Parisi and Justin Ball, *The Future of Fusion Energy* (London: World Scientific, 2019).

171 **need other measures:** We will also have to remove methane. See Katherine Bourzac, "Clear the Air," *Science News,* November 19, 2023.

171 **$7 trillion a year:** Simon Black et al., "Fossil Fuel Subsidies Data: 2023 Update," International Monetary Fund Working Paper, August 24, 2023.

172 **remain in the ground:** In his 1938 novel, *Ein Mord, den jeder begeht,* Heimito von Doderer speaks nicely of "progress reeking of oil."

172 **had to discredit scientific solutions:** Adolf Hitler, *Hitler's Second Book: The Unpublished Sequel to Mein Kampf,* ed. Gerhard L. Weinberg, trans. Krista Smith (New York: Enigma Books, 2010), 16, 21, 74, 103. Stalin promoted discredited agricultural science: Edouard I. Kolchinsky et al., "Russia's New Lysenkoism," *Current Biology* 27, no. 19 (2017): R1042–47.

172 **They finance propaganda:** See Naomi Klein, *This Changes Everything: Capitalism vs. the Climate* (New York: Simon & Schuster, 2014).

173 **the political party that denies:** Matthew T. Ballew et al., "Climate Change in the American Mind: Data, Tools, and Trends," *Environment* 61 (2019): 4–18.

173 **answers our frivolous queries:** "Since we do not have any way of making computers wise, we ought not to give computers tasks that demand wisdom."

Joseph Weizenbaum quoted in Timothy Garton Ash, *Free Speech: Ten Principles for a Connected World* (London: Atlantic Books, 2016), 178.

174    **disproportionately white males:** Matthew Ballew et al., "Which Racial/Ethnic Groups Care Most About Climate Change?," Yale Program on Climate Change Communication, April 16, 2020; Aaron M. McCright and Riley E. Dunlap, "Cool Dudes: The Denial of Climate Change Among Conservative White Males in the United States," *Global Environmental Change* 21, no. 4 (2011): 1163–72.

174    **One reason the election was so close:** Traci Burch, "Did Disfranchisement Laws Help Elect President Bush?," *Political Behavior* 34, no. 1 (2012): 1–26.

175    **we are less free:** On climate denialism, see Naomi Oreskes and Erik M. Conway, *Merchants of Doubt: How a Handful of Scientists Obscured the Truth on Issues from Tobacco Smoke to Global Warming* (New York: Bloomsbury, 2010); James Laurence Powell, *The Inquisition of Climate Science* (New York: Columbia University Press, 2011); Spencer Weart, "Global Warming: How Skepticism Became Denial," *Bulletin of the Atomic Scientists* 67, no. 1 (2011): 41–50.

175    **spoke of "significant roughness":** Johann Wolfgang von Goethe, *Gedenkausgabe der Werke,* ed. Ernst Beutler (Zurich, 1949), 13:1.

176    **"clamor and combinations":** James Madison, *Federalist* no. 10, November 23, 1787.

176    **reversed with vertiginous rapidity:** On the attractions of Stalinism, see Marci Shore, *Caviar and Ashes: A Warsaw Generation's Life and Death in Marxism* (New Haven: Yale University Press, 2006); François Furet, *Le passé d'une illusion* (Paris: R. Laffont/Calmann-Lévy, 1995); Richard Crossman, ed., *The God That Failed* (New York: Harper, 1949).

179    **think it was a Jewish attack:** Victor Klemperer recalled this in *I Will Bear Witness 1942–1945: A Diary of the Nazi Years,* vol. 2 (New York: Modern Library, 2001). His diaries were originally published in German in 1955.

179    **Thousands obliged by invading the Capitol:** Jian Wang, "The U.S. Capitol Riot: Examining the Rioters, Social Media, and Disinformation" (master's thesis, Harvard University Division of Continuing Education), January 5, 2022; Mallory Simon and Sara Sidner, "Capitol Hill Insurrection: Decoding the Extremist Symbols and Groups," CNN, January 11, 2021.

180    **worried that the stock price:** Jeremy W. Peters and Katie Robertson, "Fox Stars Privately Expressed Disbelief About Election Fraud Claims," *New York Times,* April 24, 2023.

180    **three contradictory propositions:** Amna Nawaz, Courtney Norris, and Frank Carlson, "How Disinformation Around January 6 Riot Has Downplayed Violence, Divided Americans," *PBS NewsHour,* January 5, 2022.

180    **questioned vote counts:** Brandon Tensley, "The Racist Rhetoric Behind Accusing Largely Black Cities of Voter Fraud," CNN, November 20, 2020.

180    **Trump's big lie threatens:** On Trump's continuity of big lying, see Tal Axelrod, "A Timeline of Donald Trump's Election Denial Claims, Which Republican Politicians Increasingly Embrace," CNN, September 8, 2022.

181    **insurrectionists are forbidden:** Analysis of the clear language of the Fourteenth Amendment; from all conceivable angles can be found in William Baude and

Michael Stokes Paulsen, "The Sweep and Force of Section Three," *University of Pennsylvania Law Review* 172 (2023). See also my essays on this topic on my Substack *Thinking about . . .*

182    **getting close enough to engineer a coup:** I spell out this logic in "Not a Normal Election," *Commonweal*, November 2, 2020.

182    **"free market of ideas":** A classic optimistic formulation is John Stuart Mill, *On Liberty* (1859; reprint Indianapolis: Hackett, 1978), 42.

183    **But it does not:** This was made clear to me in Daniel Markovits's analysis of the tradition in his unpublished dissertation "Toleration" (University of Oxford, 1998).

183    **outcompetes real news:** A crucial case was the 2016 election. See Andrew Guess, Brendan Nyhan, and Jason Reifler, "Selective Exposure to Misinformation: Evidence from the Consumption of Fake News During the 2016 U.S. Presidential Campaign," Center for the Study of Democratic Politics Working Paper (January 2018), 2, 4, 8; Hunt Allcott and Matthew Gentzkow, "Social Media and Fake News in the 2016 Election," *Journal of Economic Perspectives* 31, no. 2 (2017): 232. It remains the case that fake news outcompetes real news.

183    **and yet believe the most outrageous lies:** Cynicism and naïveté are neighbors. Hannah Arendt wrote of a "mixture of cynicism and gullibility" as characteristic of "mob mentality." *Origins of Totalitarianism*, xi, also 144.

183    **"build an environment":** Peter Pomerantsev, lecture at Swedish Academy, March 22, 2023. See also his books *This Is Not Propaganda* (New York: PublicAffairs, 2019), and *How to Win an Information War* (New York: Faber & Faber, 2024).

183    **affix the term *big lie* to Trump:** I was able to do so only because of a push through and therefore access to major media, some of which were the following: my appearance on *Reliable Sources,* CNN, January 11, 2021; "The American Abyss," *New York Times Magazine,* January 9, 2021; my appearance on *The Rachel Maddow Show,* MSNBC, January 7, 2021; my January 7, 2021, post on Twitter, ("1/10. The claim that Trump won the election is a big lie . . ."); my appearance on *The Mehdi Hasan Show,* MSNBC, January 6, 2021; "Authoritarians Like Trump Need Elections to Hold Power. They Just Don't Need Votes," *Washington Post,* December 12, 2020; "Trump's Big Election Lie Pushes America Toward Autocracy," *Boston Globe,* November 11, 2020.

184    **The peak year for newspaper subscriptions:** See Sarah Naseer and Christopher St. Aubin, "Newspapers Fact Sheet," Pew Research Center, November 10, 2023.

185    **local coverage or local color:** See Eric Wemple, "Could the Local News Crisis Get Any Worse? Look at Scranton," *Washington Post,* December 14, 2023.

186    **"the true enemy of the people":** Trump, Twitter, February 17, 2017 ("The FAKE NEWS media . . ."); Trump, Twitter, April 5, 2019 ("The press is doing everything . . ."). For other examples, see William P. Davis, " 'Enemy of the People': Trump Breaks Out This Phrase During Moments of Peak Criticism," *NYT,* July 19, 2018.

186    **bound by gag orders:** Theresa Brown, "The Reason Hospitals Won't Let Doctors and Nurses Speak Out," *NYT,* April 21, 2020.

187    **substitute Facebook for local newspapers:** Forty-four percent of Americans get

news from Facebook, according to Pew Research Center, cited in Olivia Solon, "Facebook's Failure," *Guardian*, November 10, 2016.

187   **we drift toward:** Judy Woodruff, Frank Carlson, and Connor Seitchik, "How the Loss of Local Newspapers Fueled Political Divisions in the U.S.," *PBS News-Hour,* August 2, 2023.

187   **"There is no error so monstrous":** Lord Acton to Mary Gladstone, April 24, 1881, available at the Online Library of Liberty, oll.libertyfund.org.

188   **"freedom which cannot be legislated":** James Baldwin, *Notes of a Native Son* (Boston: Beacon Press, 1955), 15.

188   **"horizon of truth":** Quoted in by Krzysztof Michalski, *Eseje o Bogu i śmierci* (Warsaw: Kurhaus, 2014), 13. For approximations, see Leszek Kołakowski, "Filozofia egzystencji i porażka egzystencji," in Leszek Kołakowski and Krzysztof Pomian, eds., *Filozofia egystencjalna* (Warsaw: PWN, 1965), 22, originally composed in 1963; Kołakowski, *Obecność mitu* (Paris: Instytut Literacki, 1972), chaps. 2 and 4, composed in 1966; Kołakowski, *Metaphysical Horror,* rev. ed., ed. and trans. Agnieszka Kolakowska (Chicago: University of Chicago Press, 2001), 55 and 117. See also Marcin Król, *Pakuje walizkę* (Warsaw: Iskry, 2021).

188   **truthful, risky speech:** See Michel Foucault, "Discourse and Truth: The Problematization of Parrhesia," lectures of 1983, available at Foucault.info.

189   **twenty-five years in prison:** "Russia Sentences Opposition Activist Vladimir Kara-Murza to 25 Years in Prison," NPR, April 17, 2023.

189   **novelist Victoria Amelina:** Charlotte Higgins, "A Murdered Writer, His Secret Diary of the Invasion of Ukraine—and the War Crimes Investigator Determined to Find It," *Guardian,* July 22, 2023.

189   **find and publish it:** The diary is reproduced in Volodymyr Vakulenko, *Ia peretvoriuius'* (Kharkiv: Vivat, 2023), 25–74; Victoria Amelina's foreword is at 3–23.

189   **the premise that nothing is true:** For a deeper analysis, see Peter Pomerantsev, *Nothing Is True and Everything Is Possible: The Surreal Heart of the New Russia* (New York: PublicAffairs, 2014).

190   **"journalism is the freest profession":** Hans Rauscher, "Hugo Portisch im 95. Lebensjahr verstorben," *Der Standard,* April 1, 2021.

190   **a firehose of digital information:** "Where is the knowledge we have lost in information?" asked T. S. Eliot in 1934.

191   **"most deserve to express themselves":** Simone Weil, *La personne et le sacré*, 33.

## SOLIDARITY

197   **Survivor testimony is now important:** An example of the use of testimony in a recent standard work is Doris Bergen, *The Holocaust: A New History* (London: History Press, 2009).

197   **dismissed as irrational:** See Peter Baldwin, ed., *Reworking the Past: Hitler, the Holocaust, and the Historians' Debate* (Boston: Beacon Press, 1990); Charles Maier, *The Unmasterable Past: History, Holocaust, and German National Identity* (Cambridge, Mass.: Harvard University Press, 1988).

198   **"organize the service of truth":** Havel, "Power of the Powerless," 90.

198   **"We have waited more than 340 years"**: Martin Luther King, Jr., "Letter from a Birmingham Jail," April 16, 1963.

199   **"until the revolution of 1776 is complete"**: John Lewis, "Speech at the March on Washington," August 28, 1963.

200   **under the wise motto**: *Gazeta Wyborcza* was first published May 8, 1989, with the slogan "Nie ma wolności bez Solidarności."

201   **"the powerful realization"**: Havel, "Power of the Powerless," 53.

201   **"The free individual who affirms"**: Charles Taylor, "Atomism," in *Powers, Possessions, and Freedom,* ed. Alkis Kontos (Toronto: University of Toronto Press, 1979).

202   **previous commitments now seemed senseless**: Martin Šimečka, speech at Eurozine conference, Vilnius, May 9, 2009.

202   **would take over**: Thus a number of them made what I would consider to be great errors of judgment concerning both economic inequality and the war in Iraq. See Marcin Król, *Byliśmy głupi* (Warsaw: Czerwone i Czarne, 2015).

203   **"There's class warfare, all right"**: Warren Buffett quoted in Ben Stein, "In Class Warfare, Guess Which Class Is Winning," *NYT,* November 26, 2006.

204   **Digital oligarchs distract us**: Franklin Foer made an excellent case in his *World Without Mind: The Existential Threat of Big Tech* (New York: Penguin, 2018).

204   **lies about global warming**: Nick Robins-Early, "Twitter Ranks Worst in Climate Change Misinformation Report," *Guardian,* September 23, 2023.

204   **that they will live forever**: For a novel drawing from the immortality conceit, see Gary Shteyngart, *Super Sad True Love Story* (New York: Random House, 2011).

204   **"a little while"**: The apposite biblical passage is Job 24:17–24: "For the morning is to them even as the shadow of death: if one know them, they are in the terrors of the shadow of death. He is swift as the waters; their portion is cursed in the earth: he beholdeth not the way of the vineyards. Drought and heat consume the snow waters: so doth the grave those which have sinned. The womb shall forget him; the worm shall feed sweetly on him; he shall be no more remembered; and wickedness shall be broken as a tree. He evil entreateth the barren that beareth not: and doeth not good to the widow. He draweth also the mighty with his power: he riseth up, and no man is sure of life. Though it be given him to be in safety, whereon he resteth; yet his eyes are upon their ways. They are exalted for a little while, but are gone and brought low; they are taken out of the way as all other, and cut off as the tops of the ears of corn."

204   **The finitude of our time**: Nietzsche has the nice dictum "This life, your eternal life!" *Nachgelassene Fragmente Frühjahr 1881 bis Sommer 1882*, pt. 5, vol. 2 of *Nietzsche Werke: Kritische Gesamtausgabe* (Berlin: Walter de Gruyter, 1973), 411. Compare Max Frisch in his 1964 novel *Mein Name sei Gantenbein:* "Now is not now but always" *(jetzt ist nicht jetzt, sondern immer)*.

205   **eight years shorter**: These figures vary a bit from year to year. I am relying on end-of-year 2021 data in Shameek Rakshit et al., "How Does U.S. Life Expectancy Compare to Other Countries?," *KFF Health Tracker,* October 10, 2023.

205   **would ensure that they did**: See Emmanuel Saez and Gabriel Zucman, *The Tri-*

*umph of Injustice: How the Rich Dodge Taxes and How to Make Them Pay* (New York: Norton, 2019).

206 **interaction with life:** J. B. Lamarck, *Hydrogéologie* (Paris: 1802); Charles Darwin, *The Formation of Vegetable Mould, Through the Action of Worms, with Observations on Their Habits* (London: John Murray, 1881), discussed in Stephen Jay Gould, *Hen's Teeth and Horse's Toes* (New York: Norton, 1984), 120–33; W. Vernadsky, *La Biosphère* (Paris: Félix Alcan, 1929); Pieter Westbroek, *Life as a Geological Force* (New York: Norton, 1991); Tim Lenton and Andrew Watson, *Revolutions That Made the Earth* (Oxford: Oxford University Press 2011).

206 **no other planet:** A new study of the co-evolution of Earth and life, as yet unpublished, has been completed by Olivia Judson. See her "Our Earth, Shaped by Life," *Aeon*, November 22, 2022, and "The Energy Expansions of Evolution," *Nature Ecology and Evolution* 1, no. 0138 (April 28, 2017).

206 **another several decades:** For a helpful meditation, see Bruno Latour, *Où atterrir?* (Paris: La Découverte, 2017).

206 ***first* have to master:** Jason Parisi and Jusin Ball, *The Future of Fusion Energy* (London: World Scientific, 2019), 354.

207 **The logical sequence is simple:** Parisi and Ball, *Future of Fusion Energy,* 356.

208 **hinder scientific thought:** A good example, aside from global warming, is vaccination. I am aware that there are complexities, but the digital reduces actual knowledge to binary nonsense. David A. Broniatowski et al., "Weaponized Health Communication: Twitter Bots and Russian Trolls Amplify the Vaccine Debate," *American Journal of Public Health* 108, no. 10 (October 2018): 1378–84.

208 **look away from our phones:** As a result of their media preferences, younger people are actually exposed to less factual information about global warming than their elders. Nina Horaczek, "Die Klimawandelleugner-Lobby," *Der Falter,* February 19, 2019.

208 **for example, Nebelivka:** "The Nebelivka Hypothesis" exhibition at the 18th International Architecture Exhibition of the Biennale di Venezia brought together new technology with old arguments. See https://forensic-architecture.org/investigation/the-nebelivka-hypothesis.

209 **like the rings of a tree:** David Graeber and David Wengrow, *The Dawn of Everything* (New York: Farrar, Straus & Giroux, 2021), 298.

209 **are divided peremptorily:** Józef Tischner, *Spowiedź rewolucjonisty. Czytając „Fenomenologię ducha" Hegla* (Kraków: Znak, 1993), 164.

210 **capitalism collapsed into Great Depression:** On lessons learned, see John Maynard Keynes, *The General Theory of Employment, Interest, and Money* (1936; reprint London: Macmillan, 1973).

211 **When the word *freedom* is conceded:** Fanon thought that language was a marker of when we are "being-for-others." Conceding the word *freedom* to the market means "being-for-others" when the other in question is an abstraction or a social convention. Frantz Fanon, *Black Skin, White Masks,* trans. Richard Phillcox (New York: Grove Press, 2008), 1; originally published in French in 1952.

212 **direct-to-consumer drug advertising:** C. Lee Ventola, "Direct-to-Consumer Pharmaceutical Advertising: Therapeutic or Toxic?," *P&T* 36, no. 10 (2011): 669;

Neeraj G. Patel et al., "Therapeutic Value of Drugs Frequently Marketed Using Direct-to-Consumer Television Advertising, 2015 to 2021," *JAMA Research Letter,* January 13, 2023; Ola Morehead, "The 'Good Life' Constructed in Direct-to-Consumer Drug Advertising," unpublished ms., 2018.

212 **Prevention is the most important part:** Some of this has to do with the profitability of specialization. See K. E. Hauer et al., "Factors Associated with Medical Students' Career Choices Regarding Internal Medicine," *Journal of the American Medical Association* 300, no. 10 (September 10, 2008): 1154–64. On the important but forgotten field of geriatrics, see Atul Gawande, *Being Mortal: Medicine and What Matters in the End* (New York: Macmillan, 2014), 36–48.

212 **no *Leib*, only a *Körper*:** The Japanese novelist Haruki Murakami wrote of a "relationship from wound to wound." We bind wounds, and wounds bind us.

212 **standard matrix of billable categories:** The good ones complain about this constantly. See also Jerome Groopman, *How Doctors Think* (New York: Houghton Mifflin, 2007).

214 **five years in the Gulag:** Julius Margolin, *Journey to the Land of the Zeks and Back: A Memoir of the Gulag,* trans. Stefani Hoffman (New York: Oxford University Press, 2020), 314; originally written in Russian in 1947. Golfo Alexopoulos describes the Gulag as a place where millions were quantified out of existence in her *Illness and Inhumanity in Stalin's Gulag* (New Haven: Yale University Press, 2017), 106 and passim.

214 **In the Warsaw Ghetto:** An extraordinary guide to life and death in the Warsaw Ghetto is Barbara Engelking and Jacek Leociak, *The Warsaw Ghetto: A Guide to the Perished City,* trans. Emma Harris (New Haven: Yale University Press, 2009). See also T.B., "Waldemar Schön–Organizator Getta Warszawskiego," *Biuletyn Żydowskiego Instytutu Historycznego,* no. 49 (1964): 85–90; Tatiana Berenstein, "Praca przymusowa Żydów w Warszawie w czasie okupacji hitlerowskiej," *Biuletyn Żydowskiego Instytutu Historycznego,* nos. 45–46 (1963): 43–93. I set this out in *Bloodlands: Europe Between Hitler and Stalin* (New York: Basic Books, 2016).

215 **contradictions and lies:** On the historical origins, see Jennifer Burns, *Goddess of the Market: Ayn Rand and the American Right* (Oxford: Oxford University Press, 2009).

216 **the good of everyone:** This comforting thought, for which there is no factual basis, perhaps persists in Anglo-American thought thanks to John Locke, who wanted to believe that pursuing our own ends was our way of pursuing God's. We can dismiss God from that line of reasoning and be left with the pleasant notion that (somehow) it will all work out. See Craig Calhoun, "Morality, Identity, and Historical Explanation: Charles Taylor on the Sources of the Self," *Sociological Theory* 9, no. 2 (1991): 248–50.

216 **makes us pessimists:** See Rutger Bregman, *Humankind: A Hopeful History,* trans. Elizabeth Manton and Erica Moore (New York: Little, Brown, 2020), 14 and passim.

217 **larger economic logic:** See Tony Judt, "Captive Minds," *New York Review of*

*Books,* September 30, 2010. He is alluding to Czesław Miłosz, *Zniewolony umysł,* translated into English by Jane Zielonko as *The Captive Mind* (New York: Knopf, 1953).

217    **American tax dollars:** These examples can be found in Roger McNamee, *Zucked* (New York: Penguin, 2019), and Martin Burckhardt, *Eine kurze Geschichte der Digitalisierung* (Munich: Penguin, 2018).

218    **a giant step toward oligarchy:** Shane Goldmacher, "How David Koch and His Brother Shaped American Politics," *NYT,* August 23, 2019; Lateshia Beachum, "Kochs Key Among Small Group Quietly Funding Legal Assault on Campaign Finance Regulation," Center for Public Integrity, November 15, 2017.

219    **to submit to a single value:** See Isaiah Berlin, *The Crooked Timber of Humanity* (Princeton: Princeton University Press, 1990), 13–16.

219    **a weird, cyborg form:** For a more sophistical argument, see Virginia Eubanks, *Automating Inequality: How High-Tech Tools Profile, Police, and Punish the Poor* (New York: St. Martin's, 2017).

220    **to create a mystical harmony:** The notion that one's own "rational" pursuit of interests corresponds with a higher divine "reason" was characteristic of a number of eighteenth-century thinkers. It is one of the ironies of twenty-first-century discourse that people who call themselves "enlightened," and who believe themselves beyond religion, rest their account of reason on two articles of faith characteristic of discussions that are now a quarter millennium old: that people are naturally "rational" and that their unreflective collective "rationality" somehow corresponds to some greater good.

221    **blurs into gray:** This point is nicely made from observation of the early Soviet Union by George Shevelov, "Youth of the Fourth Kharkiv," written in Ukrainian in 1948, published in Polish in *Kultura* in 1951, and available in abridged form in English at *Kultura,* https://kulturaparyska.com/en/topic-article/mlodziez -czwartego-charkowa.

221    **the most dangerous people:** Adam Michnik, *W cieniu totalitaryzmu* (Warsaw: Agotra, 2019).

222    **If we accept a single value:** Consider Learned Hand's 1944 speech: "The spirit of liberty is the spirit which is not too sure that it is right; the spirit of liberty is the spirit which seeks to understand the mind of other men and women; the spirit of liberty is the spirit which weighs their interests alongside its own without bias; the spirit of liberty remembers that not even a sparrow falls to earth unheeded; the spirit of liberty is the spirit of Him who, near two thousand years ago, taught mankind that lesson it has never learned but never quite forgotten; that there may be a kingdom where the least shall be heard and considered side by side with the greatest."

222    **dismissed as fools:** In his novel *The Schirmer Inheritance* (New York: Knopf, 1953), Eric Ambler writes that "the sadness of evil men is that they can believe no truth that does not paint the world in their colours."

223    **members of the politburo:** The most sophisticated defense of Leninism was György Lukács, *History and Class Consciousness,* trans. Rodney Livingstone (Cambridge, Mass.: MIT Press, 1968); originally published in German in 1923.

224     **or ever new values:** "The ethical world is never given; it is always in the making."
        Ernst Cassirer, *An Essay on Man* (New Haven: Yale University Press, 1944), 85.

224     **false tragic choice:** "If you play freedom against society, you lose both in the
        end." Ralf Fücks, *Freiheit verteidigen: Wie wir den Kampf um die offene Gesell-
        schaft gewinnen* (Berlin: Carl Hanser Verlag, 2017).

224     **"There is no incompatibility":** Friedrich Hayek, *The Road to Serfdom* (1944;
        reprint New York: Routledge, 2001), 148.

225     **"contradictory virtues in the souls of saints":** Weil, *La pesanteur et la grâce*, 170.
        Graham Greene has his narrator Bendrix describe saints as "outside the plot,
        unconditioned by it." *The End of the Affair* (London: Penguin, 1951), 186.

# CONCLUSION: GOVERNMENT

227     **Achilles fighting Amazons:** Adrienne Mayor, *The Amazons: Lives and Legends
        of Warrior Women Across the Ancient World* (Princeton: Princeton University
        Press, 2016).

227     **Scythians of the Black Sea coast:** Alfonso Moreno, *Feeding the Democracy: The
        Athenian Grain Supply in the Fifth and Fourth Centuries BC* (Oxford: Oxford
        University Press, 2007).

227     **merged the two cultures:** For elegant reflections on the ancient history, see
        Charles King, *The Black Sea: A History* (New York, Oxford University Press,
        2012); Neal Ascherson, *Black Sea* (New York: Hill & Wang, 1996).

227     **cult of Artemis:** Edith Hall, *The Adventures of Iphigenia in Tauris* (Oxford:
        Oxford University Press, 2012).

228     **hottest summer in history:** "NASA Announces Hottest Summer on Record,"
        NASA press release, September 14, 2023.

229     **"rashysty," a Ukrainian neologism:** On the sources and meanings of the word,
        see Timothy Snyder, "The War in Ukraine Has Unleashed a New Word," *New
        York Times Magazine*, April 22, 2022.

229     **all have their origin:** David W. Anthony, *The Horse, the Wheel, and Language:
        How Bronze-Age Riders from the Eurasian Steppes Shaped the Modern World*
        (Princeton: Princeton University Press, 2010); David Reich, *Who We Are and
        How We Got Here: Ancient DNA and the New Science of the Human Past*
        (New York: Oxford University Press, 2018).

229     **"We rely not upon management or trickery":** Funeral oration as recorded by
        Thucydides in his *History of the Peloponnesian War.*

230     **good for various reasons:** "The ethical is not a homogeneous domain, with a
        single kind of good, based on a single kind of reason." Charles Taylor, "Diver-
        sity of Goods," in Stanley G. Clarke and Evan Simpson, eds., *Anti-Theory in
        Ethics and Moral Conservatism* (Albany: SUNY Press, 1989), 237.

231     **jagged colors of a broken stained-glass window:** I was inspired in this argument
        by Isaiah Berlin's characterization of Romanticism. For example, in *The Roots
        of Romanticism* (Princeton: Princeton University Press, 1999), 26, he offers sim-
        ilar images. (The essay in question was originally a lecture delivered in 1965.)

See also Berlin, *The Crooked Timber of Humanity* (Princeton: Princeton University Press, 1990), 236–237, which reproduces an essay from 1975. Joseph Raz nicely invokes an "ultimate imprecision" in his *The Morality of Freedom* (Oxford: Oxford University Press, 1986), 409.

231    **A fascist philosopher:** On Ilyin, see Snyder, *Road to Unfreedom,* chap. 1. See also Philip T. Grier, "The Complex Legacy of Ivan Il'in," in James P. Scanlan, ed., *Russian Thought After Communism* (Armonk, N.Y.: M. E. Sharpe, 1994), 165–86; Daniel Tsygankov, "Beruf, Verbannung, Schicksal: Iwan Iljin und Deutschland," *Archiv für Rechts- und Sozialphilosophie* 87, no. 1 (2001): 44–60. Articles by Ilyin on fascism: "Pis'ma o fashizm': Mussolini sotsialist'," *Vozrozhdenie,* March 16, 1926, 2; "Pis'ma o fashizm': Biografiia Mussolini," *Vozrozhdenie,* January 10, 1926, 3; "Natsional-sotsializm," in *Vozrozhdenie* (Paris: 1933), 477–84; "O russkom' fashizm'," *Russki Kolokol,* no. 3 (1927) 60: "fascism is a salvationary excess of patriotic arbitrariness."

231    **repeatedly cited by Vladimir Putin:** Putin cited Ilyin on September 30, 2022, regarding the invasion of Ukraine, but he has a long record: address to Federal Assembly, April 25, 2005; address to Federal Assembly, May 10, 2006; transcript of radio program *Russkaia Gazeta,* December 15, 2011; "Rossiia: natstional'nyi vopros," *Nezavisimaia Gazeta,* January 23, 2012; address to Federal Assembly, December 12, 2012; meeting with representatives of different Orthodox patriarchies and churches, July 25, 2013; remarks to Orthodox-Slavic Values: The Foundation of Ukraine's Civilizational Choice conference, July 27, 2013; transcript of the meeting of the Valdai International Discussion Club, September 19, 2013; interview with journalists in Novo-Ogariovo, March 4, 2014; meeting with young scientists and history teachers, Moscow 2014.

231    **"The Priest and the Jester":** Leszek Kołakowski, "Kapłan i błazen. Rozważania o teologicznym dziedzictwie współczesnego myślenia," *Twórczość,* no. 10 (1959): 65–85, reprinted in Zbigniew Mentzel, ed., *Pochwała niekonsekwencji: Pisma rozproszone z lat 1955–1968* (London: Puls, 1989), 2:161–80.

232    **our task was to see the clash:** Weil, *La pesanteur et la grâce,* 246.

232    **The forms of freedom:** "While not denying that governments can and do, pose a threat to liberty, there is also another conception that regards them as a possible source of liberty." Raz, *Morality of Freedom,* 18.

234    **You were not born free:** I am perhaps being unfair to Rousseau, who makes this claim at the beginning of his *Social Contract* (1762). He meant that we are born free in the sense that something is lost when we are enslaved. My critique here is of the straightforward sense of the expression: we are free as ourselves; there is a clear distinction between each individual and society and each individual and the world; society and the world must be the problem.

235    **the choice of no government:** Hannah Arendt said that "the abstract nakedness of being nothing but human" was the "greatest danger." Simone Weil made the point that it is absurd to speak of rights that cannot be claimed. The ability to claim rights is part of what I am calling sovereignty.

235    **all-too-predictable coup attempt:** The prediction: Timothy Snyder, "Not a Normal

Election: The Ethical Meaning of a Vote for Donald Trump," *Commonweal,*
November 2, 2020.

235    **Silicon Valley supermen:** I use Nietzsche's "superman" here ironically. The people I have in mind actually resemble Nietzsche's last man. On these categories,
see Krzysztof Michalski, *The Flame of Eternity* (Princeton: Princeton University Press, 2011).

236    **conservative-liberal-socialists:** Leszek Kołakowski, "How to Be a Conservative-
Liberal-Socialist: A Credo," *Encounter,* October 1978, reprinted in *Modernity
on Endless Trial* (Chicago: University of Chicago Press, 1990).

237    **differences in value commitments:** There is more to be said about this than I can
manage in this general guide to basic institutions. See Thomas Nagel, "Moral
Conflict and Political Legitimacy," *Philosophy and Public Affairs* 16, no. 215
(1987): 239.

237    **"responsive to all of its citizens":** Robert A. Dahl, *On Democracy* (New Haven:
Yale University Press, 1998).

238    **The closure of voting booths:** For examples from the 2016 election, see Carol
Anderson, *White Rage: The Unspoken Truth of Our Racial Divide* (New York:
Bloomsbury, 2017), 151, 163.

238    **allow the very richest:** Martin Gilens and Benjamin I. Page, "Testing Theories of
American Politics: Elites, Interest Groups, and Average Citizens," *Perspectives
on Politics* 12, no. 3 (2014): 564–81; Jacob S. Hacker and Paul Pierson, *Winner-
Take-All Politics* (New York: Simon & Schuster, 2011).

239    **Memory laws are passed:** Timothy Snyder, "The War on History Is a War on
Democracy," *New York Times Magazine,* June 29, 2021. For background, see
Nikolai Koposov, *Memory Laws, Memory Wars: The Politics of the Past in
Europe and Russia* (Cambridge: Cambridge University Press, 2017).

240    **"veil of ignorance":** See John Rawls, *A Theory of Justice* (1971; reprint Cambridge, Mass.: Harvard University Press, 1999).

240    **we must know some basic facts:** Charles W. Mills, *Black Rights/White Wrongs:
The Critique of Racial Liberalism* (Oxford: Oxford University Press, 2017).

242    **the "avowed object" of democracy:** Thomas Jefferson to James Madison, December 28, 1794.

242    **a republic rather than a democracy:** James Madison, *Federalist* no. 10, November 23, 1787.

242    **The Supreme Court has ruled:** For example, *Arizona Free Enterprise Club's Freedom PAC v. Bennett,* 131 S. Ct. 2806 (2011).

243    **the least protected:** I tend to think that even supporters of campaign finance
reform are too respectful of an incoherent view of freedom of speech. So long as
freedom of speech is regarded as "negative," as a matter of barriers, we will
again and again see the wealthy platformed to complain about this or that rule
being applied to them. Compare Robert C. Post, *Citizens Divided: Campaign
Finance Reform and the Constitution* (Cambridge, Mass.: Harvard University
Press, 2014); Lawrence H. Tribe, "Dividing *Citizens United*: The Case v. the
Controversy," *Constitutional Commentary* 30 (March 2015): 463.

244    **The American Founders were amateur historians:** A helpful introduction to references that would have been more available to the Founders than to us: Simon Goldhill, *Love, Sex, Tragedy: How the Ancient World Shapes Our Lives* (Chicago: University of Chicago Press, 2004), 193–214.

245    **The toughness needed to face the past:** For my further thoughts on memory laws, see "War on History." For a positive proposal, see Meira Levinsohn, *No Citizen Left Behind* (Cambridge, Mass.: Harvard University Press, 2012).

246    **I finished this book in 2023:** Alert readers will notice citations and references to subsequent events. I submitted this manuscript after returning from Ukraine in September 2023. During subsequent rounds of edits I was able to insert material.

248    **pay every American adult:** For the evidence that basic income for adults helps children, see Rutger Bregman, *Utopia for Realists: How We Can Build the Ideal World* (New York: Little, Brown, 2014).

249    **clean air, food, and shelter:** Again, even the strictest devotées of market economics agree that this is a good idea: "There can be no doubt that some minimum of food, shelter, and clothes, sufficient to preserve health and the capacity to work, can be assured to everybody." Friedrich Hayek, *The Road to Serfdom* (1944; reprint New York: Routledge, 2001), 148.

249    **Potable and available tap water:** The availability of potable water is an element of freedom some of us take for granted. Steven Solomon, *Water: The Epic Struggle for Wealth, Power, and Civilization* (New York: HarperCollins, 2010).

249    **only by sound policy:** See Heather Boushey, *Finding Time: The Economics of Work-Life Conflict* (Cambridge, Mass.: Harvard University Press, 2016).

250    **Four out of five Americans:** *World Urbanization Prospects: The 2018 Revision* (New York: United Nations, 2019).

252    **the Clayton and Sherman acts:** I have in mind the laws themselves rather than the Bork interpretation, which is convenient for bad actors, contrary to the intentions of the legislators, and inimical to functioning markets.

252    **This hinders good choices:** See Paul Mason, *PostCapitalism* (New York: Farrar, Straus & Giroux, 2015).

253    **roughly the same percentage:** Data for Czechoslovakia are drawn from the entry for the Czech Republic in Institute for Crime and Justice Policy Research, *World Prison Brief*, PrisonStudies.org, and from "Prisoners in 1989," *Bureau of Justice Statistics Bulletin*, May 1990.

253    **peaked in 1991:** Gary Lafree, "Social Institutions and the Crime 'Bust' of the 1990s," *Journal of Criminal Law and Criminology* 88, no. 4 (1998): 1325–68. See also Randolph Roth, *American Homicide* (Cambridge, Mass.: Harvard University Press, 2009).

253    **no freedom dividend:** Matthew Friedman, Ames C. Grawert, and James Cullen, "Crime Trends, 1990–2016," Brennan Center for Justice, 2017.

254    **About 1.7 million Americans:** See estimates from the Sentencing Project, Prison Policy Initiative, and *World Prison Brief*.

254    **theater, and art:** On prison art, see Nicole R. Fleetwood, *Marking Time: Art in the Age of Mass Incarceration* (Cambridge, Mass.: Harvard University Press,

2020); Winfred Rembert (as told to Erin I. Kelly), *Chasing Me to My Grave: An Artist's Memoir of the Jim Crow South* (New York: Bloomsbury, 2022).

255    **such hypertrophic responsibility:** Compare Lisa Guenther, *Solitary Confinement: Social Death and Its Afterlives* (Duluth: University of Minnesota Press, 2013), 222.

256    **immobility that gripped:** Elizabeth Hinton, *America on Fire: The Untold History of Police Violence and Black Rebellion Since the 1960s* (New York: Liveright, 2021), 132.

256    **"silent operation of laws":** James Madison, *National Gazette,* [c. January 23,] 1792.

256    **"Can any condition of society":** Thomas Jefferson to Thomas Cooper, September 10, 1814.

256    **titanic inequalities of wealth and income:** As Paul Mason points out, inequality eventually makes taxation impossible, which makes governance impossible—which makes freedom impossible. See his *PostCapitalism*.

256    **Americans lose about $1 trillion:** Alan Rappeport, "Tax Cheats Cost the U.S. $1 Trillion per Year, I.R.S. Chief Says," *NYT,* April 13, 2021.

257    **tax rate was 91 percent:** Tax Foundation, "Historical U.S. Federal Individual Income Tax Rates & Brackets, 1862–2021," TaxFoundation.org, August 24, 2021.

257    **the most important liberal:** A nice introduction to Mill and then to discussions of freedom of expression is Isaiah Berlin, "John Stuart Mill and the Ends of Life," in Vincent Blasi, ed., *Freedom of Speech in the History of Ideas* (St. Paul, Minn.: West Academic, 2016).

257    **believed in the welfare state:** See my foreword to Isaiah Berlin, *The Sense of Reality* (Princeton: Princeton University Press, 2019).

257    **a secure minimum income:** And so we find a juncture between the March on Washington and *The Road to Serfdom*.

258    **single-payer health insurance:** Christopher Cai et al., "Projected Costs of Single-Payer Healthcare Financing in the United States," *PLOS Medicine,* January 15, 2020; Elizabeth H. Bradley and Lauren A. Taylor, *The American Health Care Paradox* (New York: PublicAffairs, 2013); Lovisa Gustafsson, Shanoor Seervai, and David Blumenthal, "The Role of Private Equity in Driving Up Health Care Prices," *Harvard Business Review,* October 29, 2019.

258    **Seven hours a day of screen time:** Simon Kemp, "Digital 2022: Time Spent Using Connected Tech Continues to Rise," DataReportal, January 26, 2022.

259    **take drastic measures:** Alice Marwick and Rebecca Lewis, "Media Manipulation and Disinformation Online," Data and Society Research Institute, 2017; Tamsin Shaw, "Invisible Manipulators of Your Mind," *New York Review of Books,* April 20, 2017.

259    **"The system is based on lies":** Havel, "Power of the Powerless," 28.

260    **most consistent in censoring people:** A point made by Zeynep Tufekci in *Twitter and Tear Gas* (New Haven: Yale University Press, 2018), 235.

260    **Human children need human schools:** See José van Dijck, Thomas Poell, and

Martijn de Waal, *The Platform Society: Public Values in a Connective World* (Oxford: Oxford University Press, 2018), 121.

260 **schools without screens:** Sergei Brin, Larry Page, and Jeff Bezos, for example, attended Montessori schools. See the homepage of the American Montessori Society.

260 **for their children:** Jaron Lanier, *Ten Arguments for Deleting Your Social Media Accounts Right Away* (London: Bodley Head, 2018), 12.

260 **more than $10 billion:** Nicholas Kardaras, *Glow Kids* (New York: St. Martin's, 2017).

264 **"affirmative steps to improve the methods":** Quoted in Garton Ash, *Free Speech: Ten Principles for a Connected World*, 80.

264 **The Norwegian constitution:** Article 190.

264 **views be challenged:** Garton Ash, *Free Speech,* 190.

266 **cover any of these beats:** Charles Bethea, "Shrinking Newspapers and the Costs of Environmental Reporting in Coal Country," *New Yorker,* March 26, 2019. On news deserts, see Penelope Muse Abernathy, "The Expanding News Desert," USNewsDeserts.com, n.d. See also Margaret Sullivan, *Ghosting the News: Local Journalism and the Crisis of American Democracy* (New York: Columbia Global Reports, 2020).

266 **discovering and receiving the truth:** Weil, *La pesanteur et la grâce,* 114. Compare Martin Burckhardt: "The free act of creation has costs; the replication of these efforts has none." *Philosophie der Maschine* (Berlin: Matthes & Seitz, 2018), 70. He is referring to Walter Benjamin, whose work I was reading in Moscow those three decades ago.

266 **"circulation of newspapers":** James Madison, in *National Gazette,* [c. December 19,] 1791. See Lee McIntyre, *Post-Truth* (Cambridge, Mass.: MIT Press, 2018), for discussion.

271 **"blind veneration of antiquity":** James Madison, *Federalist* no. 14, November 30, 1787.

272 **"There was a time":** Frederick Douglass, "What, to the Slave, Is the Fourth of July," speech delivered in Rochester, New York, July 4, 1852. See David Blight, *Frederick Douglass: Prophet of Freedom* (New York: Simon & Schuster, 2018).

273 **more people with life sentences today:** In 2021, the number of people sentenced to life in prison was 161,512 and the number serving a virtual life sentence (fifty years or more) was 42,353. "No End in Sight," Sentencing Project, 2021. In 1969, the total prison population was 197,136. U.S. Department of Justice, Bureau of Justice Statistics, *Historical Statistics on Prisoners in State and Federal Institutions, 1925–1986* (Ann Arbor: Inter-university Consortium for Political and Social Research, 1989).

273 **"You guys are oppressing yourselves":** Racism can become "the instrument by which democracy in the nation was done to death, race provincialism deified, and the world delivered to plutocracy." W. E. B. Du Bois, *Black Reconstruction* (New York: Harcourt, Brace & Co., 1935), 241. A persuasive modern documentation is Heather McGhee, *The Sum of Us* (New York: OneWorld, 2022). See

also Volodymyr Yermolenko, "Russia, Zoopolitics, and Information Bombs," Euromaidan Press, May 26, 2015.

273    **bit of courage:** Consider W. E. B. Du Bois: "There is but one coward on earth, and that is the coward that dare not know." "The Study of the Negro Problem," *Annals of the American Academy of Political and Social Science*, 1375, January 2, 1898, 27. He was invoking Kant's dictum "Dare to know."

# Index

gravity, 28, 68–69, 84, 100, 167, 169–170,
232, 270–271
Gubits, Danny, 269

Haraway, Donna, 69–70
"Harlem" (Hughes), 256
Havel, Václav
background, xix, 63–66, 80, 95
Charter 77 and, 71–72
on ideology, 219
on "living in truth" and dissidence, 76,
77–78, 161, 181, 259–260
on machines and digital future, 70, 84, 97
on normalization, 103
"The Power of the Powerless," 65–66,
71–72, 76, 78, 95, 134, 201
as president of Czechoslovakia, 94–95,
201, 253
prisoners released by, 253
on solidarity, 198, 200, 201
on sovereignty, 66
on unpredictability, 66, 68–69, 84, 94
Hayek, Friedrich, 10, 224, 252, 257
health care, 37–38, 85, 115, 130, 211–214,
249–250
Heidegger, Martin, 55
Helsinki Final Act (1975), 72, 73
Hitler, Adolf, 24, 43, 121–122, 162,
172–173, 178, 210
holocausts, 5–7, 24–25, 81–82, 197
Homer, 110–111, 112
Hood, Wilson, 118
Hughes, Langston, 256

*Iliad* (Homer), 110, 112
Ilyin, Ivan, 231
imperial mobility, 97–98, 124–129
intermittent reinforcement, 102–103
*Iphigenia in Tauris* (Euripides), 112

Jan 6th Capitol insurrection, 179–181
Jefferson, Thomas, 34–35, 37, 38, 242,
245–246, 256
Jesus, 26–27
Johnson, Lyndon B., 131
Jordan, Barbara, 256
journalism, 182–187, 190, 233, 265,
266–267
Judt, Tony, 44–45, 83

Kant, Immanuel, 45
Kara-Murza, Vladimir, 189
Kennedy, John F., 131
Key, Francis Scott, 29
King, Martin Luther, Jr., 118–119, 136,
198–199, 258
Kołakowski, Leszek
background, xix, 80, 82, 83, 121
on government, 236
"The Priest and the Jester," 231–232
on rules, 231–232
on truth, 188
on unpredictability, 97, 99
on "world of values," 80–83, 231
Kołakowski, Tamara, 81–82
*Körper*, 22–23, 25, 43–44, 47, 57, 60
Kosciuszko, Tadeusz, 245

law of freedom, 41, 68–69
law of life, 68–69
law of necessity, 41, 68–69
*Laws* (Plato), 154
Left, xviii, 235–236
*Leib*, 21–23, 25–27, 43–44, 45–46, 47, 51,
56–58, 60
Lenin, Vladimir, 10, 12, 124
Lewis, John, 118, 199
liberation, x–xii, xv, xvi, 60, 79, 117, 150,
201
libertarianism, 70, 215–220, 243
*The Life and Adventures of a Haunted
Convict* (Reed), 89
living in truth, 77–78, 161, 162–163, 182.
*See also* truth
Livy, 54
local news, 184–187, 265–267
Locke, John, 36–37
Luther, Martin, 26

Madison, James, 242, 256, 266, 271
Margolin, Julius, 214
Marx, Karl, 12
Marxism, 11–12, 13, 64, 69–70, 72–73,
122–124, 162
Marynovych, Myroslav, 76–77
mass incarceration. *See* prisons
mathematics, 67, 100, 230–232, 261
Mebrahtu, Y. F., xv
*Mein Kampf* (Hitler), 24, 121–122, 172, 178

# About the Author

TIMOTHY SNYDER is the Richard C. Levin Professor of History and Global Affairs at Yale University, where he also serves as faculty adviser for the Fortunoff Video Archive of Holocaust Testimonies. As a permanent fellow at the Institute for Human Sciences in Vienna, he co-founded Documenting Ukraine, which supports Ukrainian scholars, journalists, and artists as they chronicle war. He chairs the academic council of Ukrainian History Global Initiative, a multiyear, interdisciplinary, and international project on the deep history of the country. He also teaches in the seminar Reading the Other at the Borderland Foundation in Krasnogruda, Poland. Snyder has received a number of distinctions, including state orders from several countries. He has appeared in documentaries and other films, and does regular television, radio, and other media work. His twenty books, appearing in forty languages, have inspired poster campaigns, films, sculpture, a punk rock song, a rap song, a play, and an opera. His words are quoted in protests around the world.

timothysnyder.org
X: @TimothyDSnyder
snyder.substack.com